The History of
Motor Cycling

The
History of
Motor
Cycling

introduced by
Barry Sheene

MA6437

Cyril Ayton, Bob Holliday, Cyril Posthumus and Mike Winfield

ORBIS PUBLISHING · LONDON

Chapters 1–5 written by Cyril Posthumus, chapters 6–9 by Bob Holliday, 10–11 by Cyril Ayton and 12–16 by Mike Winfield.

Picture Acknowledgements
The publishers are grateful to the following for their permission to reproduce the photographs in this book: R. Adams; All Sport; Michael Bailie; BBC Hulton Picture Library; V. Belli; BMW; Bonetti; Bosch; Jack Burnicle; Daimler-Benz; M. Decet; Donington Collection; Ducati; Dunlop; Richard Francis; N. Georgano; John Gichigi/All Sport; C. Gorman; J. Greening; Harley-Davidson; J. Heese; R. Holliday; Honda; Imperial War Museum; Kawasaki; Keig Collection; Mansell Collection; C. May; Mitsui Machinery Sales (UK) Ltd.; Mondial; A. Morland; Don Morley; Moto Guzzi; Moto Laverda; Motor Cycle; National Motor Museum; N. Nicholls; NVT; C. Posthumus; Publifoto; Quattroroute; Rizzi; Science Museum; E. Thompson; V. Tosi; Triumph; F. Varisco; M. Woollett; Yamaha; Zündapp.

© 1979 by Orbis Publishing Limited
First published in Great Britain by Orbis Publishing Limited, London 1979

Revised edition published 1983

Printed in Italy
ISBN 0-85613-517-8

Contents

Foreword

I have been interested in motor cycles as long as I can remember. Everything about them has fascinated me since I was old enough to take an interest in the parts that adorned my father's workshop. I had my first bike when I was five and from then on I wanted to know everything possible about motor cycles – how big were they, how fast, how did they work? I was also intrigued by how the motor cycle had developed from the primitive motorised bone-shakers of the late nineteenth century into the sophisticated superbikes of the seventies.

Although there was plenty to read to tell me some of the things, there was nothing to paint the whole picture and this has remained true until today. *The History of Motor Cycling* tells the story of the motor cycle industry from the earliest days, right through to today. This is no text book, however, because the authors' lively style brings every man, machine or event to life. Of most interest to me is the way that the book explains the enormous part played by motor cycle sport in the growth of the industry. Racing bikes are closely related to their road-going counterparts, so that as soon as a new development is successfully tested on the track it begins to find its way on to the road.

After reading this book, I can see why so many of the early manufacturers disappeared and why the whole shape of the industry has been so vastly transformed over the last twenty years. Gone are the days of the Ariel, the BSA, the Matchless and the AJS: these great names have been replaced by the likes of Suzuki, Honda, Kawasaki and Yamaha – all companies which had the sense to interpret the market and the tenacity to bend it to suit themselves.

The illustrations in *The History of Motor Cycling* have obviously been chosen to highlight the milestones in the motor cycle's career. In many cases, two-wheeled classics have been tracked down and photographed specially for inclusion in the book. These, together with the easily readable story, make this work an absolute must for me.

For historians, collectors and all people with even a passing interest in motor cycles, *The History of Motor Cycling* must be essential reading.

BARRY SHEENE MBE

Chapter 1
Yearning (1869-1896)

Above: a prophesy of the progress of steam, as depicted by the artist Alken in 1828. The painting, entitled 'A view in Regents Park 1831' was luckily one prophesy that did not come true

The first motor cycles were literally cycles fitted with motors. In contrast with the automobile their early history has been woefully neglected until comparatively recently, and thus many dates and claims conflict. Yet cars and motor cycles are closely akin, and their evolution followed a very similar pattern. Bicycles came before petrol engines, and steam engines came before both, so it was natural that the very first attempts at motorising a cycle were by steam.

Indeed, when the first experiments took place, the term 'cycle' had yet to be invented, for the two-wheeler had not advanced beyond the stage of the 'boneshaker'. This was the English nickname for the *vélocipède*, a French machine which was descended from the 'hobby horse' or *Draisienne*, invented by the German Carl von Drais in 1817. Exponents of this crude pioneer form of two-wheeled personal transport had to propel themselves along by paddling their feet on the road, a wearisome and rupturing process which speedily set ingenious inventors seeking suitable alternatives.

Racks, 'crutches', levers and treadles were all tried, but surprisingly it was not until 1861 that Frenchman Pierre Michaux and his sons Ernest and Henri, makers of *Draisiennes* and perambulators, popularised the idea of fitting the front wheel spindle of a two-wheeler with cranks and pedals. 'Turning like the handle on a grindstone,' as 'Papa' Michaux explained it. The spine frame, following *Draisienne* style, was of solid diamond-section wrought iron, forked at the rear end. A 'spoon' type rear brake was ingeniously worked by twisting the handlebar, and the graceful Michaux *vélocipède* with pedals was an immediate success.

'Velocipeding' boomed, the Michaux factory at Bar-le-Duc became the largest *vélo* producer in Europe with an annual output soon exceeding four hundred machines, and man had gained a new personal mobility without the need for stabling and feeding a horse. The British and Americans quickly adopted the Michaux layout, although pedalling such machines with iron tyres on the unmade roads of the 1860s probably justified the sobriquet 'boneshaker'. The sheer effort required also set imaginative minds yearning for some power source to replace aching human legs. It was the age of steam, but steam engines as epitomised by early rail and road locomotives were massive affairs with great cast iron cylinders, vast flywheels, and heavy connecting rods. The limited materials and machining facilities of the day demanded generous margins, and inhibited the construction of small, light engines.

Pierre Michaux himself was interested in the challenge. He and a French engineer named Perreaux tackled the problem together. L. G. Perreaux was certainly versatile, his inventions included a six-chambered firearm in 1836, a river lock system in 1841, and a powered circular saw in 1843, and he set to with zest to develop a light, steam 'power pack' for installation on a normal Michaux *vélocipède* with front pedals. His double-acting engine had a single brazed steel cylinder, a light steel piston, and twin flywheels. Steam was generated by a transverse cylindrical multi-tube boiler, fired by alcohol fuel through a series of burners, with two shallow flues discharging rearward.

The final drive was by twin belts from the flywheels to pulleys on both sides of the rear wheel. Water tanks were fitted behind the boiler, and a steam pressure gauge was installed where the rider could easily see it – ahead of the steering head. The Michaux-type saddle was mounted on a fore-and-aft spring blade, disturbingly close to the boiler. To get under way the rider first pedalled off, then brought the engine into action with a regulator; possibly he relied on the engine to help slowing down as well, for no brake features on the machine as preserved today in the Robert Grandseigne Collection in France.

Perreaux patented his *vélo-à-vapeur* in December 1868, and completed it for testing in 1869, claiming to have reached 15kph. Apart from the danger of a spill with those burners and hot steam, the main limitation was in boiler capacity, the steam generated being very quickly used up, and rendering the Michaux-Perreaux an ingenious but impractical experiment.

A close contemporary of Perreaux was Sylvester Howard Roper of Roxbury, Massachusetts. The American may, indeed, have preceded the Frenchman in getting a steam motor cycle

The Holly Horse Dealer—

working, although dates are maddeningly vague. However, a machine claimed to have run in demonstrations in eastern USA at fairs and circuses by one W. W. Austen from 1867 onwards was built by Roper, while Roper himself produced a very similar machine to which the date 1869 is appended. The basis

Left: Henri Michaux in action on his Velocipede of 1869. The Michaux family had been building such machines since 1861 and production eventually reached 400 machines a year

Below left: this cartoon depicting an early 'hobby horse' appeared in the Horse Dealer in 1819

Right: in 1819, Maurice Rosseau presented this painting of a 'hobby horse'

Below: the American Roper steam motor cycle of 1869, powered by a charcoal-fired, twin-cylinder engine

of the Roper was an American 'boneshaker' built by the Hanlon brothers, themselves noted 'velo-gymnasts' at the same fairs.

The hickory spine of the Hanlon machine supported a compact steam unit with twin oscillating cylinders, driving the rear wheel direct in locomotive style by delicate-looking connecting rods and cranks, one per side. The piston valves were

3

worked by eccentrics from the crankshaft, and a deep boiler-cum-charcoal fire hung down between the wheels, giving a centre of gravity lower than that of the Michaux-Perreaux. Roper confidently dispensed with pedals altogether, although he, like Perreaux, was obliged to sit in uncomfortably close proximity to the boiler.

An angled flue discharged behind the saddle, and interesting design refinements on the surviving Roper in the Smithsonian Institution, Washington, include flexible boiler mounting, an extended saddle with its base forming a water reservoir, and use of the handlebars – Michaux-style – as controls with cords. A forward twist opened the regulator, a backward twist closed it and applied a 'spoon' type brake on the front wheel. In fairground publicity Roper claimed that his two-wheeled steamer could be 'driven up any hill and outspeed any horse', but he, too, must have encountered the problem of carrying sufficient water for a worthwhile journey.

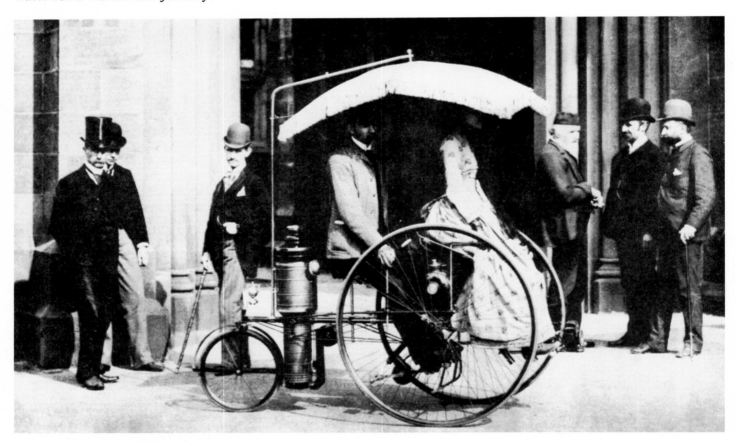

It is perhaps significant that on subsequent steam vehicles, Roper turned to four wheels, whereon the machinery and boiler could more easily be installed. Perreaux also abandoned his 'quart-into-pint-pot' efforts, devising a much less appealing steam tricycle with belts driving the single front wheel. Undoubtedly there was less merit in such vehicles than in a motorised two-wheeler, whereon the power unit and auxiliaries have to be packed between the two wheels. The rider, moreover, has to balance his machine and bank it on corners, demanding good balance and stability, while lightness is another vital factor, restricting engine size.

In an age of innovation, several other inventive engineers took the easier road in motorising three and four-wheelers, and while these met with some success in France and the USA, Great Britain's 'horsey' legislation soon killed off any such enterprises. Two promising tricycles, the Meek of 1877 and the

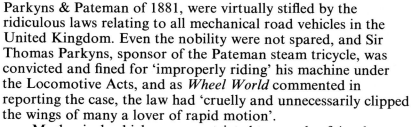

Parkyns & Pateman of 1881, were virtually stifled by the ridiculous laws relating to all mechanical road vehicles in the United Kingdom. Even the nobility were not spared, and Sir Thomas Parkyns, sponsor of the Pateman steam tricycle, was convicted and fined for 'improperly riding' his machine under the Locomotive Acts, and as *Wheel World* commented in reporting the case, the law had 'cruelly and unnecessarily clipped the wings of many a lover of rapid motion'.

Mechanical vehicles were restricted to speeds of 4mph on open roads and 2mph in towns by the Locomotive Acts of 1861 and 1865, while each 'locomotive' was obliged to have a crew of three, one walking sixty yards ahead and bearing a red flag to warn the public of their approach. To avoid frightening horses, steam vehicles had to stop on sight of one, and were forbidden to blow their whistle, release steam or emit smoke likely to frighten the animal. Quite how they managed this if mounting boiler pressure opened the safety valve at the crucial moment, the legislators neither specified nor concerned themselves about!

An 1878 Amendment dispensed with the red flag, but many councils still expected it. The man in front now had to walk only twenty yards ahead of the vehicle. Such strictures made difficulties enough for the huge, cumbersome traction engines of the time, but for any experimental light steam car or motor cycle things were impossible. Pedal-powered cyclists and tricyclists were not affected, of course, and were frequently fined for 'furious riding' at alleged speeds of 15mph and more.

Enlightened America did not suffer such repressions, and thus the next development of interest in powered two-wheelers came from Philadelphia in 1884. By then the *vélocipède* or 'boneshaker' had been succeeded by the ludicrous 'Penny-farthing' or 'Ordinary' bicycle, with a huge front driving wheel some four feet in diameter, and a rear wheel a quarter the size, or less. While much trickier to mount and ride, it was a lot faster, especially with thin solid rubber tyres, and less exhausting than the old 'boneshaker'. The latter was quickly ousted from favour among the younger and more athletic riders, but one US manufacturer, Star, decided to reverse things, and produced what amounted to a 'Farthing-penny' with the small wheel in front for steering, and the huge rear wheel the 'driver'.

The Star layout did not endure long, but in 1884 an Arizona engineer, Lucius D. Copeland, contrived to fit an inverted single-cylinder steam engine of an estimated ¼hp, together with lightweight boiler and gasoline heater, around the lofty steering column. A flat leather belt, with jockey adjustment, drove the rear wheel via a huge pulley. A brief speed burst at close on 15mph before running short of steam encouraged Copeland to seek finance and market his motorised 'high wheeler'. He exhibited and demonstrated it in eastern and western states to no avail, and he had to follow Perreaux's and Roper's example and rebuild his machine as a tricycle before he finally found a backer.

Meantime other hopeful inventors sought alternative power sources. Compressed air, clockwork, 'weights and levers', carbonic acid gas and hydrogen gas were among suggested propulsives. Hydrogen (ie coal gas) had been used by Etienne Lenoir in his four-wheeled, gas-engined 'break' on which he drive the six miles from Paris to Joinville in 1862. A bizarre yet prophetic proposal to use this same gas in a motor cycle was patented in 1879 by an Italian, Giuseppe Murnigotti of the city of Bergamo.

His vast *bicicletta a motore* had two parallel cylinders, slightly angled from horizontal, mounted on a narrow platform

Left: Arizona engineer Lucius D. Copeland had little success with his steam-powered two wheelers, and it was not until he built this tricycle that he found backing

Below: the untidy Michaux-Perraux tricycle succeeded the steam-powered two-wheeler of 1869, but suffered the same problem of limited range

with gas reservoirs hung low on each side, and a forked front
end containing the large-diameter front wheel. This was driven
direct by long connecting rods from the engine, one each side,
while the smaller rear wheel was steered by an overhead arm,
held in the left hand of the rider, seated low between the wheels
on the platform, while his right arm controlled the machinery!
Behind him was a second seat, just cleared by the steering arm,
but with no apparent room for the passenger's legs.

The engine specification included rotating valves jointly
controlling the admission of gas and flame from the burners, and
the first four-stroke action (ie induction, compression, firing,
exhaust) ever specified on a vehicle. An actual machine was
never built, and if complying with Murnigotti's specification it is
doubtful that the engine would have worked. From the rider's
point of view this was probably as well, since with that rear
wheel steering and the weight he had to balance, he would
scarcely have got beyond the first corner.

6

Murnigotti claimed that with $\frac{1}{2}$hp from the engine, his *bicicletta* would have easily exceeded 20kph (12$\frac{1}{2}$mph), although he hedged his bets by also designing a rear-drive three-wheeler with a similar power unit! Nonetheless, his 1879 patent specified the first gas-burning internal combustion four-stroke engine, albeit on paper only.

The Italian had no claim, however, to have invented the four-stroke principle. This had been outlined by the French scientist Alphonse Beau de Rochas back in 1862 and a new, working application had been patented in 1876 by two Germans, Dr Nicolaus Otto and Eugen Langen, of Deutz, near Cologne. Murnigotti 'borrowed' the principle for his fanciful design, while at the same time the principal aides of Otto and Langen, Gottlieb Daimler and Wilhelm Maybach, were putting in some solid, hard graft, experimenting exhaustively and finally producing a working four-stroke gas engine which was marketed for stationary use by the Deutz Engine Company.

The so-called Otto four-stroke cycle of piston and valve action in a cylinder, which remains unchanged today, over one hundred years later, is as follows: INDUCTION: Piston moves down to inhale air and gas through inlet valve; COMPRESSION: Piston moves up to compress air-gas mixture, all valves closed; FIRING: Piston is impelled downwards by firing of mixture, all valves closed; EXHAUST: Piston moves up to expel burnt gases through open exhaust valve.

The Deutz four-stroke stationary engines ran on coal gas supplied from the mains, but the visionary Gottlieb Daimler foresaw the vast potential of such an engine on a moving vehicle carrying its own fuel. Murnigotti's hydrogen gas, carried in cumbersome reservoirs, was only one step better than the steam *vélo* with its need to carry both boiler fuel and water tanks, whereas a liquid fuel of high volatility – or ability to gasify – such as benzine would enable a vehicle to travel perhaps 25 or more miles on just one gallon, thereby requiring only a small tank. But Otto and Langen did not want their two key men experimenting with such an engine while the Deutz works were thriving by making gas engines. Differences of opinion resulted in Daimler leaving in 1882 to conduct full-time research into liquid fuel engines, and he soon persuaded Maybach to join him in the venture.

The fuel Daimler chose to work with was then commonly called benzine, and chiefly served as a cleaning fluid for clothes. More broadly known as petrol, it is one of several distillates of petroleum, or 'rock oil' (*petra* meaning rock, and *oleum* meaning oil), which is found in the ground or, in modern times, under the sea bed, in many parts of the world. Although it is believed that the existence of petroleum and its by-products has been known of for over four thousand years, only within the last hundred years has it served as one of mankind's most valuable commodities by giving him unparalleled personal mobility.

This 'miracle' fuel, available in such abundance, made the internal combustion engine a practical proposition, but while the contributions of Daimler and Maybach to motor cycle design were of enormous importance, it is humbling to realise that they were, in fact, *incidental* to their aim of producing a four-wheeled, passenger-carrying horseless carriage. The fact that the Otto cycle had been anticipated by Beau de Rochas sixteen years earlier enabled Daimler to employ the principle without licence complications, and he and Maybach installed themselves in the former's garden shed at Canstatt in his native Swabia to perfect their liquid fuel engine.

Two years' hard work saw their goal within reach, and the

Below: things were rather difficult for the wheeled traveller before the self-propelled vehicle came along. This Aellopedes design of 1839 was perhaps taking the enthusiasm of the traveller a bit too far

Overleaf: a scene at Daimler's workshop in Bad Canstatt with their Einspur in the foreground

first engine completed was a small, air-cooled, single-cylinder unit of 264cc. It had 'mushroom' valves, the inlet being automatically operated by suction of the piston, and set directly above a cam-operated exhaust valve – a system widely used later on, and referred to simply as ioe (inlet-over-exhaust). This engine gave about ½hp and was designed to turn at 750rpm, an unprecedented crankshaft speed in those 'gas engine' days. Daimler, dubious of untried electric ignition at such a rate of rotation, devised what was termed a *gluherohezuendung*, meaning a 'glow plug' or 'hot tube'. This projected into the cylinder, and was heated on the outside by a Bunsen-type burner. Seeking a 'hot tube' material able to withstand constant heat, Daimler experimented with ceramics, nickel and steel strips before finally settling for platinum.

The carburettor, or 'fuel atomiser', was of float type, devised by Maybach, and this remarkable little engine had two flywheels, one each side of the crankshaft, all enclosed in a cast aluminium crankcase. The cylinder had no cooling fins, but temperature was controlled by a power-driven fan.

Having completed their engine, Daimler and Maybach wanted to test it as quickly as possible, but as it was too low-powered to put into a four-wheeled carriage, they decided to build it into a motor cycle. It may seem surprising that they made no attempt to adapt it to a ready-made bicycle, but in 1884 the bicycle was still in the 'Penny-farthing' stage, with the first equal-size wheeled, rear-drive 'safeties' only just coming into fashion in England, where they were invented.

Without more ado the inventive pair, anxious in any case to preserve secrecy, set about building their own machine in the Canstatt workshop. They did not use metal tubing, but fashioned the frame out of hard wood, with steel reinforcement plates and coach bolts to hold it together. The engine was installed vertically in the modern manner, using pendant wooden stays and cross-pieces to support it. The boneshaker-style main frame members were in two parts, with the upper end of the engine protruding between them, and a horse-type saddle on top. The wood-spoked, iron-tyred wheels may well have been purchased from a local carriage works, and the engine drove the rear wheel through a belt with a moveable jockey pulley serving as a crude clutch. Adopting the handlebar 'twist' control earlier employed by Michaux and Roper, Daimler used cords which simultaneously withdrew the 'clutch' and applied a rear brake.

They called it the *Einspur*, or 'one-track', but played safe by fitting two small support wheels, one on each side, since the

Top left and above: Gottlieb Daimler and the ½hp engine which powered the Einspur bike. Unfortunately, the saddle of the Einspur was directly over the engine, making things rather uncomfortable for the rider

Top right: Dr Nicolaus Otto who, along with Eugen Langen, patented the four-stroke cycle for the internal combustion engine. Hereafter, it was always referred to as the 'Otto cycle'

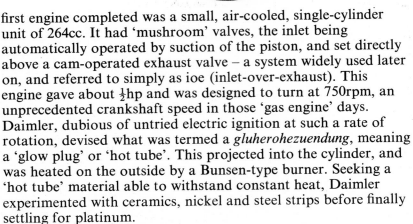

saddle was too high for the rider's feet to reach the ground easily. It was crudely and hurriedly built, but Gottlieb Daimler's *Einspur* was the true father of all modern motor cycles. Its specification as laid out in the patent application was remarkably modern, including as it did a centrally-located, petrol-burning engine with flexible mountings, float-type carburettor and fan-cooling, cradle-type frame, 'twist grip' coupled control of clutch and brake, and equal-sized wheels.

It is generally accepted that Paul Daimler, the 17-year-old son of Gottlieb, rode this machine from Canstatt to Unterturkheim village and back, a distance of about seven and a half miles, on 10 November 1885, during which it is said that the hot engine set fire to the saddle! It is also believed that Maybach rode the *Einspur* during a programme of modifications made during the winter of 1885–86. Daimler devised a primitive two-speed transmission, replacing the belt drive with an internally-toothed rim on the rear wheel, and introducing a belt

Above: to avoid contravening Otto's patents, Erith engineer Edward Butler used a two-stroke engine for his three-wheeled machine. The vehicle was provisionally patented in 1884 but was not completed for another four years

primary drive and a countershaft with pinion engaging with the final drive ring – but changing speed meant that the rider had to stop each time.

There was obviously much room for development, but unfortunately Daimler turned his full attention to building his first car, and the *Einspur*, having served its purpose as a test-bed, was left to gather dust. In later years Daimler sometimes said he regretted not developing his motor cycle further, as a cheap form of transport for the masses who could not afford a horseless carriage. The *Einspur* itself was destroyed in the great fire at the Daimler factory in 1903, and only meticulously built replicas of the later version of the machine remain today.

A 'near miss' by a brilliant British pioneer was the Butler 'Velocycle', provisionally patented a year before Daimler's *Einspur*. Edward Butler's machine had three wheels rather than two, yet it was closer to a motor cycle than a car with its single seat between the two front wheels, and important for its use of a two-stroke engine. The $2\frac{1}{4} \times 8$in bore-and-stroke, water-cooled petrol engine had two horizontal cylinders, one each side of the driven rear wheel, with the piston rods pointing forward, driving big curved overhung cranks which connected directly with the rear wheel.

Butler chose the two-stroke principle both to avoid contravening Otto's four-stroke patents, and because the idea of a power impulse in each cylinder at every revolution appealed as being more effective. He followed the Clerk pump-type arrangement patented by Dugald Clerk in 1880, wherein the injection of a fresh charge of mixture coincided with the discharge of burnt gases on the down-stroke of the piston. On the up-stroke the gases were compressed, then ignited by an electric spark to begin the next down-stroke.

The mixture was compressed at the lower, ie fore-end of the horizontal cylinders, into a reservoir, and ducted therefrom to the upper 'explosion chamber'. Butler's sparking plug comprised two platinum electrodes on a porcelain base, and his low-tension ignition system worked on the 'electrostatic' principle, like a Wimshurst machine. On later two-stroke engines, crankcase compression became the norm and mechanically-operated valves were dispensed with, but Butler prescribed oscillating sleeve valves, driven by a chain. A surface-type wick carburettor was used, and a hollow rear mudguard also served as the water tank for the cooling system.

The Velocycle, alas, was not built, but a drawing of the machine was displayed, together with explanatory literature, both at the 1884 Stanley Cycle Show and the 1885 Inventors' Exhibition in London. Butler was seeking investors, but none came forward until 1887, when a syndicate was formed and Butler got the go ahead to build a trial machine, to be called the 'Petrol-Cycle'. He revised his original 1884 design in various ways and took out another provisional patent late that year. Construction was completed by mid-1888 and then tests over private roads in East London were made by the inventor. As a result, he made further changes, using rotary-type valves, and changing his ignition to a Ruhmkorff coil and battery; he also devised the world's first float-feed carburettor, four years before Maybach's similar device on a car engine.

Butler then discovered – presumably during an encounter with the Law – that the Locomotive Acts restricting speeds of mechanised vehicles in Britain to 4mph on open roads and 2mph in towns applied equally to the Butler Petrol-Cycle. He had imagined that this crippling piece of legislature applied only to steam vehicles and was naturally dismayed, the more so when the syndicate decided as a result to concentrate on development of his engine for use in boats and for stationary purposes. Butler soon rallied, however, and revised his design still further. He scrapped the two-stroke principle with its need for compressor pumps and chambers, fitted a flywheel, reduced the stroke to six inches, and converted to four-stroke action. A radiator was fitted and the direct rear wheel drive was replaced by an epicyclic reduction gear enabling the engine to turn at 600rpm

Below: Ayrton Perry's electric carriage was one alternative to steam propulsion in the early part of the nineteenth century. However, the problem still exists with battery power that it limits the range of the vehicle

Right: John Boyd Dunlop's son, Johnny, was not too happy with the ride of his little bicycle, so his father designed inflatable tyres for it. The Dunlop name is still world famous for tyres today

and produce a speed of 12mph. The coil ignition was given a rotary spark distributor – another Butler first.

It was all in vain, for the syndicate, short of capital, abandoned all development work, and the Petrol-Cycle was left idle. In 1896 it was cleaned up and demonstrated, and shortly afterwards H. J. Lawson, out to make a 'corner' in motor designs for his famous British Motor Traction Company, purchased the patent rights. He failed to exploit them, however, and the Butler enterprise finally died after thirteen years.

Ironically, while Gottlieb Daimler romped on to fame with his automobiles, and Edward Butler reconciled himself to his job with a firm of engineers in Kent, their respective *Einspur* and Petrol-Cycle designs had minor effect only in advancing the motorised bicycle theme for nine whole years. Further innovations and ideas flowed, of course, as patent records richly testify. In 1887 E. H. Owen built a four-stroke tricycle with chain drive. A year later J. K. Starley, son of the 'father of the English bicycle', built an electric tricycle which he took to Deauville, France, to evade British law. He achieved a steady, silent 8mph but soon expended the batteries.

Another Briton, J. D. Roots, followed the Butler theme with a water cooled, two-stroke-engined tricycle in 1892. The Roots engine, mounted 'upside down' behind the rear wheel and driving it through a bevel and pinion, operated on Joseph Day's patented 1891 system, employing the crankcase compression which subsequently was almost universally adopted on two-stroke motor cycle units. In 1892, also, Félix Théodore Millet, eldest of ten children, built a radical prototype with what was called a 'stellar' engine, built into the front wheel of a two-wheeler. This unit was the ingenious precursor of the WW1 rotary aero-engine, having five radial cylinders with a fixed central crankshaft driving the wheel direct. Rotation was supposed to cool the cylinders (which had no fins), and Millet

Above: although Karl Benz was involved with the development of the motor car, his employment of Hans Geisenhof later prompted the young Bavarian to build a two-stroke engine for the Hildebrand machine

Below: Félix Théodore Millet built a bike in 1892 with a radial five-cylinder engine fitted into the front wheel. After experiments, Millet decided to manufacture another version in 1895, this time with a powered rear wheel

had taken out his first patents for such an engine in 1888, when he fitted one to a tricycle.

Millet tried out his experimental 1892 machine with another novelty – the engine rode in an 'elastic' wheel, formed by a series of circular spring blades on a steel rim. It was an early attempt to alleviate the appalling bumps in the average road of the 1890s, which played havoc with the delicate mechanisms of the machines, let alone those of their unfortunate riders! Relief was on the way, did they but know it, for John B. Dunlop had patented his pneumatic tyre (originally invented by R. W. Thomson in 1845) in 1888, and already his 'pudding wheel' as opponents derisively called it, was making history by winning numerous cycle races.

Concurrent with such efforts, there came a final spate of steam-powered cycles to punctuate the decade between 1884 and 1894. One such was made in 1889 by two Munich brothers, Heinrich and Wilhelm Hildebrand, whose keenness for cycling was countered by the many forbidding hills in their native Bavaria. They used a Serpollet-type steam unit in a duplex frame of notable structural neatness. A fellow German, von Meyenberg, in 1893 gave his steamer two speeds and employed a backbone frame containing fuel for the burners. Yet another steam cycle was the Dalifol of 1893, built by Georges Richard, a Frenchman destined for greater fame in the car world, where he became a partner in the Richard-Brasier double victory in the Gordon Bennett races of 1904–05, and later produced the Unic taxi-cab. His Dalifol borrowed Butler's idea of a hollow rear mudguard for water storage.

If, then, no great stride was taken in the evolution of the motor cycle before 1894, clearly nimble minds were contributing experience and theories and building up a fund of knowledge which one day would make the motor cycle practical for all to buy and ride. Only Britain, hamstrung by her antiquated laws, hung back and 'missed the bus' when at last it came.

The year 1894 was of outstanding interest in motor cycle history, bringing new developments from three countries which were important, not for any success, but for the experience they provided and the lessons they taught. In Germany the Hildebrand brothers had teamed up with two fellow Bavarians, Alois Wolfmüller and Hans Geisenhof of Landsberg, near Munich. Both were clever engineers, Geisenhof having valuable former experience working with Karl Benz on his projects.

In 1892 Geisenhof had constructed a small two-stroke petrol engine for the *gebruder* Hildebrand, but it proved underpowered and unreliable, so he and Wolfmüller produced a much larger parallel twin four-stroke unit. This proved too heavy on being installed in a 'safety' cycle frame, which promptly broke, so the quartet devised a new frame, based on that of the old Hildebrand steamer of 1889. The horizontal engine fitted very neatly within the bounds of the twin-tube open duplex frame, with the fuel tank on the down-tubes, and the result performed well enough for the design to be patented in the month of January 1894.

The quartet then formed a new company, the *Motorfahrrad-Fabrik Hildebrand & Wolfmüller* at Munich and, with abundant capital, the partners resolved to get their new motor cycle into production as soon as possible. The Hildebrand & Wolfmüller, or H & W for brevity, was a truly remarkable motor cycle. The first to be given the generic name 'motor cycle' (*motorrad* or *motorzweirad* in German), it also had the biggest engine ever fitted to a production two-wheeler in ninety plus years of history, the bore and stroke of the two

Above: the ignition apparatus for Edward Butler's Petrol Cycle of the 1880s. He originally designed a two-stroke machine but this was eventually abandoned in favour of the four-stroke principle. This is the coil ignition system which was given a rotary spark distributor – another Butler first

horizontal cylinders being 90 × 117mm, giving 1489cc.

The pistons were linked in steam locomotive style by long connecting rods direct to cranks on the rear wheel spindle which embodied an epicyclic reduction gear. No flywheel was fitted, the solid disc rear wheel itself serving that purpose, and the designers resorted to broad rubber straps, looking like razor strops, on each side to help the pistons on their return strokes. Ignition was by a platinum hot tube, as pioneered by Daimler, and petrol from the tank was fed to a surface carburettor. Automatic inlet valves were employed, while the two exhaust valves were actuated by long rods and a cam on the rear wheel.

H & W emulated Butler and Dalifol in making the rear mudguard serve double duty as a water tank for engine cooling, and design details were well thought out, one frame tube serving also as an oil tank, while a neatly fabricated exhaust silencing box was mounted ahead of the engine. The machine from Munich was also the first motor cycle to have pneumatic tyres. These were specially made by the German firm of Veith of Hochst, near Darmstadt, under arrangements made by Heinrich Kleyer representing the Dunlop company.

In contrast to such modernity were the primitive braking arrangements. This comprised a primitive steel 'spoon' working on the front tyre – application of which automatically closed the throttle – and, initially, a barbaric sprag below the engine, pedal-operated to scrape on the road! There was a rotating 'thumbscrew' throttle to control engine speed, but no clutch at that time, so that starting the H & W was an athletic procedure, the rider pushing the machine hard until it fired, then leaping into the saddle while simultaneously trying to adjust the throttle setting, a tricky procedure.

Although the big twin-cylinder engine produced only about 2½hp at 240rpm, the machine could attain 28mph, which must have been frighteningly fast in 1894, even though steam trains easily doubled that speed on smooth steel rails. With orders to the value of over two million marks in hand, the Hildebrand and

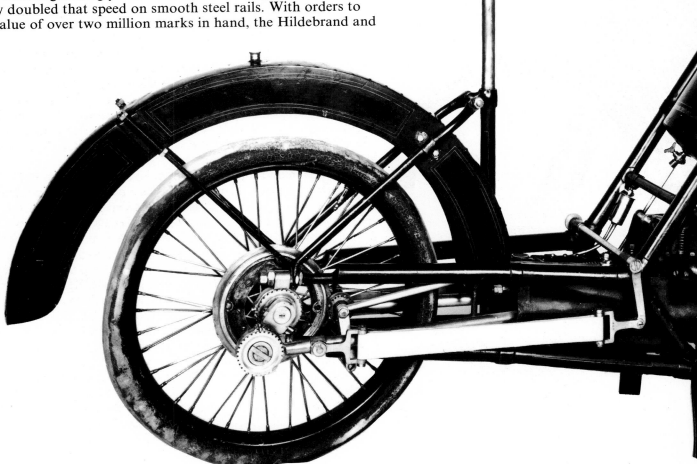

Below: the remarkable Hildebrand & Wolfmüller four-stroke, twin-cylinder bike of 1894. The white band running parallel to the cylinders is in fact a rubber strap which helped the piston on its return stroke

Wolfmüller company arranged for the erection of a new factory in the Colosseum Strasse able to house 1200 employees, while using a smaller plant for assembly of the *motorrad*, and many local engineering workshops for the manufacture of parts.

A demonstration machine was sent to Paris, and several French cycle manufacturers attended a special gathering arranged by Pierre Giffard, proprietor of the progressive *Petit Journal* which had promoted the Paris-Rouen run of 1894, the world's first motoring contest. With an expert German rider from the Munich works, who had spent most of the previous day 'tuning' the H & W to ensure that it gave of its best, the *motorrad* looked impressively easy to ride. A Paris-based Englishman, H. O. Duncan, who was partner with Louis Suberbie in a thriving cycle business, was invited to try it, and later wrote:

'I took the machine in hand and after the first few explosions, imitated the German rider by vaulting into the saddle. I have never forgotten the first sensation of riding a bicycle propelled by its own power. The feeling of travelling over the ground without effort was delightful. The machine did not seem to go fast enough and I fumbled with the thumbscrew until the motor began to move more quickly. I had evidently touched the right spot where the mixture was best, and soon found myself in a part of the country unknown to me. I thought of turning back, but then it occurred to me that if I stopped the motor I might never get it to start again! To tell the truth, I *couldn't* turn! The machine was running too fast, and the more I worried the thumbscrew the worse it behaved. At one moment the motor would drop to a crawl, then suddenly pick up and dash forward at such a speed that all I could do was to keep steering straight. . . . I continued until I came to a cross road and took the one I thought would lead me back to the starting point . . . and at length burst upon the astonished company. . . . I shut off the petrol supply and dismounted as gracefully as I could. . . . From that moment I became a staunch believer in the motor-bicycle and predicted a great future for it.'

Duncan, Suberbie et Cie secured a licence to build the H & W in France. They decided that its very Teutonic name would be no help to sales, and agreed instead to call it 'La Petrolette'. Their works manager, T. C. Pullinger, who later joined the Sunbeam Motor Co, did not enthuse as he considered the design needed more development. However, the firm had received over fifty orders, and decided to put a hundred machines into production.

To publicise their new product, Duncan decided that three Petrolettes would be demonstrated at a cycle race meeting at Lille in the spring of 1895. However, a fire broke out at the hotel where they were stored on the evening before, and all three Petrolettes were damaged, the noise of their pneumatic tyres exploding alarming the public and causing exaggerated comments on the extreme dangers of the new petroleum motors. The Lille display had to be cancelled. Meanwhile the parent company in Munich was seeking further markets and Wolfmüller took two machines to Italy for himself and the future motor manufacturer Giovanni-Battista Ceirano to ride in Italy's very first car and motor cycle race, held on 28 May 1895 from Turin to the village of Asti and back.

In a race over 62 miles of decidedly rough and hilly roads, the two H & Ws did very well to finish second and third, being headed only by a Daimler car. Two Petrolettes then contested the big Paris-Bordeaux-Paris road race a fortnight later, both failing to reach the halfway mark. The shortcomings of the

design were now becoming drastically apparent. The hot tube ignition was extremely troublesome, while the poor flywheel effect of the rear wheel made for erratic running, with the rider 'jerked backwards and forwards like a Guy Fawkes in a springless donkey cart' as the disenchanted Duncan wrote.

Both the German and French factories soon found that the selling price was well under the cost of production, and things worsened when the first customers to receive their machines complained of dire starting and other difficulties. As deliveries increased, so the complaints mounted up, and when one complainant demanded a refund Duncan, Suberbie et Cie unwisely took him to court and lost the case. The upshot was that many other dissatisfied customers also demanded their money back, and similar troubles were being experienced by Hildebrand & Wolfmüller in Germany.

Early in 1897 both the French and German ventures collapsed, but while Duncan was fortunate to sell off the Petrolette business to a buyer who resolved to have nothing to do with motor cycle manufacture, the German firm went into liquidation. It was a hard lesson in the dangers of taking up 'half-hatched' designs and in the importance of full and thorough development before plunging into manufacture. Unfortunately, in a movement where enthusiasm often outweighs business sense, many other firms would perpetrate similar errors in the future.

One, indeed, did so simultaneously with H & W. In that same Paris-Bordeaux race of 1895 in which the two Petrolettes broke down, another motor cycle took part, and also failed. This was the five-cylinder, rotary-engined Millet in a new and even more ingenious guise. Its creator, Felix Millet, had found an interested supporter for his revolutionary project in Alexandre Darracq, partner in the big Gladiator cycle concern and a man with a keen eye for business. Millet had abandoned his front-drive *velo-à-pétrole* of 1892 and produced a more practical version with the rotary engine in the rear wheel.

Ignition was by an induction coil and lead-acid battery, the latter sharing space in a neat if mysterious bin set low between the wheels with the fuel mixing arrangements. The rear mudguard followed time-honoured fashion in doubling as a reservoir for the fuel, the front wheel rode in horizontal and vertical stays as a change from the more usual cycle-type forks. Pneumatic tyres were fitted, while a lever-operated central prop stand was surely the first of its kind. Millet claimed over 34mph (55kph) for his machine and declared that it carried sufficient

Top left: the first Wolseley was this tricycle manufactured in 1896. The Bolée type machine featured a horizontally opposed, twin-cylinder engine of 1255cc

Above: Edward Joel Pennington and friends aboard the Pennington Torpedo of 1896

Right: another of the infamous Pennington designs was this tandem of 1895. Note the chain steering linkage between the forks and the rear handlebars

fuel for a twelve-hour run. One fears its tank never ran empty, for this ingenious motor cycle suffered the usual pioneer's fate in having too many *eanuis mécaniques*, and Millet wisely retained pedalling gear to enable his riders to get home after the inevitable breakdown – as in the Paris–Bordeaux.

A disappointed Alexandre Darracq, who had built the Millet with the object of putting it into production at his Gladiator works, changed his plans and sought his fortune in other spheres, making it in automobiles, while the unlucky Millet died in poverty.

The third 1894 innovation, less sophisticated than the H & W or the Millet, came from Italy, where Professor Enrico Bernardi of Verona had studied the internal combustion engine since 1874. His first efforts ran on gas, but in 1884 he turned to *benzina* (petrol) and patented a crude belt-driven tricycle. In 1889 he produced a four-stroke engine which he called the *Lauro* after his son. It was a single-cylinder, water cooled unit of 265cc

– very close to Daimler's 264cc – but novel in having overhead inlet and exhaust valves (a first for Italy?), float-type carburettor and air and fuel filters.

In employing the *Lauro* to motorise a bicycle, Bernardi simply mounted it horizontally on a single-wheeled *carrello* or trailer, and attached it by twin stays to the rear frame tubes of an ordinary pedal cycle. On setting off, the rider exercised remote control of the engine with a rubber bulb, which when pressed, worked a diaphragm which in turn actuated the throttle! The entire auxiliary unit weighed 30kg (66lb), which the rider had to balance; clearly the Professor's engine contributed more to the history of motor cycle design than his mode of transmission.

For several years from 1894, engineering and technical journals in Britain, the USA and on the continent carried numerous paragraphs with enticing news to the effect that the so-and-so company of such-and-such town 'had perfected an inexpensive new petroleum bicycle, with a power unit weighing only 20lb, and a range of over 200 miles on one filling . . .', or 'A new motive power of peculiarly strong design, giving a performance superior to a gasolene engine, noiseless and emitting no noxious vapors, has been patented by . . .'. The theorists, optimists and cranks were at work, and having a field day, and until motor and motor cycle design gelled and settled down to one broad pattern, gullible investors were all too easy meat for such 'flannel' merchants.

The entry lists for two important pioneer motoring contests are eloquent of the unrealistic proposals made by 'inventors' with no knowledge or experience of real engines, but who were anxious to file their ideas as patents, 'just in case they worked'. The Paris-Rouen Trials of 22 July 1894, attracted no less than 102 entries (but only seventeen starters), and apart from steam or petrol engines, the following comfortably vague but impressive-sounding forms of motive power were listed: gravity, hydraulic, compressed air, 'Baricycle' (moved by weight of the passengers), multiple system of levers, mineral oil, 'automatic', system of pendulums, system of pedals, combination of animate and mechanical power, *liquides combinés*, semi-electric, electric, electro-pneumatic, gas and pendulum, constant propulsion, self-acting and high-pressure gas. How many actually worked is not known.

America's first motor race, the Chicago-Waukegan held in November 1895, attracted about 100 entries of 'motocycles', as all vehicles were called irrespective of the number of wheels they had. In the event only two started, and in a re-run six vehicles turned up. Among the non-runners were vehicles powered as follows: city gas, spring motor, kerosene motor, compressed air, storage system, naphtha, electro-turbine, acetylene, ether, 'vapor' engine, carbonic acid, hot air, and the very coy 'details not ready to reveal'.

Among this blithe selection were several two-wheelers of academic interest. The Lybe spring motor had a large steel drum spring which recouped the energy expended on level and uphill runs by re-winding on downhill sections, with both arm and foot power assisting. 30mph was claimed, and, according to reports, the inventor, D. I. Lybe of Sidney, Iowa, believed his machine 'will afford a mild and pleasing form of exercise, in addition to its speed advantages'.

Above and below: Enrico Bernardi of Verona built this interesting articulated powered bike in 1893. The little single-cylinder-powered attachment revved between 280 and 500rpm and produced just under half a horsepower. This vehicle was the first motor cycle built in Italy

Above: an issue of Nature in 1897 depicted the De Dion tricycle like this

Right: Comte Albert de Dion and Georges Bouton seen in their workshop. As well as building engines for their own cars and bikes, they manufactured units for other companies. Thus, De Dion-Bouton helped many others to build their own powered vehicles and get the industry into its stride

The Remington Company, better known for its rifles, also built bicycles at that time, and proposed to fit a kerosene motor to one for the race besides marketing a range of motor tricycles. C. C. Riotte of New York actually built his kerosene bicycle, the engine of which was extremely simple, being attached or removed 'at a moment's notice' from just aft of the rear wheel, which it drove direct through a crank. A battery which 'never polarises or requires recharging' furnished the ignition spark, and the motor operated, 'almost noiseless and without smell', at speeds up to 25mph.

Another New Yorker, Lewis B. White, ran his bicycle on compressed air, the rider compressing it himself as he rode along. The pedals worked two pistons which forced water, 'greatly compressed', through a compressed air chamber to actuate a 'motor wheel' turning the rear wheel. The Twombly ether motor cycle from Portland had a generator like a steam boiler below the saddle, containing 4lb of ether, heated by

burning gasolene. The vaporised ether – 'a third more powerful than steam' – worked two small motors weighing only 2lb each without pistons, which turned the rear wheel by connecting rods and cranks. The ether was then run to a condenser tank and thus 'used over and over again'. 60mph and a 100 miles range were generously claimed.

No machine was more aptly titled, however, than the Pennington 'hot air' motor cycle, entered for the race by Thomas Kane & Co, and built by the Racine Motor Vehicle Co of Wisconsin. These companies were mere victims of the highly plausible Edward Joel Pennington, a financial adventurer – this age would call him a 'con man' – from Chicago who masqueraded as an inventor and reaped all too rich a living for several years by 'milking' gullible financiers and members of the naive and unsuspecting public.

His four-stroke motor cycle had an unfinned single-cylinder of $2\frac{1}{2} \times 6$in bore and stroke, hung on unsightly stays behind the rear wheel, and driving forward by a long open connecting rod and crank attached to the wheel spindle. Controls and a fuel

21

feed pipe passed through the retaining stays, and ignition was electric via a coil spring in the cylinder 'of light untempered steel wire', and with a small primary battery producing 'a long, mingling spark'. The petrol was uncarburetted, no flywheel featured, and the cylinders required no cooling, said the inventor, since while one end produced power and therefore heat, the other acted on the principle that 'rapid evaporation produces cold', and thus he could dispense with a water jacket.

The single-cylinder engine turned at 500rpm, producing one horsepower, and could be doubled up to make a 2hp twin, or quadrupled to make a 4hp four. It has been estimated that a Pennington motor cycle could only have run for a few hundred yards, but it was while on an (inevitably) short demonstration run that the machine hit a bump and was airborne for a foot or so. Pennington promptly exploited this by designing the now famous publicity poster, showing the machine and rider leaping 65 feet over a river, with astonished but admiring boatmen

Left: an 1895 De Dion tricycle and, right, a section of its single-cylinder engine, with the petrol feed shown in detail. The power unit looks remarkably solid and burstproof

Above: Robert Bosch whose company introduced the low-tension magneto to the motor cycle before the end of the 19th century

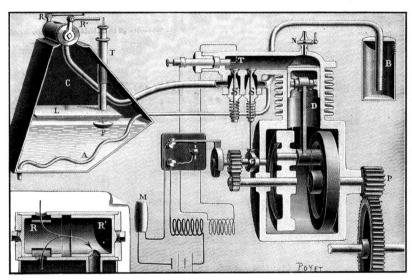

directly underneath! The machine's one apparent virtue, however, was the fitting of fat cushion tyres which, had some early rubber concern put them into production, might well have saved pioneer motor cyclists much discomfort.

The city of Munich – today the home of BMW – where Hildebrand & Wolfmüller gave the German motor cycle industry so falsely promising a start, attracted quite a coterie of engineer/inventors in those pioneer days. Two radical prototypes, at least, would seem to have drawn their inspiration from the H & W, but dates and data are regrettably vague. One machine, built by Ludwig Rubb and Christian Haab in 1895 or 1896, had an unusual power unit resembling a compound steam unit, with two pistons on a single long connecting rod, in a double-length cylinder. This was divided centrally by a secondary 'head', with the connecting rod passing through in a 'slide fit' type of arrangement.

This unorthodox twin served as a stressed member of the frame between the steering head and bottom bracket, seemingly pioneering a practice often credited to the British P & M patent of the early 1900s. Another apparent first on the Rubb & Haab was its low-tension magneto, which had just been introduced by the Stuttgart electrical firm of Robert Bosch. Mystery concerns the final drive, for the sole illustration to hand of this remarkable motor cycle indicates either that it had a very neat shaft drive, passing through one of the rear frame side tubes, or that the machine was incomplete when photographed.

Another Munich design, the Heigel-Weguelin of 1896, also used a Bosch magneto, while its engine, a much simpler 4 × 4in air-cooled single, also served as the frame down tube in the famous 'P & M' style, suggesting some possible liaison with Rubb & Haab, or a familiarity with their design. Moreover, the Heigel-Weguelin definitely had open shaft drive, with open bevels and pinions at both ends. No flywheel was fitted, and with a single speed this motor cycle, of which at least one was seen in London, was reputedly a poor hillclimber. It is of interest that Hildebrand & Wolfmüller had prepared a shaft-drive replacement for their unsatisfactory direct-link drive, but liquidation overtook them in 1897 before completion.

Interest in the motor cycle mounted elsewhere – in France, USA, Belgium, even in legally-shackled England – but nowhere more significantly than at Puteaux, in Paris, where two people of widely contrasting social background but with a common interest, the aristocratic Count Albert de Dion and the clever artisan Georges Bouton, were hard at work developing a new petrol engine. The Count had long taken an interest in mechanical things, and it was after admiring the workmanship of a model steam engine that he met the makers, Bouton and Trépardoux, and formed a business association with them in the year of 1882.

Jointly the trio built several successful steam carriages, a lighter quadricycle and a tricycle which promised good business. That was in 1889, however, just when Daimler and Benz in Germany had got their respective petrol-engined cars working. To the disgust of Trépardoux, a staunch *vaporiste*, de Dion lost all interest in steam, and enthusiastically took up the new-fangled internal combustion engine. 'How can a motor function on a series of explosions?' snorted Trépardoux, and walked out, but the De Dion-Bouton *petrolistes* pressed on and, with the Daimler single-cylinder engine as used in the *Einspur* as inspiration, they set out to produce a small engine which could be put to practical use.

Like the Daimler of nearly ten years earlier, their unit had an aluminium crankcase enclosing twin flywheels on each side of the crankshaft, and an automatic, suction-operated inlet valve directly over the cam-operated exhaust valve. Unlike the Daimler, which rotated at 750rpm, the De Dion engine turned twice as fast, at 1500rpm – and, indeed, Bouton inadvertently found during tests that it was capable of over 2000rpm without harm owing to the lubricating oil circulating faster and maintaining a constant film.

That first De Dion-Bouton single had a tiny air-cooled cylinder of 50 × 70mm bore and stroke, giving 138cc; the head was detachable, and both it and the cylinder carried cooling fins, the pair being held together by four long bolts screwing into the crankcase. Eschewing the troublesome hot tube, the partners employed battery and coil ignition, with an ingenious make-and-break mechanism which gave much initial trouble but eventually worked efficiently. Light and simple, the little engine gave only about ½hp, but they quickly installed it in a pedal-tricycle for testing.

At the historic Paris-Bordeaux-Paris event of 1895, while two surviving De Dion steamers ran unsuccessfully in the race, the firm's new motor tricycle attracted much attention in the pre-race exhibition in the Place de l'Etoile, alongside the two H & W Petrolettes and Millet motor cycle entries. While the De Dions were too new yet to race, the Petrolettes and Millet both ran, and retired. 1896 brought a different story for the much derided 'motor cycle' class, for with their bores enlarged

Top and top right: Milanese engineer Edoardo Bianchi built this quadricycle in his small workshop and utilised a De Dion engine; it was in production between 1899 and the turn of the century

Above and right: the first Raleigh was manufactured in 1899 and used a single-cylinder Schwann engine

to 58mm and output raised to around ¾hp, the De Dions quickly made their mark on the racing scene.

In the 171-mile Bordeaux-Agen-Bordeaux race in May a single De Dion vanquished a single Hildebrand & Wolfmüller, and finished fourth overall. Six De Dions then finished 1-2-3-4-6-8 in the Paris-Mantes (with a lone H & W seventh), and in the big Paris-Marseilles contest one finished an impressive third overall behind two Panhard-Levassor cars, out of 32 starters, with another fifth. In the words of famous motor racing historian Gerald Rose: 'The little De Dion tricycles showed by their admirable performance in the long race that they were very far from being the playthings which some people considered them to be'.

These first successes ushered in many more in subsequent races, but the greatest impact on motor cycle history was made when Messrs de Dion-Bouton announced that they were placing their engine into production, not only as the power source for

their own tricycles, but to sell as a proprietary power unit for other manufacturers to buy. Here was the answer to the problem encountered by so many would-be manufacturers, for producing an efficient engine was a formidable task requiring a machine shop and skilled labour. To purchase one 'over the Puteaux counter' was simply a matter of finding the necessary francs, and then adapting it to a cycle frame. The 'clip-on' motor cycle was born, and the remarkable De Dion-Bouton engine precipitated a veritable flood of new marques, and set a hesitant motor cycle industry firmly on its feet.

Chapter 2
Building to sell (1897-1904)

Left: a De Dion-engined Riley tricycle of 1899. It was fitted with a free-pedalling clutch on the back axle so that the chain was not continually in action. This machine is on display at the Donington Park museum

Until 1896 the motor cycle had been a challenge to engineers. The sheer feat of getting one to function was sufficient and future objectives were simply to make it run longer and more efficiently, without thoughts of building more to sell at a profit. Only Hildebrand & Wolfmüller had plunged wholeheartedly into producing motor cycles as a business and, as the next twelve months confirmed, they burned their fingers badly. But the coming of the proprietary, or 'loose' engine in the jargon of the motor trade, changed all that, and numerous small French cycle and engineering factions set out to produce their own motor cycles around De Dion-Bouton's excellent heart.

In Britain, too, would-be manufacturers had a tonic, but one of a different kind. On Saturday, 14 November 1896, there took place in southern England an event of immense importance to the nascent British motor and motor cycle industries. The Emancipation Run staged that day between the Hotel Metropole, Whitehall, and the Hotel Metropole, Brighton, celebrated the end of many years of bigoted and outdated restrictions on the use of British roads by mechanical vehicles.

Numerous pioneer motorists and supporters, including Sir Charles Rolls, Sir David Salamons, Henry Hewetson, the Hon Evelyn Ellis, F. R. Simms, H. J. Lawson, J. H. Knight, W. C. Bersey and J. D. Roots, had actively campaigned for many months for the lifting of the archaic 4mph speed limit (2mph in towns), which had been in force ever since 1865. They founded the Self-Propelled Traffic Association, enlisted press and political support, and in 1896 the 'Locomotives on Highways' Bill, seeking relief from that ludicrous speed limit and the obligatory 'usher' walking ahead, went before Parliament.

The Bill became an Act in November, nicely coinciding with the staging of London's first Motor Show, at the Imperial Institute in South Kensington. Parliament's concessions were grudging enough, the speed limit for 'light locomotives' being raised to 12mph, but it meant they were freed at last from 'the man in front'. The actual Emancipation Run from London to Brighton was badly organised, and took place in cold, wet weather. Its promoters, led by H. J. Lawson, were frankly more interested in the motor car than the motor cycle, but a Beeston tricycle, ancestor of the Humber, competed as did two Bollée tricars which came over from France and made quite a race of the Run, to finish first and second.

It is believed that a Dalifol steam cycle also came over, to be found abandoned many years later at the Southern Railways depot at Newhaven. Since in the sloppily maintained entry list a 'French steam bicycle' figured as number eighteen, this is highly probable, although the reason for its abandonment at Newhaven may never be known. The machine was rescued, restored, and is today in the London Science Museum.

It was noticeable that no Pennington motor cycle appeared, although the persuasive Mr Pennington had brought over his machine from Chicago, and achieved a group coup by selling the design rights, together with other useless patents covering a tandem, a quadricycle, his ignition system etc, for the impressive sum of £100,000. The purchaser was H. J. Lawson, creator of the British Motor Traction Company, The Great Horseless Carriage Company, and other dubious concerns formed to secure a stranglehold on the British motor industry by acquiring all possible patents with shareholders' money. It is recorded that the Count de Dion, when over in England, asked Pennington if he might try his motor cycle, and was told he could only do so indoors, on a wooden floor. The Count insisted that he wished to try it properly on the road, but was refused permission by the anxious Pennington.

The Pennington's absence from the Brighton run, added evidence that the purchase of the American's patents was a distinct lapse on the part of the normally shrewd Lawson. Fortune further deserted the financier in subsequent years, his monopolistic machinations ending with a term of imprisonment for fraud. Yet in founding the British motor industry, even with such dubious objects, Lawson indirectly did the nation a service. He brought over from the continent not only the Daimler car and Bollée tricar but also the De Dion tricycle, all three being built under licence by British firms who thereby gained an inside knowledge of continental practice which would have taken years to acquire from scratch.

Before all this could take effect, however, a major from the Royal Engineers was to give Britain the unexpected honour of producing the world's first four-cylinder motor cycle, and what might also be called the world's first 'superbike'. Major, later Colonel, Henry Capel Lofft Holden began work on his powered two-wheeler many months before the Emancipation Act, which argues either prescience or optimism on his part. Variable gears were still well over a decade ahead, so Holden relied on sheer power to overcome the inherent inflexibility of direct drive. Like Hildebrand & Wolfmüller, he used long exposed connecting rods and cranks direct on the rear wheel spindle, but his engine differed greatly from the Munich product.

The four cylinders were in two horizontal pairs, each like a straight, unfinned pipe, closed at each end. In each pipe was a very long piston with a crown at each end. Explosions took place at alternate ends of the cylinders, giving an impulse on every stroke. Bore and stroke were 54 × 114mm, making a total capacity of 1047cc. Stout gudgeon or 'crosshead' pins as on a steam railway engine, projected through slots in the cylinder walls to engage with the connecting rods. Automatic inlet valves were fitted, but the mechanically operated exhaust valves, lacking any convenient rotary motion in the engine to drive them, were actuated via a camshaft, chain-driven from the machine's rear wheel.

This camshaft also drove a distributor for the battery and coil ignition, and an oil pump. Carburation was by a surface-type instrument, and one of the two exhaust pipes was diverted through the fuel tank to assist vaporisation. The entire power unit was neatly enclosed by sheet metal covers, and the frame was an adaptation of the Crypto 'Bantam' cycle, with unequal sized wheels, 24in at the front and 16in at the back.

Above and below: the world's first four-cylinder motor cycle was the machine built by Major Henry Capel Lofft Holden. Its engine had two sets of twin cylinders and was mounted low in the frame

Above right: a procession of vehicles start off for Brighton from Northumberland Avenue, London, on the Emancipation Day Run in 1896. They were celebrating the abolition of the Red Flag Act

Pedals working through a hub reduction gear were retained on the front spindle, and the rider's saddle was mounted well forward for him to pedal-start the machine.

The Holden's engine turned at only 420rpm, when an output of around 3hp and a 24mph maximum were realised. It proved reasonably reliable, and by all accounts functioned in a quiet, mannerly fashion. Limited quantity production by a Kennington firm was planned in 1898, but overheating problems persuaded the Colonel reluctantly to change to water cooling the following year. This added to the already considerable weight of the Holden, and when production of the first batch was at last under way, the light motor car had realised such a stage of comfort, reliability and reasonable price that the costly Holden had little chance. Three examples were exhibited at the 1901 Stanley Show, and one was ridden from London to Petersfield and back, some 106 miles, without trouble, but that marked the swansong of the world's first 'super-bike'. An 1897 example survives today in the Science Museum in London.

Within a mere dozen years of Daimler's pioneer *Einspur*, therefore, motor cycles with vertical and horizontal single-cylinder engines, flat twins, horizontal twins, flat fours and rotary 'fives' had already appeared. A British-built one-off, unusually named the Hertschman after its creator Arthur Hertschman, an engineer with the Dunlop Rubber Company in London, added a four-stroke air-cooled parallel twin to the list. The two separate cylinders were inclined, clamped one each side of the frame down-tube from steering head to bottom bracket, and final drive was by chain. The frame was pure bicycle, and the machine's other novelty lay in the cooling, which consisted of 'air jackets' around the cylinders with great mouths for intake of air above the heads, and vents to discharge it lower down, once it had passed around them.

In France, while the first De Dion-eingined machines such as the Bougerie, Bouilly, Garreau and La Parfaite, were coming onto the roads, there were fresh developments. In 1897, a Paris firm, Labre et Lamaudière, produced a true 'micro-motor', a diminutive 64cc four-stroke single, claimed to reach 2000rpm and to weigh only $17\frac{1}{2}$lb. Its final drive was by belt with two pulleys, the largest driving the rear wheel, the smaller, with a controllable jockey pulley, serving as a primitive clutch-cum-starter gear. Battery-electric ignition featured, and the claimed overall weight in a normal cycle frame was 66lb.

Another design of greater ultimate significance came from one Hippolyte Labitte, who inadvertently made possible the biggest motor cycle success story of the pioneer years. Like de Dion he aimed to build a compact high-speed single-cylinder engine and, inevitably, the layout was similar, with overhead inlet and side exhaust valves, the former automatically operated, with four retaining bolts combining the head, cylinder and crankcase, and twin flywheels, although these were exposed and not inside the crankcase on Labitte's design.

It was pure chance that, late in 1896, Labitte took his engine along to the Paris workshops of the brothers Michel and Eugene Werner, Russian emigrés who had started a business dealing in phonographs and cinematographs. Michel had gone to Amsterdam to view an early film projector called the Kinetoscope, made by the American Edison-Bell company. It was driven by a small electric motor, and the Amsterdam importer had taken one of these motors and fitted it over the front wheel of a pedal cycle, using dry batteries for power and driving the wheel by belt.

He intended it as a publicity gimmick for advertising the new kine-show, and Werner was impressed by its possibilities. On his return to Paris he found that Labitte had left his petrol engine for the brothers to examine, with a view to its use driving a kinetoscope. Michel quickly fitted it to a pedal cycle, first at the back, then horizontally at the front, and finally vertically, in front of the steering head. He was really experimenting, like the Dutch agent, to produce an unusual advertising gimmick, but the motorised bike seemed so promising as a cheap form of transport that they publicised it as the Werner 'Motocyclette' at a price of 1000 francs – which was precisely the sum they had paid Labitte for his engine.

They were inundated with inquiries and orders, abandoned their film projection work and established a small motor cycle assembly plant in the Rue Richelieu in Paris. For a supply of cycle frames they drew up a contract with the Scot, Alexander Goven, of the Hozier Engineering Company in Glasgow, and in 1897 a dozen 'Motocyclettes' were built and sold. By 1898 sales exceeded three hundred, even though the machine had definite shortcomings. The weight of engine made the steering heavy, while the 'sideslip' so dreaded by automobilists in those days was far more dangerous on a Werner. An upset on the greasy stone setts of the typical French town all too often meant that the spirit supplying the hot tube ignition would catch fire, while riding a Werner invariably meant a libation of hot oil on the rider's face and clothes from the engine in front of him.

Then the famous, or infamous, English financier H. J. Lawson came into the picture. Hearing of the Werner's success in France, he acquired the British rights for £4000, and one of his concerns, the Motor Manufacturing Company (MMC) of Coventry, began building Werner Motocyclettes in 1899. Whatever Lawson's influence elsewhere, he was good news for the Werner brothers, who were able to expand their factory and improve the design, mainly by replacing the troublesome hot tube by trembler coil and spark ignition. The upshot was a Werner sales record of over 1000 machines sold during 1900 and wide acceptance, fortified by the countless De Dion-engined machines of other makes also in circulation, that a motor cycle was no longer a capricious toy, but could at last provide

30

Below: a replica of the 1902 Paris–Vienna-winning Werner single, marketed in 1903 in 2½hp form. The Werner company set the style with central engine-mounting, low in the diamond-type frame, from 1901

dependable and reasonably inexpensive transport.

While the Werner was becoming news, De Dion-Bouton were widening their activities still further. Adding to their loose engines, tricycles and a new light car which they were developing, they found time also to market a motor cycle of their own manufacture. Its engine was located between the rear wheel and the saddle down-tube and, while it was reliable enough, it made little impact, probably because the makers lacked the time to develop it further. Production ended in 1899, the London De Dion agent, S. F. Edge, loftily remarking that 'the motor cycle was not a satisfactory vehicle except for amusement, and would never compete with the tricycle'.

Dozens of manufacturers, large and small, in France, Germany and Britain, proved how wildly wrong he was. The coming of the *moteur* De Dion on the open market had precipitated a bewildering variety of permutations on engine location in a simple cycle frame. With the bottom bracket

'taboo', being occupied by the all-important pedal gear, all manner of alternative positions were tried; units were hung ahead of the frame triangle, inside it, between it and the rear wheel, over the back wheel, behind it, on one side or other, and in unit with the saddle down-tube, with drive belts writhing at all angles. Many of the early 'kit' bikes were frankly a mess and not particularly viable as motorised transport.

Moreover, by the law that all good things are inevitably copied, De Dion soon found their loose engine market challenged by rivals making similar units. Clement, Aster and Buchet of France joined in, as did Sarolea of Belgium and ZL (Zurcher et Luthi) of Switzerland, while Fafnir of Germany and MMC of Britain built De Dion engines under licence. More engines brought more makes to exploit what looked like rapidly becoming a boom. Famous British cycle makers who early obeyed the urge to motorise their products included Excelsior, Eadie (forerunners of Royal Enfield), Raleigh and Matchless.

Below: Riley were the first British company to manufacture engines with mechanically operated inlet valves. The system was incorporated in three single-cylinder engines, of $2\frac{1}{4}$, 3 and $3\frac{1}{2}$hp. This is the 1903 3hp Riley Forecar

Holland, new to the game, contributed the Burgers-ENR and the Eysink, both with their own engines, and the Fafnir-powered Simplex. France fielded the Clement, Peugeot and Rene-Gillet among others, Switzerland the Motosacoche – one of the neatest 'clip-ons' ever, designed by the Dufaux brothers of Geneva – Italy the Bianchi, Carcano and Figini, and Austria-Hungary the Laurin-Klement, under Werner licence.

In so cosmopolitan a boiling-pot of ideas, all was confusion for a time, and design anarchy reigned. With horsepower strictly limited, lightness and simplicity seemed vital factors, yet lightness on pre-20th century roads all too readily meant breakages, and only the strongest survived. Inevitably, engine sizes began to rise. The De Dion air-cooled range was widened from $1\frac{1}{4}$ to $1\frac{3}{4}$hp, to $2\frac{1}{4}$, and then $2\frac{3}{4}$hp by 1899, and rival engine makers followed suit. As to simplicity, that meant crude transmissions, with plain belt and pulley drives which helped to damp out the appalling vibration but were prone to slip in oil and wet, rather than more positive but heavier, costlier, chains and sprockets.

There was no clutch to assist get-away, nor gears to help on hills. When his little engine began to falter on a gradient the rider helped with energetic pedalling, an exercise wryly known in Britain as 'lpa', meaning 'light pedal assistance' as per the optimistic manufacturer's catalogue. Often it was anything but light, and hard pedalling in heavy protective clothing able to keep out wind, rain, dust and cold made early motor cycling a game for strong young men with a mechanical bent to nurse the recalcitrant machine along and to overcome the numerous petty troubles afflicting even the simplest design. In short, the man who went motor cycling in those pioneer days was essentially an enthusiast who took the rough with the smooth, and enjoyed the novelty of independent personal transport, no matter how erratic. Fortunately, there were many such people who were sufficiently adventurous and thereby ensured the perpetuation of two-wheeled transport.

In the end, sheer experience dictated the general format of the motor cycle, and by the start of the twentieth century the bold, complex, praiseworthy unorthodoxies of Holden, Rubb & Haab et al had to yield to less appealing, simpler, cheaper designs. Single cylinders, single speeds and belt drives held sway, although mercifully a few non-conformists remained to disturb the *status quo* and stimulate extra interest. There is, alas, neither room nor adequate data to record all the refreshing novelties that ingenious engineers proposed; shaft drive, overhead valves, clutches and variable gears, spring frames, unit construction, were all included. Suffice it to say that most features of the modern motor cycle were foreseen many years ago. Only the lack of suitable materials, prohibitive cost, and the buying public's resistance to the unorthodox and the unproven, forestalled their introduction.

The new century brought a further important nation into serious motor cycle production. The saying that the automobile is European by birth and American by adoption applies equally to the motor cycle, despite Roper's pioneer steam cycle experiments. The effects of Daimler's petrol machine and other early 'probes' took a long time to reach American shores, and even then reaction was largely sceptical. 'You can't get people to sit over an explosion' snorted Colonel Albert Pope, the country's leading cycle manufacturer, when one of his engineers, Hiram Maxim (who built a petrol tricycle in about 1897) tried to interest him in the internal combustion engine.

Yet, ironically, Pope's own Columbia motor cycle, built at

Hartford, Connecticut, in 1900, was one of the USA's first production models, using their own ioe single-cylinder engine in a standard Columbia bicycle frame. Contemporary with it was the Orient from Waltham, Massachusetts, which had a French Aster ioe engine in a loop frame. Drip feed lubrication from a glass-walled oil tank was a novel feature, and final drive was by a flat leather belt and a huge pulley. Early, too, was the Holley, designed by a 19-year-old from Bradford, Pennsylvania. George M. Holley built his own ioe single in 1900, even making his own patterns and castings, and fitted it into a light cycle frame. Instead of hanging it on the frame by clips and lugs he embodied the unit in the saddle down tube, forming a special inverted U-member wherein the cylinder was bolted to the frame, thus giving it more stability within the structure of the entire machine.

Holley used a big flywheel, and final drive was by chain with a big sprocket to give a high gear; his intention was to race

his machine in what was probably America's first motor cycle road race, from Boston to New York in 1901. What is more, he won that race, and in recalling it years later, he said 'That was quite a ride. Cobblestones, mud, sand, chickens and people, but the engine kept purring and I arrived right on schedule. Of course, with the layer of mud and dust on my face even my own mother wouldn't have recognised me!' The Holley motor cycle soon went into production, and by 1903 was even being exported to Europe, although George Holley gained greater fame for his carburettors made for the motor industry.

May 1901 brought the famous Indian motor cycle, a product, like so many, of a cycle maker. A Swedish immigrant, Carl Hedstrom, built a $1\frac{3}{4}$hp ioe single-cylinder engine, broadly following De Dion pattern, but with a spray-type float carburettor and battery fed jump spark ignition. It was a light, fast-turning little engine which performed well when fitted into an Indian bicycle frame at the instigation of the manufacturer, George M. Hendee of Springfield, Massachusetts. Whether by coincidence or agreement, Hedstrom fitted the engine at a rearward incline just as on the Holley, though using a simpler bracket to connect cylinder head and saddle pillar than Holley's U-piece. This rearward-inclined engine became a fashion widely followed in the United States.

The Indian was distinguished by a 'camel back' petrol tank on the rear mudguard, and had single-speed chain drive, as on the Holley. Production figures complete the success story; the Hendee Co built three Indian motor cycles in 1901, 143 in 1902,

and they had a waiting list which lasted for seventeen years!

During the next three years the US industry gathered momentum fast. Royal, Mitchell, Wagner and Marsh were all born by 1901, Merkel and Yale by 1902, and Reading-Standard, Thiem, Thor, Rambler, Tribune, Curtiss and Harley-Davidson by 1903. The Curtiss was an early venture by Glenn L. Curtiss, later famous for his aircraft, while the Harley-Davidson has flourished through the years, and is today the sole surviving major American make of motor cycle.

William Harley and Arthur Davidson of Milwaukee began work on their motor cycle in 1901, while still studying. They made the patterns and did the machining on a borrowed lathe, with Arthur Davidson's elder brothers Walter and William – both of them toolmakers – also helping. A friend who also joined in was Ole Evinrude, destined for world fame for his outboard motor boat engines. By 1903 the first machine was ready for trial. Its ioe single-cylinder engine was inclined forward in a loop frame, with final drive by belt, and somehow it epitomised all future Harley-Davidsons in being exceptionally sturdy of construction.

Arthur did the testing, the bike went well, orders began to come in, and soon a small wooden works was erected by the Davidsons' father, after which H-D, like Indian, never looked back. Their 1904 output was eight machines, but this became

Far left: Harry Metz set up the Orient company in America in 1900. This is his side-valve Aster-engined 'Mohican' of 1901

Left: a De Dion single-cylinder engine of 1899

Below: a 1905 1¾hp Indian designed by Carl Hedstrom and built in Massachusetts

fifty by 1906, 450 by 1908, and well into four figures within seven years of their founding.

Back in Europe, it was in 1901 that logic prevailed, and the motor cycle engine was placed low down and centrally in the frame, where the bottom bracket of its bicycle forebear was located, and where the lowest centre of gravity is achieved. The concern incorrectly credited with pioneering this was Werner, but because they had the foresight to patent their method of fixing, and vigorously fought any rival marque which essayed to copy them too closely, the myth has been perpetuated. As major manufacturers, Werner certainly set the fashion, but they most certainly did not invent it.

The ancestor of all petrol motor cycles, Gottlieb Daimler's *Einspur* of 1884, had its crankcase in the middle of the frame, and among other makes who followed the same logic before Werner were Hertschman, Heigel-Weguelin, Oméga, Gibson and Kerswell. There was also the special case of Joah Phelon and

Above left: the Laurin & Klement model TL of 1902 used a 498cc engine

Top: William S. Harley; above, William A. Davidson; above right, Arthur Davidson; right, Walter Davidson Snr. They were the founders of the Harley-Davidson motor company

Top right: a 1902 Neckarsulm with clip-on 1½hp Zedel engine. Later on, the bikes were renamed NSU

Far right: the Frederick Reginald Simms War Machine of 1899 which was powered by a single-cylinder, 238cc engine

Harry Rayner, two Yorkshiremen from Cleckheaton, who in 1900 patented their particular system of engine location, replacing the down tube between steering head and bottom bracket. Like Werner and the central engine, they were not the first to employ the system, but the first to patent it. A special clamp on the cylinder head was bolted to a stout frame-eye behind the steering head, the four holding-down bolts of the De Dion type engine taking the frame stresses.

Rayner later withdrew, and Phelon was joined by Richard Moore, the engine mounting system thereafter being known as the P & M for Phelon & Moore. The Humber Company of Coventry, shaking themselves free of tricycle and quadricycle entanglements by 1902, began building motor cycles with engine location and all-chain-drive under P & M patents, and the renowned 'Sloper' position endured throughout P & M's motor cycle manufacturing career, which only ended in 1965.

The 'new Werner' system, as it was called, appeared late in 1901, and subtle copies, circumventing the patent, began appearing in 1902–03. Still more new makes of motor cycle came along; Adler, Opel, Durkopp and NSU in Germany, Buchet and

Terrot in France; Puch in Austria; FN and Minerva (engines as well as motor cycles) in Belgium; Ormonde, Rex, Royal Enfield, Singer, Ariel, Rover, Coventry Eagle, Quadrant and Riley from the island of Great Britain.

Of the foregoing, the NSU came from a long-established Penny-farthing and safety bicycle factory at Neckarsulm on the River Neckar, hence NSU. Their first motorised bicycle used the Swiss Zedel engine, but within a few years they were selling their own proprietary engines as well as producing a wide range of notably sturdy motor cycles. The first powered two-wheeler by Opel, sewing machine and cycle makers, was a very run-of-the-mill belt-drive single, and fame only came their way in the automobile world. Adler, too, made cars, and today thrive in the typewriter and computer world.

The marque Buchet of Levallois sold proprietary engines built for them by Alexandre Darracq before they took up complete motor cycle manufacture. They claimed to have made the world's first full overhead valve engine in 1898, forgetting, or perhaps ignorant of, the admittedly primitive Bernardi of 1889. Puch was another old cycle firm which motorised one of its bikes as a prelude to producing big, sturdy machines. Yet another cycle maker, who also produced small arms when wars required them, the Fabrique Nationale des Armes de Guerre of Liège, Belgium, followed fashion by making a 'clip-on'. Unlike most, they made their own FN engine, a neat little 133cc ioe unit which went so well that their first year's output, in 1901, was 300 machines.

The British Ormonde, an early ancestor of the Velocette, was built in a modest basement in London, where a handful of fitters assembled motor cycles around Belgian Kelecom engines, located betwixt saddle tube and rear wheel. The first Royal Enfield had its engine in the 'old Werner' position over the front wheel, but with a bootlace belt snaking its way back to the rear wheel to the peril of the rider's nether limbs. The Singer, yet another cycle marque, graduated from three to two wheels, and was most unusual in having its engine within the front or rear wheel to choice.

It was a self-contained 'motor wheel' made by Perks &
Birch, the complete single-cylinder unit with surface carburettor,
Simms-Bosch magneto, fuel tank and rear drive being
accommodated within a cast alloy wheel. This ingenious 'power
pack' was bought for exclusive use by Singers until 1904. Unlike
many unconventional designs, this one worked well and
achieved a fair measure of popularity.

In general, the 1900–1904 period could be regarded as the
'apprentice years' for British motor cycles, most of which lagged
behind the continentals in design. Nor were the new
contraptions favourably received by some influential factions.
In 1901 the well-informed monthly magazine *Engineering*
described the motor cycle as 'a form of entertainment that can
appeal only, one would think, to the most enthusiastic of
mechanical eccentrics', and further commented: 'Much as we
admire the boldness of those who design an engine-driven
vehicle which will not stand upright of itself, and the ingenuity

with which the details are worked out, we think it doubtful
whether the motor cycle will, when the novelty has worn off,
take a firm hold of public favour'.

Happily *Engineering* was wrong. Indicative of the
near-boom conditions, motor cycles at the combined Stanley
and National Shows in London had jumped from eight in 1897
to eighteen in 1899, over 100 in 1901, and 376 in 1903, by which
time still more *debutantes* of interest had their 'coming out'.
J. A. Prestwich, a Londoner whose early interest, like that of the
Werners, lay in cinematography, introduced a new British
proprietary engine, the JAP. The first one had the time-honoured
ioe valve arrangement, inherited from De Dion-Bouton, but in
1904 JAP took a jump ahead with a pushrod overhead valve unit.

Then the ancestor of the Norton, the Energette, had
appeared in 1902, having a French-designed, British-built 143cc
four-stroke Clement-Garrard engine clipped to the front
down-tube. James L. Norton produced a few, including an
open-framed ladies' model, but concentrated more on making
cycle parts and chains for other manufacturers; his fame was to
come later in racing. Another newcomer destined for fame was
Triumph, a Coventry firm founded by two German residents in
England. Siegfried Bettmann and Mauritz Schulte began by
building bicycles, but in 1902 they clipped a Minerva engine
experimentally to one of their frames. Being well made, it went

and sold well, to the tune of 500 in its first production year, 1903. They then announced an 'all-British' 3hp Triumph with the new 293cc JAP engine for 1904, and by creating and jealously guarding a reputation for reliability their future was safeguarded for over sixty years.

Exotic designs had a lean time in those hard commercial days, but Colonel Holden's pioneer 'four' inspired others. In 1903 Charles Binks of Nottingham produced a very neat air cooled in-line four-cylinder of about 400cc, which could be set sideways or in line to choice, in a reinforced cycle frame with chain final drive and a spring bucket seat in place of a saddle. Binks later made his name in carburettors, but his 'four' reappeared in 1904 as the Evart-Hall, that London firm proclaiming in their catalogue: 'Speed, 4 to 50mph. Hills – you need not consider them. Engine started before you mount by simply pushing switch or foot lever; you then take your seat, both feet being on the ground, raise the lever which operates the clutch, and you glide away with feet on rests. Tight places in traffic have no terrors, as you release clutch, stop engine, and put foot or feet on ground. To start again, connect clutch. . . .'

At £70 this futuristic machine seemed a veritable bargain, but soon, alas, had disappeared, like so many 'ideal motor cycles' after it. Other design exotics included W. Starley's clever 1903 model built by Swifts, with single-cylinder engine set across the frame, worm drive to the bottom bracket, clutch and two-speed gear, and chain final drive. A rare London machine, the Aeolus, sported shaft drive, while the French Ader of 1903 had both shaft drive and a big transverse vee-twin engine, uncannily forecasting the Italian Moto-Guzzi models of similar

Far left: a model of the 1901 150cc Royal Enfield. Note the long drive belt which takes the power from the front-mounted engine to the rear wheel

Left: J.A. Prestwich built complete motor cycles between 1904 and 1908, but he is better known for his proprietary engines. This is a 1904 JAP 293cc, 3hp, ohv unit

Above the first Triumph produced in 1902 used a Minerva engine

Below: a 1901 Singer Auto Wheel

layout of seventy years later.

By 1904 the real motor cycle was shaking itself clear of the motorised bicycle theme. Engines were bigger, frames were getting stouter and stiffer, wheels were stronger, and forks were acquiring extra bracing and sometimes even springing. Following car trends pioneered by Mercédès in 1901, the automatic inlet valve was yielding rapidly to mechanical operation, the first tentative clutches were appearing on dearer models, and the twisted rawhide driving belt had given way to a thicker vee-belt compounded of rubber and canvas, though chain drive was becoming an ever stronger rival. Brakes were being improved, Weller of London – later to make AC cars – using an internal expanding hub type as early as 1903. The Bowden cable was coming into use for brake and engine controls, and the twist grip, first used for throttle control in racing by Werner, was adopted by Indian of the USA in 1904 for that year's range of machines.

On the legal side, police persecution became a big bone of contention in Britain, with speed traps and strong anti-motoring and motor cycling factions adding to the harassment. The raising of the speed limit from 12 to 20mph in 1903 brought some relief, although even 20mph was well below the capabilities of many machines. The noise of many motor cycles was a butt for much criticism by those who found the hard bark of a single-cylinder engine unpleasant, and exhaust cut-outs were made illegal that same year.

The new Motor Car Act also made registration of all vehicles compulsory in Britain from the beginning of 1904, both cars and motor cycles being required to carry registration plates at front and rear. This provided a useful pointer to the relative popularity of the two classes of vehicle, with 22,126 motor cycles on the register against 18,340 cars by mid-summer of 1904. This was rather surprising considering the greater exposure of the motor cycle, the relative lack of refinement, and the athletic requirements of its rider compared with those of the car driver. But purchase price and operative costs came into it, and the growing popularity of the sidecar, which made the motor cycle into an inexpensive carriage for two, and sometimes three, gave it the majority.

Below: a 1902 2¾hp Humber with its neat inclined engine; its gearing was by primary and secondary chains. The machine is fitted with pedals for starting and assisting on uphill gradients, while a freewheel clutch is also employed for coasting. This actual bike was in use until 1920

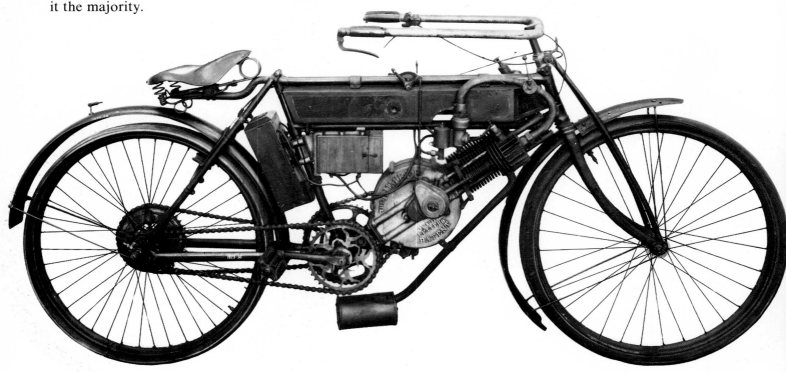

The sidecar evolved as a more practical substitute for those abominable devices, the trailer chair and the forecar. In the former, a basket-work affair drawn by a normal motor cycle, the unfortunate passenger had no communication with the rider, but collected all the dust, mud, exhaust fumes, hot blobs of oil in the face, and the racket of the engine. In the latter, he or she escaped these discomforts and had a fine view of the road ahead, offset by being closest to the accident, with a large mass of iron-ware threatening his back. The sidecar, in contrast, offered more enclosure, in a body generally made of wickerwork and later of metal sheet.

It was fixed to a light tubular frame attached to one side of the solo motor cycle, with an extra wheel for support, and a big advantage was that it could be disconnected in a few minutes by deft use of a spanner. The combination, as the motor cycle and sidecar came to be called, thereby helped in the demise of the tricycle and tricar, both of which posed storage problems only

Above: M. Denis's Lurzuin-Coudert arrives in Paris during a stage of the Paris–Bordeaux endurance trial of 1904. These endurance events were gruelling affairs and a good test of the stamina of those early motor cyclists and their machines

one stage less than those of a car. With only two wheel tracks against three, its comfort was also relatively greater.

Credit for inventing the device has gone to diverse pioneers – Oakleigh, Liberty, Mills & Fullford, Trafalgar and Montgomery – but in truth it was scarcely 'invented' by the motor cycle trade at all, being inherited direct from earlier cycling days. One Richard Tingey is credited with first attaching a lightweight wheeled 'chair' to the side of a bicycle, and quite a few were built before the motor cycle even became a practical possibility. When it did, and sufficient reliability was achieved to contemplate carrying an extra passenger, the 'borrowing' of the same idea was inevitable.

The complexities of modern road travel, with its traffic lights, multiple speed limits, pedestrian crossings, 'passing' lanes, lighting regulations, parking zones and all the other problems were unknown to the pioneer motor cyclist, who had his own set of worries, and whose main concern was to keep going at all. The conditions under which he rode give added testimony to his fibre. There were no such things as tarred, concrete or macadamised roads, and a smooth surface was a rarity. Bumps, potholes and wracking vibration were the norm, with deep cart ruts and gutters to catch the unwary.

In dry weather the motor cyclist not only left his own dust cloud astern, but rode into the one raised by the vehicle ahead. It penetrated eyes, nose, ears and clothing, while in the wet the mud did the same. Rain-filled ruts and puddles, struck by wheels, sprayed over the rider's legs and menaced the electrics, while in town the greasy cobbles and the eternal plaster of horse manure increased the perils of the 'dreaded sideslip'. The lack of

Below: the Alcyon machine of French ace Prevost pictured during the Circuit des Ardennes event of 1905

Right: M. Joostens in action on his 9hp Korn tricycle during the gruelling Circuit des Ardennes of 1902

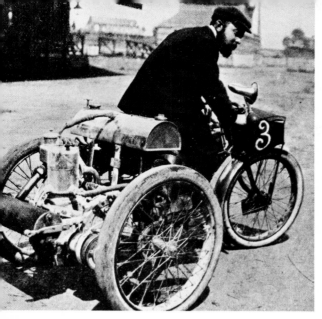

clutch and gears made traffic a nightmare, and any complete stop meant a wearying dismount and restart.

Horses needed a wide berth lest they start nervously from the noise, while the rider all too readily wielded the whip at the passing motor cyclist or motorist disturbing his way. The prejudice against 'those damned motorbikes' was at its most damaging in court. Country folk relied on the horse to haul and carry, farmers depended on them, and bred them, all 'gentry' rode horses, and all magistrates were 'gentry'. Small wonder that the offending motor cyclist got short shrift from such biased justice, especially with a 12mph speed limit to transgress up to 1903, and a 20mph limit thereafter; he was virtually guilty before going into dock.

A mean-minded bench composed of local gentry, farmers and traders saw a useful council income from the string of unfortunate law-breakers, and the police as upholders of the law joined in the persecution. Across the Channel similar prejudices prevailed with variations in their application. Germany and Holland had crippling speed limits, in Switzerland some cantons forbade mechanical vehicles altogether, while Italy was too poor to have many mechanical vehicles, and those they had were regarded as playthings or eccentricities of the wealthy. Only in France was the outlook more enlightened; she had glorious straight, well-maintained roads and a progressive outlook, plus the moral superiority of having popularised if not actually invented both the car and the motor cycle. Both were vital to her industry and trade.

In the United States there were no laws or lawmakers to stifle automotive development; some farmers and residents might raise objections, save that they themselves often found the 'new-fangled' machinery useful over such extensive land areas. A major limiting factor was the absence of a proper road system. Most towns had a stretch of well-surfaced way which expired a mile or so beyond the last houses, after which the road deteriorated badly. Large patches of sticky 'gumbo', mud and sand, were not conducive to long journeys on anything but the time-honoured horse and wagon, and only the launching of a proper trans-American road campaign (in which, incidentally, Colonel Pope of Columbia cycles and motor cycles was a leading instigator) gave American motorists and motor cyclists future hopes. In all aspects of motor cycling much had been done by 1904, but much had yet to be done.

Unlike the automobile, which found early maturity and stamina thanks largely to bold manufacturers participating in motor races, motor cycle makers had little opportunity or encouragement to pit their products against rivals in the formative years of the industry. In contrast with fast, powerful cars, frail, stuttering motor cycles scarcely able to muster 2hp presented a poor spectacle in the great town-to-town road races of pioneer days. At best they were minor sideshows, granted a class to swell the entry list, and inevitably with two and three-wheelers jointly classified in continental events as *motocycles*, the tricycles dominated. They had more room to carry bigger engines and more fuel, while their third wheel gave them more stability and the advantage of two driving wheels instead of one.

From their first appearance in the 1895 Paris-Bordeaux-Paris race, and first victories in Paris-Mantes and Paris-Marseilles of 1896, the De Dion-Bouton tricycles grew progressively more powerful, faster and more successful. In the four years from 1897 to 1900 they virtually dominated the *Motocycle* class, leaving meagre chance for any gallant two-wheeler venturing to compete with them. Often the hectically fast *mototris*, as the French termed them, outpaced the voiturettes and light cars as well, for their power-to-weight ratio was much better, and the coterie of specialist riders highly skilled and venturesome.

In 1897 the De Dion 'circus' won in Marseilles–Nice, at La Turbie, in the Criterium des Motocycles, in Paris–Dieppe and Paris–Trouville, and only in the last-named race did a solitary De Dion-Bouton two-wheeler run. Ridden by Osmont, its sixteenth place overall is eloquent of its relative impotence. The next two seasons saw the De Dions romping on to further successes, and if sometimes their victory march was disturbed by a Buchet, Gladiator, Perfecta or a Soncin, these, too, were all *mototris*. They spread to Italy, England and Germany, and wherever they went they eclipsed the underpowered two-wheelers and left them trailing in their dust.

Yet during that tricycle era there were interesting facets. In a German mixed race in 1898 from Berlin to Potsdam, a Beeston

Humber *mototri* proved the winner, beating a Daimler car and a Clément tricycle in a rare British victory. In Italy a young man named Ettore Bugatti built and tuned his own Prinetti e Stucchi motor tricycle with De Dion-type motor, scoring four wins in 1899 and three more in 1900. In those same two years another young man, Carlo Maserati, eldest of six brothers, designed, built and rode a Carcano motor cycle for the Marquis Carcano de Anzano del Parco; he won one race at Padua, won the motor cycle class of the big 138-mile race from Brescia to Cremona, Mantua, Verona and back, and scored two other, lesser wins. Both young men later gave their names to world-famed racing cars, the Bugatti and the Maserati.

At Crystal Palace track in London, a former racing cyclist, S. F. Edge, won four races in one day on his De Dion *mototri*, covering 34 miles 540 yards in one hour during one event. In each race he defeated another *De Dioniste*, Charles Jarrott. Both riders became famous in motor racing and the motor industry, and in his book 'Ten Years of Motors and Motor Racing', Jarrott recalls the 1899 Paris-Bordeaux race in which he and Edge rode De Dion tricycles. Having had but two hours' sleep the night before, he began the race feeling tired and, after an hour or two, hungry as well. His goggles, too, gave little protection to his eyes, but then he was overtaken by one of the

Above: Laurin & Klement of Czechoslovakia were among the best known of the early manufacturers. This is their vee-twin CCR model of 1904

Above left: the Coupe Internationale event of 1904 was ruined when saboteurs threw nails on the course causing innumerable punctures. At a depot somewhere between Dourdan and Foret-le-Roi, pit crews tackle the problem of yet another puncture

Above right: one of the best known of the early motor cycling pioneers was Charles Jarrott. He is seen here on his De Dion-engined tricycle prior to a record breaking attempt at the Canning Town race track

cars, which had started later:

'I think it was Charron, but it took me little time to realise that he was travelling faster than I was, and as he came by I made a desperate effort and dropped in behind him, and thereby obtained the benefit of his pacing, thus being drawn along behind the car with no wind resistance to overcome. It was a desperate game as he, on a car fitted with springs, was able to take every inequality of the road, *caniveaux*, gutters and *pavé* at top speed, whereas I, on my little machine without springs of any sort, found these obstructions terrifying, as I had no opportunity of seeing them before I struck them. It was all very thrilling while it lasted, and I stuck grimly on for miles. And then my engine began to over-heat, and to my despair I gradually dropped back. In the meantime, however, I had passed a number of motor cycles, and was in a very much better position. . . . Then another car came along, but I found that another motor cyclist had followed my example and was safely tucked in behind it. . . . Within ten miles from Poitiers, however, the heavens seemed to open and the rain came down in sheets. This was bad, but to my consternation my tricycle began to go very badly and my motor to misfire. It gradually became worse and worse, and then with a sudden jerk it stopped altogether. By this time I was reduced to a condition of absolute despair. Tired to death, aching all over, and my eyes causing me the most excruciating pain, I flung myself down in the road by my machine and there lay oblivious of everything. . . .'

Jarrot later restarted, but did not finish the race, hitting a huge rocky boulder which had been placed in the road by some miscreant for the benefit of the racing cars and buckling a front wheel too badly to continue.

As their engines grew from $2\frac{1}{2}$ to 4hp, from 4 to 6hp, and then to 8hp, the tricycles became dangerously fast, and historian Gerald Rose in 'A Record of Motor Racing' wrote: 'By 1900 the motor tricycle had become a formidable machine with a two-cylindered engine of 6 or 8hp, with huge tyres, spring front forks, dropped handlebars, and upon which the daring rider, crouching on the tiny saddle, could outpace the most powerful racing car upon straight stretches'.

The Paris-Roubaix race of 1900 foreshadowed their demise, two *mototris* becoming entangled and crashing into the crowd gathered at a corner. Several spectators were injured, including the wife of the Deputy of the local *Département*, who promptly proclaimed a ban on all racing in his region. This was later rescinded, but the writing was on the wall for the tricycle, it rapidly lost favour, and virtually disappeared after 1902, apart from short sprint and hillclimb events.

It was in 1901 that the two wheeler at last began to assert itself, thanks chiefly to the Werner factory taking up road racing. The biggest race of the year, Paris-Berlin, had a *Motocycle* class in which, inevitably, the fierce De Dion-Boutons took the first five places. Next home, however, and winner of what was termed the *Motociclette* class, came a little 1.5hp Werner ridden by Rivierre, while two Laurin-Klement singles from Austria gave the class an international flavour, but had to retire.

After this initial 'dabble', the Werners and the L-Ks turned up again for the Paris-Vienna classic of 1902. This gruelling $615\frac{1}{2}$-mile, four-day event involved the scaling of the Arlberg pass, some 6000ft above sea level, over appalling roads. The Clément works rider Derny was leading the two-wheelers when he lost control and careered downhill, shouting for help. Miraculously the driver of one of the Clément cars, de la Touloubre, managed to grab Derny's coat and drag him from

his machine in passing. Bucquet on one of the new
centrally-engined Werners got through to score an outstanding
victory over the tricycles, followed by Labitte, he who had
designed Werner's first engine, and two Laurin-Klements.

Bucquet also won the Circuit du Nord, in which all
machines had to run on alcohol, which was then a somewhat
neglected fuel, while Labitte scored in the Criterium de
Provence. Then came an important new international road race,
the Circuit des Ardennes in Belgium, with a special two-lap,
106-mile event for tricycles and motor cycles. For once the
two-wheelers outweighed the *tris* numerically, twenty to three,
and an interesting entry resulted. France sent two new
narrow-angle vee-twin Cléments, two Lamaudières, and single
examples of Impetus, Gognet and Automoteur. Belgium
defended with six Minervas, all with mechanically-operated
inlet and exhaust valves, five Antoines and a Saroléa, and
Edward J. Arnott, motor cycle sales manager for S. F. Edge's

London business, became the very first of a long, long string of
British riders competing in continental circuit races, his mount
a 2hp Werner.

Of course the tricycles took the first two places in their last
big race, with Derny's vee-twin Clément third, winning the
motociclette class. Behind came the Belgian Elskamp (Minerva),
Arnott on the Werner, the Saroléa and the other Clément.
Derny capped his success with more wins on the Clément at
Laffrey and Mont Ventoux hillclimbs, and with three wins in
three major races the French motor cycle industry was well
pleased with itself.

Contemporary with these road events a new form of racing
had sprung into popularity in several countries, using the short,
fast tracks with banked corners built for cycle racing. In Paris
the Parc des Princes, Velodrome d'Hiver and the Buffalo
stadium all staged meetings; others were held at Lille and other
towns, America ran several popular 'meets', while in Britain the

Top left: the French Griffon team rider Lamberjack in action during the Coupe Internationale race of 1904

Left: two early racing motor cyclists, messrs Martin and Hooydonk, in action at the Crystal Palace race track in 1902

Top: Charlie Collier, one of Britain's best known pioneer racers. Together with his brother Harry, he was a driving force behind the Matchless company

Above: the Griffon team pictured at Dourdan after the abortive Coupe Internationale of 1904. First home was Demester (left) while team-mates Lamberjack (centre) finished fourth and Inghibert (right) third, but the race was declared null and void after nails strewn on the road ruined it

Crystal Palace, Herne Hill, Canning Town and Plymouth cycle tracks all ran motor cycle events.

As in modern speedway, the motor cycles raced in a series of short heats and a final; good 'captive', paying audiences were available, there was plenty of excitement in the many starts and on the banked corners, and in France a series of so-called 'World Championships' was staged. The machines for these *vélodrome* events were often developments of the special 'pacers' on which the rider sat bolt upright, sometimes with a board as well as a *coupe vent*, or windbreak, to shield the racing cyclist right behind him. With no rules to comply with, these pacing machines became grotesquely over-powered and over-size, with massive single or vertical twin engines of up to two litres, devised by doubling up two singles. The next stage, inevitably, was to race these monsters on their own without the *coupe vent* and the rider crouched down and really trying. With so much power on such courses, speeds of around 60mph became almost commonplace.

In England, famous early specialists on the short cycle tracks included Harry Martin (Excelsior), the Collier brothers, Charles and Harry, on their Matchlesses, T. H. Tessier (BAT), and J. F. Crundall (Humber), while the French aces such as Cissac, Marius Thé and Rigal frequently came over – at a fee – with their huge machines for special races and demonstrations. Such meetings were the first to be organised on a commercial basis, with the object of making a profit rather than simply catering for enthusiasts, with gate-money as an incidental. Although they contributed little to the future of motor cycle racing, the competitors in these short, sharp contests learned invaluable 'wrinkles' about engine tuning which were of subsequent benefit.

Encouraged by their road racing successes, the Clément concern concocted a special sprint machine by doubling up two of their narrow-angle vee-twins on a common crankcase to make an awe-inspiring 1200cc V4. This ferocious beast gave some impressive demonstrations in the hands of Maurice Fournier, who attained a speed of around 68mph on one occasion, this probably standing as an unofficial world speed record. A valuable by-product of those vélodrome races was the evolution of the crash helmet. Following the death of a prominent American rider at Boston, the organisers enforced the wearing of leather protective helmets.

These were both heavy and unsafe, but a Frenchman named Wannson invented a lighter headgear containing an inflatable ring which was pumped up, after being fitted with an ordinary cycle tyre inflator. It was strapped around the chin by webbing, and the first well-known rider to use one was Alessandro Anzani, the Italian-born, Paris-based rider/designer who later produced many famous engines, including the three-cylinder unit with which Bleriot flew the English Channel in 1910.

On the road racing front, 1903 was a year of great promise with two classic events taking place. As is well known, the Paris-Madrid combined car and motor cycle race was stopped at Bordeaux following several bad accidents involving drivers and spectators, but Bucquet and his 3hp Werner, novel for its twist-grip throttle control, came through unscathed to win the two-wheeler class. Werners missed the second Circuit des Ardennes race, which brought a new French make, the Griffon, to the fore. It had a Zedel engine capable of 3000rpm and a 60mph maximum, and one ridden by Demester emerged the convincing winner. His team mate Lamberjack further demonstrated the marque's potential in a speed attempt with a twin-cylinder model at Dourdan, where he achieved a speed of 65.10mph (105kph).

With ever increasing interest in the Gordon Bennett series of car races which began in 1900, the French decided in 1904 to hold a similar race, the *Coupe Internationale*, for motor cycles, with similar rules restricting entries to a maximum of three machines per nation. A 34-mile course around Dourdan was prepared, five laps having to be covered, making a distance of 170 miles. France held an eliminating race to decide which makes should represent her, three twin-cylinder Griffons gaining the honour by outpacing the Peugeot entries.

Germany sent three Progress machines to be ridden by Mraz, Muller and Tolksdorf, Austria was represented by two Laurin-Klements, unusual in having their magnetos mounted upside down, below the vee-twin engine but within the loop frame. A Humber-based Jurgensen represented Denmark, ridden by Nils Petersen, and Britain sent three machines of three different makes, a Staines-built Lagonda (forerunner of the much more famous car) to be ridden by Rignold, a Quadrant for Silver, and a JAP to be ridden by Hodgkinson and built by J. A. Prestwich with one of their new overhead-valve engines.

The dozen runners became eleven when Muller's Progress was damaged in a pre-race fire, but the rest went off at two minute intervals from the needlessly early hour of 6am. Vondrich (Laurin-Klement) led the first lap from Petersen and Demester, but other machines were badly damaged by punctures, and it transpired that some unknown, ill-disposed persons had sprinkled the course liberally with nails. Both Tom Silver and Hodgkinson stopped on the first lap, and on the second only six machines came by. Vondrich still led, but Demester on the Griffon caught him and, when Vondrich punctured his tyres, team mate Toman moved up into second.

Thus they finished, with the Griffons of Inghibert and Lamberjack third and fourth, with Vondrich the only other survivor, fifth. The leader's average was 45.1mph, and the French crowd were congratulating themselves on a home victory when news came that, following protests by the official British representative and others, the race was declared null and void. Not only had the nails spoiled the event, but there were serious discrepancies in the weight limits and on the restrictions on using components made only in the country represented.

Thus the first International Cup ended in anti-climax and acrimony, although 'void' or not the French made the most of their 'victory' in the 'motorcycle Gordon Bennett'. The third Circuit des Ardennes was more successful, a tense race ending in a narrow 'home' victory for Kuhling on a Belgian Minerva, from Griet on a French Alcyon and a Peugeot. The latter marque, a branch of the famous pioneer car firm, was growing more prominent in motor cycle racing, as demonstrated a few weeks later when Lanfranchi won the Gaillon hillclimb. Winding up the season was the similar Chateau Thierry event, in which a new make, the Magali, set a new record ridden by Collomb.

Apart from racing, there was growing international interest in long-distance reliability events. In 1903 the Auto Cycle Club (known today as the Auto Cycle Union or ACU) was formed by several influential British motor cyclists and motorists, and that same year they organised a ten-day, 1000-mile Reliability Trial. This started each day from Crystal Palace, radiating out to different parts of the country, but with too numerous classes, some important abstentions, an inconsistent marking system and bad weather, the results were inconclusive. Moreover, the rural police en route made the best of a rare opportunity, trapping

literally dozens of riders for exceeding the statutory 20mph limit and causing much ill-feeling. The following year the Trial was repeated, but occupying only seven days and covering much more of England. Despite their early shortcomings, these ACC Trials were the direct forerunners of the International Six Days Trial, an event of unsurpassed prestige.

France followed Britain's example in 1904 by staging a long-distance trial from Paris to Bordeaux and back, attracting sixty starters and only twenty-three finishers, with bad weather to add to the difficulties. A Belgian Minerva ridden by Olieslagers, and a French Bruneau gained the major honours. The Italians, too, took up 'durability' town-to-town trials in which speed, regularity between stages, and hillclimbing ability all counted. In such an event, the 1903 Milan-Genoa, a chain-driven Quagliotti shone, while in 1904 the *Gazzetta dello Sport* organised a long distance affair from Milan to Nice and back. It was headed by Tamagni on a Marchand.

Left: the Canning Town track was typical of the various racing circuits which sprung up around the turn of the century. This is J.F. Crundhall, winner of the Five Miles Handicap event held at Canning Town on Easter Monday, 1904

Below: ideal for back seat drivers; this is the 400cc Phoenix of 1904 complete with unusual rear basket seat

Chapter 3
Into Gear (1905-1912)

More power, more flexibility, more comfort, were three prime needs on the average motor cycle from any country by 1905. In quest of power, it was too easy to increase the bore and stroke of the existing single-cylinder units, for the greater thump and vibration of a big single taxed the transmission and frame cruelly. Higher efficiency or more cylinders with more frequent, smoother power impulses were the options, and the year brought some notable advances.

Several vee-twins appeared, mostly of sixty degrees which fitted neatly into the diamond frame structure. The Americans with much rugged terrain to cover, particularly felt the need for more power, and the rearward incline of their average 'single' simply invited the addition of a forward cylinder. Carl Hedstrom of Indian, then the style leaders, did just that in 1905, producing a lively 500cc twin, still with ioe valves, but with twist-grip control for throttle and ignition, and a spring front fork in place of the old rigid type.

Other US makers followed, while in Europe, NSU of Germany, Puch of Austria and Peugeot of France all produced $3\frac{1}{2}$hp (500cc) twins with ioe. This wide adherence to suction-operated automatic inlet valves may seem surprising, but makers clung to the system for its simplicity and reliability compared with mechanical operation. Riders were sometimes less appreciative; too strong a return spring prevented even slow running, but too weak a spring prevented high engine revs, yet ioe persisted practically up to World War 1.

With racing experience behind them, Clément of France produced road variations of their fast 3hp twin, which the British licensees, Garrard, marketed in England. The XL'All concern of Birmingham introduced a 4hp twin from two 2hp cylinders, advertising it with the slogan: 'Have two strings to your bow and never be stuck; have reserve power and never pedal'. Princeps and Iris also marketed twins, the Iris a 5hp unit with water cooling.

Abroad, there were more exciting multis, the Paris Salon seeing two significant new models from Werner and FN unveiled for 1905. The Werner Frères' prize exhibit was a neat new air-cooled vertical twin in $3\frac{1}{4}$ and 4hp versions, with automatic inlet and mechanically operated exhaust valves. Unlike modern practice, the pistons rose and fell alternately, a single gear and belt drive were retained, but new spring front forks with rocking bottom links featured, and the machine sold at a reasonable £45 for the $3\frac{1}{4}$, and £47 for the 4hp model.

Left: an unusual feature of the vee-twin-cylinder Iris machine of 1905 was that it utilised water cooling

Below: a close up of the vertical-twin, 3¼hp Werner engine of 1905. It was air cooled with automatic inlet and mechanically operated exhaust valves

The Werner vertical twin might well have checked the march of the 'single' more effectively but for the untimely death at 46 of Michel, the younger of the Werners. His brother Eugène's interest waned, while he lost much of his capital investing in useless Russian bonds. He died in 1908, and with him died the splendid Werner enterprise which had pioneered the working utility motor cycle, popularised the diamond frame with central engine location, dominated racing for two seasons, and built the first practical vertical twin.

That fruitful Salon had further surprises, including another vertical twin. This was the Brussels-built Bercley, which had side-by-side mechanically-operated valves, and measured 616cc. It had an extra central crankshaft bearing for rigidity, with the pistons rising and falling together in the manner popularised on the Triumph vertical twin some thirty years later. Unlike the Werner, which was produced for over two years, the Bercley never made the impact its clever design merited.

FN's exhibit was still more radical. Having thoroughly familiarised themselves with the production of small, simple motor cycles and proprietary engines, the Belgian arms factory did a complete *volte face* from austerity to luxury, producing an exquisite 363cc in-line, air-cooled, four-cylinder motor cycle with shaft final drive. This was the *chef d'oeuvre* of Paul Kelecom, hitherto a builder of proprietary singles. The diminutive separate cylinders had a bore and stroke of 45 × 55mm each, and automatic inlet valves, Simms-Bosch high-tension magneto ignition, and FN's own spray-type carburettor were employed.

The FN propeller shaft for the final drive passed through the offside lower frame tube, recalling the ancient Rubb & Haab and anticipating some of today's exotic multis. The duplex front forks were early examples of their kind, with leading link telescopic springing, the coil spring being enclosed in a tube, while the rear wheel brakes comprised a car-type drum with both internal expanding shoes and external contracting band.

Unlike the British Holden, Binks and Evart-Hall fours, which failed to live up to expectations, this FN four was a great success. Kelecom progressively enlarged the engine to 412cc, 491cc, and eventually to 748cc, as well as introducing a clutch and two-speed gear by 1910, but the basic four-cylinder, shaft-drive format was unchanged right up to 1923. This was the world's first properly working and satisfactory 'super-bike' – 'super' not for high performance, since its 1905 maximum was about 40mph, but for smooth, comfortable, quiet progress to astonishing new standards for the time. FN added impact to their Salon unveiling by showing the begrimed machine which had just been ridden all round Europe on a demonstration tour by M. Osant.

Two more air cooled in-line fours quickly followed the FN

Above: at the Paris Salon in 1905, FN introduced their new machine. It had an in-line, four-cylinder engine of 363cc, and final drive was by shaft

in 1905. One came from the Mlada-Boleslav factory of the Laurin-Klement concern in Bohemia, in what was then Austria-Hungary but today, of course, is Czechoslovakia. The L-K's engine was set unusually high in order to accommodate the magneto, upside down, below the crankcase--an eccentricity also practised by L-K on their International Cup racing twins. Transmission on the 'four' was by clutch and chain final drive with single speed. Called the Type CCCC, it was a big, ugly, powerful machine catering for a small, exclusive market in its own country and in Germany.

The third 'four' came from the German Durkopp marque of Bielefeld. Rated at 4½hp, it was again an in-line with separate finned cylinders and shaft drive in FN style. The engine was of T-head type, however, while the magneto was enclosed in an extension of the crankcase and driven off the flywheel. This machine did not last long, but the concern still thrives today as roller bearing manufacturers.

Ingenious new engines abounded that year. There was the Rivièrre, a rehash of the Millet rotary theme with three or four cylinders, the Boudreaux '1-stroke' engine and the Bouchet, able to run on acetylene gas. Of greater potential was the Bichrone, an early effort at a proprietary two-stroke on the Clerk system with separate pumping cylinder, and fitted by several continental makes including Griffon. A prophetic device was the Autofauteuil. This had small wheels, an enclosed 427cc engine below the saddle, an open frame with footboards, and a *fauteuil* (an armchair) for sitting on instead of a saddle. In short, it was a forerunner of the scooter, which only caught on successfully almost half a century later.

In Britain a fresh configuration for two-cylinders on two wheels was the horizontally opposed or flat twin layout, as popularised through the years by Douglas and still used today

Above: a far cry from today's luxury saddles, but in 1904 it represented a great advance in motor cycle comfort. This advertisement appeared in The Motor Cycle of 1904

by BMW. It was pioneered on the Benz *kontra* and Lanchester car designs in around 1896 and in fact it was after studying the Lanchester engine at a Crystal Palace motor exhibition that a Bristol engineer, John Joseph Barter, set out to develop a smaller unit suitable for a motor cycle.

With assistance from Walter Moore, later renowned for his ohc Norton and NSU racing engines, and P. J. Kerswell, another Bristolian who anticipated Werner with the central, vertical engine position, Barter evolved a working unit which he called the Fée. It was fitted to a pedal cycle for testing and, following various modifications to the design, Barter formed Light Motors Limited late in 1905. The name Fée was anglicised to Fairy, and a 200cc flat-twin motorised version was marketed, followed by a 2½hp.

Some of the engine castings were made by another Bristol firm, Douglas Brothers, and when Light Motors unfortunately failed in 1907 Douglas took over, with Joseph Barter joining them as works manager. In its transition from Fée to Fairy, and then to Douglas the engine grew from 200 to 340cc, imparting the machine with some necessary zest. Even so, the first 2¾hp Douglas, introduced late in 1907, proved hard to sell initially, although the marque eventually achieved the success it deserved.

Another new twin, a conventional vee but of significance, came from Matchless. It used the 6hp JAP engine, but its novelty lay in a practical rear springing layout featuring swinging arms and coil springs, while at the front were leading link forks with tension springs. This was a creditable attempt at offsetting the execrable road conditions of the time. Another

London-built machine, the BAT, had used a spring frame since 1903, but the overall cost of such machines encouraged the appearance of 'spring fork' kits and other aids to comfort from accessory makers.

These auxiliary attachments consisted of rocking arms and tension or compression springs, which could readily be adapted to rigid front forks. Examples included the Coalway and the LAC, which fitment cost a mere £1 6s 6d in 1905! An intriguing plunger-type 'air spring' for front or rear wheels, or both, was produced by the Sharp company, while Hallé, whose main agent was none other than the Hon Charles Rolls, marketed a sprung hub at six guineas. Spring saddle pillars and sprung handlebars were other palliatives to the bumps of the day, but an increase in the fitting of spring forks by manufacturers was the best sign that something really was being done.

There was keen demand, too, for 'free engine' devices to ease the gruelling acrobatics of setting off, and for variable gears to give the hard-pressed engine a chance on hills and in slow traffic. The German NSU concern made an excellent two-speed epicyclic drive which fitted on the end of the engine shaft, and Bradbury of Oldham made it under licence in England. A. W. Wall's Roc concern, in which Sir Arthur Conan-Doyle of Sherlock Holmes fame was the main backer, produced an equally good two-speed epicyclic rear hub gear, like an oversize cycle gear. Oppermann and Kent's products were other optional fitments, while a variety of expanding pulleys and rather elementary clutch devices were available, the Bowden being one of the best.

Phelon & Moore, those Yorkshire individualists, introduced a new two-speed gear comprising two primary chains with two clutched sprockets of different diameters, engaged by expanding rings on the countershaft giving a clutch action. In combination with P & M's chain drive, the machines were brilliant at hill-climbing, and the gear was soon adopted under licence by Royal Enfield. The distinguished firm of Werner also used a twin-chain, twin-sprocket final drive on an otherwise depressing tricar they marketed in 1905, the interesting point about it being that the gears were changed through cone clutches by a rocking pedal – the world's first footchange.

Among other developments of interest were the flexible oil pipes offered by Bowden, whose covered flexible cables were already making handlebar control layouts so much simpler, a proprietary internal-expanding rear brake, and some more spring front forks, notably the French Truffault pattern, and the Italian Marchand design of sturdy leading-link type, with long narrow springs enclosed in the front tubes. A new and unusual approach to frame springing came in the Zenith Bi-car. It had a low frame of twin tubes, with coil springs interposed, the upper tubes supporting the wheels and the lower the rider and a curious tubular 'pyramid' supporting a 3hp Fafnir engine and the steering column, with car-type hub centre steering.

By mid-1905, motor cycle sales eased off, faltered, and began to drop, and the first few qualms swept the trade. Had the boom brought over-production and excessive competition? New machine registrations of over 12,000 by June were a comfort, however, so interest focused instead on the big race in France, the second for the International Cup or the 'motorcycle Gordon Bennett'. The formation of a new ruling body, the Federation Internationale des Clubs Motocyclistes (FICM) would, it was hoped, avoid a repeat of the 1904 fiasco, and the race rules and the circuit near Dourdan remained unchanged.

Entries were again restricted to three machines per nation,

and France, Austria-Hungary, Germany and Britain all nominated teams again whereas Denmark, disgusted at the 'rule bending' the previous year, abstained. To select the best runners it was necessary to stage eliminating trials, and the French were over generous to their home teams in holding these on the actual race circuit, thereby giving them invaluable extra practice. The British had a special problem, however, for apart from the 20mph speed limit, English law forbade the closure of public roads for speed events – yet the Auto Cycle Club had received no less than eighteen would-be entrants.

Fortunately, qualifying trials for the car Gordon Bennett contest were being held in the Isle of Man (which had its own government) in late May, and the ACC were able to agree arrangements to 'borrow' the circuit at around the same time. Thus racing motor cycles ran on 'Mona's blessed Isle' for the first time, using the so-called 'St John's Circuit', $15\frac{3}{4}$ miles round, between Ballacraine, Kirkmichael and Peel.

The eighteen applicants included Matchless, Westlake, JAP, Rignold, Humber, Barry, Ariel, Barnes, Quadrant and Roc motor cycles, and in the three laps, $154\frac{1}{2}$-mile 'dress rehearsal' race the first three home were J. S. Campbell (Ariel-JAP), Harry Collier (Matchless-JAP) and C. B. Franklin (JAP), this trio thus representing Britain in the actual race in late June. The French runners were Demester (Griffon), Giuppone (Peugeot) and Cissac (Peugeot), Germany was represented by Muller, Menzel and Jahn with single-cylinder ohv Progress machines, and the Austrian trio comprised Toman and Vondrich on Laurin-Klements, and Nikodem on a Puch, all of them with vee-twin cylinder layouts.

The maximum weight limit of 50kg (110lb) for a machine was highly unpopular, obliging makers to skimp on every component to save a few precious ounces, while after the machinations of 1905 the foreign contestants were on their guard against any 'hanky-panky'. Weighing-in was a tense affair with rival factions watching with eagle eyes, and the regulation insisting on all components being made in the country the machine represented caused some difficulties. The Austrian Puch was found to be using a British chain, while queries were raised on the Griffon using a Swiss Zedel engine, until it was

Below: the Peugeot team pose for the photographer prior to the start of the Circuit des Ardennes of 1905

established that this was actually made in ZL's French factory.

With observers pointedly sent by the visiting teams to police the course and check that no short cuts were made at corners and that rules were fairly observed, the atmosphere was not exactly one of international harmony. From the start Demester and Giuppone led for France, whereas Jahn's Progress proved so awkward to start that its rider threw it down in a temper, thereby adding to his delay by bending a pedal crank! The Germans were having trouble with oil leaking into their fuel tanks, and were not in the running. Toman crashed his Laurin-Klement, Campbell's Ariel had plug and other troubles, Franklin's JAP broke an inlet valve, and Collier's Matchless had tyre troubles.

On lap two Vondrich on the old-fashioned looking Laurin-Klement took the lead from Demester, and the latter burst a tyre on his third lap, changing the whole wheel with the aid of a following tender rather than repairing the old. Collier on the Matchless, last surviving Britisher, was spasmodically fast but retired on lap five, and the race finished in the order Vondrich, Demester, Giuppone. Then protests flew, and Demester was disqualified by a rule which the French themselves had imposed, banning the change of wheels. So Austria won the Cup and the French, hoist with their own petard, retired from the competition in high dudgeon.

There was comfort for them in the Circuit des Ardennes, where the Griffons scored a double in both the under-50kg *motociclette* and *motocycle* classes. The latter allowed any weight and any number of wheels, but fortunately the racing tricycle was at last extinct. A healthy entry of nineteen contested the *motociclette* race, Griffon, Alcyon and Peugeot facing ZL, Saroléa and Adler. Bucquet, the old master, won for Griffon, but a fast newcomer, René Thomas (later famous in motor racing) staved off Demester's Griffon to finish second, only to be disqualified as his Alcyon was ten grammes overweight. So Griffon emerged first and second, followed by ZL, Peugeot and Adler, while Tabuteau on the bigger Griffon easily won the heavy class from a Peugeot.

That concluded the meagre road racing season of 1905, but racing was still popular on the short cycle tracks in Britain and

Top: M. Bucquet, known as 'the old master', winner of the 1905 Circuit des Ardennes on his French works Griffon machine

Above: Griffon rider Tabuteaux pushes off at the start of the 1905 Circuit des Ardennes

Right: a competitor in the 1905 Circuit des Ardennes cutting back part of his footrest in order to save weight. Greater love hath no man than to forfeit his own comfort for the sake of a few ounces

France, and in Paris Anzani scored a notable win in the 100km Hydra Cup, riding a 250cc Buchet-engined Alcyon and beating the Peugeot team. The French also staged an eight-day road road endurance event, the 2000km Tour de France Motocycliste, covering most of *la belle France* and giving Cissac (Peugeot) victory over the rest of the specialists.

It was at the Parc des Princes vélodrome in Paris that Peugeot also set a new world's Hour record in December 1905. Giosue Giuppone was the rider, covering 63 miles 1078 yards in the time, which was thought by many to be an absolute speed record. Several two-wheelers had in fact exceeded that figure over shorter distances, but the all-out speed record for *motocicles* stood, somewhat anachronistically, to Victor Rigal's 8hp de Dion-Bouton tricycle at 109.09kph (67.63mph). Such records were in any case unofficial, but this did not diminish interest in them, while the prestige of breaking any 'record', unofficial or not, always made good advertising copy.

Such happenings waned somewhat in importance as winter brought signs that the trade depression might worsen to a slump. Those forlorn *addenda* to makers' advertisements, offering 'a few shop-soiled and last year's models' at reduced prices, betrayed the anxious mood, and manufacturers drew in their horns. Although still dominant in racing, the French motor cycle industry began a gradual lapse into indifference and stagnation, and has never really regained major international status since. The chill economic breeze also hit the USA, casualties including Colonel Pope's Columbia motor cycles and the Holley, Royal and Mitchell. In contrast, while several Italian car enterprises perished, Italy's motor cycle industry remained buoyant and, indeed, gained new recruits in Borgo and Frera, both founded early in 1906. Though both are long defunct, the welcome Latin leaning towards racing saw both their names prominent, and Borgo became pioneers in the use of aluminium pistons, scored many racing successes, and reaped such a volume of piston business that they had to abandon motor cycle production.

When sales are poor, design innovations are few, and 1906 echoed the nervousness in the trade. More spring forks were announced, the feature soon becoming the rule rather than the exception except on the smaller utility bikes. Rex introduced a particularly neat telescopic pattern, while Triumph's new 'rocking' design, nicknamed the 'crash' fork, had a horizontal spring at the top and a fore-and-aft motion which inadvertently varied the wheelbase. It did not seem very scientific, but it lasted right through World War I and into the 1920s.

Ignition improved by leaps and bounds with the coming of the high-tension magneto, evolved by F. R. Simms in collaboration with Robert Bosch of Stuttgart. The spray carburettor, such as the French Longuemare and the English B & B (Brown & Barlow) also became firmly entrenched. Brakes and tyres also improved, pedal gears were slowly disappearing, and the motor cycle had reached a stage in dependability where a rider could achieve a 200-mile journey without mishap, and take it more or less for granted.

The Berlin Show early in 1906 provided a surprise, the motor cycle section including no less than four different makes of in-line four, all broadly following the FN theme! They were the aforementioned Durkopp, the Amandus Gluser with shaft drive, the Burkhardtia with twin flat belts, and an Austrian make, the Bock & Hollaender, with shaft drive and two speeds. There was also an Opel vertical twin, and if little came of all these they do indicate that design enterprise was not lacking even when times were bad.

Right: an early poster advertising John Bull tyres

Below: another early period advertisement this one being for Brampton chains

BRAMPTON'S Chains, Pedals, Saddles,

58

On the racing front, the season's major contest, the International Cup, again proved unsatisfactory. After the Laurin-Klement victory in 1905, organisation of the third *Coupe* passed automatically to the Austrian national club. A 39 mile circuit was worked out around the town of Patzau, near the Bohemian border, and once again France, Britain, Germany and Austria-Hungary nominated teams. Only four British makes – Matchless, JAP, Westlake and Quadrant – applied to enter, and the eliminating trials took place, not in the Isle of Man this time, but in the private grounds of Knowsley Park, north of the city of Liverpool.

A useful four and a half mile circuit was laid out, and 27 laps had to be covered, the result according to the weekly magazine *The Motor Cycle* being 'undoubtedly the best motor cycle race ever held in Great Britain'. The two Collier brothers, Charles and Harry, led all the way on their 7hp twin-cylinder Matchless-JAPs, C. B. Franklin the Irish rider was third on a 6hp JAP, while Morewood (Westlake) and Butt (Quadrant) had to retire their machines.

Peugeot, Griffon and Alcyon decided to give the controversial *Coupe* a miss, so Réné-Gillet represented France with three neat ioe vee-twins ridden by Taveneau, Fauvet and Lautanne. Germany's colours were again carried by Progress, and Austria's by the well known Puch marque from Graz. The Patzau course had to be covered four times, totalling $155\frac{1}{2}$ miles, and proved a very rough, rugged affair with some severe bends, forbidding boulders lining the road, and, to the consternation of many riders, a rather too accessible lake.

Again Austria won, the crash-helmeted Nikodem on his Puch twin leading all the way to win comfortably from his team mate Obruba. Britain did better this time with Collier taking third place on his Matchless, followed by the German Retienne (Progress). All three Gillets, Wetzka's Puch, and the other British runners retired, and once again there were protests and grumbles, mainly concerning Puch's contravention of the rules in having sidecar tenders laden with spares patrolling the circuit during the race.

Nikodem's runaway victory stood, however, and the British contingent returned home thoroughly fed up with the International Cup and its regulations. The maximum weight limit of 110lb was the biggest bone of contention, restricting design to its simplest essentials – rigid forks, no gears, minimal brakes, lightened flywheels, skimpy wheels and tiny saddles. The British wanted a race of their own, run to sensible rules, and already proposals had been made for such an event in the Isle of Man. In charge of the British contingent was the Marquis de Mouzilly de St Mars, a master linguist, a skilled diplomat, and a staunch anglophile despite his French name. He, too, agreed that the Cup rules were untenable, and a fruitful discussion ensued on the train journey back from Patzau.

Before the party had reached England the framework for a new race, the Tourist Trophy or TT, had virtually been worked out. It would be held in the Isle of Man which had proved so satisfactory for the 1905 eliminating trials and for the car TT, and the Marquis de Mouzilly de St Mars would contribute a special trophy for it. . . .

Meantime, there were signs that road racing was spreading elsewhere in Europe. In Spain a German Wanderer ridden by Vidal won the Sportsmen's Club Cup at Urbano, while a Goricke ridden by Escoda took the Sama Cup, a combined road trial and race in the Tarragona area. In Italy Carlo Borgo on a Borgo won the Milan-Como road race, beating an Adler. In

France a new event, the Reims GP, fell to Taveneau on an International Cup René-Gillet. And in Belgium the fifth Circuit des Ardennes gave the Griffon team a walkover in the order Giuppone, Cissac, Demester, with a Saroléa taking the touring class. In Britain the sport was very healthy, with abundant hillclimbs, trials, track races and club events.

Salesmen hoping for improved conditions in 1907 were disappointed. The depression continued, emphasised by a marked drop in new UK registrations from 11,039 in 1906 to 8142 in 1907. Nor were all these British motor cycles, for German NSUs and other foreign makes were being imported in sizeable numbers. There were few new models. A Dennell motor cycle appeared with an in-line, three-cylinder JAP engine. Ariel produced a new single with sprung fork, mechanically-operated side valves and magneto ignition. A new proprietary engine, the 3¼hp water cooled Green, appeared. A. Drew patented a new front fork with side-linked compression springs, calling it the Druid; the pattern lasted for over twenty years.

Abroad, NSU of Germany tried an impoverished market with a new motorised bicycle, clipping a 1¼hp motor to a light frame with spring fork, tensioned belt drive and a weight of 86lb. Reception was discouraging so they concentrated on their bigger singles and twins, becoming one of the busiest factories in Europe. The Dutch Eysink marque from Amersfoort took a leaf from Werner's book and offered a 3½hp ioe vertical twin, but it didn't last long. America had a promising new big single in the Iver-Johnson from a famous maker of pushbikes and revolvers.

If a poor year for innovations, 1907 was momentous in the history of motor cycle racing. On Tuesday 28 May, the first Tourist Trophy contest duly took place. The emphasis then was greatly on the 'touring' in reaction to the farce of the International Cup. There were no limits on weight or engine capacity, but there *was* a restriction on fuel consumption, single-cylinder machines being rationed to one gallon per ninety miles, and multi-cylindered bikes to one every 75 miles, with a compulsory ten-minute stop halfway for refuelling.

Proper tyres, saddle and mudguards had to be fitted, and 5lb of tools were to be carried. Prizes for the two classes were £25, £15 and £10 for first, second and third, and the fastest winner also received the Marquis de Mouzilly de St Mars' Tourist Trophy, a beautiful silver figure of Mercury, 2ft 10in high. The 15.8-mile St Johns circuit was used, and the entry list totalled 26, the nineteen singles including Triumph, Matchless, Rex, Roc, Brown, GB, Silver and JAP machines plus two NSUs, the sole foreign contenders. The seven multis, all vee-twins, comprised two Rex, two Vindecs, and single examples of Norton, Kerry and BAT.

With machines released in pairs at one minute intervals there was little passing for spectators to see, but the races were a great success, even though the organisers did not escape controversy. Reaping the benefit of his cycle track and International Cup experience, Charles Collier on a 3½hp, 500cc Matchless-JAP was first home in the singles class, averaging 38.5mph and 94½mpg over the 158 miles. Two Triumphs followed, and Geiger (NSU) was fifth, making the best foreign performance. The multi class fell to Rem Fowler on a 5hp twin-cylinder Peugeot-engined Norton at 36.2mph, leading a Vindec and a Rex. It was objected that Collier had used his pedal gear to help on the hillier spots in the race, although no rules forbade this, and while he was not penalised the upshot was a ban on pedals in 1908 – a first fruit for the Tourist Trophy in improving design.

Above: a famous make bearing an unfamiliar engine. This Norton model of 1907, featuring a 5hp Peugeot engine, was used by Rem Fowler to win at the first Isle of Man TT

Above: H. Rem Fowler, winner of the first ever Isle of Man multi-cylinder TT, on his 5hp Peugeot-engined Norton twin of 1907. His average speed for the race was 36.22mph

Shortly after the first TT, another historic event took place – the opening of the world's first artificially constructed race track, at Brooklands, Surrey. This great work was conceived and paid for by Hugh Locke King, and built on his land between Weybridge and Byfleet between 1906 and 1907. It was designed by the self-same Colonel Holden who had produced the Holden four-cylinder motor cycle back in 1897.

Roughly egg-shaped, with high banked turns and two straights, the Brooklands outer circuit measured 2.77 miles round, and the entire surfacing was in concrete, averaging seven to nine inches in depth and laid on bare, packed sand. Locke King aimed to provide not only a venue for racing, but also a high speed track suitable for the British motor industry to test and develop its products. With a force of over 600 workmen, the whole track was completed within eight months, a remarkable feat which included taking the steep banking over the River Wey on a bridge built on the then new and revolutionary Hennebique system of reinforced concrete.

The entire project was initially car-orientated, with organisation by the newly formed Brooklands Automobile Racing Club (BARC) who held the first race meeting on 6 July 1907. Motor cycles did not race there that first season, one reason advanced being that extended full-throttle work was beyond the capability of their engines, which would seize up. This betrayed both a lack of confidence in, and ignorance of the

durability of motor cycles over seventy years ago, but
fortunately minds were changed and the first of countless
Brooklands motor cycle races was held as part of the 1908
Easter meeting. A two-lap event, it was won by Will Cook riding
a 984cc NLG built by North London Garages, with Peugeot
vee-twin engine. He averaged 63mph and was chased home by
E. Kickham (984cc Leader), with Charles Collier third on his
1906 International Cup Matchless.

While 1907 thus ushered in two new developments of vast
importance to future motor cycle development, it also marked
the sixth and last running of an established continental race, the
Circuit des Ardennes in Belgium. The event attracted thirty
entries, and resulted in a surprise final victory for the Werner
motor cycle, only a few months before the factory closed its
doors. The rider was Contant, and his machine was a new
vee-twin, suggesting that Werner's vertical twin was not suitable
for speed work. Second and third came Bucquet (Griffon) and
Peteers (Minerva), while FN, Saroléa and Peugeot all secured
impressive class wins.

The Spanish Sama Cup event was again held at Urbano, a
new French make, Magnat-Debon, taking the honours, and late
in 1907 interest centred on news that America was claiming
fantastic speeds for a fantastic motor cycle, built and ridden by
Glenn L. Curtiss at Ormonde Beach, Daytona, Florida. Surely
the world's first 'drag special', Curtiss's bike had an air cooled
40hp V8 engine intended for use in a pioneer aircraft, but
mounted experimentally in an extended and much trussed motor
cycle frame, with shaft drive through exposed bevels. The
intrepid Curtiss took it over a four-mile stretch on the famous
beach, being clocked at a claimed 26.4secs through the flying
mile. That meant an astonishing 137mph, which many experts
frankly rejected and which never gained official recognition.

A most important 1908 debutante in the motor cycle world
was the twin-cylinder, two-stroke Scott, a design which set new
standards in swift, smooth, relatively silent performance. One of
the 'immortals' of motor cycling, Alfred Scott of Bradford had
been experimenting with two-strokes since 1902, and his 1908
production model was an eye-opener. Designed from first
principles instead of following convention, it had an open duplex
triangulated frame which recalled the Hildebrand & Wolfmüller
of 1894–97, but differed vastly in other respects.

Its forward-inclined parallel twin-cylinder engine initially
measured 58 × 63mm (333cc) and had deflector-type pistons on

*Above left: a group of Oxford University
undergraduates pose on their machines prior
to a race meeting at Brooklands circuit in 1908*

*Above: Giuppone on the works Griffon
undergoes a pit stop during the 1907 Circuit
des Ardennes. He went on to win the event in
convincing fashion*

180 degree cranks. The heads were water cooled, with the radiator above them on the frame, and a 'breadbin' petrol tank on the saddle tube. A P & M-style, two-speed, all-chain transmission with Werner-style rocking pedal footchange, and front forks with telescopic springs were other features and – incredible novelty for 1908! – a kickstarter was mounted near the rear wheel spindle, spinning the engine through a length of chain. The Scott's low speed exhaust note was an entrancing purr, but like a true feline it concealed formidable performance, breaking into a fierce 'yowl' and out-accelerating most contemporary four-strokes, as future racing successes confirmed.

The eternal quest for variable speeds brought a fresh solution in the Zenith 'Gradua' gear, designed by F. W. Barnes. The expanding pulley principle was not new, but in the Zenith adaptation the rear wheel spindle moved forward or back in guides, actuated by a hand winder on the tank. The engine pulley contracted or expanded, providing 'infinite' variation between about three and a half and seven and a half to one, and if the system was crude it was remarkably effective. Norton brought out a new 'big single' of 633cc; Triumph, then very much the leading British make, introduced a special 'TT replica' of their side-valve single-speeder; Motosacoche of Switzerland marketed a neat 450cc vee-twin, and NSU built a 'pocket' 300cc twin, with a new method of taking up belt slack with a lever-operated cam plate.

On the sporting side, the second Isle of Man TT was eagerly awaited. The Auto Cycle Club had become the Auto Cycle Union (ACU), the national governing body in motor cycle sport, and they secured 37 entries, with the race pattern as in 1907. Of special interest were two FN fours with hand-operated clutches, and two NSUs with epicyclic two-speed engine pulleys, but the big excitement was the struggle between Collier's ohv Matchless and Jack Marshal's side valve Triumph in the 'singles class. Marshal won by two minutes, with another Triumph third, while Harry Reed (5hp Dot) headed the multis, pursued by a BAT with one of the FN 'fours' an impressive third.

Abroad, road racing seemed moribund, but the Reims GP

Above: Jack Marshall wins the 1908 Isle of Man TT on his single-cylinder Triumph at a speed of 40.49mph

Right: Jack Marshall looking relaxed after his winning Isle of Man ride in 1908. His overall time was 3 hours 54.50 minutes. Charlie Collier, riding a Matchless, finished second

took place again with the usual Griffon victory, Dieudonné scoring after the veteran Bucquet crashed and broke a leg. There were sundry track race meetings in Germany in which the Progress rider Georg Retienne dominated, while in England racing at Brooklands got going in earnest. The special value of the track was emphasised, however, when Charles Collier's TT Matchless broke the world One Hour record, covering 70 miles 105 yards; the successful machine was proudly displayed on the Matchless stand at the Stanley Show that year.

Trade picked up notably by 1909, as indicated by a rash of new makes in all countries. America had the Excelsior, Flying Merkel and the Emblem, all with sturdy frames and beefy engines as demanded by the long, rugged roads of the USA. America's first 'four', the Pierce, also appeared; a top-quality shaft-drive, FN-style, in-line, air-cooled unit, but with T-heads and ugly if practical large-diameter frame tubes also serving as fuel and oil tanks. Two speeds were available in 1910 but the Pierce was costly to make as well as to sell, and did not last beyond 1913.

Britain, too, had a new 'four', the Wilkinson-TAC. A product of Wilkinsons, the famous sword (and razor blade) makers, and designed by P. G. Tacchi, design was à la FN, but with cantilever leaf frame springing, a three-speed gearbox, hub brakes front and rear, leading-link low pivot forks, and a sumptuous leather armchair instead of a saddle. Several variations were made, but this ambitious dream bike had died by 1913. Other names poured forth: New Hudson, Blackburn, Regal, Royal Ruby and Premier from the UK, Ultima from France, Gilera and Della Ferrera from Italy, and even a Japanese machine, the Miyapet, all in 1909 alone.

The Isle of Man TT saw changes too. The fuel limit was dropped and the singles and multis ran together in one race for the Trophy, the former limited to 500cc and the latter to 750cc, singles then being considered faster! Two American Indian twins and the continental ace Giuppone on a Peugeot brought special interest, and though the latter finished well down, one of the Indians, ridden by Lee Evans, shattered everyone by taking the lead. Not until after half-distance did Harry Collier catch it on his Matchless-JAP twin to win, with a Triumph third.

After years of tolerating fixed drive and performing athletic run-and-jump starts, motor cyclists in 1910 found themselves

Top: the four-cylinder TAC engine of 1909. The engine was used in the Wilkinson machine of that period and was very similar to the FN unit from Belgium

Above and left: two views of the four-cylinder Pierce of 1911. The Pierce was the first four-cylinder machine produced in America, and made its debut in 1909

Below: in 1910, A. W. Wall produced his Autowheel, a 'clip-on' engine of one cylinder which drove a small wheel clamped alongside the rear wheel of a bicycle

Bottom: spectators watching the Isle of Man TT races of 1910 from their unprotected vantage point at Ballacraine

faced by a veritable plethora of 'free engine' devices: Phillipson, Mabon, NSU, Kerry, VS, Armstrong, Fitall – the choice was wide and varied, some with the clutch in the rear hub, others on the rear wheel pulley or on the engine shaft. It was the first vital step towards the separate two and three-speed gearboxes which just had to come. There was also an outbreak of 'sit up and beg' handlebars, aesthetically deplorable though undoubtedly comfortable; there were more new forks, experimental rotary valves, cleaner frame lines, more mechanically operated valves and fewer ioe engines.

The TT commanded its usual attention, but the ACU cut the twins' capacity advantage down from 750 to 670cc. It made no difference, for the Collier brothers on their Matchlesses mopped up the race, Charles preceding Harry, with a string of Triumphs behind. Remarkably, there was a race near St Petersburg in Russia, won by a German Wanderer, while Brooklands staged its first long-distance race that season, for TT bikes over 163 miles. A. J. Moorhouse on an Indian twin won outright at 56.72mph, and F. A. McNab's Trump-JAP was the first single home.

1910 also brought the first all-motor cycle show at Olympia, with vast crowds and some important new makes and models. The Birmingham Small Arms Company, parts suppliers to the trade for several years, introduced the BSA, a sturdy, conventional 499cc side valve, but quiet-running, flexible and well made. Another quality British bike, the Rudge Whitworth, also appeared, coincidentally identical in engine size but more sporting, with pushrod-operated overhead inlet valve and side exhaust, both facing forward, and clean, rakish lines. The ingenious A. W. Wall produced a new kind of 'clip on' auxiliary motor called the Autowheel. Its engine, with one cylinder from

an FN four, drove a small wheel clamped alongside the rear wheel of the bicycle. Other newcomers included the Connaught, with 300cc two-stroke engine running on petroil, and the London-built PV with neat spring frame.

The 1911 TT was quite sensational. The ACU changed the course to the full mountain 'car' circuit, 37¾ miles of winding, undulating narrow roads, mostly unmetalled, and including a cruel six-mile climb up from Ramsey to Snaefell mountain. Then they cut the capacity of the twins again, to 585cc, and introduced a new race, the Junior TT, for up to 340cc twins and 300cc singles, the big bikes' race becoming the Senior. Finally they moved the dates from September to June, where they have remained ever since.

The change of circuit caused tremendous flutter, making variable gears essential. Many competitors opted for two or three-speed epicyclic rear hub gears, but some up-to-date countershaft gears also featured, as did the Zenith Gradua, while Rudge adopted the broadly similar Mabon variable gear on which both front and rear pulleys expanded or contracted in sympathy with each other, thereby avoiding the Gradua's sliding rear spindle.

In the Senior race, the British had a severe shock when a team of three 585cc Indian vee-twins cleaned up and took the first three places. Luck played its part, for Charles Collier's Matchless was leading when he punctured, refuelled away from the pits in his haste, and was disqualified, but even so, the fierce red Indians with their two-speed countershaft gearboxes and all-chain drive gave clear warning that the European industry should put their transmission house in order. The 500cc Rudges with variable gears only managed twenty-first and twenty-second places, but a Scott twin two-stroke ridden by Frank Philipp gave notice of things to come by making the fastest lap. The Junior race was less exciting, although NSU and Alcyon challenged fourteen British makes, P. J. Evans winning on a vee-twin Humber from a Matchless single.

Below: Charlie Collier (Matchless) chases the NSU of Boldt (32) during the Isle of Man TT meeting of 1911

Bottom: a TT Indian of 1911. It had a 585cc vee-twin engine with overhead inlet and side exhaust valves. The claimed top speed was around 50mph

America's challenge in racing extended that year to Brooklands, where Indian's great ace Jake de Rosier and Charles Collier of Matchless fought an epic match race. The American won heat one with some clever slipstreaming, lost heat two when a tyre burst, and won the final when the Matchless ignition cut out. The Indian's average was 80.59mph, and Collier gained compensation for his narrow defeat a few days later, when he set a new motor cycle speed record at 91.37mph.

European road racing also began to wake up. The French ran a race from Marseille to Nice, won by a Réné-Gillet, and another from Paris to Reims, in which Naas on a Griffon beat a Réné-Gillet and a 3½hp TT replica Triumph. This model also made its mark in Italy, Vailati winning the President's Cup at Brescia, and Pusterla, the 201-mile Italian Championship race, both on Triumphs. A Triumph also won the 'feature' race at the second St Petersburg meeting in Russia, over forty versts, or about twenty-seven miles.

In reaction to America's TT triumph, Olympia 1911 went down in history as the 'Variable gear Show'. The single-speeder was irrevocably doomed, save on small, cheap lightweights, and of the 275 motor cycles exhibited, 83 per cent were offered with some kind of variable gear. Douglas fitted a proper countershaft two-speed to their flat twin, with clutch and kickstart as optional extras, while another important two-speeder was the AJS, an important newcomer from Wolverhampton named after Albert John Stevens, eldest of several enthusiastic brothers.

After producing Stevens proprietary engines for several years, the brothers were encouraged by the new Junior TT to fit one of their neat little 292cc side-valve singles into a light diamond frame with countershaft two-speed gear and belt drive. Two of these AJS machines took fifteenth and sixteenth places, after which they put the model into production with optional chain or belt drive. The Levis 211cc, two-stroke single-speeder also made its debut – a design of far greater potential than its specification suggested. There was the NUT (Newcastle upon

Tyne) from Tyneside, new quality vee-twins by Lea-Francis and Clyno, and a pleasing new side-valve Rover single, with the magneto behind the cylinder.

America's market also bloomed with a fresh influx of chain-drive singles and twins such as the Dayton, Jefferson, Monarch and Flanders. There was also the weird 'underslung' Militaire with car-type chassis and steering, side wheels, three speeds and choice of one or four cylinders. More enduring was the first Henderson four, odd-looking at first with its FN-like 1068cc engine close to the rear wheel, with an empty space ahead for footboards and the feet of the unfortunate pillion passenger, seated *ahead* of the rider. It went much better than it looked, making some impressive endurance runs, but the Henderson gradually assumed normality and became one of America's best known four-cylinder machines, many examples managing to survive until the present time.

By 1912 motor cycles were getting cleaner, lower and ever more efficient, British products particularly so. The 'model of the year' was undoubtedly the new Sunbeam from Wolverhampton, with 350cc side-valve engine, two-speed countershaft gearbox, fully enclosed primary and final chain drives, and quality right through to its impeccable finish. A big 8hp, all-chain, three-speed AJS was another notable, Douglas tidied up their flat-twin and gave it mechanically operated valves, and Williamson produced what amounted to a 'pumped up' Douglas flat-twin of 984cc, Douglas themselves making the engine which could be air or water-cooled to choice depending on the customer's preference.

The interest in road racing widened further. The IoM TT was gratifying in that two outstandingly original British designs came into their own. Alfred Scott's splendid yowling twin two-stroke won the Senior race hands down, Frank Applebee in the saddle, while flat-twin Douglases took first, second and fourth in the Junior, riders being Bashall, Kickham and Stewart. The TT over, there began what came to be known in the '20s and '30s as the 'Continental Circus' – the cross-channel forays by British riders and motor cycles which brought so much success and prestige to the industry. The French really made an effort to revive old glories, although a row between organising clubs caused the cancellation of a proposed French Grand Prix, and disturbed entries elsewhere.

In the Reims GP, British rider Graham Fenton (Triumph) won the 500cc class, but Péan's 350cc Peugeot won overall. 'New boy' Freddy Dixon crashed when his New Hudson's handlebars came adrift in the first mile, and Singer and Rudge entries were also out of luck. Then came a 280-mile 'GP de France', not to be confused with the French GP, and held at Fontainebleau. 1911 TT winner O. C. Godfrey won on his Indian twin after over six and a half gruelling hours in the saddle, heading a Triumph and an Indian single. Sidecar racing also came into vogue, Vanella winning the class in France on an outfit built by the French René-Gillet company.

France's third big race was an abortive attempt to revive the International Cup title of 1904–06. However the Cup itself had been lost in Austria after Puch won it in 1906, but they staged a new race at Le Mans, and attracted Douglas, Rudge and New Hudson from England in opposition to Peugeot, René-Gillet, Terrot and Alcyon. A British one-two-three resulted in the order Bashall (Douglas), South (Rudge) and Bailey (Douglas), while a René-Gillet again won the sidecar race. Nor was that all. A Rudge ridden by Vailati won the 314km Milan road race, while the first motor cycle Targa Florio,

Top: a close-up of the single-cylinder, 3½hp, 500cc Rover engine of 1911

Above: Ed Kickham takes the finishing flag at the end of the Junior TT of 1912, in which he set the fastest lap at 41.76mph. The winner of the race was W.H. Bashall on a Douglas

Above right: a Henderson Four of 1912. This particular example is on display in the Harrah Museum. It used an in-line four-cylinder engine which produced 7hp

Right: two competitors in the Senior TT of 1912, I.B. Hart-Davis and J.L. Emerson, race uphill out of Ramsey Town

that epic Sicilian long-distance mountain race, fell to Revelli on a Tourist Trophy Triumph.

The ACU's International Six Days Trial was assuming an ever-increasing importance, and the 1911 event in the north of England had seen both Douglas and P & M teams finish without loss of marks, the rival makes sharing the team prize. The 1912 event moved down to the south-west, centring on Devon, and again the single-cylinder P R M 'Slopers' shone, making the best overall performance and scoring four gold medals with five machines. Rover were next best with three golds, and AJS, Indian and Royal Enfield followed.

British domination in this branch of motor cycle sport had caused one German club in Munich to ban British machines on the grounds that they 'diminished the home industry's chances of success'. The result of the subsequent 500-mile Bavarian Trial, in which British machines were admitted, rather bore this out, since a P & M and a Triumph made the two best performances, heading an NSU and an FN. Undoubtedly the British motor cycle industry had made up for its sluggish start a decade earlier, and was now well in the ascendancy – a position which must seem almost incredible to modern eyes, when Britain scarcely has an industry left.

Chapter 4
On the Road (1913-1921)

Although the coming of the 'free engine', followed so quickly by variable gears in their diverse forms, made motor cycling both easier and more pleasant, it was not instantly hailed by everyone with unhallowed joy. Old hands at motor cycling who had grown up with single gears and fixed drives saw few faults in them. They liked their simplicity, could cope from long experience with the caprices of drive belts, and regarded the new devices as extra complications and fresh sources of trouble. The fact that with fixed drive they invariably had to stop their engine at any traffic halt, then pedal hard or 'run and jump' to restart, deterred them not, any more than having to return to the bottom of a hill if their uphill charge was baulked halfway up by a cart. They were used to it.

Chain drive was received with equal mixed feelings by the cautious element, who favoured the rubber-cum-canvas belt which obligingly absorbed much of the jerky engine action and general vibration. Its defects were shown up further with a 'free engine'. All was well on the level, but the average compromise drive ratio of, say, $4\frac{1}{2}$ to 1 for all conditions, made getting under way on an incline a tricky business and, if the motor did not stall, the belt fastener all too often would pull out. 'Sooner have the fixed gear and do the old run-and-jump' was the frequent first reaction. Technical ignorance also prejudiced it, a wide contention being that, because an engine got unduly hot when worked hard through a single speed, it would get even hotter if running faster on a lower gear, regardless of the fact that it was running lighter. With such factors to consider, it was small wonder that the smaller makers, to whom sales were all important, should hang back before adopting the unknown and unproven 'new fangled' gears.

Only time could wear such prejudices down. Those 1911 and 1912 TT wins by chain-drive two-speeders helped enormously, as did countless reliability trials involving hill-climbing, from the major ACU and Scottish Six Days events down to the most modest of club affairs, but the gearbox was slow in coming. When Sturmey-Archer and Armstrong both developed three-speed hub gears, elaborations of their old two-speeders but with clutches, these were eagerly adopted as a simpler answer, but here, too, there were snags. They needed frequent lubrication, lost adjustment quickly and were just too fragile to withstand the erratic power thrusts of the single-cylinder engine.

Many then copied the 1912 Douglas chain-cum-belt drive, using a separate two-speed countershaft gearbox driven by a primary chain, with belt final drive. It was a good compromise but, if the pulley on the countershaft picked up excessive oil or was wet, the belt would slip. Also, as engine power increased, so belts began to slip in the dry as well. The message was plain and unavoidable: it had to be chains eventually, even though they gave a harsh, snatchy drive with none of the belt's damping qualities. So, engineers cushioned the transmission with 'cush' drives and other shock-absorbing devices, and gradually the system was perfected, but all this expended a dozen years of exhaustive trial-and-error, so that not until the mid-1920s was there consistency at last in motor cycle transmissions.

Yet, the tenet 'What you don't have, you don't miss' applied then as ever and, despite the wide experimentation in transmission systems, distinct advances in engine efficiency, frame design and comfort made the 1913–14 period extremely stimulating. The fast sporting motor cyclist had a good choice of fast sporting motor cycles, the more serious devotee and the

family man had a wide selection of sturdy, reliable machines able to haul a sidecar, and the man seeking cheap 'get to work' transport could choose from several economical lightweights. In most motor cycle producing countries, there was now something for nearly everybody.

Whatever the stratum, there was something of interest. The 276cc Veloce machine was the successor to the Ormonde of 1900–05 and the forerunner of the much revered Velocette. A Birmingham-based cycle maker of German origin, Johannes Gutgemann, had built the Ormonde frames and when the company failed he took it over, redesigned the machine and

72

relaunched it as the VMC. In the then-current sales depression it flopped, but a few years later he tried again with the new 276cc Veloce. This had inlet-over-exhaust valve location (both mechanically operated), automatic lubrication and magneto ignition. The two-speed gearbox was in unit with the engine and located in front of it (the engine ran backwards), while final drive was by belt.

A foot gearchange was an advanced Veloce feature, and the firm began its long interest in racing by tackling the 1913 Junior TT, albeit abortively, with a bored-out 344cc edition. It also produced a larger 'Colonial' model with 499cc side-valve engine, and then a new 206cc two-stroke with the choice of single speed and belt drive, or two speeds and chain drive. To distinguish this from the larger machines, Mr Gutgemann – who by then had changed his own name to Goodman – called it the Velocette, and it sold so well that two-strokes became the firm's staple product right into the 1920s.

More proprietary engines came forward to challenge JAP, White & Poppe, Stevens and the continentals such as Motosacoche, Moto-Rêve and Saroléa in a wide market. An offshoot of John Marston Ltd, which owned Sunbeam, was the Villiers Engineering Company run by Charles Marston, the son. Like the Veloce, its first engine of 1912 was a 349cc four-stroke with overhead inlet valve and a unit-construction two-speed gearbox. This was behind the engine, however, and embodied a gear-driven magneto, cone clutch and kickstarter. It was an advanced little engine, but at the 1913 Olympia Show Villiers' main exhibit was a 70 × 70mm, 269cc two-stroke of simpler concept. Its production was apparently sanctioned only reluctantly by John Marston, but it proved such a success that the four-stroke was dropped, and Villiers became the premier suppliers of engines for lightweight motor cycles for the next forty years and more.

Another two-stroke to appear in 1913 was Pearson & Cole's Peco, a 349cc three-port unit, while Precision was yet another name to be reckoned with. It offered wide design variety, ranging from the intriguing 175cc Junior with horizontal ohv and two speeds in unit, to a water-cooled 3½hp engine and a lusty vee-twin. Made to Green's patents, the 3½hp had vertical overhead valves operated by pushrods, the radiator being formed in a square around the cylinder barrel with the cooling surfaces facing outwards. The 6hp, 800cc vee-twin had pushrod-operated vertical overhead valves, and was used in sprint and racing motor cycles and cyclecars.

Another 'over the counter' four-stroke single or twin was the Blumfield, but when Sunbeam, already rated as a kind of 'Rolls-Royce' in quality and manufacturing standards, decided

Left: one of the bikes which established the reputation of Velocette was their 1913 2¼hp model. Very advanced for its time, it featured adjustable mechanical lubrication, two-speed gears and chain drive. It weighed a mere 101lb

Above: around this time, Villiers were making headway in the world of engine production. This is their 248cc two-stroke unit, in this case fitted to a 1915 Juno

Top right: Moto Rêve were based in Switzerland but also had a plant in England. This is their 1911 vertical-twin, two-speed machine

to market a new twin in 1913, it opted for the well proven 770cc
side-valve JAP engine. Other twins were swelling the market for
sturdy, amply powered solos and combinations. Royal Ruby
and Hazelwood also favoured JAPs, but Bradbury, builders of
bikes in Oldham, with a great name for hill-climbing, made
their own. AJS and Clyno, both using the 770cc Stevens
vee-twin, could boast enclosed side valves, and all these twins
had countershaft gearboxes and chain drive, often fully enclosed.

Olympia 1913 had lots of surprises. Triumph, bastion of
four-strokes, brought out a 225cc two-stroke with the
fashionable unit construction two-speed which they called the
'Baby'. Built to their standards, it sold for years. The firm also
added a 550cc version to its four-stroke singles, with sidecar
customers in mind. BSA, too, did a '550' with three-speed
countershaft gearbox and Sunbeam a 500cc version of its
side-valve single. A well known sidecar maker, Montgomery,
turned up with a 688cc flat-twin engined motor cycle, while

Humber astonished with a weird three-cylinder 6hp model
looking like a flat-twin, but having a front cylinder of 78 × 78mm
(370cc) and two rear cylinders, each of 55 × 78mm (185cc) with
concentric cranks and sharing a common combustion chamber.
The aim was to eliminate the couple inherent in the flat-twin
with a two-throw crank but, not surprisingly, the Humber
'three' soon disappeared.

The subsequently hallowed name of Brough also became
prominent. William E. Brough of Nottingham had built motor
cycles since 1902, graduating to a 500cc single by 1908, a
vee-twin by 1911 and a flat-twin by 1913. This 496cc unit
anticipated Douglas, the flat-twin 'kings', in having ohv, while
its two-speed gearbox lived under the rear cylinder, with belt
final drive being somewhat anticlimactic on an otherwise
up-to-date performance bike. Among its feats was the premier
award three years running in the London-Edinburgh trial,
ridden by none other than W. E. Brough's second son, George.
He also raced one in the 1913 TT, and at Brooklands and

elsewhere, acquiring a taste for fast motor cycling due to attain full, rich fruition a few years later.

Royal Enfield produced a delightful little 340cc Motosacoche-engined vee-twin with ioe, dry-sump lubrication, enclosed valve gear, two-speed gearbox and all-chain drive. That pioneer marque Excelsior stuck to singles, however, and from around 1910 took up export trade in a big way, some sixty per cent of its output going to Australia, New Zealand and the Straits Settlements. In such places, power was at a premium, and the Excelsior big single, free engine single-speeder grew progressively from 500 to 650cc and finally to 800cc, becoming perhaps the ultimate 'plonker'. Rudge Whitworth ran them close, however, with a 750cc model, and such machines were in great demand for sidecar work.

The Germans at this time were expressing dissatisfaction at the inability of their motor cycle industry to stop the invasion by British motor cycles of their markets. Several concerns had

Above left: this 1910 Bradbury 3½hp used its single-cylinder engine as an integral part of the frame structure

Left: an example of a 1913 50-degree vee-twin Precision engine. Of 654cc, the unit developed around 6hp at 2000rpm. The whole unit weighed just 84lb

Top: a 1913/14 Matchless 7hp, 996cc tourer. Its 82 × 94mm bore and stroke engine had overhead inlet and side exhaust valves

Above: a view of the NSU stand at the Motor Cycle Show at Olympia in 1913

deserted motor cycles for cars, which were more profitable, but were now returning in an effort to reinstate the Fatherland's products to their rightful status. There was rather too much talk at that time of 'the Fatherland', accompanied by some disturbing sabre-rattling which boded ill for the future unless common-sense prevailed. Austria, on the other hand, seemed to welcome its cosmopolitan variety in motor cycles, with Belgian FNs, Swiss Motosacoches and Moto-Rêves, Italian Freras, and German NSUs and Wanderers all being popular. Its main home product was the Puch (which, however, used a British Precision engine, a B & B carburettor and Armstrong gears) and another make, the Vienna-built Niesner. This employed a German Fafnir engine, British Druid forks and a British carburettor, saddle and various other fitments.

The French, much more interested in cars and ludicrous, spidery cyclecars at that time, had little that was new, although Peugeot at last switched from ioe to mechanically operated side valves, and Herdtle-Bruneau surprised with a new water-cooled vertical-twin with side valves and an enclosed friction drive in the transmission.

In the United States – whose marauding Indians had largely precipitated the swing to variable gears by their unprecedented 1911 TT victory – the motor cycle industry also enjoyed the boom conditions and had multiplied impressively. Not only were there more makes, but most of them were large and powerful. In that vast land of seemingly limitless expanse but surprisingly undeveloped roads, horsepower became the prior need, and with the extra advantage of cheap gasoline, America had become the breeding ground of the big twin.

Some singles were made, of course, while even belt drive lingered awhile, but the thrust from two husky cylinders tore belts to pieces and chain drive was soon preponderant. The 1912–1917 period marked the American motor cycle industry's peak, and with their abounding power, all-chain drive, two or three-speed gearboxes and excellent brakes, their machines became world leaders, sought in all other countries and imitated in many. Indian and Harley Davidson were the largest producers and they set the fashion, the former being the faster, the latter the rock-steady 'goer'. The basis of both was a 45 degree vee-twin engine with pushrod-operated overhead inlet valve and side exhausts, in sizes from around 740cc to 1000cc.

Most other US makers followed the same format, the number of makes in those golden years being surprisingly high, with Excelsior, Pope, De Luxe, Jefferson, Pirate, Yale, Feilbach Limited, Emblem, Michaelson, Dayton, Reading-Standard, Thor, Iver-Johnson, Flying Merkel, Monarch and AMC all marketing twins. Quite a few used the same engines, for Thor, Spacke and Joerns-Thiem all supplied proprietary units, while, as in Europe, gearboxes, clutches and the like could be 'bought out'. Not that there was dull conformity. Some makers, such as Iver-Johnson and Reading-Standard, had side-by-side ('flathead') valves. Indian, Pope, Flying Merkel, Jefferson and Iver-Johnson were among those with spring frames. In fact, there was wide variety in fork design with bottom link, top link, leaf springs and coils all being used.

Bold makers like Feilbach and Peerless used shaft instead of chain drive, others like Jefferson sported full overhead valves, while Cyclone went the whole spectacular hog and produced the world's first road-going twin with overhead camshafts and inclined valves. The 61cu in (1000cc) engine, designed by Andrew Strand and built by the Joerns company, and domed pistons, roller-cum-ball main bearings and roller big ends, while all cam and magneto drives ran in double-row ball bearings. The makers claimed 100mph for these magnificent, expensive machines, which were finished in bright yellow as standard. Nor were they just performers on paper, for Cyclones were raced successfully in a period when competition was intense between Indian, Harley-Davidson, Excelsior and others.

In Europe, meantime, road racing was having its finest season yet. The French Motor cycle Grand Prix was at last to take place, uninterrupted this time by gallic inter-club squabbling, on the Amiens circuit in Picardie where the car Grand Prix also took place. An impressive international field was promised for 13 July, even at the fee of six pounds per machine. 'With this race,' said *Automoto*, with an obvious tilt at the Isle of Man Tourist Trophy, 'France brings back to the Continent of Europe the prestige of staging the greatest International race of the season, and one in which it is hoped that French machines will relive former glories'.

Clearly, however, the Isle of Man TT would only with

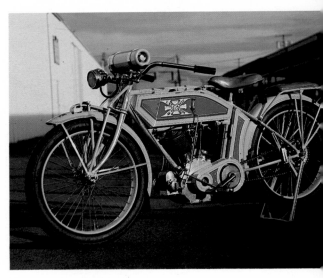

Top left: a 1913 Excelsior 7C Series 61. Excelsiors were manufactured in Chicago under the wing of the Schwinn bicycle conglomerate

Above: the vee-twin-cylinder engine layout was very popular with motor cycle manufacturers in the period before and during World War I. The Americans in particular favoured this system. This is a vee-twin Emblem of 1917

Top right: Yale of Toledo, Ohio, built bikes between 1902 and 1915. This is their 950cc, vee-twin, two-speed bike of 1912

Right: another machine built in Ohio was the Flying Merkel of the Miami Cycle & Manufacturing Company of Middletown. This is one of their famous 980cc vee-twins which featured spring mechanical starting

difficulty be ousted from its status as the year's major road race. After the 1912 Mountain circuit shock, makers returned in record numbers in 1913, with 103 entries for the Senior and 44 for the Junior race. The ACU had complicated things and lengthened the races by splitting them over two days, with an overnight stop for the machines in a guarded marquee, riders being permitted to work on them only after the starter had released them on the second day.

On paper, the Rudges with their overhead inlet valves and Multi variable speeds should have won, but ill luck and a young tester from Scott's factory named Tim Wood foiled them. After a dramatic struggle, Wood won Scott's second Senior TT by just five seconds from A. R. Abbott (Rudge), with Indians third and fourth. Suffragettes spread broken glass around on parts of the course before the Junior TT, which went to the new NUT twin from Tyneside, ridden by Hugh Mason. Trouble dogged the faster flat-twin Douglas bikes, but one finished second ahead of

an Ivy machine and a German manufactured NSU.

Despite French hopes, their 392-mile Grand Prix at Amiens proved a British benefit in the Senior class. Only one French bike, a Peugeot twin, figured in the first eight finishers, the winner being Irishman Tom Greene on a works Rudge Multi from a Triumph, BSA, Triumph, Peugeot and BSA. France fared better in the 350cc class with a win by a French Clément (although the rider was the Englishman Graeme Fenton), followed by two Swiss Motosacoches.

The revived Coupe Internationale had its fifth running in

August at Le Mans, bringing another Anglo-French success for the Briton Jack Woodhouse on a 500cc Clément. This was a compact ohv vee-twin with two speeds and chain drive, and it comfortably outpaced a Terrot and a Triumph at 54mph. Terrot won the Junior event, Indian and BSA took the two sidecar classes and the 250cc race had no finishers at all when the one Alcyon starting retired. Interestingly, a massed start was held for each class at this meeting, probably for the first time anywhere.

That busy season brought other events of interest. Rudges did well in Italy, E. Vailati winning the extremely gruelling 638-mile Circuit de Po, in which only fourteen survived from 57 starters; F.A. Rowlandson, Rudge's own competition manager, was second. The latter then won the Cremona 500cc race, making excellent publicity for Rudge on their important Italian market. Then Isody (BSA) won the Circuit de l'Eure and Pernette on a British Premier won the Champagne GP at Reims. Switzerland's fast Motosacoche bikes were a thorn in the side of both British and French rivals, with Lavanchy winning the Fontainebleau race, Riva at Brescia, and Bordino, later a Fiat car racing ace, at Umbro, all on '500s', while on Motosacoche '350s' Vuillamy was first at 'Eure and Malvisi at Umbro.

That the Swiss built very good racing machinery was emphasised by the Moto-Rêve 500cc twins, which won both the Turin GP and the Italian Championship at Cremona. In a new race, the 158-mile Spanish TT on a course between Bilbao and San Sebastian, British teams had a field day. Frank Applebee, 1912 TT winner, won the Senior event on a Scott, heading a Triumph and a Rudge, while Douglases were first, second and third in the 350cc race. Back in Britain, Brooklands also laid on something special that season – a six-hour scratch race, no less, with numerous classes for solos and sidecars. Mechanical toll among the fifty runners was pitiless and in a survival of the fittest J. R. Haswell (500cc Triumph) won at 58.62mph, with Cyril Pullin (Rudge) and H. Mason (NUT) second and third. while Zeniths took both the 500cc and 750cc sidecar classes.

Indicative of the widening popularity of road racing, major motor cycle events also took place in India, South Africa, Australia and Georgia, USA. The 300-mile Indian TT from Calcutta to Gaya went to a Royal Enfield. The Durban-Johannesburg of 1913 inaugurated a South African marathon scarcely equalled for severity. About 400 miles long, it was run over an appalling ox wagon trail traversing the Gold Reef and the Drakensberg mountains, with boulders, 'black cotton' soil, precipices, fierce rainstorms, wandering horses and oxen thrown

Top left: the start of the 1913 Isle of Man Senior Race sees Tim Wood and his Scott machine get under way. He went on to win the race in fine style

Top right: a detail shot of the vee-twin Indian Hendee Special's unusual primary drive and self starter

in. There were two overnight stops, and of 63 starters first home of under a dozen survivors was A. McKeag (Bradbury), averaging all of 28.44mph.

The West Australian TT was easy in contrast, offering rough roads but only 150 miles of them, a rider named Norton winning on a TT Triumph. And in the USA, the Savannah TT was staged over the American Grand Prix car circuit in Georgia, Bob Perry (Excelsior) winning from a Flying Merkel and a Thor. The term 'TT' was, it will be noted, gaining wide international acceptance, even though the 'Tourist' aspect was meaning less and less as the years passed.

Motor cycle sales had rocketed ever upwards since 1910, when 36,242 were registered in Britain alone. By the end of 1913, the figure was 97,784, and despite all the grim happenings of 1914 it rose still further to 123,678 during that year. When it is remembered that thousands of British motor cycles were also exported then to all parts of the Empire and many other

countries, the achievements of an industry which hardly existed twelve years earlier become still more impressive – and its virtual demise sixty years later all the more depressing.

Interesting models which appeared during 1914 included a 500cc edition of the popular flat-twin Douglas, and two other flat-twins by Wooler and ABC. The latter initials denoted the 'All British (Engine) Company', founded at Brooklands by Granville Bradshaw to build aero-engines. In 1913, he also built a 496cc flat-twin motor cycle with overhead inlet valves, two racing in that year's TT without success. By 1914, a 350cc version appeared, and ohv heads were also under development.

In America, a remarkable Indian twin, the Hendee Special, appeared; it was virtually a 'superbike' with electric starter operated through a chain-driven motor-generator and two six volt batteries. The 'all-electric' Indian was dropped a year later as being too far ahead of its time. . . . America was much ahead of Europe in lighting, electric head and tail lamps featuring on several US models by 1914, whereas Europeans seemed reconciled to acetylene lighting, the gas being produced in a generator by introducing water on to solid lumps of carbide – a smelly, messy and not very reliable process.

Above: Tom Peek's Peerless heads W. Creyton's Ariel through Kirkmichael village during the 1913 TT

Above right: victor of the 1913 Junior Race was Hugh Mason who is seen here with his NUT

79

In Britain, P & M were in the news with a new 6hp twin. This was a logical development entailing an extra cylinder at 90 degrees to the famous 'Sloper' unit. The result harmonised well, and a worm-driven magneto, 'hot spot' carburettor, enclosed oil-bath primary and final chains and footboards all featured, while – greatest novelty of all – this P & M had four speeds. The Cleckheaton engineers contrived this by combining their twin-chain primary drive with a cleverly designed, countershaft two-speed gearbox.

However, P & M also featured in another news item. 'The largest motor cycle order ever placed by the War Office, for 20 motor cycles to be used by the Royal Flying Corps, has been received by Phelon & Moore Ltd.' It didn't seem much of an order, in comparison with a French report which said 'The German Army has at its disposal in the event of mobilisation 20,000 motor cycles, 50,000 cars and 7700 lorries'. Other snippets of information were equally disturbing. There was talk of

military manoeuvres, and of vacancies for motor cyclists in the Army Service Corps and the Signal Service, apparently offering 'plenty of excitement'.

Interest in the 1914 TT in June could not be repressed, however. The ACU had tightened up the rules, making crash helmets compulsory and insisting that all competitors cover at least six practice laps. Technical innovations were rife, and good 500cc singles were getting near 5000rpm and 80mph; one Douglas had twin carburettors, and all others had overhead valves. The Junior side-valve AJSs had internal expanding rear brakes and four speeds, devised as on the aforementioned P & M twin by combining two primary drives with a two-speed countershaft gearbox (both were anticipated by Douglas in 1912); the ABCs had twin ignition; the New Hudsons had coupled brakes. The Tourist Trophy was fulfilling its role as a test centre for motor cycle development.

Top: the crowd closes in around 1914 Senior TT winner Cyril Pullin and his Rudge machine

Above: another Rudge rider at the 1914 Senior TT was J.W. Anderson seen here at the pits in front of the Grandstand

80

Top: E. Williams and AJS cross the line to win the 1914 Junior TT at the Isle of Man

Above: a 1914 Douglas flat-twin of the type raced by the factory prior to World War I. Machines of this make achieved great fame during the hostilities between 1914 and 1918

The four speed AJSs were the sensation of the Junior, the two brothers Eric and Cyril Williams placing first and second, while the 500cc race brought deserved victory to Rudge at last. Cyril Pullin rode the winning machine, while a dead heat for second place between Howard Davies' Sunbeam and Godfrey's Indian made the 1914 Senior TT a memorable one. Race followers could not know that it would be the last for six years. The assassination of an Austrian archduke in the Balkans seemed infinitely remote . . .

In August, the first International Six Days Trial was to take place in France and Switzerland, based at Grenoble, and there was some grumbling about the course and the entries. Meantime, the Italian Malvisi riding a British Ariel had won the exhausting 1500-mile Tour of Italy, beating a Frera and a Borgo. A little two-stroke Levis scored a 250cc class win in the annual French race at L'Eure, while Colver on a TT Matchless won the Senior race and Frank Smith of the Clyno concern won the 750cc sidecar race.

New four-valve racing Della Ferrera machines made their mark in Italy, winning Senior races at Cremona, in the Italian TT, and in the Appenines race, and the Junior event in the new Italian GP held near Turin. Malvisi (Motosacoche) won the Senior race, BSA picked up a Senior win at Fontainebleau, and Peugeot announced an exciting new racing vertical-twin with four valves operated by twin ohc, as on the famous Peugeot Grand Prix car. Engine and gearbox were in unit, and on its very first outing this new French bike broke the flying kilometre class record at 76.09mph. It was intended, of course, for the second French GP at Le Mans on 15 August, for which a colossal entry had been received. Eleven British makes – Matchless, Rudge, Scott, BSA, ABC, Blackburne, Douglas, Triumph, Rover, NUT and Calthorpe – were down to face Griffon, Réné-Gillet, Magnat Debon, Peugeot, Terrot, Clément and Gladiator in the Senior race alone, with NSU, Terrot, Douglas, NUT, Motosacoche, Gladiator, Ivy, Alcyon, Clément and Peugeot in the 350cc class. What a tremendous race it promised to be . . .

The ominous news item continued, though: a call for volunteer despatch riders and advice to tourists on the continent to contact the AA, warning them of the risk of machines being commandeered for military purposes. Then, on 2 August, the Germans marched into Belgium, and it was war. No French GP, no International Six Days, no Brooklands meetings, no Olympia Show; all such events became trivia in the terrible years ahead.

The switch from peace to an all-out war footing took time. Motor cycle factories still made motor cycles, and motor cyclists still rode them, unless they were already in the forces, or had their machines 'impressed' for military use. The motor cycle was undoubtedly going to be of immense value in the war, virtually replacing the horse for communications purposes. With no extensive telephone communication in fighting areas, and with vital missives to be delivered speedily, the motor cycle despatch rider soon became indispensable.

Substantial orders for DR machines were placed by the War Office with Douglas and Triumph for the Army and Navy, and with P & M for the Royal Flying Corps (later RAF). The Allied needs were enormous, with Russia, Belgium, Italy and the Middle East as well as the home forces and the colonies, all clamouring for motor cycles. Many civilian machines were commandeered at first, although too many were panic acquisitions which proved unsuitable for the appalling conditions encountered on the fronts.

Most widely used, and most popular of all the Allies' WD bikes were the 4hp Triumph and the 2¾hp Douglas. Triumph's engine was a development of its race-proved 85 × 88mm 499cc single. Early examples had a single speed, but by 1915 the Sturmey-Archer three-speed countershaft gearbox with kickstarter and belt final drive were employed, as were the famous fore-and-aft pivoting 'clash' forks with top coil spring. A magnificent reliability record earned these machines the nickname 'the Trusty Triumph'.

The Douglas earned equal affection as the 'Duggie' to many

Above: A.W. Wall marketed this Autowheel in 1910, using a single cylinder from the FN four engine. The complete 'power pack' was attached alongside the rear wheel

Right: Clyno, who were subsequently involved in car production, produced this 5/6hp sidecar outfit in 1912

thousands of 'Don R's. It had basically the same flat-twin engine which began life as Barter's Fairy eight years earlier, but now measured 57 × 61 mm (349cc) and drove through a two-speed gearbox and final belt. Douglas later also built many larger, 593cc, machines for sidecar work, and overall it is estimated that the Bristol factory turned out about 25,000 motor cycles for the services during World War I, as well as many stationary engine generating units.

Numerous other makes served 'under the colours' in diverse ways. Special Scott, Clyno and Royal Enfield sidecar outfits were built as mobile Maxim machine gun mounts, medical units also made wide use of sidecars, and AJS, Rudge Multi, Sunbeam, Premier, New Imperial, Matchless, Rover, Sunbeam and Zenith all supplied motor cycles in appreciable numbers. Belgian FN machines, both solo singles and four-cylinder combinations, were used by the Belgian and Russian forces, the latter also favouring Rudge Multi solos. France had a choice of Peugeot, Réné-Gillet, Terrot and several British makes, while Italy favoured the big 1140cc Frera twins for heavy work and the smaller side-valve Bianchis for solo despatch riding.

The rugged American all-chain-drive machines such as Indian and Harley-Davidson were widely used; Henderson fours also served well, while in contrast the little 270cc Cleveland two-stroke was employed on US base communications work. On the other side, NSU, Wanderer and Brennabor motor cycles were used by the Germans, the Wanderer being a particular favourite. This product of a Chemnitz factory had a 4hp, 600cc vee-twin engine, bottom link front forks, a spring frame with the coil springs housed in the frame tubes between the saddle and the rear hub and a reversed wedge tank with the deeper section at the rear, ensuring complete drainage of petrol. Austrian-built Puch singles and twins were also widely used by the armed forces of the Central powers.

While civilian needs became secondary to the war, motor cycles were still built and sold for private use in Britain until, in November 1916, the Ministry of Munitions banned all production of cars and motor cycles for civilian use 'for the duration'. Although there was, of course, no 1914 Olympia Show, 1915 models were duly announced, with the inevitable reservations on delivery dates. Some promising designs were lost, such as a vertical-twin, side-valve Triumph and P & M's new vee-twin. Emphasis was naturally on economy, and frugal two-strokes and small four-strokes predominated, although Rudge-Whitworth introduced an improved 500cc Multi and a new 7hp twin. Lea-Francis also had a fine 6hp twin with very neat gate-type hand gearchange, but with luxury frowned upon, Quadrant announced a small two-stroke, unique in having a poppet side-valve in the exhaust port.

Premier also sprang a surprise with a 322cc in-line, twin two-stroke called the Pony. It was in unit with a three-speed countershaft gearbox and set in a duplex frame with cylindrical petrol tank forming the top member. £45 seemed a modest price, but few if any can have been made in those grim times. Interesting, too, was the Allon 584cc parallel-twin two-stroke, which was virtually a doubling up of their reliable little single. It had a one-piece crankshaft, chain-cum-belt drive with a separate three-speed gearbox, and rim brakes front and rear. Not released until mid 1916, its career was a short sad one.

Levis built some experimental units including a 422cc flat-twin two-stroke which ended up driving ships' ventilation fans, and a 211cc two-stroke two-speeder with unit construction, all-chain drive and inside flywheel. The war killed it, although

The latest despatch "SEND MORE MEN!"

Age 18 to 45

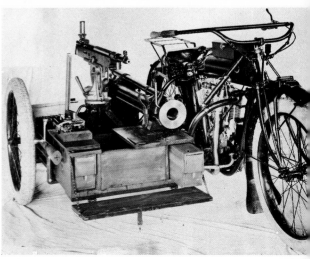

Above left: a call to arms by the South Australian Government in World War I

Left: a vee-twin Indian of World War I

Top left: Christmas Eve 1914 sees the motorcycle-equipped army on manoeuvres

Top right: a 1916 P & M war model of 498cc

Above: a 1915 Harley-Davidson 988cc outfit

Royal Enfield managed to market and sell a less radical 225cc two-stroke with chain drive, two speeds and foot change. Many garages and small engineering works were able to obtain proprietary engines such as the Villiers, Peco, JAP, Precision, Metro or Dalm, build them into simple frames and sell in those days of short supply. Thus, several unfamiliar new names replaced established old ones (engaged on war work) in the buyers' guides, names such as Hockley, Elmdon, Consul, Juno, Kumfurt, Gaby, Raynal, Ladies Pacer (made in Guernsey) and various others.

With the specialist periodicals containing instructive but

depressing articles on subjects such as 'Running on paraffin' or 'Cutting down on running costs', any news item of a sporting nature was seized upon avidly. Thus, two Combined Services race meetings at Brooklands in 1915 attracted much attention. The main concrete track had suffered severely from the pounding of heavy RFC lorries, but a series of sprints was arranged along the Railway Straight one day in August as a 'morale booster'. All the competitors were in the services, and with a 'slow' race, a plug-changing contest and timed Test Hill climbs as extra attractions, a good time was had by all.

A second, similar meeting was held a month later, with equal success, and this encouraged a third gathering in October, this time to boost morale of the Farnborough aircraft factory workers. Apart from some record breaking activities by D. R. O'Donovan, the famous 'tuning wizard' with Norton machines, that concluded Brooklands' somewhat unexpected wartime activities. There was much domestic racing in the USA, of course, until that country also joined the war in 1917. Small batches of delectable racing versions of the Indian, Harley-Davidson and Excelsior twins, all with overhead valves, were built for sale, and these fierce machines contested a prodigious number of races, mostly on short tracks, success being about equal between the three, with Flying Merkel and Cyclone occasionally intruding. Single-cylinder ohv machines were also raced on board tracks, but all activity ended after 1916 by mutual agreement.

When the war finished in November 1918, an exhausted world gradually returned to normal life. Factories geared to intensive war production took months to switch to peaceful commodities, such as motor cycles. Discharged servicemen eager to spend their gratuities on a new machine found very few available, and long waiting lists for them. They also found that prices had risen considerably since 1914. Conditions in 1919 were chaotic, with serious shortages of coal, and all the materials that make up a motor cycle or car – iron, steel, sheet metal, brass, copper, rubber, aluminium, wire *etc*. Supplies were rationed and makers and their customers had to wait.

Some concerns like Douglas and Triumph had assembly lines which had simply to be switched from DR to civilian machines, but with no more 'priorities' they, too, suffered from the universal shortages. Advertisements were enticing. 'Place your order Now,' said Bradbury. 'Register your name for earliest delivery,' said Clyno. 'It is coming – the perfect motor cycle – worth waiting for,' said Raleigh. 'Join our waiting list,' said Zenith. 'Coming events cast their shadows before,' said Scott. 'Deliveries by March,' said Coulson-B in February. But there weren't. Coulson-B was just one of dozens of new makes which mushroomed on the British market, and much the same conditions prevailed in France, Belgium, Italy and even defeated Germany. Big firms engaged for the past four years on armament work or aircraft, ships, tanks, guns or what-have-you were all hungry for new outlets to sustain their overgrown factories. At the same time, small firms or individuals enthusiastic about motor cycles would laboriously scrape up some capital and launch shakily into manufacture. Between them all, large and small, they contributed over fifty new British makes in 1919 alone, over forty more in 1920, and over fifteen in 1921. Many were simple assemblers of bought-out parts, whereas others produced machines in their entirety. There was a vast, almost dangerous optimism pervading all, for the war was over, money was plentiful and pleasure was back on the agenda.

Considering their technical backgrounds, some of the

Above: a Scott 3¾hp, two-stroke, water-cooled engine of 1919. This parallel-twin-cylinder inclined engine was used by the company for many years and the same basic design was utilised by George Silk for his custom-built machines of the 1970s

Right: board-track racing was very popular in America in the early 1920s. This superb shot is of a big twin-cylinder Harley-Davidson

newcomers seemed assured of success. The famous Sopwith Aviation company took on manufacture of a new ABC motor cycle; Beardmore, the shipping and locomotive giant, acquired an all-new Precision design from F. E. Baker; Hawker, Martinsyde and Bleriot, great names in flying, all put their names on motor cycle tanks; Gnome-Rhone had built aero-engines, as had BMW of Munich; the mighty Krupps armament firm, Mauser of rifles fame and Spandau the machine gun makers – they all tried building motor cycles, yet only BMW among them survives today.

Despite all the problems, with labour troubles and unemployment thrown in, Britain managed to stage an Olympia Show in 1919, perhaps prematurely, for many of the exhibits were pre-war designs 'warmed up'. Clyno showed a new 8hp 'Peace' model, Matchless its almost indestructible 'Victory' Model H big twin, painted in revolting Army khaki, and BSA and Sunbeam also showed big twins. There were some

interesting spring frames, many proprietary two and four-stroke engines to keep the assemblers busy, while undoubtedly the sensation of the Show was the new ABC built by Sopwiths.

Starting with a clean sheet of paper, Granville Bradshaw had produced a 398cc flat-twin ohv engine, installed transversely in a cradle frame in unit with a four-speed gearbox. Chain drive, a twist grip controlled clutch, quarter elliptic springing and hub brakes front and rear completed an almost ideal specification, and production got under way as quickly as possible. The Gnome-Rhone factory in France also arranged to build the machine under licence, and lost no time in developing a full 500cc version.

As 1919 rolled into 1920, motor cycle production at last began to flow, and orders were gradually fulfilled, but prices had risen so sharply in the meantime that many orders were cancelled, and few new ones were forthcoming. A £65 motor cycle in 1919 had all too often become a £130 one in 1920, and the nice new boom quietly petered out. In the middle of it came the scooter 'bubble', inspired by the Autoped, an American wartime austerity device with two tiny wheels, a 155cc engine attached to one side of the front wheel, and a platform for the rider but no saddle. The Autoped was hailed as the new 'Everyman's (and woman's) Runabout'.

Much ingenuity went into some designs, but others were crude and ill-conceived. Two-strokes, four-strokes, side-valve and overhead-valve, gear, chain and belt drive, spring and rigid platform frames, seats or standing room only, full enclosure or stark exposure – variety was wide, but one vital thing proved lacking in most of them – reliability. Too frail, too limited, the first scooter age died within two years; Skootamota, Autoglider, Kenilworth, Silva, Marseel, Hack, Grigg, Autosco, Unibus, Reynolds Runabout, Tankette, Whippet, Stafford, Kingsbury, even the German Golem built by DKW and the Krupp, had come and gone. More than a quarter-century later, the species would be revived, successfully this time.

With all the euphoria of peace, Olympia shows and new models, an essentially sporting movement like motor cycling required one other sign that normality had returned – a resumption of racing. Almost inevitably it was the French, inventors of road racing, who first revived it after World War I. Following a preliminary hill-climb or two to 'get into gear', the long-established Circuit de L'Eure at Vernon was revived. Peugeot sent a pair of its sensational 1914 twin-cam eight-valve vertical twins, with which Péan and Perrin duly scored first and

second in the 224-mile 500cc race. An ohv Motosacoche beat two Alcyons in the Junior event, and two G-Ls, a new French marque with a MAG engine and many British components, beat a Rover in the 750cc sidecar race, wearing sparse but elegant aluminium sidecars.

In Britain, competition resumed in 1919 with much zest, countless sprints, hill-climbs and trials taking place. 'Soldiers' outings' arranged by clubs were a sign of the times, and the year's big events were the Scottish and ACU Six Days Trials, which produced the usual multifarious class wins. In 1920, things moved in earnest, with the revival of the Isle of Man TT. Some manufacturers, grappling with production problems, stayed away, and the Senior event attracted only 27 runners, with Indian, Norton and Sunbeam the main protagonists. George Dance, ace sprinter, set the pace on a works side valve Sunbeam, but a broken inlet valve halted him on lap three, whereupon Manxman Duggie Brown (Norton) took over, until T. C. de la Hay gradually overhauled him to score Sunbeam's first Tourist Trophy victory.

The Junior race saw a dramatic finish in which Cyril Williams, with a twenty minute lead on a works ohv AJS, stopped four miles from the finish with a broken engine shaft. He pushed, paddled and coasted home, and still won from two Blackburnes and a 2¼hp Levis two-stroke which also won the newly inaugurated Lightweight (250cc) class. France offset the TT with two race meetings that season though neither had the glamour of the Manx classic. Péan's Peugeot twin galloped off with the 500cc race at Lyons, while Alcyon cleaned up the other classes, but things went awry in the Grand Prix at Le Mans.

Douglas, Verus and ABC contingents went from Britain to rival the Peugeots, Alcyons, Motosacoches and three interesting new Bleriot eight-valve vertical twins. Alexander's Douglas looked a sure 500cc winner until second gear stripped, and Jolly's Alcyon inherited first place, the sole survivor of twenty starters, indicative of the destructive circuit and the fragility of early post-war racing motor cycles. Englishman Kenelm Bartlett won the Junior race on a Verus, and a Thomann beat a Motosolo in a dull 250cc race.

Brooklands track also came back to life in 1920, the war-time scars partially healed, although the course was distinctly bumpy. The joint car and bike meeting due on Easter Monday was postponed a week through heavy rain. Two BMCRC races were billed, and both were won by the new transverse flat-twin ABC ridden by Jack Emerson, beating a Matchless each time. America, too, was quickly back in the swing of racing, although her main international achievement in 1920 was a new absolute motor cycle speed record, set at Daytona beach by Gene Walker on a 997cc eight-valve Indian. He was clocked at 103.56mph through the kilometre, adding over 8mph to Le Vack's figure set at Brooklands a year earlier.

Having staved off a clamorous 1919 clientele, grappled with tremendous 1920 supply problems, and at last got his production line moving steadily, the bewildered manufacturer found himself facing 1921 with sliding sales and sliding prices. That post-war slump was short and sharp, and hammered home the risks of over-production and over-charging – even if the latter was unavoidable. By the cruel law of the business jungle, many smaller enterprises weak on capital and credit went to the wall, while the chastened survivors trimmed their prices and output.

While Europe was weathering all these traumas, the American industry was wilting under completely different circumstances. Of all those splendid vee-twins of the 1912–1917

Top left: a prototype of the Royal Enfield four which did not get into production. This 836cc, three-speed machine was constructed in 1919

Top right: this unusual machine is a Grigg 1¾hp scooter manufactured in 1922 and is one of only three still in existence

Above: an ABC of 1919, which utilised a horizontally opposed twin-cylinder engine of 398cc producing 3hp. A spring frame and four-speed gearbox were other features that made ABC a marque ahead of its time

Left: another example of the scooter was the Stafford Mobile Pup of 1920

period, only Harley-Davidson, Indian and Excelsior (exported as the American X) survived, together with the Henderson four. The rest were all victims of Henry Ford's genius in making his Model T car so amazingly cheaply that none but the most rabid motor cycle enthusiasts could resist it. The US police, telephones, fire and other public services, plus wide overseas demand for the almost unbreakable 'Yank bikes', kept the remaining United States motor cycle industry busy, but their golden age had gone.

Withal, there were those surprises that enliven any period, boom or slump. From Denmark, remarkably, came an advanced 750cc four-cylinder motor cycle, the Nimbus. With its in-line air-cooled engine and shaft drive *à la* FN, it differed in its cradle frame built up of flat welded-steel members, fortified by an integral cylindrical petrol tank, and by its swinging link rear coil springing. No fly-by-night, this sturdy Dane was built steadily for years, the basic design lasting almost in the 1960s.

Left: D.R. O'Donovan was nicknamed 'The Wizard' for his ability to tune motor cycle engines to a fine pitch and then use them for record-breaking purposes. He is seen astride his Norton which became known as 'Old Miracle'

Below: a Triumph Model H sidecar outfit of 1915. It featured a side-valve engine of 550cc, and in solo form was produced in thousands for despatch rider duties during the war

Right: a 2¾hp Neracar of 1921. It was the brainchild of New Yorker C.A. Neracher and was an attempt to produce a 'two-wheeled motor car'

Much shorter was the life of a British four, the 1920 Superb, which offered light-alloy construction and an overhead-camshaft head, but withered and died for lack of capital. The strange Anglo-American Neracar lasted longer. Brainchild of a New Yorker, C. A. Neracher, this attempt at a two-wheeled car had an open pressed-steel chassis with low-pivot geared-up steering, enclosed working parts save for the protruding cylinder, and friction drive giving five speeds. With varying engines and transmissions this transport for both sexes was built at Kingston, Surrey, until 1926.

The Triumph company produced first an all-chain edition of its famous side-valve Model H with a coil-spring transmission damper, and then a spanking new 500cc ohv single. Designed by Harry Ricardo and F. B. Halford, this virile newcomer had four valves and a light-alloy piston, and was known as the Ricardo or 'Riccy' Triumph. George Brough, son of William, launched the Brough-Superior, a big twin, superb in line, manufacture and finish, in side and overhead-valve forms, and destined to gain the unofficial title 'the Rolls-Royce of motor cycles'. Villiers outpaced their copiers by devising a flywheel magneto. 'Speedmen' could have the 500cc side-valve, single-speed Norton in lean and hungry form as the BS, or Brooklands Special, tuned by 'Wizard' O'Donovan to give a guaranteed 70mph, while the BRS, or Brooklands Road Special, could do 65mph – all this with a derisory 20mph speed limit still in force in Britain, providing the police with periodic brisk exercise in apprehending malefactors and enriching the Crown reserves.

Racing compensated, as ever, though. The very rapid pushrod ohv AJS continued its winning streak in the TT, 1914 winner Eric Williams taking the Junior again in 1921, with three more 'Ajays' in train, all now with normal three-speed gearboxes. Luck again played its part, for Jim Whalley (Massey-Arran) burst a tyre when fighting for the lead on the last lap, finishing fifth with a bleeding nose, flat tyre, gearbox stuck in second and holding a broken exhaust pipe. G. Prentice on a side-valve New Imperial beat off the two-strokes in the Lightweight class, while the Senior was won sensationally by a Junior AJS, ridden by Howard R. Davies, who staved off two Indians to score the only Senior Tourist Trophy victory ever gained on a 350 machine.

Britain had a second big race that season, the first (and regrettably last) 500 Miles on the outer circuit at Brooklands. A splendid but gruelling, machine-breaking grind, it brought a first, second and third sweep for American big twins, Le Vack's

Indian heading Freddy Dixon's Harley-Davidson and Harveyson on another Indian. A fine fourth, and class winner, was Horsman's 500cc Norton, and other class winners were a 750cc Coventry-Victor, a 350cc Ivy and a 250cc New Imperial. The sustained thunder of over sixty motor cycles with wide open exhausts, for over seven hours on a summer Saturday proved too much for local residents, whose forceful complaints helped to kill the '500', and led eventually to compulsory silencers at the Brooklands circuit.

On the European continent, a formidable new combination, Alec Bennett and a 500cc side-valve Sunbeam, won the French Grand Prix at Le Mans after Edmond's new ohv Ricardo Triumph ran out of fuel. T. C. de la Hay on another Sunbeam was second after a model team performance, with Sgonina's 'Ricky' Triumph third. A twin-cylinder ohv Alcyon won the Junior race, some 10mph slower than the Sunbeams, and a JAP-engined Yvels won the Lightweight after Milner (Levis)

was unfortunately put out of the race by a flying flint.

Another new race was the Belgian GP, held at the classic Spa-Francorchamps circuit, and arousing tremendous spectator interest. Le Vack and Dixon on Indian singles strove might and main to displace Hubert Hassall, but his Norton evaded them to win at 56.5mph. The new Belgian marque, Gillet, took the first two places in the Junior race to loud acclaim from the enthusiastic Belgian spectators who had come to witness the event.

A team of ABC transverse flat-twins, built by Gnome-Rhone to full 500cc capacity, ran at Le Mans and Spa with small success, but in the misleadingly named GP de France at Provins, Naas won the Senior race for ABC, heading two Alcyons, with two more ABCs following. Clearly, with so much technical interest and so many makes competing, the immediate future for international road racing was highly promising. Britain, France, Belgium and Switzerland were all active, and news came that Italy, too, would soon be challenging, not with the British

Top left: C. Williams pushes his overhead-valve AJS in to score a dramatic win in the 1920 Junior TT. His average speed for the event was 40.74mph

Left: J.W. Shaw's 500cc Norton in action during the Senior TT of 1920

Above: competitors line up for the start of the 1921 Isle of Man Senior TT, won by H.R. Davies on a 360cc AJS

machines which many of her best riders had to use if they were to win, but with new Italian products.

The remaining major event of 1921 was the International Six Days Trial, which began to live up to its 'International' title. Switzerland having made the best performance in the 1920 event, it became her privilege to host the 1921 Trial. Thus, the Six Days took place on Swiss soil, and in rigorous mountain conditions the local boys again won, their team consisting of a 350cc Condor and two 1000cc Motosacoche twins. The British team were runners up, and class winners included AJS, Scott, Condor and Motosacoche.

Chapter 5
In Top (1922-1929)

Left: although early New Imperial models used Precision and JAP engines, the Birmingham company began to make its own engines by the mid 1920s. This is a single-cylinder, 350cc New Imperial model of 1924

While the British, French and Belgian motor cycle industries generally overcame the many early post-war difficulties and were able to resume regular production, defeated Germany faced crippling extra problems. Since the Armistice, the Germans had suffered considerable privation through economic and political chaos and massive unemployment. Unlike drivers of cars, for which special permits were required, German motor cyclists were able to use their machines, although the high prices of petrol, oil and tyres were a natural and drastically effective rationing system in the first months of peace.

In order to encourage production for export, the German Government gave priorities in coal, iron, steel and other metals to many factories, but such materials were so scarce that makers had to resort to extremes of ingenuity and improvisation to build any motor cycles at all. Yet they contrived it somehow, and around such proprietary engines as were available dozens of very basic lightweights were born in industrial towns like Berlin, Nuremberg, Leipzig, Munich and Cologne. One firm, the Berliner Kleinmotoren AG, produced the excellent 174cc Bekamo two-stroke unit with charging pump below the crankcase, supplying many hundreds to small firms.

Bekamo were among those who earlier tried to make motor cycles with a reinforced wooden frame, although the weight cruelly taxed the tiny engines. Another much used over-the-counter engine was the 100cc two-stroke DKW, built by an enterprising concern in Schopau, Saxony, who also produced an early moped with their engine fixed on a carrier above the rear wheel. Improvisation was the order of the day until supplies improved, but progress was repeatedly retarded by chronic inflation and fresh financial crises.

By 1922, however, some measure of stability was achieved, and during the next five years over 250 new German makes of motor cycle emerged. Some were backyard efforts, some came from small workshops with perhaps a staff of six, and some from large firms seeking work for their factories and employees. The Bayerische Motoren Werke, makers of BMW aero-engines during the war, was one such concern. They began with a very utilitarian 148cc motorised bicycle, the Flink, following up in 1922 with a 500cc flat-twin, four-stroke engine in Douglas style. This they supplied to other makers such as Helios, Victoria, SMW, KC, Heller etc, until BMW's chief engineer, Dr Ing Max Friz, followed Granville Bradshaw's example on the ABC, turned the engine round 90 degrees and installed it transversely in the frame, driving through a three-speed gearbox and final

shaft. Thus was born the famous BMW marque, with Zündapp one of only two survivors today of all those mushrooming firms of the early '20s.

Descended from the DIAG armaments firm which made Spandau guns among other things, the D-Rad was another newcomer with a flat-twin engine which achieved prominence later. Opel, the famous car make, added to the legion of lightweights, while Mauser took the 'car on two wheels' approach. Their *Einspur* or 'one-track' was a serious attempt to develop a two-wheeler giving adequate personal protection, with a windscreen and light folding hood, and two seats in tandem, enclosed to waist height. Instead of handlebars, a half-wheel was fitted, the frame was cantilever-leaf sprung, and small retracting support wheels were fitted each side. The engine, a side-valve 500cc 'single', was water-cooled, with the radiator embodied in the nose. The machine was rather heavy, although it performed well enough for a French company to build it under licence until 1927 as the Monotrace (this also meaning 'one-track').

A more eccentric 'car on two wheels' was the 640cc Megola, an apparent throwback to Felix Millet's designs of the 1890s, but with some clever features. It had a similar air-cooled, five-cylinder, rotary 'star' motor, a masterpiece of quart-into-pint pot packaging, housed in the front wheel. Drive was through epicyclic gearing giving a 6:1 ratio, and mixture was fed from a carburettor on one side, through the hub and crankcase, then to the cylinders by piping. Fuel came from a header tank above the carburettor, and a very exposed magneto was mounted on the

Above: this is the highly unusual Megola of 1921. It was perhaps the most unorthodox machine ever made on a commercial basis, and was powered by a side-valve, 640cc, five-cylinder rotary 'star' engine mounted in the front wheel. Some 2000 were made before the company eventually folded in 1925

Right: the first of the famous Moto Guzzi models; it had a horizontal single-cylinder, 498cc engine with air cooling, a three-speed gearbox and chain final drive

opposite side. A shapely curved 'spine' frame was fabricated in sheet metal, forked at the rear to accommodate the wheel and support semi-elliptic springs on each side, and an armchair seat completed the two-wheeled car effect. With that engine turning six times faster than the front wheel, gyroscopic forces surely affected its steering, yet the Megola withstood the acid test of racing, won several events, and reached 90mph on the Avus straight, outside Berlin.

For cheap personal transport, motor cycles were wanted all over Europe. The industry spread to Budapest, Hungary, where the well-designed Meray machine was produced right up to World War II. Many German motor cycles were imported into the new Republic of Czechoslovakia, formerly part of Austria-Hungary, but the Czechs soon began production themselves of lightweights such as the Eisler and CAS, and the larger 750cc Itar flat-twin used by their Army.

In Italy the industry took great strides forward, especially when lightweights were freed from road tax in 1922. A flood of 'mini-motos' ensued, but more significant larger arrivals included the Moto-Guzzi, Garelli and Benelli. A talented engineer, Carlo Guzzi, was lucky to find an enthusiastic and wealthy sponsor in Giorgio Parodi, and the 'GP' prototype, soon renamed the Moto-Guzzi, was out and about by 1921. Of sporting concept, it had a 498cc air-cooled, single-cylinder engine laid horizontally, in unit with a three-speed gearbox and chain final drive. A Marelli magneto, twin sparking plugs, dry sump lubrication, and an outside flywheel featured, and right from the start the 'Gootzie' was low, lean and fast. G. Finzi won its first race, the motor cycle Targa Florio, late in 1921 even before production models had reached their buyers, and the make has never looked back.

Racing also set Garelli on the road to fame. With nothing better to do in 1919, the Italian Army organised a timed regularity run or 'Raid' (from Genoa to Trieste, Verona and back)

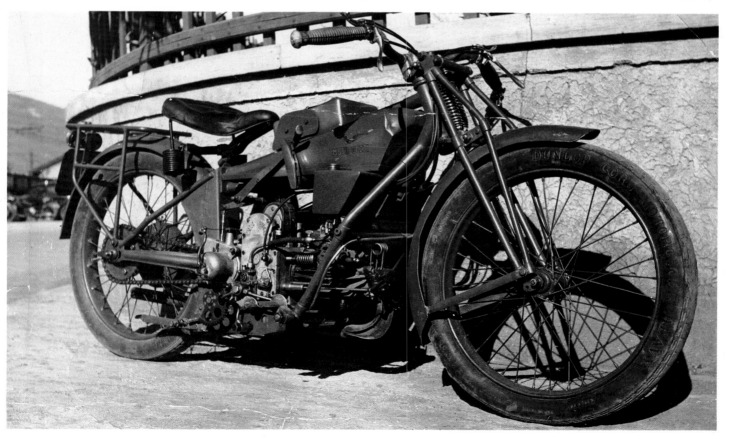

for motor cycles. Adalberto Garelli, who had built his first twin-cylinder, two-stroke, belt-drive prototype back in 1913 when working for Bianchi, prepared an improved chain-drive machine with which Girardi won the 'Raid' outright. Encouraged, the combination then contested the 'Raid Nord-Sud' from Milan to Naples, and won again, defeating two Sunbeams, a Motosacoche and a Douglas. The new *marca* went on to win the Torino-Salo, Lario and other races, while production got under way in a big new factory at the village of Sesto San Giovanni.

The Garelli 'split-single' two-stroke engine had two parallel cylinders in one casting, and two pistons on one crankpin, one cylinder compressing the gases into the other. The makers extracted remarkable power from this unit, which scored many further racing successes, outstanding among them being the 1922 350cc French Grand Prix at Strasbourg. By such efforts, Italy found herself 'riding high' on the motor cycle wave in the '20s decade, and foreign imports decreased notably while her own exports rose.

Design enterprise was not always so rewarding. The sophisticated British ABC transverse flat-twin won races in Britain and France, broke records, and did well in hill-climbs and trials, but production had been too rushed by Sopwith in hopes of scooping the market. The promised 'ideal bike' at around £60 in 1919 had become a fine but fractious £160's worth by 1921, and many orders were cancelled. Insufficient development time meant inflicting teething troubles such as fragile valvegear and poor starting on to customers, and despite every effort by Bradshaw to cure these defects, Sopwith's decided to cut their losses, and a brilliant design died – for being too soon rather than too late.

In an essentially conservative movement where the customer cannot afford to risk his hard-earned cash on experimental designs, breakaways from convention far more often brought failure than success. One example was the GSD (Grant Shaft Drive) with which R. E. D. Grant pursued the shaft drive will o' the wisp. He showed it at Olympia in 1922 with a 350cc two-stroke White & Poppe engine installed transversely to take the drive through a car-type three-speed gearbox, then tried a flat-twin, oil-cooled Bradshaw engine in ABC style, but there were no takers.

The Pullin-Groom was a praiseworthy effort by racing motor cyclist-cum-engineer Cyril Pullin to break away from the old tubular frame and forks formula. It had a frame formed from two big pressings welded together, pressed steel forks and an early form of enclosed coil spring-cum-damper telescopic suspension units front and rear. The 216cc two-stroke engine lay horizontally, and an epicyclic two-speed gearbox and total enclosure gave rich promise of cleaner, easier utility motor cycling. Too dear, too experimental, too 'cissy' were the harsh verdicts that doomed it by 1924.

There was also the Peters, built in the Isle of Man. Uncannily modern, this machine had cantilever-type rear springing and a saddle tank projecting forward to support and enclose the steering head, the 347cc two-stroke engine deriving upper support from a bracket welded to the tank. The oil tank also acted as the seat tube, and there was no front down-tube in this ancestor of the modern 'cantilever' lightweight. Belt drive was something of a let down, but chains and three speeds soon replaced it, and with mudguards devoid of ugly stays and partial engine enclosure the looks were well above par.

There was a general cleaning up of design during 1922,

Above: a close up of the 349cc, single-cylinder, overhead-valve, oil-cooled Bradshaw engine of the mid 1920s

Top right: the legendary Stanley Woods, hero of countless races and winner of no less than ten Isle of Man TT races

Above right: in the early 1920s, motor cycle racer and engineer Cyril Pullin attempted to break away from the traditional tubular-frame-and-forks formula. The Pullin-Groom machine used a two-stroke, 216cc engine, which was mounted horizontally in a pressed-steel frame

together with a more sensible level of prices. One or two British makers had seemingly taken a hard look at the better French designs at the Paris Salon, both Triumph and Rover appearing with unit construction of engine and three-speed gearbox. The former applied it to a new 350cc side-valve model with unusual overhanging crankshaft and outside flywheel, the latter to a pleasing new ohv '250' with saddle tank and front fork dampers. Zenith and Douglas offered 'all-chain' models, Norton introduced a beautifully proportioned pushrod ohv '500', and Scott announced a three-speed model at last, with internal expanding brakes as well. Barr & Stroud launched a range of sleeve-valved proprietary engines, and Bradshaw a 350cc ohv 'single' and a 500cc flat-twin, both with oil-cooled cylinder barrels, while P & M produced a sporting version of their classic side-valve 'Sloper', giving it the pleasing name of Panther, a name which would endure for many more years.

From America came a surprising Harley-Davidson, a 584cc

flat-twin-aimed at the European market. They offset it with an even larger edition of their famous big twin, with 1208cc engine! From Belgium came the very antithesis, the tiny Clément 43cc single with miniature pushrod ohv, intended as a clip-on and anticipating the modern under-50cc moped. From Scotland came a surprising number of motor cycles; the New Gerrard with Villiers, JAP or Blackburne engines, the Gri with combined rotary-cum-poppet valvegear driven by chain, the Royal Scot with Barr & Stroud engine, the Victoria with diverse bought-out engines, and others.

On the sporting side, 1922 was remarkable for the debut of three future racing stars, Wal Handley, Stanley Woods and Jimmy Simpson. Between them, this doughty trio won fifteen TTs and countless Continental GPs during the next quarter-century. Handley was employed as a junior road tester by the OK company when, at eighteen, they sought a 'stand in' rider at short notice for the TT. A new 250cc class, the Lightweight, was inaugurated that year, and Handley (OK-Blackburne) duly gave notice of future performances by haring off into the lead and setting the fastest race lap on his first round. Then he broke down and G. S. Davison on a much lightened two-stroke Levis went on to win from two other very fast British machines, a Rex-Acme and a Velocette.

The concurrent Junior TT was another AJS benefit, Manxman Tom Sheard winning from team-mate Grinton – but only after Le Vack on a remarkable new twin-ohc JAP-engined New Imperial had retired when leading. Young Irishman Stanley Woods (Cotton) came fifth despite a refuelling fire, a broken pushrod and no brakes. Said *The Motor Cycle*: 'Watch Woods'; how right they were. For the six-lap Senior, Sunbeam's new Canadian star Alec Bennett on their new 77 × 105.5mm

side valve 'long-stroke' machine was unassailable. Despite an unscheduled stop for oil he won by over seven minutes from a Triumph Ricardo, two Scotts and a Norton.

After the TT, several riders made for the continent and that other classic, the French Grand Prix. Again utilising the car GP circuit, the 1922 race was at Strasbourg, and there two of the TT winners, Bennett and Davis, repeated their respective Senior and Lightweight victories. The Junior race was sensational, with the strange new Garellis coming from Milan with their raucous double-piston two-strokes. To French surprise, the Italians wiped the floor with the experienced Alcyon and Terrot opposition, Visioli, Gnesa and dall'Oglio scoring a triumphant one-two-three. With Fiat also scooping the car GP, it was a bad meeting all round for the French!

Above: in 1922, Harley-Davidson sprung a surprise by unveiling their new flat-twin model. It was powered by a 584cc engine, and was aimed specifically at the European market. In time, however, Harley-Davidson returned to their traditional vee-twin formula

Having made their point, the Garellis returned home, contenting themselves with first places in the Lario, Cremona, Ticino and Tigullio races and then shaking the racing world again with an outright win in the Grand Prix of the Nations at the new Monza track near Milan. This race attracted British, French, Swiss, Belgian and Italian runners, and Naas (500cc ABC) led until past half-distance when his frame broke. Brandish (Triumph) took over, only to break a tappet, whereupon Gnesa's 350cc Garelli howled through to victory from Fieschi (Douglas) and Morabito (Sunbeam), both 500s.

The Belgian GP at Spa also had its dramas. Alec Jackson, a private British entry on a Sunbeam, won the 500cc race in drenching rain from a Triumph and a Norton, only to be told he was disqualified for having changed a plug on the course for one offered by a spectator. This contravened the regulations and made Antoine (Triumph) the new winner, although few recognised such a petty decision. A Belgian Rush, ridden by an Englishman, E. Remington, won the Junior event, and Geoff Davison on his faithful Levis scored a 250cc 'hat trick', with Wal Handley (OK) second despite a drowned magneto.

Another new race, the Ulster GP, joined the calendar, staged over the 20½-mile Clady circuit in Northern Ireland and attracting a large and wildly enthusiastic crowd. It was run as a handicap but with scratch class winners, and Hassall (Norton) was first 500cc and overall winner, with Handley (OK), Andrews (Trump) and Metcalfe (Brough Superior) the other class winners. Testifying to their versatility, racing motor cyclists also took part in the 1922 International Six Days Trial, held again in Switzerland. The local riders repeated their 1921 success, but the British team, comprising Alec Bennett (Sunbeam), G. S. Davison (Levis) and F. W. Giles (AJS) were second, with a Swedish trio on Husqvarna machines third.

Prices were still coming down by 1923, and the belt drive was really on its way out. Even the excellent Rudge Multi ended production late that year, being replaced by a 350cc four-valve, four-speed chain drive model of great potential. Villiers now made two-stroke engines in 150, 250 and 350cc size, all with flywheel magnetos providing sparks and electric light. Francis-Barnett introduced a Villiers-engined lightweight with triangulated, bolt-up frame which could be assembled from a collection of tubes in twenty minutes.

A rare 'mini-ABC' was the Economic, with transverse

Below right: the Martinsyde factory was situated quite close to the Brooklands track and so, not surprisingly, the local machines competed there on many occasions. This is their 1000cc vee-twin seen with the team at the Surrey track in 1922, a year before they were bought out by Bat

flat-twin, 165cc, two-stroke engine of US origin, foot clutch and friction-cum-belt drive. A tempting price of under £29 was offset by a speed of just 20mph. Coventry-Eagle, Cedos, Mars and Brough-Superior all sported saddle tanks long before these became 'the rage', the last-named resplendent in best quality nickel plate, of course, while the big JAP '90 bore' ohv, twin-cylinder engine underneath made this the 1923 'speedman's most desired machine. FN of Belgium shattered both traditionalists and idealists by changing from shaft to chain drive on their famous fours after eighteen years, on grounds that chain drive was now fully reliable and much cheaper.

Eloquent of the happy-go-lucky attitude then was the special straight-through copper exhaust pipe which 'young bloods' could fit to their machines. One such was called the 'Zoom-Zoom', made specially for 2¾hp Douglases – 'No back pressure, pleasing note, improved appearance' said the advertisement, and all for thirty shillings. Noise made the motor cycle unpopular in some quarters, as per one letter in a London newspaper: 'Far in the distance rises a sound that drowns all others, and makes speech and hearing impossible for many minutes. Is the motor cyclist a maniac or a fiend? Whether alone, disguised in overalls and goggles, or with a sidecar and a few encumbrances therein, never does he pass without a roar and rattle. Nothing but Death can stop his mad career, but does he stop his own ears with cotton wool?'.

Perhaps the excitement and glamour of racing, or just reading about it, was partly to blame. The sport was certainly booming in Britain, for while the law forbade closing the roads for circuit racing, many sprints and hill-climbs were run on stretches of the highway with police permission, and were attracting ever-increasing crowds. Spectator control was haphazard, and many authorities feared a major accident one day. It came, in fact, at Kop Hill in 1925, when first a motor cycle, then a car crashed, injuring one spectator and endangering

Below: A.E. Taylor's passenger gets dangerously close to the scenery as their Blackburne outfit charges on in the 1923 Sidecar TT

Bottom: Stanley Woods and Cotton chase P. Walker's Excelsior through Governor's Bridge hairpin in the 1923 Junior TT. Woods went on to win, and is seen celebrating, right, with his many fans

others. Contests on public roads thereafter were firmly banned.

Meantime, however, there was the 1923 TT, now with still more innovations. This time there was a three-lap Sidecar TT with a capacity limit of 600cc, while the 250 and 350cc races were lengthened to six laps (226½ miles). In the Junior event AJS's long run of good fortune broke at last. Jimmy Simpson led at meteoric pace, and then broke down – a fate that was frequently his – after which Stanley Woods won on a Cotton, leading an AJS and a Douglas.

The Lightweight fell to the Scotsman Jock Porter (New Gerrard), while the Senior, run in miserable wet for the first time since 1912, brought success for a new ohv Douglas with experimental disc brakes, ridden by Tom Sheard. Next home were a new ohv Norton and an Indian ridden by the redoubtable Freddie Dixon. That tough Yorkshireman also won the Sidecar TT, beating two Nortons, on a Douglas fitted with his famous part-banking sidecar, often acclaimed as the first of its type, but anticipated both in the USA and Germany.

The Continental Circus was now part of the regular round for many Britons after the Manx races in June, and new events were being added each season. Of the 'regulars', the French GP (this time at Tours) brought another fine Douglas 500cc victory for Jim Whalley over two ohv Nortons. Frank Longman (AJS) won the Junior, and Davison notched up yet another Lightweight first on his remarkable two-stroke Levis, beating a Cotton. The Belgian GP was at Dinant that year, instead of Spa, and was remarkable for the pace set by Freddie Dixon on an Indian single. Despite a big international field he led the 500cc race by an ever increasing distance, with two Saroléas the only survivors from his hot pace. Huynens (FN) won the Junior event, and the peerless Wal Handley took the 250cc honours on a Rex-Acme, dogged by Davison's reliable Levis.

At Monza, the Italians had a severe 'tit for tat' shock when the Frenchman Gillard simply ran away with the 500cc GP of the Nations. His mount was a revised four-valve, single-cam version of the Peugeot vertical-twin, and he won by over twelve minutes, the best Italian bike, a Guzzi, being fourth. The Garellis which triumphed at Strasbourg the year before could do no better than four-five-six in the 350cc race, won by the Italian Gnesa on a British AJS from two Belgian machines; thus are racing situations changed in a mere twelve months.

The second Ulster GP gave Handley a deserved overall and 250cc class win with a Rex-Acme, with Shaw (Zenith) and Joe Craig (Norton) garnering the other class wins. A dull and very

exhausting endurance race was the Spanish 12 Hours at
Guadarrama, won by Jim Whalley on a 500cc Douglas. The
two-stroke Garellis won several lesser races in Switzerland,
Austria, Germany, Spain and in their homeland, while the new
Peugeot twins scored in several French events unattended by the
'Continental Circus' from Britain.

In place of the late, lamented 500 Miles Race at Brooklands,
the BMCRC instituted the 200 Miles scratch event, run annually
for several years. Le Vack was the hero of the day in the
inaugural race, winning the 350cc class on a New Imperial and
the 1000cc class on a Brough-Superior. Brooklands track was
also the scene for two successful attempts on the motor cycle
absolute speed record. Freddie Dixon achieved 106.8mph
(171.8kph) in September on a 989cc Harley-Davidson, only to be
pipped a month later by C. F. Temple riding a 996cc, ohc,
vee-twin British Anzani special, which blasted through the
measured kilometre at 108.48mph (174.6kph). In another sphere

of competition, it was Sweden's turn to run the International Six
Days Trial, and the home-based Husqvarna team won outright.
Runners-up were Britain, represented by Kershaw (New
Imperial), T. C. de la Hay (Sunbeam) and Giles (AJS), with
Switzerland third, only fifteen contestants finishing without loss
of marks.

By 1924 twist-grip throttle control was widely used in motor
cycle racing, and gradually it was adopted on road machines as
well. With mechanical lubrication and improved steels, overhead
valves were now reliable, and several more makes announced
pushrod ohv models; P & M for their new Panther, New

*Top left: the great Freddie Dixon seen at
Brooklands in May 1923 on one of his many
record-breaking attempts. His passenger,
however, seems a little uninterested in the
proceedings*

*Above: George Brough's own JAP-engined
Brough-Superior, Old Bill, on which he took
51 firsts in a row in sprint and hill-climb events*

Hudson, Raleigh and Royal Enfield. BSA digressed with their famous 'round tank' side-valve '250' at a mere £39 10s, then followed up with a new 350cc sports ohv roadster, while Rudge introduced a 500cc edition of their four-valve four-speeder.

Then Matchless sprung a surprise with a 350cc overhead camshaft engine, a form of valve operation hitherto used only on racing machines. The Matchless was unusual in having the camshaft disposed fore-and-aft, with the enclosed vertical drive shaft behind the cylinder and the carburettor on the offside, facing forward. It also had a saddle tank, and although the first British make to 'go ohc', the Matchless merely foreshadowed an infinitely more important interpretation, the Velocette. This was announced in September 1924, the former two-stroke specialists turning 'sporting' with a superbly designed 348cc engine, its camshaft across the head and driven by shaft and bevels. Swiftly plunged into the crucible of racing, the 'cammy Velo' was to emerge a frequent TT winner in future years, and a splendid road machine, the design enduring right into the '50s.

Chater-Lea and OEC in Britain also produced ohc engines, but without the Velocette impact. Continental engineers also appreciated the value of fewer moving parts and improved head formation, and the German Kuechen ohc proprietary engine was an excellent example, while the Italians favoured it on the tiny high-speed ohv units they were so good at making. The one snag was the cost of machining the drive gears in comparison with that of producing pushrods and rockers.

When Alec Bennett won the 1924 Senior TT, it marked Norton's first Isle of Man win since 1907. His machine had pushrod-operated ohv, as did the 588cc sidecar outfit ridden to victory by George Tucker in the second Sidecar race. Thereafter it was Norton's golden year. Bennett went on to win the Belgian GP at Spa and the French GP at Lyons, while Joe Craig, later to become Norton's racing team manager, won the Ulster GP both on handicap and overall. Using JAP ohv engines, the very race-minded New Imperial concern equalled Norton's double in the TT. Ken Twemlow won the Junior from a Dot and an AJS, while brother Eddie ran off with the Lightweight TT, twelve minutes ahead of the second place Cotton. There was also an Ultra-Lightweight TT that season, Jock Porter (New Gerrard) winning for Scotland from two Cottons.

In July the Swiss GP on the Meyrin circuit outside Geneva drew an excellent international field. Graham Walker won the Senior race on an ohv Sunbeam, staving off the fast Italian Luigi Arcangeli on a Motosacoche. T. C. de la Hay made it a real

Top centre: G.H. Tucker averaged 51.31mph while winning the 1924 Sidecar TT

Top right: Claude Temple poses with his OEC-Temple-Anzani on the Brooklands circuit in 1923. His Hubert Hagens-designed, ohc, 996cc Anzani-powered bike had around 60bhp at its disposal and Claude captured many world records

Sunbeam day by adding the 350cc event to their bag, while a locally built Condor beat a two-stroke Velocette in the Lightweight race. Racing also picked up in Germany, where E. Zuendorf on a Zenith beat a BMW in the *Wanderpreis von Deutschland* run over a circuit centred on Swinemunde.

Italy's big day came in the GP of the Nations at Monza, where Mentasti and Visioli on the Guzzi flat singles, now with four valves and ohc, avenged France's 1923 win with a triumphant one-two, beating Norton and Peugeot. In Spain it was Douglas's turn again, their ohv flat-twins scoring a grand slam in the first Spanish GP at San Sebastian. They took the first five places, in the order Mateos, Anstice, Whalley, Naure and Santos, while French Alcyons placed one-two in the Junior.

Britain also won the International Six Days Trial at last. The event was held in Belgium, over a rather unsatisfactory route in the industrial areas, and the team comprised Arter (James), Wilson (Sunbeam) and Giles (AJS). Norway's representatives on Triumph, Husqvarna and Harley-Davidson machines equalised on performance, but were unlucky to lose marks for riding foreign machines. The Belgians, on two FNs and a Saroléa, were third. Completing a very satisfactory year for Britain, the absolute speed record was twice broken, both times by Le Vack on his 1000cc Brough-Superior. Choosing the Arpajon road outside Paris as the venue, he raised Temple's figure to 113.61mph (182.8kph) in April, then improved it to 119.05mph (191.5kph) in July.

During the year 1925, midway through the decade, motor cycle design tended to mark time. The definitive frame-engine-transmission format had been reached, internal expanding brakes were fast driving the rim-type away, electric lighting was at last ousting acetylene with its wretched generator and rubber piping, and new straight-tube forks by Webb and Brampton displaced the curved blade types. During the twelve months 581,288 motor cycles were registered in Britain alone, a figure rising as production rose ever higher.

Triumph stirred up the price war with a new 500cc side-valve, the Model P, at under £43. Matchless and Raleigh took up BSA's 'round tank' challenge in the utility '250' class, producing similar side-valvers at roughly similar prices. Douglas then upset the applecart with a fully equipped 350cc all-chain flat-twin, the EW, at a mere £43, while still running off batches of the old 2¾hp with belt drive at £35. It was jungle law again, with the big firms cutting to the bone, while the smaller ones fell out. Many old-established makes with ill-equipped and/or under-capitalised factories had already abandoned the struggle – Bradbury, Beardmore-Precision, Hobart, Hazlewood, BAT, McKenzie and Martinsyde among them, Quadrant and Connaught were ailing, and Clyno, Lea-Francis and Rover were concentrating on cars.

At the 1925 Olympia Show Banquet, Sir Harold Bowden warned that 'within ten years Germany would be the most prosperous country in Europe unless Great Britain recognised her tasks'. That year, indeed, three prominent new German makes, Standard, Stock and Taunax, were founded, while both the Hess and Cockerell marques built four-cylinder machines; clearly enterprise was in the wings, awaiting the call. A new Spanish 'national' motor cycle factory at Baddalone was announced. Its products were to be called Patria, and would include a 250cc, two-stroke lightweight and a big in-line 'four'; nothing came of this project, and not until after World War II did the Spanish found a proper motor cycle industry.

The 1925 racing season was marred by deaths and disputes.

Left: Raleigh of Nottingham are best known for their bicycles, but they built some good-quality motor cycles between 1919 and 1933, including this side-valve, 248cc model of 1926. They later switched to moped production

Below: one of the famous 'round tank' BSAs. This is a 1925 2¼hp, 249cc machine which was popular as a work horse for the British Post Office's messengers

Italy lost her Guzzi star, Guido Mentasti, in a road crash, then suffered a second blow when the veteran Mariani was killed in an Italian race. At Spa in the Belgian GP, Britain's Jack Hollowell died after hitting an iron gate-post at a point still known today as Hollowell Corner; but things began on a bright note in the TT, when a rider-turned-manufacturer, Howard R. Davies, won the Senior TT with his own JAP-engined HRD, beating Longman's new 500cc AJS and Bennett's Norton.

The HRD had made its debut at Olympia the previous autumn as a high-performance sports model, and with second place on another HRD in the Junior TT, Davies' cup was surely full. Then Wal Handley, unbeatable on his day, was first home both in that Junior race and also the Ultra-Lightweight, riding Blackburne-engined Rex Acmes. The 250cc race proved another New Imperial benefit for E. Twemlow, while the third and last pre-war Sidecar TT went to Len Parker's Douglas outfit.

For their 1925 Grand Prix, the French followed the car

107

classic to the new Montlhéry course near Paris. Despite this apparent advantage, a very meagre crowd attended to see their Peugeot twins well trounced by Simpson's 500cc AJS, Craig's Norton and Whalley's Douglas. Then J. H. Stevens, son of George of the AJS family, gained a surprise 350cc win with Hollowell (AJS) second. Stevens later declared he had been credited with a lap too many and that Hollowell was the true winner, but the organisers would not change the results.

The Belgian GP began farcically. Just before race day an internal dispute arose between the organisers and the FN company, who were suspended for contravention of some ruling in an earlier event. FN took the case to a civil court, which ruled that they should be allowed to race. The Belgian Motorcycling Federation thereupon cancelled the race 'to preserve their authority', leaving foreign visitors stranded. Hotel costs and return fares were guaranteed for competitors, however, and the race was run a week later, with FN graciously standing down.

Below: ex Rolls-Royce employee Michael McEvoy produced motor cycles from his own Derby factory between 1926 and 1929. This is the vee-twin McEvoy of 1927, which used a 998cc JAP engine. This is believed to be the machine which lapped Brooklands at 124mph in 1929 in the hands of George Patchett

The Senior event proved another Bennett/Norton victory, but was marred by Hollowell's fatal accident, and the other winners were Handley and Porter (250cc New Gerrard).

Ulsterman Joe Craig again collected the Ulster GP for Norton, with a Royal Enfield and a Cotton as Junior and Lightweight class winners, while AJS went out to Monza for the GP of the Nations, where wet weather and a slippery course caused much attrition. Hough and Simpson (AJSs), Handley (Rex Acme) and Arcangeli (Sunbeam) all retired, and the overall winner was the dashing Tazio Nuvolari, destined to become the world's greatest racing driver but then riding a 350cc Bianchi. Two more Bianchis followed him home, with the 500cc class going to the much slower GR, ridden by Count Gino Revelli, leading a Moto-Guzzi. In the 250cc class, normally an Italian

speciality, the persistent Jock Porter affronted them by beating their best by over six minutes.

The new Bianchis, known as the *Freccie Celeste* or 'Blue Arrows', took over Italy's 350cc class vacated by the Garellis. They had twin gear-driven overhead camshafts and were very fast, winning several other Italian races that year. In Spain the San Sebastian Three Hours was won by Mateos (Douglas),

Top: Walter Handley and Rex-Acme-Blackburne on their winning way in the 1925 Junior TT

Above: J.H. Simpson rounds Ramsey Hairpin with his 3.49hp AJS outfit in the 1925 Sidecar TT

Above right: Dougal Marchant poses with his Chater-Lea machine in 1924

privately owned Sunbeams won both the Austrian and Hungarian TTs, and C. T. Ashby (ohv Panther) won the German TT at Kolberg. Britain also scored another win in the International Six Days, held in the south-west corner of England, the trio of Arter (James), Kershaw (New Hudson) and Giles (AJS) defeating German, Dutch and Norwegian teams.

In record-breaking, an ohc Chater-Lea ridden at Brooklands by Dougal Marchant became the first '350' in the world ever to exceed 100mph, while later in the year Claude Temple (OEC-Temple-Anzani) went over to the Montlhéry banked track and set a new world's hour record at 101.98mph.

With that combination of optimism and determination required by a motor cycle manufacturer, 1926 saw new makers coming in as others went out. Two specialist British newcomers were McEvoy and AJW, both building sports singles and inspiring big twins for a limited clientele. Michael McEvoy of Derby was an engine and supercharging expert who was soon experimenting with Roots blowers on his JAP-engined twin. A. J. Wheaton of Exeter chose the British Anzani eight-valve, ohv engine for his first AJW twin, using Royal Enfield wheels, hubs and brakes, and a Jardine gearbox. Later, he also turned to JAPs. Both makers probably derived more pleasure than profit from their motor cycle ventures.

The ohv big twin, as immortalised by the Brough-Superior, held a particular fascination over sporting manufacturers, and another to succumb to it was Coventry-Eagle, who in 1926 produced a splendid 980cc JAP-powered ohv 'Flying Eight', with part leather-clad tank and polished aluminium chain guards. Like the McEvoy it used Enfield wheels and Jardine gears, and cost £35 less than Brough's SS100.

An ardent advocate of the 'two-wheeled car' was Sir Alliott Verdon Roe of Avro aircraft fame. To prove his contentions he built his own Saro 'runabout' in 1926, using a 350cc Villiers engine, three-speed gearbox and shaft drive. The low chassis had the wheels attached on one side only, with oleo leg springs and spun aluminium wheels with 10in brakes. Narrow steering arms controlled the front wheel through a drag link, and the scooter-like body largely covered the wheels and carried a windscreen and a comfortable seat at just above hub height. The centre was open for easy access, and Sir Alliott claimed he could ride his runabout in gusty winds with arms folded.

New and interesting was the Bradshaw-designed P & M Panthette. This had a 246cc, vee-twin engine mounted transversely, a four-speed gearbox in unit, car-type gear-change and chain drive. Detail work was impressive, with fully enclosed valvegear and a steel 'backbone' top tube, but high price and unorthodoxy were against it and, sadly, it soon was dropped.

In Germany the motor cycle was booming, with a strong national effort to reduce British imports of machines, engines and gearboxes. At the 1926 Berlin Show British exhibits were barred, but several interesting domestic proprietary engines were shown, notably the Velox, Kuhne and the 'K', with unit construction. BMW produced an ohv edition of their 500cc, transverse flat-twin, and DKW a 496cc, twin-cylinder parallel two-stroke with power cooling fan. The lightweight market was dominated by the 119cc Stock, actually an old American Evans design with crude belt drive and pedal gear, but selling at an unbeatable *deutschmark* equivalent of £22, electric light included.

In the racing world, the newly invigorated Germany added a Grand Prix at the Avus track for the Continental Circus to contest. In contrast, the Isle of Man TT programme was pared back, the Sidecar and Ultra-Lightweight events being discontinued. 1926 was the year the Italians came – three twin-cam Bianchis, a Garelli two-stroke and two Guzzi horizontal 'singles', one a 500, the other a new '250'. With the latter, Pietro Ghersi very nearly won the Lightweight, an extra fuel stop giving the race to Paddy Johnston's Cotton. Then Ghersi was excluded by a stupid rule – he had used a plug of different make from that specified on his entry form!

The Bianchi and Garelli entries fared poorly in the Junior TT, which marked the first victory for the ohc Velocette, ridden by the master, Alec Bennett. Simpson (AJS) and Handley (Rex Acme) followed, and it was Handley who provided the fireworks in the Senior, riding a fierce Rex Acme with vee-twin, ohv Blackburne engine. Despite a long stop on lap two with plug

Above: Alec Bennett is congratulated after winning the 1927 Senior TT with one of the first ohc Nortons. Shaking his hand is G. Albert, while the rider standing behind is Alec's team-mate, Jimmy Shaw, who finished fourth

Below: British pioneer aviator A.V. Roe built this ingenious Saro runabout in 1926, although the public were less than impressed by its seemingly double identity of car and bike

Right: Pietro Ghersi with his horizontal-single-cylinder racing Moto Guzzi seen in 1925

Far right: a scene at the Motor Cycle Show of Olympia in November 1927. DGW was the name applied to DKW machines imported into Britain at that time, but they reverted to the old initials twelve months later

trouble, he tore back into second place behind Woods' Norton.

Results of the Continental races emphasise the quality and quantity of competition in those far off days. Of the 500cc races, Bennett (Norton) won the French GP at Strasbourg, Simpson (AJS) the Belgian GP, Stelzer (BMW) the German GP at Avus, Moretti (Guzzi) the Italian TT, Varzi (Sunbeam) the GP of the Nations, and Graham Walker (Sunbeam) the Ulster GP – six races, five different makes! The 350cc class was also well shared out; Simpson (AJS) won at Avus, Longman (AJS) at Spa; Handley (Rex Acme) at Ulster, Rolland (Terrot) at Montlhéry, and Nuvolari (Bianchi) at Monza. Among the '250s' Jock Porter and his New Gerrard found a doughty new opponent in Syd Crabtree's Crabtree-JAP, Jock winning at Spa and Avus, Syd at Strasbourg and Ulster.

The first Dutch TT, held at Assen, was a nationals-only race won by Piet van Wijngaarden (Norton), with BSA and New Imperial taking class wins, while the Bol d'Or, in those days a

gruelling 24-hour race with but one rider per machine, went to Francisquet (Sunbeam). Taking a change from racing, Graham Walker rode a Sunbeam in the British team for the 1926 International Six Days Trial, with Phil Pike (Norton combination) and J. Ledstone (James). The Trial took place on British soil, and the British team scored the first of four successive wins, only meeting defeat again in 1930 at the hands of the Italians. In record-breaking spheres, the two-wheeler 'world's fastest' took another smack when Claude Temple on the big Anzani-powered OEC-Temple went to Arpajon and added over 2mph to Le Vack's 1924 figure, leaving it at 121.41mph.

In 1927 several motor cycle manufacturers realised that the saddle-type petrol tank was both attractive and convenient. The popularity of ohv meant tall engines, which in turn meant unnaturally high top frame tubes if a reasonable tank capacity was to be achieved. A saddle tank, straddling the tube with its sides often flanking the valve gear was a useful answer. Velocette, Ariel, Excelsior, New Hudson, Zenith and New Henley all joined Coventry Eagle, HRD, OEC, Chater-Lea and other established wearers.

Ariel gave their formerly rather untidy range a major 'wash and brush up'. A new cradle frame giving a low saddle position, central spring forks, saddle tank, and their own pushrod ohv and side-valve engines brought them into fashion, aided by very

111

competitive prices; they were on their way to becoming one of the most popular marques. At the 1926 Olympia Show Banquet a leading topic had been the silencing problem on motor cycles, and several makers heeded this. Racing motor cyclist Herbert Le Vack had joined New Hudson, endowing them not only with new sports lines and extra knots, but also a thorough silencing system with an expansion chamber ahead of the crankcase and twin tailpipes to two more silencers.

P & M adopted a similar scheme, and Dunelt fitted larger silencers. BSA produced the first of their 493cc ohv inclined engine models – the beloved 'Slopers' which were noted for their silence. Triumph replaced the four-valve Ricardo sports with the two-valve 'TT', Calthorpe made an ohc '350', and Sunbeam introduced their classic two-port 500cc pushrod ohv Model 90, and a 350cc Model 80 equivalent.

Velocette's 1926 Junior TT victory made the 1927 Isle of Man week very ohc-minded, more so when Norton wheeled out their new ohc '500' designed by Walter Moore, late of Douglas. With Alec Bennett and Stanley Woods astride them they proved unassailable, even though Woods' clutch failed when he was leading, Bennett won his fourth TT at record speed. A quiet Scot named Guthrie was a surprise second on a Le Vack-tuned New Hudson, with a Triumph third. In the Junior, the legendary Freddie Dixon on an HRD, goggleless and with footboards as ever, followed the meteoric Handley round until a piston on the latter's Rex Acme melted on the last lap. So Dixon won from Harold Willis on a 'cammy' Velocette, with Simpson third on a new AJS, also with ohc, but chain-driven with a Weller tensioner. Moto-Guzzi had another stab at the Lightweight race, and only Handley (Rex Acme) denied Arcangeli the chequered flag. Ashby (OK) was third, while Bennett on another OK made fastest lap but retired.

The subsequent Continental round was pretty much a 'cammy parade'. Joe Craig won the French GP, Woods the Dutch, Belgian and Swiss GPs, and J. W. Shaw the Ulster, all on the latest Nortons. Among the 350s, Simpson scored with the 'cammy Ajay' in the Belgian, Swiss and German races, while Longman won the French GP on a Velocette. Demonstrating that there was life in the old pushrods yet, however, Graham Walker, on the newest two-port Sunbeam, won the 500cc German GP at the new Nürburgring circuit from Stanley Woods, while the diminutive Charles Dodson (Sunbeam) won his first 'classic', the 350cc Ulster race. Even Brooklands inaugurated a 'Grand Prix' that season, albeit minus international representation; the big names won just the same, Bennett won the Senior, Simpson the Junior, and Handley the Lightweight.

By 1928, no less than 712,583 motor cycles were registered in Great Britain; more than in any other country and amounting to over one-third of the world total. It was Britain's decade without question, although a counter statistic has cruel irony: Japan had a total of 7670 motor cycles in circulation that year, about sixty per cent of them British, whereas in 1961 Japan had 4,860,589, very very few of them being British. But back in those bonanza years it could not be said that British manufacturers sat back complacently. The last years of the '20s were as fertile and imaginative as in the late '10s when they had the French industry to compete with. There were perhaps too many ohv sports singles, but motor cycling is preponderantly a young man's activity, and young men in any era like going fast and cutting a dash.

Some manufacturers also enjoyed 'cutting a dash', none more so than that talented showman George Brough, whose

996cc, vee-four shown at Olympia in 1927 put the name 'Brough-Superior' on everyone's lips. It was the sensation of the show, even if Brough hardly contemplated selling many. It had four separate 249cc air-cooled cylinders with side valves, believed of JAP origin, paired at 60 degrees on an aluminium crankcase. A single central camshaft within the crankcase operated the valves, car-type battery and coil ignition was used, and drive was via a four-speed gearbox and chain. With sweeping exhausts, the customary bright nickel tank and impeccable Brough finish, it was an aesthetic joy, while a price tag of £250 kept frivolous customers away.

At the 1928 Show twelve months later, Brough struck again. The vee-four had gone, and in its place was another 'show sensation', an all-new 900cc straight-four. This time Motosacoche of Geneva built the engine for Brough; it had side valves and a three-bearing crankshaft, and drove through a three-speed gearbox. A Draper pivot-type spring frame with coil spring below the saddle was fitted, and at £200 this 'twin headlamp' four drew at least one customer – that inveterate Brough fan, Col T. E. Lawrence – 'Lawrence of Arabia'.

In between those two shows, design in general was further cleaned up, and more saddle tanks appeared, only AJS, Sunbeam and Douglas of the major makers still defaulting. The deep new tanks, enclosed valvegear and pushrods, bigger hub brakes and tyres, two-port exhaust systems, and separate oil tanks, toolboxes or batteries filling up the gaps, combined to give the average 1928 motor cycle a more solid look, the much admired lean, low 'vintage' line departing.

Production of motor cycling's most famous four, the FN, had ended in 1927, but a year later Olympia visitors were confronted, not with the new Brough alone, but also *four* others! Two were American – the time-honoured 1200cc Henderson, and the 'new' Indian 'Four', which was virtually the old Ace in red paint. The other pair were British, entirely new, and came from those arch-enthusiasts aforementioned, McEvoy and A. J. Wheaton. The McEvoy Model 4A or 'Cyclone' had a 987cc, in-line engine with bevel-driven single ohc operating wide-angle valves in a hemispherical head, and a light alloy block with steel cylinder liners. An electric starter was a £10 optional extra.

The AJW 'Super Four' looked more dramatic, with its sleek covered-in 'bodywork' and hub-level steering, but the engine was less enterprising, being a 985cc, in-line, side-valve, water-cooled car unit supplied by British Anzani. It was mounted in a channel section chassis, with the radiator set across the engine panelling to catch the air. Catering for 'the super sportsman', a guaranteed 100mph was talked of but, like the McEvoy and, one suspects, the Brough-Superior, this AJW began and ended as what the profession terms a 'one-off'.

The novelties of that memorable show did not end there. Cyril Pullin, designer of the ill-fated Pullin-Groom, came up with a lineal descendant, the Ascot-Pullin. Stuffed full of surprises, this had a pressed steel frame, a 496cc, pushrod ohv engine installed horizontally, Moto-Guzzi style, with an integral four-speed gearbox. The brakes were hydraulic, the kickstarter was coupled with the valve lifter, and all mechanical parts were enclosed, with integral leg-shields and an optional windscreen. The object was comfort, not performance, 70mph being about its limit, and one Ascot-Pullin averaged 54mph in a nine-hour run at Brooklands with screen and legshields in place.

There were also two remarkable OECs, one the Tinkler with ohv water-cooled engine laid horizontally with the gearbox in a self-contained 'power pack', and OEC Duplex hub centre

Left: Freddie Dixon seen at Brooklands in October 1927

Below: Brough-Superior, who were famous for their show sensations, delighted the public in 1927 with their sensational vee-four, 996cc bike

steering; the other a variation with open frame in the earlier Neracar style. Yet of all these 'dream bikes', 'gimmicks' or 'design probes', only the Ascot-Pullin saw a production line – and sadly those built were being sold off at desperately low prices two years later in an effort to get rid of stock.

That same show contained many sound, conventional 1929 models. There were several new ohv '250s' at challenging prices, including the new Ariel 'Colt', a two-port Matchless, a New Hudson and even a Rudge Whitworth with 250cc JAP engine. Even the big, lordly 'Sloper' Panthers were supplemented by a sleek little 172cc Villiers-engined model, while the race-bred Cotton also acquired a two-stroke baby brother. Then Calthorpe, makers for some years of a clean ohv model with the pushrods in a single tube, *à la* Rudge and Panther, made a major effort to produce a well-styled two-port sporting ohv '350' at a really low price. By concentrating on one-model production, careful tooling and stringent pricing, they contrived to offer the

new 'Ivory' model at £47 only, with electrics extra. The neat lines and pleasing white finish to tank, mudguards and headlamp made this a best-seller.

Brighter finishes were evident elsewhere, on the Matchlesses in black and white, later with optional nickel-plated tanks, Panthers in their famous green with cream wheels an extra; Dunelts with green mudguards and cream wheels; the plum-coloured Zeniths, and Excelsiors in somewhat startling black and white checkered tanks. Such exuberances were offset by the dignity of Sunbeam's black and gold weatherproof turn-out, and the similar black and gold of the Velocettes, Rudges and AJSs.

The 1928 racing season upset a few predictions when the overhead camshaft brigade, thought to be unbeatable after

Above: a 1928 500cc Rudge-Whitworth which was piloted to victory in that year's Ulster Grand Prix by Graham Walker, who later became motor cycle curator at the National Motor Museum. This machine, which was the first bike to win a long-distance race at an average of over 80mph, was the prototype of the famous Rudge Ulster

Top: a 1928 K7 overhead-camshaft AJS which had a top speed of 75mph and a fuel consumption of 80mpg with its 349cc engine. It weighed around 240lb

Above: a close-up of the Henderson four-cylinder engine as used on their C14 Deluxe model of 1925

twelve months' further development, were roundly defeated several times by the pushrod bikes, the Isle of Man TT setting the trend. On streaming wet roads, Graham Walker's pushrod ohv Rudge led the Senior until seven miles from the finish when it broke down and Dodson's pushrod ohv Sunbeam went though to win. Alec Bennett and Harold Willis on two ohc Velocettes, fitted with ingenious positive-stop foot gearchanges, cleaned up the Junior, and OK-Supreme won the Lightweight honours, Longman up.

'Pocket dynamite' Dodson and his Sunbeam then won the Belgian and German Senior GPs, and ran second to Woods' Norton in the French GP. Walker's Rudge walked off with the Dutch TT, and then beat Dodson's Sunbeam by 200 yards in an exciting Ulster GP, the winner averaging 80.78mph. Wal Handley, who 'freelanced' from make to make, won both the 500 and 350cc classes of the Swiss (also European) GP on locally-built Motosacoches, and won the Junior Austrian GP and German TT races, both times on an AJS. George Rowley (AJS) beat a BMW and a DKW in the Austrian GP, and privateer Franconi (Sunbeam) took the Senior GP of the Nations in Italy.

Norton muscled in on the 350cc class with a 350cc near-replica of their Senior bike, winning both the Dutch and German Junior races. Frank Longman's Velocette took the '350' laurels at Ulster, and Nuvolari led a Bianchi 'double knocker' formation at Monza. After its TT success, the 250cc JAP-engined OK-Supreme went on to collect the Ulster, Swiss and Austrian races, while Guzzi on their home ground scooped the first five places at Monza in a sweeping in-line formation that sent the crowd cheering wildly.

The racing machine of those days was much closer akin to the production model than it is today, the 1927 or 1928 racer often becoming the 1929 super-sports model, as indicated by the Model 90 Sunbeam. Other examples were the new 350cc, ohc Norton road model marketed in 1929, and the saddle-tanked, 499cc Rudge 'Ulster' commemorating the marque's victories in that race. Velocette offered their 1928 TT-winning 350cc 'cammy' in production racing form as the KTT, a mouth-watering £80's worth providing dozens of private owners with an entrée into racing.

As 1929 advanced and motor cycles continued to sell in large numbers (731,298 British registrations that year, over 18,000 more than in 1928) there was little sign of the dire economic woes to come. Yet it was a year more of design refinement than of spectacular new models. Chromium plating had arrived, with its obvious advantages over nickel in eliminating the tedious chore of polishing, yet conservative makers (and buyers) would not unbend at once. Dunelt, for instance, cautiously offered it as an option, charging ten shillings extra for a chromed petrol tank and five shillings extra for a chromed exhaust system!

Scott *afficionados* were surprised, not to say affronted, by the introduction of a new single-cylinder 'Squirrel', and air-cooled at that. Its 298cc, two-stroke engine, basically one half of the 596cc twin, was inclined in a frame with normal top tube and saddle tank. At £39 basic or £42 with Maglita electric lighting (twistgrip control nine shillings extra), it was an obvious attempt by Scott to widen their market, but its career was short.

Clearly some enterprises were feeling the pinch. Howard Davies' praiseworthy HRD venture was taken over by Phil Vincent, becoming the Vincent-HRD and destined for future

Below: first seen at the 1929 bike show was the Matchless Silver Arrow, which its makers heralded as their 'ideal motor cycle'. It featured a 26-degree vee-twin unit of 398cc. Silent and smooth it was, but it lacked the outright performance that enthusiasts thought of as 'ideal' in a bike

fame. McEvoy closed down, and F. E. Baker's pretty little Villiers-engined sports lightweight was soon to be taken over by James. France reported growing interest in motor cycling, but this amounted to rebellion against high bus fares and resultant demand for diminutive *vélomoteurs* giving languid mobility on a waft of petrol. Germany was determinedly exporting lightweight DKWs and other makes in considerable quantities, the Zündapp came to Britain as the Newmount, and the sturdy Belgian FN and Gillet machines were also imported in small numbers.

As Olympia Show time approached in 1929, the economic wind chilled, and in late October came the big Wall Street 'crash' in New York, affecting finance world wide. Stocks and shares values tumbled, banks and finance houses failed, and countless investors were ruined. The shock wave quickly hit Europe, luxury shrank before the Depression, and the dismal new theme was 'economise'. All this seriously affected motor cycles of the early '30s, but did not prevent the release of important new models in late 1929.

The annual Show sensation was not a Brough-Superior this time, but the Matchless 'Silver Arrow', a model important not for what it was, but what it portended. It had a narrow-angle, monobloc, vee-twin engine of 400cc with side valves, the cylinders at only 26 degrees. The makers aimed not for power or high performance, but for smooth, silent comfort. Aided by an adjustable double coil spring frame, pivoted on Silentbloc bushes, the 'Silver Arrow' certainly accomplished this, but it was too heavy and docile for the average motor cycle fraternity. Yet it was a direct forebear of the four-cylinder Matchless 'Silver Hawk' of a year later, a machine which was to help keep British motor cycles on the crest of the design wave in those stormy, troubled years of the early 1930s.

Other developments of interest at that last show of 'the roaring '20s' included a two-port ohc Velocette, the KTP, and an excellent new two-stroke, the GTP, both with coil ignition. For an extra fifty shillings, foot gearchange as developed on their racing machines was available on any Velocette, a trend swiftly copied by other makers. Vincent-HRD and OEC offered spring frames; Excelsior had pressed steel forks on one model – a straw in the wind for the future, while further straws came in sparse new economy lightweights such as the nineteen guinea Rex Acme, plus Radco and Excelsior models with 147cc Villiers engines and two speeds.

The economic crisis loomed too late to disturb the 1929 racing season, and the TT promised another tremendous inter-make struggle. It rained before the Senior race, precipitating some alarming crashes on lap one at Greeba Bridge. Handley (AJS), Simpson, now riding for Norton, Lamb (Norton) and Amott (Rudge) all came down on the slimy road, and Lamb lost his life. 1928 winner Dodson, his pushrod Sunbeam now with footchange and saddle tank, gradually caught the four-valve Rudges and Norton's 'new boy' Tim Hunt, to win from Bennett (Sunbeam) and Tyrell Smith (Rudge).

The 'cammy' Velocette came back on form to win the Junior TT, Brooklands track specialist Freddy Hicks holding off the road racing experts to lead Handley (AJS) and Bennett (Velocette) home. Anglophiles had a severe fright in the Lightweight TT when Pietro Ghersi tore into the lead on his Guzzi, and stayed firmly in front right to the last lap. Then cruel fate gave him engine failure, and Syd Crabtree went through to win for Excelsior from a Dot and an OK, all three JAP-motored.

By coincidence, the three TT winners exactly repeated their placings in the subsequent French GP at Le Mans, while

Dodson won a third Senior victory for Sunbeam in the Belgian GP. Handley's alcohol-burning Motosacoche dominated the Junior race, and that untiring Scottish combine, Jock Porter and his New Gerrard took 250cc honours. The four-valve, four-speed Rudges really found their form at Assen, where Ernie Nott and Graham Walker placed one-two in the Dutch TT after a bloodcurdling scrap with Handley's Motosacoche. They did it again in the German GP at Nürburg, Tyrell Smith winning this time, and yet again in the Ulster GP – Walker's hat-trick, at a record speed of 80.63mph.

Normally the Ulster closed the season, but the Spaniards ambitiously took on promotion of the European GP, at a rather improvised 10½ mile circuit at Amettla, north of Barcelona. This time it was Norton's turn, Tim Hunt winning his first classic, hounded home by Walker and Dodson. The 350cc class in 1929 had been a battlefield between the AJS and Velocette teams and the meteoric Handley, sometimes Motosacoche, sometimes AJS

mounted. The score was two-all, AJS winning in Ulster and Spain, Velocette in France and Holland, Motosacoche in Belgium and Germany. Among the Lightweights, the 'Hecker-JAP' which Crabtree rode to win in Germany was a Nurnberg product, while the OK-JAPs took wins in the Grand Prix events held in Ulster and Spain.

In Italy, the polished Achille Varzi won the 500cc GP of the Nations at Monza for Sunbeam, Moretti on a twin-cam Bianchi won the Junior race, and one Truzzi (Guzzi) was the Lightweight victor. Of lesser events, Simcock (Sunbeam) won the six-hour Senior Austrian GP, Rowley (AJS) the Junior and Runtsch (OK) the Lightweight, while a 500cc, twin-cylinder, two-stroke DKW won the Hungarian TT.

If the '20s were preponderantly Britain's decade in

Left: Jim Whalley and his 250cc Cotton-JAP seen at the 1929 Belgian Grand Prix at the Spa Francorchamps circuit

Above: the start of the German Spree Prize event for sidecar outfits up to 600cc of 1929. The venue is the Berlin Trotting track for horse racing

competition, first hints of a foreign challenge from a new source came in 1929. The Brooklands rider O. M. Baldwin had captured Temple's motor cycle speed record at 124.62mph on his 996cc Zenith-JAP in 1928. Some months later Le Vack took his big Brough-Superior out to Alpajon and notched up his fourth record, at 129.07mph. The record had now been British property for seven years, when out of poverty-stricken Germany came a new and unexpected challenge. BMW had supercharged their 735cc transverse flat-twins for high speed racing, and in September Ernst Henne took one out to a fast straight road near Munich. He flashed through the flying kilometre at a speed of 216.05kph (133.95mph), and Britain had lost the motor cycle speed record to Germany. Whatever else, the 1930s certainly promised much of interest in the world of speed; however, there was no-one who could foretell the long-term effects of the economic crises of the 1920s on motor cycle production in the following decade. The subsequent years were to paint a sombre picture of cut-backs, economy production lines, and a state of general decline in the industry. Indeed many manufacturers were unable to weather the storm, and went under.

Chapter 6
Survival of the Fittest (1930-1934)

Left: when Edward Turner arrived at the Ariel company in the early 1930s, he helped to rejuvenate the ailing firm by giving their existing range of models a cosmetic uplift. One of the models which received the treatment was the little single-cylinder 250 Colt which subsequently joined the Red Hunter stable. The model pictured is of 1936 vintage

Occurring midway between the two World Wars, 1930 was a red-letter year, not only for the motor cycling movement, but for nations all around the globe whose economies were in any way influenced by the 'almighty dollar'. After a decade of mounting prosperity, the United States of America had been plunged into financial chaos when, in December 1929, New York's stock market gamblers finally overreached themselves, bringing about the devastating Wall Street Crash and the Depression.

The effects of the American upheaval quickly crossed the Atlantic to Britain and Europe and, almost overnight, the carefree, golden days of the 1920s changed into a reign of economic crisis, dole queues, hunger marches and a general atmosphere of belt-tightening.

Motor cycle manufacturers suffered in common with industry and commerce of all kinds. The impact on the US constructors was immediate, and it virtually killed motor cycling in that country. Henry Ford and his imitators, the availability of cheap gasolene, and 'keeping up with the Jones' had already turned America into a nation of motorists, and a motor cycle industry that had once supported a score or more of marques had been reduced to a bare half-dozen, relying chiefly on exports and sales to domestic police forces. During 1930, the USA exported only 10,262 machines, contrasting with nearly 17,000 in 1926 and 38,000 in 1920. The downward trend continued over the next few years, too, leaving only two firms, Harley-Davidson and Indian, sharing the market.

British and European makers faced the situation in various ways. Some, like the long-established Humber concern, abandoned two wheels altogether to concentrate on cars and commercial vehicles. A few, such as Ariel, Raleigh and Triumph, made light cars and trade delivery trucks. AJS diversified even more widely, turning out sidecars, cars, lorries and radio sets. Whether they branched into other lines of business or stuck doggedly to making only motor cycles and bicycles, all manufacturers cut their prices. Standards of quality, safety and luxury suffered, but there was no lack of innovation or engineering ingenuity, and far more attention than hitherto was paid to simplifying the methods, and reducing the costs, of production. Customers at this time were offered some of the best bargains the market has ever known.

A further inducement to sales was the widespread adoption of the easy-payments by instalments system, a form of purchase not previously favoured or exploited. Now, a first-class machine costing about £50 could be had for a £10 deposit and repayments of a few shillings a week. For a hard-pressed young man needing personal transport to find himself a job, or to travel to work, hire purchase came as a godsend. Indeed, it could be said that the Depression, despite all of its grim realities, had beneficial side effects for the motor cycle movement. It arrived just at the time when the rest of the world had begun to catch up with US production and sales techniques. In England, Austin, Ford and Morris all had near-£100 models, and there were signs that the American desertion of two wheels in favour of four might be emulated in Europe. In their endeavours to stay in business, the British and European motor cycle makers had to sharpen up their ideas, razor-strop their factory procedures and put a keener edge to cut-throat competition with their rivals.

At all events, when London's annual Motor Cycle Show was held at Olympia in the autumn of 1930, not only was there an almost complete parade of eligible exhibitors, but many of them had newly conceived and much advanced designs on

display. For the record, stand space was taken by: AJS, Ariel, Ardie (German-built duralumin frames with JAP engines), Brough-Superior (showing a 500cc ohv twin model), BSA, Calthorpe, Cotton, Coventry-Eagle, Coventry-Victor, Douglas, Dunelt, Excelsior, Francis-Barnett, Grindlay-Peerless, Indian (twin- and four-cylinder types), James, Levis, Matchless (including the new Silver Hawk 593cc ohc four-cylinder model), Montgomery, Motosacoche, Morgan, New Hudson (panelling enclosing engine base and gearbox), New Imperial, Newmount (German-built with Rudge Python engines), Norton, OEC, OK-Supreme (with 'Lighthouse' ohc engines), P & M, Radco, Raleigh, Royal Enfield, Rudge, Scott, Sun, Sunbeam, Triumph, Velocette, Vincent-HRD and Wolf. Not at Olympia, but in special displays in London dealers' showrooms, were

Top: among the many interesting machines on display at the London Motor Cycle Show of 1930, held at Olympia, was this Newmount model using a German-built Zündapp two-stroke engine. Latterly Rudge Python engines were fitted

Above: the unusually styled Ascot-Pullin of 1930. Designed by racer/engineer Cyril Pullin, it used a 496cc, overhead-valve, single-cylinder engine coupled to a three-speed gearbox

Harley-Davidson and Henderson (the American 'four' then being made by the Excelsior Mfg Company of Chicago). British marques not exhibiting included AKD, Ascot-Pullin, Chater-Lea, Diamond, Dot, New Gerrard, New Henley, NUT, Royal Ruby, SOS and The Ivy. Most of these were either dormant or at death's door, shortly to disappear and, in some cases, to be revived years later 'under new management'.

European makers seldom exhibited at Olympia. France, Italy, Belgium and Germany all had their own shows and they were not great exporters. In addition to the leading makers (Peugeot, Terrot and Rèné-Gillet in France; Moto Guzzi, Gilera and Bianchi in Italy; BMW, DKW, D-Rad, NSU and Zündapp in Germany; FN and Sarolea in Belgium; Puch in Austria and Motosacoche in Switzerland), there were scores of smaller concerns fighting for their share of the cake crumbs in their own home markets. How these highly individualistic little firms survived, some of them even to the present day, has always

Above: all roads lead to the Derby; two Indian students who made their way to Epsom to see the classic Derby horse race get a tip from a friendly policeman. Their bike is a 500cc, side-valve, German-built Ardie of 1931

been a bit of a mystery to motor cycle enthusiasts.

There was much rivalry among the English makers to see who could produce the biggest motor cycle at the lowest price and of the least weight. At the time, solos weighing under 224lb enjoyed a road tax concession of only 30 shillings per annum, and in this category, Matchless offered a 350cc model with enclosed side valves, dry-sump lubrication and a duplex-tube frame. Standard equipment included electric lighting, a

decompressor and centre prop stand. Claimed to do 60mph and finished in the company's recently adopted black-and-white livery, it was priced at £38 10s, but it was not the ultimate: a few months later it had a big brother of 500cc (suitable for sidecar work) priced at £40. Even by today's standards, the 224lb Matchless bikes must be reckoned as having been real value for money. Also in the 30 shillings tax class were an ohv 'Big Port' AJS and a 350 sv Douglas horizontal-twin, both costing £40.

Bargain hunting among the accessory suppliers' stands in Olympia's galleries also had its delights. Gamages, whose Holborn store was world famous, could supply a five-gallon drum of Super de Luxe oil (state engine make and model) for 10s 6d, carriage paid. Another well known dealer, George Grose, had Cowey speedometers, complete with drive and fittings, for 15s, and the Services Watch Company's Despatch Rider shock-proof wrist watches ('as worn by noted TT riders') cost 15s 6d, post free.

Hard times notwithstanding, the Show organisers must have been reasonably pleased with the attendance. Although it was open for six days only, the 106,000 gate was just about level with the previous year's seven-day run. Every show has its 'sensation'. That of the 1930 Olympia exhibition was not some new masterpiece of design, but a machine that should not have been there at all! On why and how it got there hangs a tale that has become a classic in the 'do-you-remember' *genre*.

Earlier in the year, the Munich-based BMW concern, which had steadily been increasing its status, had made that attack on the world's motor cycle speed record with a 750cc supercharged semi-streamlined solo on which Ernst Henne had reached a flying kilometre speed of 137.6mph. This was regarded by the pundits of the technical press as an almost impertinent encroachment on Britain's prerogatives in the sphere of speedy travel, and demands that 'something should be done about it' filled the editorials and correspondence pages. The action came, not from one of the big constructors, but from a comparatively obscure little country firm, the Osborn Engineering Company, of Gosport in Hampshire. After years of conventional machine production, OEC had evolved a highly unorthodox duplex steering system. Into a frame of this type they put a blown 996cc ohv JAP twin engine, engaged Brooklands speedman J. S. Wright to pilot it and quietly took off for Eire where, on a stretch of public road near Cork, on the eve of the show, Joe Wright was officially timed at a 150.73mph average.

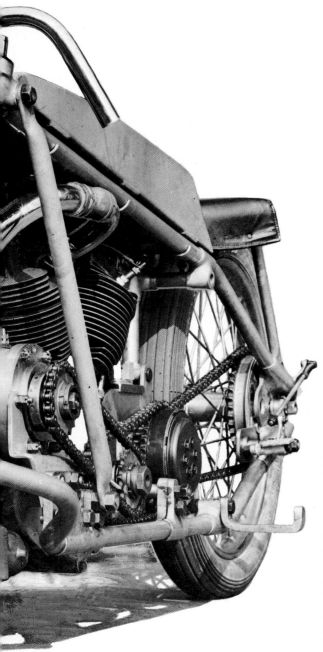

Left: Ernie Nott (Rudge) is followed by C.W. Johnston (Cotton-JAP) at Governor's Bridge during the 1930 Isle of Man Junior TT. With first and second placings in both the Junior and Senior TTs, 1930 proved a very good year for the Rudge company

Below: the famous OEC-Temple-JAP record breaker of 1930. The machine featured a highly unorthodox duplex steering system and a supercharged, overhead-valve, 996cc, vee-twin JAP engine

Below right: Ernst Henne poses with the supercharged, 750cc BMW record breaker on which he reached a speed of 137.6mph in 1930

At Olympia, the OEC-Temple-JAP, as it was called, was proudly displayed as Britain's answer to the German challenge, but not for long. The show had barely opened when knowledgeable people who had witnessed Wright's ride were saying that this was not the machine on which he had achieved the record; it had had, so they claimed, an ordinary diamond frame and a conventional girder front fork. An inquiry was held, 'misleading misunderstandings' were examined; Joe Wright *had* ridden the OEC-Duplex, but his reserve machine had produced a better result, and that was the one that went into the books, to the credit of J. S. Wright (Temple-JAP). The face of British prestige was saved.

In that other field of record-breaking, road racing, 1930 was unquestionably Rudges' year. The Coventry factory had for several seasons been building fast 500cc sports machines with four-overhead-valve engines, four-speed gearboxes and large-diameter coupled drum brakes. Company chief John Pugh had assembled a crack team of riders and technicians among

whom were the TT experts Ernie Nott, Tyrell Smith and Graham Walker, who was also the firm's advertising manager and racing *chef d'équipe*. Technical development was in the hands of brilliant engineer George Hack, who was assisted by designer Frank Anstey and Jack Amott, a rider-tuner of vast experience. However, Rudges' chances in the TT were not rated all that highly by the critics, who regarded pushrod engines as old-fashioned in an era when overhead camshafts had become the 'in thing'.

The experts were in for a shock when, for his first morning practice run, Tyrell Smith arrived at the Grandstand with Hack's close-kept secret, a 350cc mount whose four valves were set radially in a hemispherical cylinder head and were operated by an extremely ingenious linkage of six rockers with two rods. With this machine, from a standing start, Tyrell Smith clocked an initial lap in 31mins 26secs (71.9mph), knocking almost half a minute off Freddie Hicks's 1929 AJS record.

On Junior Race day, the three experimental Rudges, none of which had been ridden on the road before they reached the Island, achieved an astonishing one-two-three victory, Smith, Nott and Walker finishing in that order with less than sixty seconds separating them; Nott raised the lap record to 72.27mph. Could the Rudge trio repeat their hat-trick in the Senior? It seemed unlikely, for the 500cc machines were practically standard four-valve pent-roof jobs, and they were up against a strong Sunbeam team (captained by two-times winner Charlie Dodson); and Stanley Woods, Jimmy Simpson and Tim Hunt were on Nortons that had new ohc engines developed by the company's clever engineer, Arthur Carroll, who introduced for this year the 'square' bevel box vertical shaft drive that was to characterise the Bracebridge Street factory raceware for the next three decades.

The Raleigh company had three good riders on fast machines prepared by the original Brooklands 'wizard of tune', Dan O'Donovan, and there was a dark-horse foreign threat in Walter Handley's entry, a massive unit-construction ohc FN which had already shown its speed in European events. However, this Belgian menace failed to reach the Island and it was looking as though Walter would be a non-starter ('a TT without Handley is like an egg without salt', moaned one of the fans) when a way was found for him to take over a private owner's Rudge entry; so, he joined Smith, Nott and Walker in the Coventry firm's camp.

Never before having raced a Rudge, Handley quickly proved that, no matter what it was called, if a machine had speed he could use it. On his first practice run, he averaged over 75mph and cut fifty seconds off the lap record!

In the Senior race, under conditions that deteriorated into a downpour, Walter Handley held the lead on every one of the seven laps, ending with a race record speed of 72.24mph and a final record lap in 28mins 41secs (76.28mph), shattering the thirty-minute barrier and becoming a winner in all four of the solo classes. It was the last time that a push-rod machine won the International Senior TT. Graham Walker finished second and, with Tyrell Smith sixth, Rudges took the Manufacturer's team prize for the second time in the week.

By the end of the season, Rudges had many other racing successes to reinforce their great TT victories. Walker won the German and Dutch GPs; Smith and Nott were 500 and 350cc European Champions, respectively, and Rudge riders were first and second in the Senior Manx Grand Prix and second in the Junior. This was the first year of the Manx, which had replaced the Amateur TT, first held in 1923.

In the booming sport of dirt-track racing, the famous Australian broadsider, Vic Huxley, had won seven British open championships on his Rudge and was the outstanding speedway star of the year.

Norton had collected wins by Stanley Woods in the French and Ulster GPs, and on a 500cc model C. W. G. 'Bill' Lacey and Wal Phillips shared a '300 miles in three hours' record at the Montlhéry circuit. AJS, too, had laurels to claim. In only his second TT, a young Scottish rider, James Guthrie, won the Lightweight Race, and ex-butcher's boy, Albert Denly, took the classic One-Hour record on a 495cc 'cammy' model at

Above left: a close-up of the victorious single-cylinder, 350cc Rudge engine which made a fairy-tale debut in the 1930 Junior TT

Above: Geoff Butcher's 500cc Rudge outfit at the Scottish Six Days Trial of 1930

Right: Jimmy Guthrie winning the 1930 Lightweight TT on his AJS

Below: the dohc, 175cc Benelli racer of 1931 proved faster than many 250s of the time

108.6mph; on a 350 version, his sixty-minute stint raised the class record to a very impressive 104.52mph.

On the trials and scrambles courses, 1930's most successful men were Graham Goodman and Dennis Mansell (Norton), Len Heath and Harry Perrey (Ariel), Vic Brittain and Peter Bradley (Sunbeam), Bert Kershaw (New Imperial), Jack Williams and Geoff Butcher (Rudge), Bert Perrigo and Phil Cranmore (BSA) and Stuart Waycott (Douglas). However, in the premier long-distance event, the International Six Days Trial, Great Britain, after a four-year run of supremacy, was out of luck. Italy, with a team of Gilera riders, won the Trophy, and a French squad took the alternative prize, the Silver Vase.

In England, something started creeping into the state of the sport which was to have a distasteful effect. The 'bonus' system of cash payments for successes, originated at Brooklands, had spread through road racing to competitions of all sorts. It had wrecked the Amateur TT and was having such a disturbing effect on reliability trials that the industry, through its organisation, the Manufacturers and Traders Union, withdrew its support, except for a short list of approved events. Both the Union and the ACU strongly opposed a move to allow the use of 'dope' fuels in international races. Instead, a 50-50 mixture of petrol and benzole was agreed upon, and this formula remained in force thereafter, except for the post World War II period when the only fuel available was 'pool' petrol.

Although nobody knew it at the time, the last day of 1930 was a date of great significance, for it marked the end of the Vintage epoch. On the authority of the Vintage Motor Cycle Club, arbiters on all matters pertaining to historic machines, 'A vintage motor cycle is one manufactured between 1 January 1915 and 31 December 1930'. Machines made prior to that period are generally recognised and classed as veterans.

On New Year's Day 1931, the Road Traffic Act came into force. Replacing the Motor Car Act, it was a piece of legislation that was to have far-reaching and long-lasting effects on the British way of life, for much of it, as originally drafted, has remained Law to present times. It covered practically every facet of road and vehicle usage and introduced a new kind of traveller's guide, the advisory Highway Code. Two of the most important provisions of the new Act, that concerned all drivers of mechanically propelled vehicles, were the necessity to provide themselves with third-party insurance, and the abolition of the 20mph general speed limit that had stood since 1903. Henceforward excessive speeding was to be checked by mobile policemen armed with power to prosecute for dangerous or careless driving. The Act contained a number of measures specifically affecting motor cyclists. The minimum age for holding a motor cycle driving licence was raised from fourteen to sixteen; side-saddle pillion riding was banned; much larger rear number plates became obligatory. Quick off the mark, the Sun Insurance Office Ltd began advertising third-party cover for private motor cycles (with or without a sidecar) for the princely sum of £1 per annum.

Visitors to the Italian Show at Milan in January were able to see a double-overhead-camshaft racer of 173cc from the Benelli factory and a 500cc, unit-construction, transverse vee-twin exhibited by AJS. The latter machine was not announced in the English technical press until the following April. An excellent performer with many good points, it was, unhappily, doomed to a short life, for the famous Wolverhampton company

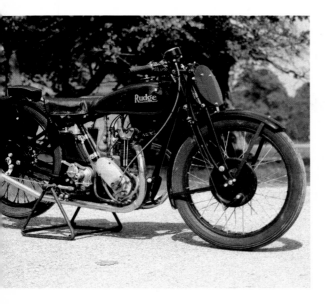

Above: a 250cc Rudge of 1932, which is a replica of the model on which Graham Walker won the 1932 Lightweight TT

Left: in 1930, Matchless launched their revolutionary Silver Hawk model. It used a narrow-angle vee-four, ohc engine of 593cc

Below: Graham Walker (Rudge) leads Jimmy Guthrie (Norton) during the 1931 Junior TT Guthrie went on to finish second

was one of the first major British motor cycle firms to find itself caught in the financial blizzard that was by now freezing the country's trade arteries. Despite having some of the best brains in the industry, a fine, well-equipped factory and a wide range of excellent and popular machines, AJS were grappling with what would nowadays be called a cash-flow problem. By July the customary full-page advertisements had ceased to appear in the trade journals. Rumours of a sell-out to BSA began to circulate, but early in November it was announced that 'There are no further developments to record in connection with the reported negotiations for the acquisition of A. J. Stevens and Co by the BSA company, which states that the discussions have been dropped'. Nevertheless the rumours continued.

During the Show, where there were neither AJS nor BSA exhibits, came the news that Matchless Motor Cycles (Colliers) Ltd had acquired the stock, goodwill and assets of A. J. Stevens. Production would continue at the Matchless factory in the London suburb of Woolwich.

BSA's reason for abstaining from the Show was the depressed state of the motor cycle market. In 1929 the number of machines in use in Britain was a record 731,298: in 1930 it had dropped to 724,319 and it was obvious that the 1931 figures would show a further decline. Indeed, the 1929 record was not again exceeded until 1950. BSA staged their own show at their Small Heath factory where the pride of a twelve solo-model range was a new Blue Star sports type, available in either 350 or 500cc capacity. With high-compression pistons, double-coil valve springs, special cams, pump-type Amal carburettors, high-level exhaust pipes and positive-stop control for four-speed gearboxes, the Blue Stars were the forerunners of a long line of successful Star models that appealed especially to fast tourists and sporting clubmen, of which latter there were increasing numbers. It is a curious fact that while the industry generally was going through very difficult times, enthusiasm for motor cycle sport was growing at such a rate that by the end of 1931 the ACU was claiming that it had 400 affiliated clubs – a record. The entry for that year's TT, at 153, was the second highest ever reached between the World Wars. The peak had been in 1923 when a four-race meeting attracted 163.

Most of the major racing firms continued their support for the Island event and there was even a return, after a three-year absence, of the Douglas company. NSU, regulars in the 1907–14 era, reappeared with ohc 500s, and Guzzi were back in the Lightweight class. Of the 21 different makes which were represented, eight were foreign.

In the TT saga, 1931 is chiefly memorable as marking the start of the Norton reign, a success story that was to span thirty years. The firm's technical wizards, Joe Craig and Arthur Carroll, had overcome earlier lubrication troubles and, on a Junior model, Tim Hunt opened the meeting with a victory run that lowered the race record by $8\frac{1}{2}$ minutes. In the Senior he made it a double, reducing Handley's Rudge record by a good ten minutes. With Guthrie second and Woods third, Norton registered the first ever Senior hat-trick by a British manufacturer, and Hunt became the first man to win the Junior and Senior Trophies in one week. Simpson, first to lap at sixty, then 70mph, put in a lap at over 80mph. In the Lightweight race Graham Walker won his long-overdue Trophy on a radial-valve machine from the Rudge factory.

An attempt during the year by the ACU to revive the Stock Machine Trial failed through lack of entries, and a determined, combined endeavour by the industry to win back the

International Six Days Trophy also came to grief. Nevertheless, despite, or perhaps because of, the Manufacturers Union restriction of trade support to certain approved open events, the sport of trials riding was flourishing, so much so that it was sometimes necessary to hold quite important meetings on Wednesdays, the weekend fixture lists being overcrowded.

At the Show, the Ariel concern displayed the Maudes Trophy among its season's prizes. Offered annually for the most meritorious officially observed test by a manufacturer, the 'Maudes' had instigated many arduous and comprehensive trials of long-distance reliability and speed. Ariel's award was for an ambitious Sevens Test of all the seven models in their catalogue, as follows: a 350 side-valve model averaged 52.58mph for seven hours, covering 368 miles 120 yards; a 350 overhead-valve machine did 115 miles on seven shillings worth of petrol and used no oil; given seven minutes in which to decarbonise a 557cc side-valve model, mechanics did the job in 4mins 19secs; a 500 overhead-valve model, scheduled to cover seventy miles in

Below: Edward Turner's remarkable square-four Ariel of 1931, which had a capacity of 497cc. This bike's engine featured an overhead camshaft operating vertical valves via short rockers, although later machines had a pushrod valve system. The last bikes also had engines bored out to 1 litre

Right: the Brough-Superior four-cylinder of 1932, which used a modified 796cc Austin Seven engine and shaft drive. Note the twin rear wheels, and the ammeter placed by the battery. This was a popular position for such units on machines of that vintage

seventy minutes, did 80 miles 276 yards, averaging 68.7mph; a 550 side-valve 'sloper' model was driven for seventy minutes in each of its four gears, non-stop; a 500 overhead-valve 'sloper' and sidecar outfit made seven ascents and descents of seven famous hills, including Porlock, Beggars' Roost, Bwlch-y-Groes and Allt-y-Bady; a 600 'Square Four' covered 700 miles in under 700 minutes, averaging 62mph.

The famous Henderson 'four' was a 1931 casualty, the American Excelsior company having ceased to make motor cycles. However, George Brough was offering a BS with an Austin Seven car engine and shaft drive to twin rear wheels. Another 'four', a sad example of what might have been, was a 630cc ohv in-line-cylinder prototype that had been devised by the Stevens brothers but had not satisfied their critical standards. It came to light as part of the AJS assets but, although undergoing favourable Press tests, it was never developed and became a museum piece preserved by the Birmingham dealers, the Colmore Depot.

Before the year was out an honorable name that had passed into limbo reappeared when the London firm of Writers Motor and Cycle Works revived the Zenith marque, using big-twin and single-cylinder, JAP engines.

One of the most important of the Continental motor cycle exhibitions; the Milan Show, customarily held in January, nearly always included interestingly new machines, not only from the Italian factories but also from constructors from other countries who used the occasion as a curtain-raiser to test reactions to innovations that they expected to put into full production in readiness for the spring buying season. The 1932 event was no exception and, in addition to a number of British firms, other non-Italian exhibitors were Sarolea, Gillet, Motosacoche, FN, BMW, NSU, DKW and D-Rad.

Signs of designers' increasing preoccupation with multi-cylinder engines were much in evidence, particularly in the Moto-Guzzi range. By now by far the largest and most progressive of Italy's manufacturers, Guzzi had two years earlier produced a supercharged 500cc, four-cylinder racer/record-breaker, of remarkable complexity and ingenuity. Now they had an unblown ohv 500 three-cylinder machine, with the monobloc unit lying horizontally in a rear-sprung frame. It was not intended for racing but was equipped as a super-luxury *gran turismo* model. An expensive piece of machinery, the *Tipo Tre Cilindri* remained in production barely a year, but its 120-degree

crankshaft layout antedated MV's famous world-beating triple-pot racers by 34 years.

Another anticipation of things to come was the name given to a neat little 175cc ohv single shown by the Turin firm of Pellini and Ferrari, which had been building Simplex motor cycles since 1921. They called their new model the 'Golden Wing', more than forty years before Honda used a similar name for their flat-four. Luigi Pellini continued making high-class motor cycles until Italy entered World War II. Between 1899 and the 1960s, the Simplex name was applied to four different makes of motor cycle, the other three having their factories in Amsterdam, Birmingham and New Orleans.

Gilera, second to Guzzi in terms of output and prestige (for two successive years their men and machines had won the International Six Days Trophy), had a big Milan display, and Bianchi decorated their stand with a huge photo of Mussolini riding one of their 175cc models. *Il Duce* was a keen motor cyclist and held the number one membership card of the Moto Club d'Italia. With his encouragement – and eagerness to push his country to the forefront – Italian motor and motor cycle construction was making tremendous technical advances.

On the other hand, British manufacturers got no help at all from the authorities. Indeed, it seemed at times as though the government had an anti-motor cycle phobia, imposing stricter silencer regulations and firmly rebutting well-argued pleas for road-tax reductions. In view of the nation's economic plight, encouragement for low-priced, cheap-to-run, utility machines – 'mounts for the millions', or Everyman models, as they were termed – would have been logical. Paradoxically, however, the types in most popular demand were the more expensive ohv sports and clubman's 350s and 500s. At one end of this widely divergent scale George Brough went blithely on his individualistic way, having no great difficulty in finding customers for his SS100 996cc ohv twins at £180 apiece. By contrast, £20 (£5 10s 3d down payment) was all that Royal Enfield were asking for their new Cycar, which had an immensely strong pressed-steel frame enclosing the 148cc two-stroke engine and three-speed gearbox. With electric lighting, integral legshields and many other useful features, it weighed only 168lb and was quite the cheapest form of personal mechanical transport available. Yet it never attained the quantity-production output for which it had been planned, although it remained on the market for some five years.

At no time in motor cycle history were prices, in relation to value, lower than they were in 1932. On all sides manufacturers knocked pounds off the costs of their existing models and many followed the Royal Enfield example, introducing new utility lightweights at almost ridiculously low figures. Villiers two-stroke engines predominated in this field. Douglas brought out a Bantam model with their own 150cc unit mounted horizontally in the frame. They also produced an attractive Golden Star Model, having a 250cc transverse, flat-twin, side-valve engine in unit with a four-speed (silent third) constant-mesh gearbox and spiral-bevel shaft-drive. Coventry-Eagle dropped four-stroke engines altogether and offered a 250cc version of their pressed-steel framed Silent Superb. The mighty Triumph company produced a fully-equipped (with legshields) ohv 147cc 'sloper' at £28 10s. Even the lordly John Marston Sunbeams went through an economy purge. A new 350cc Model 8 cost £58 10s; for an extra £10 there was a high-performance edition, the Model 80. Both had two-port heads, enclosed rocker gear and double-coil valve springs. Also

Below: a 1932 500cc ohc Norton featuring the camshaft drive revisions made in 1930 by Arthur Carroll to Walter Moore's 1927 design in which the magneto was chain-driven on the left side directly from the crankshaft. Continuously developed by Joe Craig, Carroll-type 'square bevelbox' Nortons dominated road racing for three decades

new was the Sunbeam Little 90, a long-stroke (90mm by 57mm) 246cc two-port ohv job at £56 10s.

One reason why the utility machine market did not expand at the rate that the trade had expected was a change in the taxation scale foreshadowed by the Chancellor of the Exchequer, Neville Chamberlain, in his April Budget. It had been confidently hoped that he would yield to heavy pressure for removal of the 15s tax on under-150cc engines, so putting Great Britain on parity with many European countries whose lightweight riders paid no tax. This argument was given greater force when the registration figures for 1931 were published. The number of motor cycles in use in Britain had fallen again but in France, Germany and Italy, where lightweights were totally exempted, they had all gone up. However, the Chancellor proposed to abolish the 224lb weight class in favour of a simple three-tier capacity scale – solos under 250cc would be taxed at £1 10s per annum; for bigger engines the fee was £3; it was also announced that the 150cc 15s rate was to be left unchanged.

Although not due to come into effect until June 1933, the new scale had an immediate influence on design and sales. Clearly, it encouraged the 250cc class; it was a disadvantage to the popular 'nifty three-fifty'; and it did no good at all for the economy lightweights. Helped by favourable insurance rates and unchanged taxation, however, sidecar combinations and three-wheeled cyclecars (officially called 'tricycles', the latter were taxed at only £4 a year if they weighed under eight hundredweight) enjoyed a boost in popularity. BSA were doing good business with their vee-twin 'trike', reduced to £100, and now introduced a four-cylinder, water-cooled version at £125. There was a Morgan four-seater family model at £95 and Raleigh had a three-seat saloon three-wheeler that was available at a cost of only £89 15s.

In all cases, where prices have been quoted, they were for new machines currently in production; under-cutting was prohibited by Manufacturers Union rules. Nevertheless, customers with time to shop around could find excellent bargains when the trade unloaded their stocks of unused, but out-of-season, clearance lines.

In all its branches, motor cycle sport was in full swing. An outstanding example of the enthusiastic spirit prevailing was seen when four south of London clubs, Bermondsey, Sidcup, West Kent and the Owls, formed the Brands Hatch Combine, making arrangements with a landowner for £1500 to be spent on equipping several acres of open ground near Farningham in Kent as a permanent grass-track venue. The first-ever Brands Hatch meeting was held on the following Easter Monday.

The road-racing season began as usual with the Irish North West 200 and Leinster 200 events, regarded by the big racing firms as warm-ups for the TT, and as the honours were pretty evenly shared between Norton and Rudge, it was expected that the Isle of Man classic would produce a tremendous battle between these two marques. For the Nortons, to be ridden by Stanley Woods, Jimmy Simpson, Jimmy Guthrie and Tim Hunt, Joe Craig had added more cylinder finning, at the same time reducing weight by a much greater use of light-alloys. The 250 and 350 Rudges were not noticeably changed but the engines of the Senior machines had radial exhaust valves. Rudge-entered in all three classes were Walter Handley, Graham Walker, Tyrell Smith and Ernie Nott.

Opening this, the 21st TT meeting, the Junior race produced a shock result. Only one of the six Norton starters finished – Stanley Woods, who led all the way, winning with a race-record speed of 77.16mph and a record lap at 78.62mph. Handley and Smith chased him home.

Handley seemed all set for a Lightweight win, having put in a record lap at 74.08mph, but his engine slowed and he finished third behind Walker who himself had had to give best to a speedy New Imperial ridden by Leo Davenport.

The Senior, a Royal occasion, being watched by HRH Prince George, was a sweeping Norton one-two-three, with Woods making it a personal double. Simpson, third behind Guthrie, set the lap record at 81.5mph. There was hardly any foreign opposition but an interesting, although non-finishing, newcomer was a unit-construction Jawa from Czechoslovakia, ridden by its designer, ex-Brooklands star George Patchett.

During the summer a gallant attempt to capture the world's speed record was mounted by three Australians, Arthur 'Digger' Simcock, Alan Bruce and Phil Irving. They had prepared a potent, supercharged, 1000cc JAP-engined Brough-Superior, 'Leaping Lena', and with it, on a public road near Tat, in

Top: Arthur 'Digger' Simcock seen in 1931 with his 1000cc JAP-engined Brough-Superior, 'Leaping Lena'. Arthur partnered Alan Bruce and Phil Irving in building this machine which attempted to beat Joe Wright's solo land speed record. It did not quite make it, however

Above: the 1932 International Six Days Trial competitors at the stopping place of Costalinga in Northern Italy. The British team was triumphant in that year's event

Hungary, Bruce succeeded in raising the sidecar record to 124.41mph but he was unable to better Joe Wright's remarkable 150mph solo figure.

Hopes that the economic recess would soon be showing signs of abating took a set-back when, in August, the papers carried an announcement to the effect that 'a receiver has been appointed to take over the affairs of Ariel Works Ltd, manufacturers of Ariel motor cycles. Motor cyclists all over the world will regret that the depression has so seriously affected this famous factory.'

It was indeed a serious blow, not only to motor cyclists all over the world, but particularly to a number of dedicated enthusiasts in the executive ranks at the Selly Oak plant, who had suddenly to find other employment in an industry where jobs were notoriously hard to come by. Ironically, Ariel went broke just at a time when it was seemingly on the crest of a wave. Second in output only to the giant BSA organisation, the firm had a range of excellent, competitively priced machines; on the staff were two of the leading motor cycle designers, Edward Turner, who had devised the Square Four, and Valentine Page, from whose drawing board came, among many other popular types, the highly successful Red Hunters.

The official receiver kept the factory ticking over while reconstruction plans were laid, but for the time being the thousands of Ariel dealers had to live in hope for machines with which to meet a strong demand.

Almost concurrently with the Ariel shock came a statement from the liquidator of A. J. Stevens, that all AJS creditors would be paid off at twenty shillings in the pound.

The contradiction between the precarious business of motor cycle making and the flourishing state of motor cycle sport was quite extraordinary. At the time when there should have been an Olympia Show (cancelled in 1932 because of the depression), Wembley Stadium was over-filled by 84,000 wildly delirious dirt-track fans cheering their heroes in the final of the England-Australia Test Match series, each side having scored two victories in earlier rounds. England won the rubber.

There was a further boost for British prestige when, after failing in the two previous years, the GB team in the International Six Days Trial succeeded in winning the trophy. At the end of a week of hard riding in the Italian Alps, Bert Perrigo (BSA), George Rowley (AJS) and Peter Bradley (Sunbeam and sidecar) beat the home-side Gilera team in the final speed test at Merano. The all-Rudge trio of Bob Macgregor, Jack Williams and Graham Walker topped the competition for the Silver Vase.

In the 'world's fastest road race', the Ulster Grand Prix, Norton, Rudge and New Imperial secured the chief prizes. The Senior Nortons of Woods (85.15mph) and Hunt were first and second, with Simcock (Rudge) third. Junior Rudge men Tyrell Smith and Charlie Manders beat Harry Pinnington (AJS), and the Lightweight victor, Ted Mellors, on a New Imperial, also won the overall handicap, the Governor's Trophy; his stablemate, Syd Gleave, was second and Harvey Pilling came third on a Rudge-engined CTS.

By mid October Ariel's future was settled. The company had been completely restructured and would be known as Ariel Works (JS) Ltd, with Jack Sangster at the head of affairs. 'Mr Jack', who had previously been joint managing director with his father, Charles Sangster, one of the firms original founders, now became virtually the sole proprietor and he re-entered the fray with a reduced range, dropping the 'slopers' but retaining the

135

popular Red Hunters and the ohc 600cc Square Four.

In their Plumstead workshops the Colliers had revived the 'cammy' AJS, in 350 and 500cc types, based on the mount George Rowley had ridden so successfully in the ISDT. Also resuscitated was another of the Stevens brothers' projects which had come with the Wolverhampton assets to Woolwich. This was a supercharged 1100cc vee-twin put together in 1929 as a world-beater but untried until now, when Reg Barber, a notable Matchless rider-tuner, began tests at Brooklands in readiness for a full-scale record attack. While this was going on, however, Ernst Henne used the Tat, Hungary, road to recapture the fastest-ever honour on his 750cc blown BMW, upping Wright's 150mph record to 151.86mph.

With the arrival of 1933, two important news items made talking points for road-race folk. First, the ACU had harkened to the demands of the ever-growing ranks of sidecar enthusiasts by promising to re-introduce the Sidecar TT – last run in 1925 – of sufficient entries were forthcoming. Secondly, the Rudge company announced it would no longer participate in competitions work. However, race machines would be ioaned to the Graham Walker Syndicate (Walker, Ernie Nott and Tyrell Smith) for certain events, including the TT. The three riders were all Rudge employees; they would be given time off from work for racing, the assistance of mechanics and sundry 'fringe benefits' but otherwise they would be on their own.

In May Joe Wright was trying out the AJS vee-twin on Southport sands where he reached a 143mph maximum and average 130mph over a flying kilometre, under not very favourable conditions.

As TT-time approached, it became clear that the required entry of at least twelve outfits for the Sidecar race was not going to materialise and the event was dropped from the programme, to remain a non-starter for a further twenty years. Support for the solo classes was, however, even better than in the previous year, in spite of general moans that the TT was losing its spectator attraction. Not for the only time in the Island's history, there were calls for a shorter course, but the ACU refused to disturb its formula and when June came round the crowds were as big as ever.

Norton swept the board with a Junior and Senior double treble, Stanley Woods leading combinations of Simpson, Guthrie and Hunt. Stanley, who broke the lap record in both classes, had then had four wins in four successive rides. The Lightweight was a victorious debut for the Excelsior 'Mechanical Marvel' whose four radial valves were operated by pairs of pushrods fore and aft of the cylinder. Syd Gleave, the winner, raised the race record but failed to beat Handley's 1932 lap record on a Rudge.

June also brought the introduction of Neville Chamberlain's revised taxation measures. With nearly a year in which to prepare for it, the industry had clambered on the favourable 250cc bandwagon and by now quarter-litre types abounded in all forms – singles and twins, two-strokes, side-valves, pushrod ohvs and overhead camshafts. Many makers opted for the 250cc Villiers two-stroke unit, notably Francis-Barnett who put this engine into a frame built up with channel-section members, enclosed most of the works and called it the Cruiser, thereby creating one of the best motor cycles of its type ever made. On the other hand, Velocette, who had begun by making high-class two-strokes and then expanded to the equally prestigious overhead camshaft 350cc K models, came out with a 250cc high-camshaft ohv, the much-loved Model MOV, destined to

Below: the ingenious 250cc Excelsior 'Mechanical Marvel' which featured four radial valves driven by pairs of pushrods. The Blackburne-engined bike, although complicated, was the machine to beat in 1933. Wal Handley, seen right, led that year's Lightweight TT, but was forced out when his engine blew-up at Sulby, so letting Syd Gleave take the chequered flag on a similar bike

father many illustrious sons with characteristics which were recognisably similar.

It was around this time that a brief and curiously worded notice was circulated to the press. It read: 'The Douglas works at Kingswood, Bristol, which recently changed hands and subsequently closed down, have been purchased by the old firm of William Douglas and Co, which existed prior to the formation of Douglas Motors (1932) Ltd.'

The affairs of the West-country flat-twin firm had for long been as chequered as the tam-o'-shanter affected by its Highland clansman trading mascot. Very much a family business, it was not easy to keep track of its numerous changes of ownership and company titles. The failure of Douglas Motors (1932) Ltd meant that the ambitious Golden Star 250 shaft-drive model became a still-born casualty, for its production was shelved when the family regained control.

Another consequence of the financial upheavals that beset 1933 was the appearance of a twin-cylinder engine of a quite

unusual kind that was to pioneer a fashion which has remained in the industry to present times. When the Ariel concern collapsed, Valentine Page took his talents to Triumph in Coventry and from there, in July 1933, emerged his 645cc ohv twin model 6/1, which had vertical cylinders cast side by side in one block.

Parallel twins were nothing new; indeed, Triumph had used a French-built Bercley engine with this formation as far back as 1913, and even before that Scott twin two-strokes had become famous. Val Page's engine was different in that the pistons rose and fell together, being connected to a three-bobweight crankshaft whose big-ends were in line. This arrangement obviated the rocking-couple disadvantage inherent in a four-stroke twin whose pistons rise and fall alternately. Page largely countered the complementary drawback of the additional reciprocating weight of the paired pistons by building the entire engine to immensely robust proportions, and mounting it in a massive duplex-cradle frame. Since the primary drive was by two

Below left: in 1933, Morgan broke away from their tradition of using motor cycle engines, and produced this four-seater powered by a Ford car engine. Electric starting and three-speed-plus-reverse gearbox were some of the luxuries offered

Below: a scene at the opening of the car and bike show at Berlin in 1933. Closely scrutinising the bike is Reich Chancellor Hitler with former crown prince Banker von Stauss and car racer Hans Stuck

Right: Carlo Guzzi, co-founder, with Giorgio Parodi, of Moto Guzzi

double-helical gear wheels, with no intermediate idler, the engine ran 'backwards'. Gears were also used to drive the single camshaft, situated behind the cylinder block in which was cast a tunnel to enclose pushrods operating semi-exposed rockers.

The prototype 6/1, paired with a sidecar specially designed for it by Harry Perrey, who had also moved from Ariel to Triumph, made its bow at the Scarborough Rally. A month later, Perrey took the outfit through the International Six Days Trial in Wales, winning a silver medal and then going on to Brooklands, where he and four other riders (among whom was the author) took turns in circling the track to cover 500 miles in under 500 minutes.

This ACU-observed test won the Maudes Trophy, but it did not win a lot of customers for the 6/1. At £75, the price was on the high side; it was too cumbersome for solo use; and it lacked certain features, such as foot gear-control, which by then had become standard practice. After a desultory life of some five years it was superseded by another Triumph parallel twin, the tale of whose fame comes later in this history.

The ISDT in which Perrey gained his silver medal was won by a German team of BMW riders captained by Ernst Henne. It was a close run thing: Britain's solo Trophy teamsters, George Rowley (AJS) and Bert Perrigo (BSA), came through without loss of marks, as did the German soloists, but whereas the BMW sidecar outfit was penalised by one mark, Peter Bradley, with

Bert Tetsall in his Sunbeam sidecar, lost two. The British A team of Fred Povey (BSA), Jack Williams and Vic Brittain (Nortons) won the Silver Vase.

With the Olympia Show due to reopen in November, there was a considerable stirring among the English manufacturers, many of whom were reporting increased sales, as compared with their 1932 results. *Motor Cycling* commented 'The corresponding improvement in the unemployment position, which has been very grave, will be appreciated. There is no doubt that for everyone concerned with motor cycling there are unmistakable signs of returning prosperity'.

In the 24 months since the last show there had been big advances in general design and in the quality of equipment. The principal 'surprise' exhibit was a 500cc ohv BSA single with fluid-flywheel transmission and preselector three-speed gear mechanism. The system worked on the same principles as had been developed by the Daimler car division of the BSA group of companies. At £70, the fluid-flywheel model was not unreasonably priced, but its novelty scared off the conservatively minded British motor cyclist and this interesting new machine never went into quantity production.

Three-wheelers were continuing to sell well. BSA reported a 70 per cent rise in sales over the previous year, the four-cylinder model having been particularly well received. Morgans broke their long tradition of using motor cycle type vee-twin engines by introducing a four-seater family model having an 1100cc water-cooled Ford car engine, complete with such luxuries hitherto unknown to Morganatics as electric starting and a three-speed and reverse gearbox.

It was during the Show that the industry lost one of its founding fathers. At the age of 76, Maurice John Schulte died at his home in Marlow, Bucks. As a young immigrant from Germany he had opened a business in London in 1893, making fittings for bicycles. With another young German, Siegfried Bettmann, he founded the Triumph Cycle Company in a small workshop in Coventry on a capital of only £650, producing their first motor cycle in 1902. Mr Schulte was the firm's first managing director and he held the post for thirty years until he parted with Bettmann in 1920 and retired to pursue his interest in philately, frequently supplying King George V with rare stamps, collected from around the world.

As the year was ending another excursion by Carlo Guzzi into the realms of unorthodox design made its appearance. This was an ohc 500cc racing vee-twin which had the cylinders arranged at an angle of 120 degrees. The front cylinder lay horizontally; the rear one occupied the position normally taken by the seat pillar. The *Bicilindrica 500* had such a purposeful look about it that the experts were predicting its threat to British single-cylinder supremacy before it had even contested a race. In its second season of track work it won the Senior TT, and through its fifteen years of continuous development it carried some of the world's fastest and finest riders. It was discontinued in 1951 but its wide-angle concept is successfully perpetuated to the present day by Ducati.

Summarising prospects and hopes for the coming season, *Motor Cycling*'s columnist, 'Carbon', wrote: '1934 will undoubtedly be a good year for motor cycling. National prosperity is on the upgrade and with improved conditions generally, thousands of would-be riders will acquire the wherewithal to invest in machines. Our top priorities must be to win back the world's fastest record and to regain the International Six Days Trial Trophy.'

Bright as Britain's prospects might be, progress towards full recovery seemed laggardly when compared with the advances being made on the continent, especially in Italy and Germany, where the two dictators were thoroughly motor-minded. Mussolini's special autostrada motorways were being copied in Germany where Hitler also introduced a remarkable concession to encourage the sales of motor vehicles – all newly purchased motor cycles and cars were exempt from any kind of tax so long as they remained the property of their first owners. That this measure would boomerang by tempting owners to hang on to their vehicles as long as possible was inevitable, but meantime the *herrenvolk* were contributing their Reichmarks to subsidise the Führer's prize plum – the 'people's car' that was to make everyone a motorist.

Be that as it may, enthusiasm for motor cycling and motor sport generally leapt ahead in Germany. By 1934 the country had become the greatest motor cycling nation in the world, with over three-quarters of a million riders. Topping a score or more of busy factories, the DKW concern was the world's largest producer of motor cycles, building machines at the rate of 20,000 a year. At sporting events – races, hill-climbs and so forth – spectator figures exceeding 100,000 were not uncommon at some of the more popular meetings.

Because of the insurmountable laws prohibiting racing on public highways, the only areas open to British promoters were the Isle of Man, Ireland and a few enclosed tracks such as Brooklands, the Crystal Palace and certain privately owned estates, where circuit length was, of necessity, restricted.

One man, however, Fred Craner, a garage proprietor and secretary of the Derby and District Motor Club, had ambitions to establish a full-scale, permanent road-race circuit on the British mainland, where spectators could enjoy a day's sport, staged on an international basis, without having to tranship themselves to other lands. Barely ten miles from his home town, Derby, in the heart of the English midlands, Fred Craner found what he wanted, an extensive private park containing a network of drives and roadways that could, with no great effort or expense, be linked to provide a serviceable race course for both car and motor cycle race enthusiasts.

The owner of Donington Park was Mr J. G. Shields and he collaborated fully with the Derby club's scheme, which had come into operation in 1933 when a series of more or less experimental races for motor cycles had been run over a 2.19-mile circuit that twisted over undulating parkland and through woods and shrubberies. It was barely wide enough for sidecars, and certainly not for cars. The amenities were sketchy – a few wooden benches on a bankside by the start-line constituted the 'grandstand', the paddock was a field enclosed by chestnut paling and tents served for the race office, refreshment room, first-aid post, etc. Nevertheless, the initial meetings were so popular with competitors and onlookers alike that the organisers pitched in and revamped the whole set-up, to such good effect that when Donington opened for its second season, in March 1934, the track had been lengthened to 2.55 miles and widened to accommodate cars. Trees and undergrowth that had created blind corners were cleared away; permanent spectator stands had been built at the best vantage points and there were vastly improved facilities for the public, competitors and officials. The success of Donington's future was assured and, until World War II halted racing, Fred Craner's baby grew in stature to become one of Europe's most popular and prestigious Grand Prix racing circuits.

140

There were, however, apprehensive feelings that the outlook for motor cycle racing in that other stronghold of the sport, the Isle of Man, might not be so rosy. The Manx Government's customary grant of £5000 towards the cost of running the TT was cut in 1934 to £3500, the £1500 balance being allocated to the RAC's Douglas-based 'round the houses' car races. On top of that came the news that Stanley Woods would be riding Guzzi and Husqvarna machines. Out came the headlines – 'Foreign Racing Challenge'; 'British Road Race Supremacy in Jeopardy'; 'Prospect of Defeat in Our Own TT this Year!'.

The challenge did indeed look formidable. The speedy Swedish-built Husqvarna twins were especially feared; a le Vack-designed Motosacoche, the wide-angle Guzzi; FN and Sarolea singles were all seen as dangers to British prestige, which by now was virtually in the sole keeping of Norton and Velocette. There was hope that a new 500cc vee-twin New Imperial might support them, but the position regarding Rudge was uncertain. The Coventry concern had struck a financial reef

Above: Donington Park, later a racing circuit proper, was originally a course which utilised the drives and pathways in the grounds of the manor. Here, a competitor comes to grief at the old hairpin during the first event in 1933, which was organised by the Derby and District Motor Cycle Club

and was going through a period of reconstruction, 'Successors to Rudge-Whitworth Ltd' being the title of a take-over company. In view of the possibility that there would be no works Rudges in the Lightweight race, Stanley Woods's choice of a 250 Guzzi seemed to indicate that at least one trophy would 'go foreign'. It was not forgotten that in the previous year Walter Handley had won both the Swiss and Belgian GPs on Guzzi's masterpieces.

There was trouble for the Husqvarna camp before they even reached the Island. Several of the machines were badly damaged when they were dropped from a dockside crane while being loaded aboard ship.

Norton had had to reorganise their squad. After a

141

crippling crash in the 1933 Swedish GP Tim Hunt was *hors de combat*. Ulsterman Walter Rusk had taken his place in the Ulster GP but had since transferred to Velocette, so Handley teamed up with the two Jims, Guthrie and Simpson, who opened the TT ball with first and second places in the Junior. Yet another one-two-three for Bracebridge Street had seemed certain until Handley fell at Governor's Bridge, sustaining injuries that ended his Island chances that year. Ernie Nott (Husqvarna) was third, with the distinction of riding the first twin-cylinder machine to take a Junior place since 1923, when Alfie Alexander was third on a Douglas.

The Junior prize-distribution ceremony saw, for the first time, the presentation of bronze, as well as silver, replicas of the Trophy to those riders who finished within the required time.

There were cheers all round the Island when the Lightweight race ended, for 'Unlucky Jim' Simpson, after twelve furious years of trying, had at last won a TT – on a class of machine he had never raced before, a Rudge. His stablemates Nott and Graham Walker made it another treble for the marque which, despite its factory problems, had mounted a magnificent comeback. Stanley Woods and his Guzzi came fourth. The two Jims repeated their Junior one-two in the Senior and Walter Rusk brought a new 495cc Velocette into third berth.

In all three races, only one place, Nott's third spot on the 350 Husqvarna, had gone to a foreign machine, but it had been a close run thing in the Senior, for Woods had made the fastest lap on his 'Husky' and was all set to collect his seventh trophy when he ran out of fuel.

It was Jimmy Simpson's last TT year. His IoM score was one trophy, four times runner-up, four third places and eight fastest laps, including the 60, 70 and 80mph records. For the remainder of the season Charlie Dodson took his team place and the little ex-Sunbeam star, in his first race on a Norton, was second to the Belgian GP winner, Walter Handley. British riders on British machines went through the Continental Circus series from one victory to another.

So, through the summer of 1934 the world in general, and the motor cycling movement with it, began to feel that the worst was over and that a prospect of 'business as usual' lay ahead.

The Stevens brothers formed a new company, using their original Wolverhampton premises to build a good-looking 250 single-port ohv which they called the Stevens. Rudge-Whitworth

Top: the Excelsior Manxman engine of 1934 was a single-cylinder, two-valve unit of 249cc

Above left: Stanley Woods with his Moto Guzzi at the 1934 Lightweight TT

Above: for 1934, Stanley Woods was Husqvarna-mounted in the Senior; unfortunately, although he took fastest lap at 80.49mph, he ran out of fuel on the last circuit

Right: 1934 was the year that the Vincent-HRD Comet came out; this particular machine is a 1939 example

Ltd dropped the 'Successors to' prefix and, with F. G. Woollard as Managing Director, reshaped their course with a number of new models, some of which had JAP engines.

At Brooklands, busier than ever, with meetings every weekend and often on Wednesdays, Florence Blenkiron won a Gold Star, the emblem awarded by the British Motor Cycle Racing Club to members who lapped the track at one hundred or more mph. First woman recipient, Miss Blenkiron's speed was 102mph on Bill Lacey's 500 Grindlay-Peerless.

For the second successive year, Norton riders scored a treble in the Senior Manx GP, perpetuating a habit that was to be repeated with almost monotonous regularity in the future.

Those two top priorities, however, the world's fastest record and the ISDT Trophy, eluded British endeavours. Over a course laid out in the Bavarian mountains, Germany again took the Six Days prize, beating the British team by a single mark.

Several attacks on the all-out record had been prepared during the year. Joe Wright had carried out further tests with the big blown AJS twin at Montlhéry but he could not improve on his Southport speeds and the machine was returned to Plumstead where it lay forgotten for many years until, in 1956, it turned up in Tasmania, minus its Zoller supercharger.

Other attempts, in which Brough-Superior machinery figured prominently, were mounted by 'Ginger' Wood, C. T. 'Tommy' Atkins and Syd Gleave, the last-named having chosen a stretch of sand in Egypt for his ride. None was successful, however, and in the middle of Show Week Ernst Henne, in a gesture of defiance, raised his own record speed to 152.9mph with the supercharged 750cc BMW at Gyon in Hungary.

Olympia 1934 is memorable for introducing a number of excellent new designs. Levis had a workmanlike 250 with chain-drive ohc gear. Douglas showed a revised edition of the aborted transverse, flat-twin Golden Star. Enlarged to 500cc, it was called the Endeavour, and its handsome lines were much acclaimed; sadly, they failed to win many customers. There were, however, two newcomers that were to prove best sellers for many years to come – the spectacular Vincent-HRD Comet and the more mundane Excelsior Manxman.

Ever since Howard R. Davies had won the 1925 Senior TT, and was second in the Junior, on JAP-engined machines carrying his own initials, the marque had always used proprietary engines, but the 500 Comet had a Phil Irving-designed unit with a high camshaft operating ultra-short, widely splayed pushrods and an unconventional form of rocker gear. The layout proved so successful that it became the basis of a long line of engines – singles and twins – with multi-purpose characteristics, from roadster work to racing and record-breaking.

Brainchild of Excelsiors' managing director, Eric Walker, the single-cylinder, ohc, two-valve Manxman, in 250 and 350 form, was primarily intended as a fast clubman's or sports mount, with optional specifications that changed it into a highly competitive racer. Although a Manxman never won a TT, it became a great favourite for lightweight events.

At a Show-time banquet in aid of the Motor and Cycle Trades Benevolent Fund, Dr E. L. Burgin, Parliamentary Secretary to the Board of Trade, said that the motor cycle and cycle industries had suffered less from world depression than most trades. Perhaps not all his hearers, thinking of the crises they had been through, agreed with him but, in fact, after five years of struggle, not one of the 35 British motor cycle marques exhibited at the 1930 Show was missing when the industry embarked on the second half of the decade.

Chapter 7
Back on Course (1935-1936)

Left: Colonel T.E. Lawrence – or Aircraftman T.E. Shaw as he was by then known – astride his sixth Brough-superior, an SS100, in conversation with his friend George Brough, outside the company's Haydn Road, Nottingham, factory in 1930. This machine was a present to the legendary Lawrence of Arabia from George Bernard Shaw, another old friend. George Brough was forced to walk with sticks at this time, after an accident in the International Six Days Trial

1935 was King George V's Silver Jubilee year and it was celebrated, say contemporary observers, 'with great splendour and rejoicing'. His Majesty's subjects were entitled to rejoice, for during their sovereign's reign they had experienced four terrible years of war, followed by an equally long and bitter struggle to recharge the run-down batteries of the national economy.

Now the worst was over; there was work to be done; the barometer was set fair, both for improved trade and for the splendid summer weather which graced that jubilee year. One major consequence of the prevailing better pay and conditions enjoyed by the population was an upsurge of the desire to possess personal transport – to be able to get out and about independently as and when one wished. For this purpose there was no vehicle more handily economical than the motor cycle.

At the end of 1934 there were well over half a million motor cycles registered in Great Britain. Of the 45,845 new machines sold during 1934, 16,960 were in the 250cc class, 13,233 were over 250cc and 5890 under 150cc. New sidecar combinations numbered 4567, about 1000 up. Rather surprisingly, because the fitting of a sidecar saved fifty per cent of the cost of solo insurance, there were more new three-wheelers than 'combos', with 5195 being registered.

So, having achieved an output increase in the twenty per cent bracket, the British motor cycle industry entered the new year full of confidence and, along with the rest of the rejoicing nation, paid scant heed to certain ominous happenings across the Channel. Italy was gearing up to declare war on Abyssinia. Spain was on the verge of civil war. Germany was about to break the Locarno Treaty by reoccupying the demilitarised Rhineland. Having recently become '*der Führer*', in absolute control of Germany's destiny, Adolf Hitler was ruthlessly fanning the sparks of revenge throughout the Fatherland – revenge for 1918, revenge for Versailles, revenge for the loss of colonies and, above all, revenge on Britain. Foreigners were given a grim demonstration of the growing strength of National Socialism at the great Leipzig Fair of 1935, where not only were weapons and munitions-making machinery openly displayed, but squads of black-uniformed SS troops paraded their goose-stepping precision drill.

Among the thousands of onlookers from other countries was a representative of a British motor cycle factory – James Leek, a senior executive of the Birmingham Small Arms Company. On returning to England he presented his directors with a momentous report. It proposed that immediate steps be taken to reorganise the company's plant and factory space in preparation for armament manufacture. Despite the lean years through which the company had passed, and without any financial support from the Government, which was still actively espousing the cause of disarmament, the BSA board took the courageous step of sanctioning the heavy expenditure which James Leek's report involved.

Thus, in 1935, did BSA, a full four years before the outbreak of World War II, resume the purpose for which it was originally formed, the manufacture of weapons of war. Within twelve months, large sections of the plant were on overtime, making rifles, machine guns and other military equipment on a scale that was to grow to fantastic proportions. This side of the company's operations, however, was conducted with a reticence in strong contrast to the publicity accorded to its normal occupation – that of making motor cycles, bicycles, cars and various other vehicles in ever increasing quantities.

One hint of BSA's affiliation with the War Office was given when a 500cc, ohv vee-twin, the Model J, specially built to the Army's specification for a training machine, was put on the civilian market.

Whatever their governments might be planning in the way of war, continental motor cycle manufacturers continued to build-up production. At the Milan Show, 48 firms displayed 227 different models and it was noticeable that the Italian preference for 175cc engines had changed in favour of quarter-litre machines. The French industry decided that business was so good that there was no need for a show at all, their designs being concentrated mainly on 250 and 500cc types of conventional 'English' pattern. In Berlin eleven domestic firms covered everything from baby two-strokes to the lordly 750cc BMWs and Zündapp flat-twins. The first-ever oil-damped telescopic front fork made its appearance on BMWs which were soon available to British buyers, for a London company, AFN Limited, had been appointed distributors for the marque. The 200cc, ohv, single-cylinder model was listed at £70; its 400cc counterpart cost £85. Side-valve 745cc and ohv, 730cc, dual-carburettor, horizontally-opposed twins cost a meagre £115 and £125 respectively.

In March 1935, British roads, where they passed through certain designated built-up areas, were subjected to a 30mph maximum speed limit. The Minister of Transport Leslie Hore-Belisha, achieved lasting renown for his orange-coloured lollipop poles, the Belisha beacons that marked the zebra-striped pedestrian crossings. Soon after, 'L' plates began to appear, distinguishing vehicles that were being driven by learners preparing to take the official driving tests which became obligatory from 1 June.

In April, an Italian machine named the Rondine (Swallow) won the 200-mile Grand Prix of Tripoli. Designed by Piero Remor and developed from one of his earlier concepts, the OPRA, it had a 500cc, water-cooled, supercharged, in-line, four-cylinder engine, set transversely across the frame. Its appearance in the following Isle of Man TT was predicted. At the same time another four-cylinder mount, the Nimbus, which had been made in Denmark since 1921, changed to a tubular frame from one of pressed steel although its original characteristics of a 750cc, air-cooled engine with shaft drive were unchanged.

Another change made in April was the renaming of Pratts petrol, on the market since the very earliest days of motoring. Henceforward, the brand would be known as Esso.

Above: Nimbus were Danish manufacturers making four-cylinder machines for the everyday motor cyclist, rather than the sports or touring rider. This 1935 example, with a 746cc engine, features a pressed-steel frame, which is both simple and strong

Right: this Zündapp KS500 of 1936 was of similar frame design to the Nimbus

Below: the BSA 500cc, ohv, vee-twin was first built specifically for military use, but was later put on the market. This Model J was first seen in October 1935

The ceremony of King George V's Jubilee was on 6 May and the newspapers were full of reviews of his twenty-five years' reign. *The Motor Cycle* turned back to its 1910 Olympia Show report to discover that at least a score of the firms exhibiting at that event were still in business – AJS, Ariel, BSA, Calthorpe, Douglas, Excelsior, FN, James, JAP, Matchless, Montgomery, New Hudson, Norton, OK, P & M, Royal Enfield, Rudge, Scott, Triumph and Zenith.

In the midst of the jubilee junketings came the sad news of the death of Colonel T. E. Lawrence, killed in a collision with a boy on a bicycle while riding his Brough-Superior SS100. Soldier, explorer and author, 'Lawrence of Arabia,' or Aircraftman Shaw, as he had become, had owned six Brough-Superiors and he left among his brilliant writings some wonderful descriptions of the sense of joyous freedom he found in fast riding on a powerful solo.

During the summer months, Sunbeam introduced a high-camshaft 250cc model, with hairpin valve springs, costing

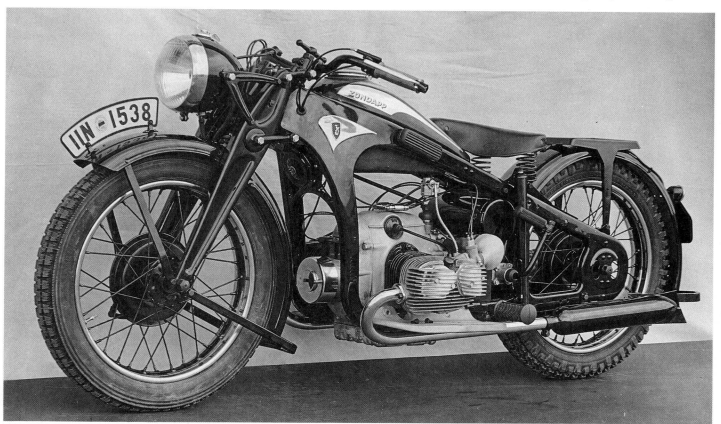

£49 10s. Velocette produced its first 500, the MSS model, based, at £59 10s on the successful MOV and MAC types. OK-Supreme came up with a neat 250cc ohv job at the same price as the 500 Velo. Overhead camshaft gear was also applied to supercharged 500cc BMWs which created a sensation at the German Grand Prix held on Berlin's Avus track. Tubular, instead of pressed steel, frames were used.

As TT time approached there was more talk about the 'foreign menace'. Not since 1911, the year of the Indian hat-trick, had a non-British machine been a winner, although there had been some near-misses, especially in 1934 when Stanley Woods all but did it with his 250 Guzzi and 500 Husqvarna. Now he was back with Guzzis in both the Lightweight and the Senior, his 500 mount being a wide-angle twin which, like the 250, had a sprung rear wheel.

Apart from Guzzi, the only other TT marques with rear suspension were Vincent-HRD and OEC, the latter firm making its last Isle of Man appearance. The German threat lay chiefly in 250 and 500cc DKWs and NSUs in the Junior and Senior races. Unit-construction ohc Jawas were confessedly experimental and and even before the Czech machines reached the Island, race manager George Patchett was pointing out some of the difficulties faced by continental entrants whose headquarters were far from Manxland. With the practicing period cut from its erstwhile fortnight to nine days, it was now almost impossible for him to obtain any replacement parts from his factory in time to fit them in readiness for the races. There was no telephone link with the mainland; detailing spares requirements by telegram in the Czech language was out of the question; it took four days for a letter from Douglas to reach Prague; and the nearest aerodrome with customs clearance facilities was at Croydon. As an aside, it is interesting to note that Czechoslovakia, apart from its Jawa and CZ models, also

produced the fascinating Böhmerland models using 598cc four-stroke and 348cc two-stroke motors.

Among the 107 entries were riders from Italy, Denmark, France, Spain, New Zealand and Australia, mostly using English machines, Velocettes and Excelsiors being popular choices. There was no sign of the promised Rondine.

Travellers from the midlands and south of England taking their vehicles to the Island no longer had to face the frustrating ferryboat voyage from Birkenhead to Liverpool for the Mersey Tunnel was now in operation, but when the advance guard of TT-ites reached Douglas they had to off-load their machines themselves and carry their own luggage, for the Islanders were in the grip of a national strike. This was settled before practicing was over, by which time Velocettes had had to find substitutes for its two star riders – Walter Handley, immobilised with an injured hand, and H. E. Newman,

Top: this Royal Enfield vee-twin was built for sidecar work with which it coped admirably, due mainly to its 1140cc, side-valve engine

Above: A.V. 'Ebbie' Ebblewhite waves Jimmy Guthrie and his Norton off in the 1935 Senior TT. Guthrie finished 4secs behind the Guzzi of Stanley Woods after a last-lap mix-up

Above right: W.F. Rusk, on his way to second place in the 1935 Junior TT, passes Signpost Corner; he took fastest lap at 79.96mph

Right: OK-Supreme advertised this 1935 Flying Cloud as 'a model for the discriminating'

hospitalised with pneumonia. It was a sad ending to Handley's career. Like Jimmy Simpson, he had competed at every meeting since 1922. He had started in 28 races, won all four of the solo trophies, been runner-up three times and was third twice. In his first-ever year he opened his score of nine fastest laps and, again like Simpson, only twice finished lower than third. He had raced nine different makes of machine, fourteen of his rides being on the Rex-Acme company's products to which he was exclusively loyal for five successive years.

For the fifth consecutive year Norton won the Junior race, with Jim Guthrie, Walter Rusk and John 'Crasher' White never seriously threatened by their rivals.

The 24-year run of British TT victories was broken in the Lightweight event when Eire's Stanley Woods led throughout on his Guzzi, setting a record lap at 74.19mph in spite of dull and misty conditions. It was the bad visibility that caused Woods' stablemate, Italian champion Omobono Tenni, to crash at Craig-ny-Baa on his fifth lap. He had lain second to Woods from the start. The Rudges of Tyrell Smith, Ernie Nott, Jack Williams and L. P. Hill were second, third, fifth and ninth. Sixteen of the 28 starters retired.

Over the next two days the weather deteriorated so badly that on Senior day, for the first time in TT history, a race had to be postponed and many people, including a number of competitors who had urgent engagements elsewhere, sailed away, thereby missing what was perhaps the most exciting Tourist Trophy of all time.

At breakfast on Saturday 22 June the Mountain course was still enveloped in thick mist, but by 10.30am conditions improved and half an hour later the stewards declared that the race would definitely start at 11.30am.

The tale of the 1935 Senior TT race is one of those epics that can never be retold too often. From start to finish – indeed, beyond the finish – it was a suspense story concerning just two men – Jimmy Guthrie and Stanley Woods.

The Norton ace had number one as his riding number. Woods, whose number was thirty, started fifteen minutes later. After one lap, at over 84mph, Jim was half a minute up on his team-mate, Walter Rusk, with Stanley in third place on his Guzzi twin. Another lap and Woods had overhauled Rusk but he was losing ground to the flying Scotsman, who raised the lap record to 85.5mph on his third circuit, at the end of which he halted to refuel. The Irishman did not stop and knocked two

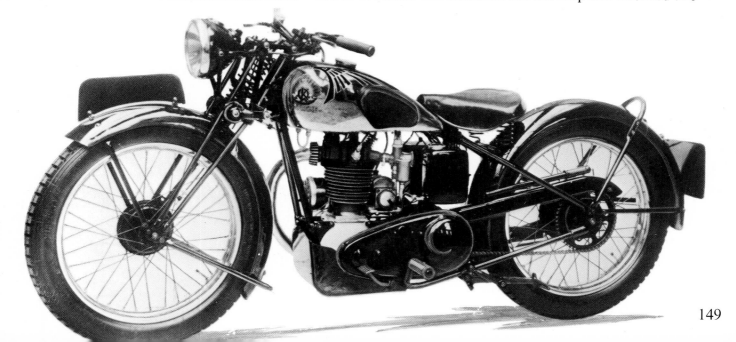

149

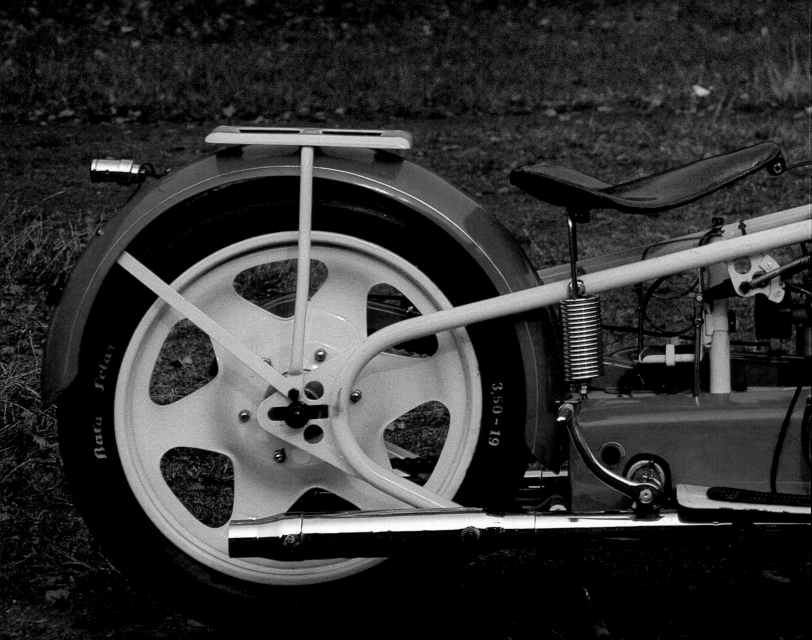

seconds off Jim's record on the fifth round. Stanley told his own story: 'At the finish of the fourth circuit I was 32 seconds behind. I did the fifth lap in 26 minutes 26 seconds, at an average speed of 85.66mph, but I only wiped off three seconds from Guthrie's lead. Another lap and I had wiped off another three seconds. I don't believe that any spectator thought for a moment that I could wipe out Guthrie's lead of 26 seconds when I started on the final circuit. I decided on one final gamble; I knew the safe revolutions of the engine – 7700 – and I decided to ignore all safety margins. I gave her her head and let the revolutions mount. Actually she exceeded 8200rpm in places – a speed of over 121mph . . . 26 minutes 10 seconds for that last lap, an average of 86.53mph'.

The foregoing passage was included in a letter Stanley Woods had written to the Ferodo company, praising the efficiency of the brake linings fitted to his Guzzi, but he made no reference to his brilliant piece of gamesmanship that contributed to his devastating win.

In those days it was not thought possible that a 500cc machine could cover seven laps of the Mountain circuit without a fuel stop. Stanley had made no mid-race top up and it was felt certain that he would need to make a stop at the end of his sixth circuit. Indeed, his pit personnel were seen to be active with the quick-filler hose in readiness for a lightning replacement. Reckoning that this would add some fifteen to twenty seconds to

Previous page: an example of the two-stroke, 348cc Böhmerland of 1937. Only a few were made, before the war killed the company

Above: a 1935 CZ of 348cc, which was one of the company's few forays into bike production before World War II; it was a limited edition

the Guzzi's known 26 seconds arrears, Norton telephoned its signal station at Ramsey to give Jim an 'all's well, steady up' message. When Woods came screaming past the grandstand he did not stop but shot over the brow of Bray Hill without so much as a glance at his pit. He didn't need to, for he had his own secret signallers installed in a private house on the other side of the Glencrutchery Road, as well as a second set of assistants in a phone box on the Sulby Straight.

When Woods failed to make his expected fuel stop, Guthrie had already received his 'ease up' signal at Ramsey and, all unaware of the Guzzi's furious progress behind him, was nursing his Norton through the last dozen miles to the chequered flag and plaudits for another victory.

While the cheers echoed, the champagne flowed and the press cameras clicked, those grandstand spectators who were still studying the scoreboard began earnestly to consult their watches. Number thirty has passed the Mountain Box; Woods is at the Bungalow; Stanley is through the Craig and he's level-pegging with Guthrie! Then the scarlet Guzzi roars over the finish line and the grandstand crowd falls silent. The loudspeakers crackle; 'This is the Clerk of the course speaking. Stanley Woods is the winner – by four seconds!'

It was an emotional epic. Feelings were torn between admiration for the Irishman's courageous achievement and commiseration for the Scot who, misled into a sense of false security, had eased up to the extent of some eight seconds after receiving his Ramsey signal; his last lap was actually nine seconds slower than his sixth.

In winning his eighth trophy – the second in the week – Woods made it hard for replica seekers. Only the leader-board men won silver statuettes. Rusk and Johnny Duncan backed up Guthrie to take the manufacturers team prize for Norton with the NSUs of Oskar Steinbach and Ted Mellors finishing fifth and sixth. The half-dozen bronze replicas went to the riders of four Vincent-HRDs, a Royal Enfield and a Velocette. For the fans who had been able to stay for the extra day, their reward was a race they would never forget.

Apart from its dramatic Senior, the 1935 TT meeting is memorable for a number of organisational innovations that have remained to the present day. For example, competitors were allowed to warm up their engines before the start. Travelling marshals were appointed to patrol the course during races. Pit attendants were given more freedom to assist their riders. The Manx flag was used by the starter instead of the Union Jack.

One of the Senior entrants who had not waited for the race was Noel Pope. He was not going to risk missing an appointment he had with timekeeper A. V. Ebblewhite at Weybridge on the following Wednesday. The object of their rendezvous was to see if author, poet and enthusiastic speed-seeker Pope could achieve his ambition to break the 118.86mph Brooklands Outer Circuit record, held since 1929 by Joe Wright. For this foray Noel had bought from the recently retired sidecar trackman, E. C. E. 'Ted' Baragwanath, the latter's famous supercharged 996cc JAP-engined Brough-Superior outfit. Shorn of the sidecar and suitably geared for solo work, it was wheeled to the Fork where, installed in Chronograph Villa, 'Ebbie' set up his stop watches and signalled the pushers-off to send Pope away on a warm-up lap. That completed, the Brough came roaring past the Vickers sheds, rode high up the Home Banking, plummeted down onto the Railway Straight, thundered around the long curve of the Byfleet Banking to reappear at the Fork having circled the 2.8-miles concrete saucer at 120.59mph. Thus

Top: Noel Pope seen at Brooklands in 1934, just before he did a two-miles-per-minute lap

Above: the great Stanley Woods on his frugal Moto Guzzi at the 1935 Senior TT. His victory could be put down to his bike's good fuel consumption and lax team work by Norton

did Noel Pope become the first holder of the BMCRC's Super Award for a two-miles-a-minute lap, a magnificent compensation for having foregone his chance of a Senior Isle of Man Tourist Trophy replica.

Noel's record did not stand for long. Two months later 'Ebbie' was timing an attack by another blown Brough-Superior. This one belonged to E. C. Fernihough. Tall, thin, bespectacled 'Ferni' was, like Pope and many other young men of the period, normally of a serious, studious turn of mind – he could write MA (Cantab) after his name – with a passion for fast motor cycles. As a member of the celebrated Cambridge Automobile and Motorcycle Club he had ridden successfully in many inter-varsity events, nearly always on small-capacity machines which he personally tuned to produce phenomenal speeds. Then suddenly he switched to the opposite extreme, fitted a blower to a big Brough-Superior, painted his mascot, a scalded cat, on the nose fairing . . . and lapped Brooklands at 123.5mph. From then on Eric Fernihough's golden dream was to recapture for Britain the world's fastest motor cycle record.

Meantime, the Norton trio of Guthrie, Rusk and White had been wiping up the continental *grands epreuves* and were getting ready for the season-ending Ulster Grand Prix which, in 1935, was named the Grand Prix of Europe. It was the first time that this courtesy title had been applied to a race in the British Isles. Hitherto, it had been given, more or less in annual rotation, to the major foreign events, the winners of which could call themselves European Champions.

Already 'the world's fastest road race', the Ulster was promising to be a real cracker. Guthrie, Rusk and Woods (on the twin Guzzi) were entered in the 500cc class. The 350 race was clearly going to be a Norton-Velocette battle, with 'Crasher' White and Johnny Duncan versus Walter Handley and Ernie Thomas, the rider who had taken over Handley's Velo entry in the Junior TT and finished sixth. The 250 class was wide open to a collection of DKWs, Guzzis, New Imperials and Rudges.

Anticipating a big crowd of spectators, travel agents Thomas Cook and Son laid on an excursion trip from London at the inclusive price of 42 shillings – which included meals on the train, a sight-seeing coach drive from Belfast to the Clady Circuit, returning after the race to Belfast, where a meat tea would be provided. For an extra twelve shillings, superior persons could travel first-class on the boat.

In the race all three capacity classes ran concurrently. Straight into the lead went Guthrie and Rusk with standing start laps at over 93mph that annihilated all records. On the second circuit the two Norton men collided at Aldergrove Corner. Rusk retired but Guthrie straightened a twisted mudguard and restarted with footrests, gear control, handlebar and front wheel rim all bent. The crash had dropped him to fourth place but, with a lap at 95.33mph, he regained the lead and finished three and a half minutes ahead of Belgian René Milhoux, on an FN. Woods was never in the picture, having struck engine trouble early on.

Bracebridge Street had to take a setback in the 350 event. Handley and Thomas were first and second. Duncan, White and local man Jackie Chambers followed. Germany's pocket-sized star, Arthur Geiss (DKW) was the 250 winner with Bob Foster (New Imperial) and Stanley Woods' business partner, Gordon Burney (Guzzi) third.

Jim Guthrie's 500cc average of 90.98mph was a world record for a motor cycle road race.

All through the summer, while racing and record-breaking

Top: the Villiers-engined Coventry-Eagle two-seater Pullman of 1936, with its pressed-steel enclosed frame

Above: Florence Blenkiron after completing her epic London–Cape Town–London expedition with her P & M and Watsonian sidecar combination. She was partnered by Theresa Wallach on the outward trip

was in full swing, an astonishing slow-speed marathon was under way. Two girls, both of them BMCRC members, Brooklands Gold Star holder Florence Blenkiron, and Theresa Wallach, had set off from London in March with the object of driving a 600 Redwing Panther, fitted with a Watsonian sidecar and hauling a trailer, to Cape Town and back. In September came the news that they had accomplished the first 7000 miles to the Cape and were preparing to tackle the return journey. This remarkable feat of courage and endurance got little attention in the technical press, which was busying itself with exciting happenings in the International Six Days Trial, back again among the Bavarian Alps. Great Britain's Trophy teamsters were George Rowley (350 AJS), Vic Brittain (350 Norton) and Peter Bradley (600 Sunbeam and sidecar). All using supercharged ohv BMWs, the German team were Henne, Stelzer and Krauss. Also competing for the chief prize were French, Czechoslovak and Italian teams.

The seventeenth ISDT developed into a tussle between the BMWs and the Jawas, and George Patchett's men had the edge when it came to the final speed test for they had lost only 23 penalty marks against the home side's 25 and so had only to average the required speeds on the last day to secure a victory. But a dropped-in valve ruined the Czechs' splendid effort and the Trophy stayed with Germany for the third year.

In alliance with race-wizard, Nigel Spring, a Norton-riding stonemason, F. L. 'Freddie' Frith crowned several years of Manx GP competition by winning the Junior event with record race and lap speeds. But for a shortage of fuel on the last lap he would have been first instead of runner-up in the Senior.

According to custom, the record-breakers made their autumnal attacks. Ernst Henne, using a blown 750cc machine, raised his own record to 159.13mph on the Frankfurt–Darmstadt autobahn. At Montlhéry, on 18 October, Jim Guthrie, aboard an alcohol-burning 500 Norton, lifted the hour record to 114.09mph, upping by over 3mph the figures set four years earlier by Bill Lacey, who had also used a Norton.

With Olympia in the offing, manufacturers began to announce their new models. Excelsior brought out a 500cc version of the Manxman. BSA had a redesigned range that included ohv Empire Star models, hailed, with prophetic truth, as will presently be revealed, as 'machines which should make a name for themselves'.

Ariel completely revised the 1000cc, four-cylinder engine, with pushrods replacing the chain camshaft drive. Coventry-Eagle had a two-seater Pullman model with a pressed-steel frame and rear suspension using two long half-elliptic springs. For the first time, BMWs were on display at an English show – singles and twins in pressed-steel frames, all with shaft drive. Ernst Henne was in attendance on the stand.

The show surprise came from AJS, in the form of a 500cc vee-four with four separate overhead camshafts operated by a single chain located between the cylinders. It was intended, said the makers, for fast touring and racing.

A breakdown of the 320 machines on exhibition showed that 277 were solos, 31 sidecar outfits and 12 three-wheelers. The most popular engine size was the half-litre – 33.5 per cent; next were 250s, 24.7 per cent; 350's 19.3 per cent; 1000s, 8.4 per cent; 150s, 6.3 per cent; 600s and over 1000s, 5.3 per cent and 2.5 per cent respectively. Over thirteen per cent of engines had more than one cylinder – 31 twins and eleven fours; 63 per cent were ohvs; 18.8 per cent side-valvers; 11.3 per cent two-strokes and 6.5 per cent had overhead camshafts.

As good tidings for Christmas came the news that those hazards for motor cyclists – tram tracks – were on their way out. More than half of London's trams were to be replaced by more modern trolley buses.

January 1936 was barely a fortnight old when Jack Sangster made a deal with the Triumph company, which had been getting into deep water by trying to make cars, motor cycles and bicycles all together in its old Priory Street, Coventry, factory. Sangster provided the capital to purchase the motor cycle side of the business and to form a separate organisation, the Triumph Engineering Company Limited with Siegfried Bettmann as chairman. Edward Turner became Chief Designer and General Manager. 'Mr Jack' invested some £50,000 in Triumph Engineering and, when he sold it in 1951 to the BSA group, he received £2.5 millions. In all those fifteen years it never failed to make a handsome profit.

Turner separated the motor cycles from the cars; leaving the old Triumph company to concentrate on four-wheelers, he set up new offices and workshops on the other side of Priory Street and there proved rapidly to justify Jack Sangster's faith that he could be as good a businessman as he was an engineer.

When the official returns of newly registered motor cycles were published in the spring they revealed another downward move – 45,311 as compared with 45,845 in the corresponding period of the previous year. Indeed, this trend continued and it was not until 1950 that the peak year, 1929, with 731,298 machines in use on British roads, was surpassed. Exports, however, were doing well; over one million pounds-worth of machines and accessories were sold abroad during 1935, Australia, New Zealand and South Africa being the best customers for Britain's products.

It was around this time that one of the industry's oldest manufacturers, Yorkshire-based P & M, launched a model forever to be remembered for its remarkable value. The 250 ohv Red Panther, complete with dynamo lighting and horn, cost only £29 17s 6d. It had a lively 65mph performance, could cover 115 miles on a gallon of petrol and, distributed and backed by the big south London dealers, Pride and Clarke, it could be yours for fifty shillings down and six shillings and ninepence a week. Tax was six shillings and threepence a quarter.

There was another success for P & M, when in April, Florence Blenkiron arrived back in England. The Redwing Panther sidecar and trailer outfit which she and Theresa Wallach had driven to Cape Town had become a write-off in a street accident. P & M and Watsonian shipped out a new combination, but Miss Wallach had become ill and had gone home by boat. Nothing daunted, Miss Blenkiron filled the sidecar with the gear previously carried by trailer and set off on her own to retrace her route to London. Arriving there, her only reward for 14,000 miles of hard driving and extraordinary pluck was a quiet little reception at South Africa House, a glass of South African wine and a pat on the back.

Edward Turner wasted no time on his transition to Coventry and in May he had three new Triumphs in production. They were the Tiger 70 (250cc), 80 (350cc) and 90 (500cc) models. They owed the basic design to earlier Val Page types but the Turner flair for style and embellishment was seen in such details as chromium-plated tanks with silver sheen panels, nacelle headlamps and totally enclosed valves for the 70 and 80 engines.

Triumph Tigers made their first competitions appearance in the Scottish Six Days Trial – and won three silver cups for faultless performances, a manufacturers team prize and the very

Top: a scene in London during 1937 shows a P & M Red Panther coping with the traffic and the wet weather. The little ohv 250 had a sparkling performance, with a top speed of around 65mph, and could manage well over 100mpg

Above: Billy Tiffen Jnr (Velocette) hard at work on the Stoney Brae section of the 1936 Scottish Six Days Trial

Right: Edward Turner's 500cc Triumph Tiger 90. This model typifies Turner's style with its high standard of finish

prestigious 'best 250cc machine' award.

Advance news of TT plans revealed that Norton would have plunger rear suspension, a new type of girder fork and twin-spark magnetos. Prototype models had carried Jim Guthrie to victory in the 350 and 500cc classes of the Swiss GP.

Velocette racers had an entirely new 'shock-absorbing frame' employing a pivotted rear fork with oleomatic 'legs' in which there were no springs; impact and recoil were controlled respectively by air compression and hydraulic (oil) valves. This arrangement was highly successful and became a regular Velo feature for the future. Another innovation from the Hall Green factory was a double-overhead-camshaft 350cc engine, the first ever British 'double-knocker', so named by the firm's race development engineer, Harold Willis, who thus translated the German term *doppel-knocke*. Stanley Woods was to ride this interesting experimental machine.

AJS had applied supercharging to their vee-four, which now had the rear cylinder heads reversed so that the exhaust ports faced forward.

Interest in supercharging was on the increase. Velocette had already tried it with the famous 'Whiffling Clara'. There had been a blown Ariel four while DKWs had their own special form of forced induction and now Vincent-HRD were also blown.

A clever combination of the radial four-valve Mechanical Marvel cylinder head with Manxman vertical shaft drive was evolved by Excelsior for the Lightweight race. Another unusual

250 was New Imperial's massive unit-construction model.

Walter Handley was *hors de combat* following a Donington crash and Walter Rusk was an unlikely starter, having suffered an injured arm in a street accident.

For the first time since 1914 there was an American entrant in the TT – Putt Mossman, who struggled manfully to qualify on his 250 OK-Supreme but was finally excluded, having failed to complete a practice lap within the required time limit.

With Italy in the throes of war with Abyssinia, there were no Italian entries and Stanley Woods had chosen to ride a DKW in the Lightweight race. His Junior and Senior mounts were Velocettes.

The expected Junior battle between Guthrie and Woods expired almost at once when Stanley retired at Kirkmichael with a broken coupling in the drive to the Velo's newly introduced double-overhead-camshaft gear. Thereafter, Guthrie and Frith circulated faultlessly, each cracking records like fireworks. The works Velocettes of Mellors and Thomas kept ahead of White's Norton, and H. E. Newman (Velocette), Steinbach and Heiner Fleischmann (NSUs) popped on and off the leader board, with Harold Daniell (AJS) not far away.

On the fifth lap came the debacle whose echoes have rippled round the halls of TT history ever since. When Frith's speed was announced he had cracked the lap record for the third time personally and for the fifth time during the race, taking it

The
SQUARE FOUR
1000 C.C. MODEL 4G £90
600 C.C. MODEL 4F £84

to 81.94mph. That was drama in itself . . . but what of Guthrie? He was posted third behind Ernie Thomas.

'Guthrie', said the loudspeakers, 'has received outside assistance and is disqualified'. His rear chain had jumped its sprockets at Hillberry and, after refitting it he had, so it was alleged, been pushed back on to the course by a marshal.

When he reached Ramsey he was stopped and told he was out of the race; but he continued and eventually finished in fifth position. There were protests and long arguments, and at the evening's prize-giving, to roars of disapproval, Clerk of the Course Loughborough reported that the stewards, after sifting

Above left: A. Geiss, third in the 1936 Lightweight TT, with his DKW

Top left: an example of the rare 192cc, 8bhp, 60mph R20 Sports BMW of 1937

Top right: winner Jimmy Guthrie receives congratulations from runner-up Stanley Woods after the Isle of Man Senior TT of 1936

Above: Ariel advertising of 1937

the evidence, realised that they had been misinformed. Had he not been stopped in Ramsey, Guthrie would in all probability have been second, and he was awarded the appropriate prize money, but the order of the first four could not be disturbed and he was officially placed fifth, behind the Nortons of Freddie Frith and 'Crasher' White and the Velocettes of Mellors and Thomas. The NSUs of Steinbach and Fleischmann were finally placed sixth and seventh.

The incident unfortunately overshadowed Frith's valiant performance. Not for a dozen years had a newcomer to the TT won on his first appearance.

The Lightweight event suffered the same afflictions as the previous year's Senior, the start being twice delayed by bad weather and then postponed to the following day, when conditions were excellent and remained so for the Senior.

On his honeymoon, and on his unit-construction pushrod New Imperial, Bob Foster took the 250 Trophy, so becoming the last man ever to win the Lightweight race on a British-built machine. Riding the four-valve ohc Excelsior, Tyrell Smith was second and Germany's Arthur Geiss brought his DKW two-stroke home third. After breaking the lap record, Woods' DKW had persistent ignition trouble and went out on the last lap when lying in second position.

Guthrie got his revenge on Woods in the Senior, his Norton (fitted with rear chain guides) beating the Velocette by eighteen seconds in a race won at the record speed of 85.80mph. The dicing between them saw the lap record repeatedly broken, finally by Woods at 86.98mph. Only half of the twenty starters finished, among the unlucky ones being Rowley and Daniell whose blown AJS 'fours' were not only difficult to handle but capricious in the carburation department.

For the International Six Days Trial, held in Germany's Black Forest area, there were 255 entries and at long last British teams were successful. Vic Brittain (350 Norton), George Rowley (350 AJS) and west-countryman Stuart Waycott (495 Velocette and sidecar) beat Germany's BMW trio by seventeen marks and captured the Trophy. One of the two British teams in the Silver Vase contest took that prize – an all-Scots squad, R. MacGregor, J. A. M. Leslie and J. C. Edwards.

With the show approaching, came details of a pushrod version of the Ariel Square Four, and Vincent-HRD announced a 1000cc big twin to be called the Rapide model. It was, in effect, two 500 Meteor engines on a special crankcase. Weighing 410lb, and with a claimed 120mph maximum, it was listed at £138.

In October Ernst Henne took a 500cc supercharged BMW with full, torpedo-shaped enclosure, to a one and a half-miles straight stretch of motorway near Rosenheim and there covered the flying kilometre at 180.97mph. Riding against a head wind in the opposite direction, his speed was reduced but the average was 169.14mph, a hefty improvement on his previous best of 159.10 with a 750cc motor.

Eric Fernihough quickly replied by taking his blown 996cc Brough-Superior to Gyon in Hungary where, at 163.82mph, he bettered Henne's flying mile record of 1mph, but he could not crack the German's 'kilo' speed.

Another kind of record was broken at the Olympia Show – the attendance for a six-day event was raised by 5000 to a total of 76,633 admissions. Mecca of British motor cyclists since the beginning of the century, it was the last time that the famous glass-domed building in Kensington would house the annual show. A newly constructed exhibition centre at Earls Court was waiting to take over.

Chapter 8
War Clouds Gather (1937-1939)

Left: many cross-country trials were organised in Germany just prior to World War II, and here a two-stroke, 100cc DKW tackles a sandy section. Such events included the Ost-Preussenfahrt, the Wiesbadener Kampfe and the Dreitagemittelburgsfahrt. These events were not so much outright sporting competitions as testing grounds for military riders who might one day be expected to ride in such conditions during hostilities

By 1937 Mussolini had established, and was developing, his North African empire. Motor cycles had played a big part in the Abyssinian campaign, conducted over terrain whose almost total lack of proper roads favoured two-wheeled, as against car, transport. Consequently, the Italian motor cycle industry was busy with large domestic orders, civilian and military, as well as with an export demand from the newly acquired territories in which the rough riding conditions called for the best kind of suspension. At the Milan Show, great advances in spring-frame construction were much in evidence. Guzzi, Gilera, Bianchi, Sertum, MAS, Miller, Astra and MM were leading makers who all had models featuring some form of rear-wheel articulation, the variety of methods including coil springs, leaf springs, bonded rubber, hydraulic struts and torsion bars.

While at war, Italy had been subjected to sanctions by the Locarno Treaty powers and, not being able to import accessories and fittings, the trade had been obliged to make its own. Thus there came about an entirely new sub-industry, supplying the carburettors, magnetos, gearboxes, forks, wheels and so forth that previously had been obtained mostly from Britain.

Despite sabre-rattling noises from the Rome–Berlin axis – Mussolini claiming the Meditteranean as *mare nostrum* and Hitler demanding *lebensraum* – the world rolled merrily along on a course of seemingly perpetual peace, with the pursuits of leisure and pleasure in high ascendancy.

In Britain petrol cost about a shilling a gallon. 'Touring' was in fashion. Hitherto little-known towns and villages became popular resorts. Everywhere sprang up roadsigns advertising 'Farmhouse Teas', 'Camping Site' and 'Bed and Breakfast, 7s 6d'. To the swiftly increasing hordes of motor vehicles was added a vast population of cyclists – it was estimated that some fourteen million Britons owned bicycles and, to accommodate them, special cycle tracks were built alongside some of the busier main roads. Morris and Ford offered four-seat saloon models at around £100. The secondhand car market was an Aladdin's Cave of goodies at give-away prices.

Motor cycles, however, still provided the most economical means of transport. It cost only twelve shillings a year to tax a 150cc lightweight; twenty-five shillings for machines over 250cc. At this time there were 37 different manufacturers of motor cycles exploiting the English market, together with a score or more makers of sidecars and three-wheelers. A Super Sports Morgan with an 1100cc ohv Matchless engine cost 138 guineas.

It was the heyday of the sporting three-wheeler; there were nearly thirty of them in the Motor Cycling Club's classic Eastertide London–Land's End trial, the total motor cycle entry for which was 215, the largest for nine years.

Motor cycle trials – and motor sport generally – were flourishing as never before, with AJS, Ariel, BSA, Matchless, New Imperial, Norton, Royal Enfield, Triumph and Velocette all maintaining expensive competitions departments and large staffs of factory riders.

In April, Eric Fernihough regained for Britain the world's fastest motor cycle title. On the Gyon road in Hungary, with his blown Brough-Superior, he raised the flying kilometre speed to 169.786mph and the flying mile to 168.581. With a sidecar, his corresponding records were 137.109 and 135.160mph.

The drama of the abdication that ended King Edward VIII's short reign had come and gone and, on 6 May, his brother was crowned George VI. The new monarch, while Duke of York, had been not only a practical motor cyclist (riding a Douglas while he was a Cambridge University student) but was also a popular patron of the sport, entering his official jockey, S. E. Wood, in Brooklands races.

There were many Coronation events that year, among them being a special Donington occasion to celebrate the inauguration of a much-revised circuit – the track had been lengthened to 3.125 miles by an extension that included the Melbourne Hairpin, overlooked by fine new grandstands. This was the course that was to provide some of the fiercest, most exciting car races ever held in England, when drivers such as Dick Seaman,

Below: the supercharged, twin-cam, four-cylinder Gilera 500 with which Piero Taruffi claimed many records, including the hour record at a speed of 121.23mph

Below right: JAP engines were not the only units popular on Morgans as this Super Sports of 1937, powered by a Matchless engine, proves

Rudolf Caracciola, Bernd Rosemeyer, Manfred von Brauchitsch and Prince Bira thrilled enormous crowds with their Auto-Unions, Mercedes and ERAs.

It was in May of that year that Italy's Dot Ing Piero Taruffi broke Jimmy Guthrie's 500cc Hour record on the Brescia-Bergamo autostrada with a fully enclosed dohc Gilera-Rondine fitted with a Roots-type supercharger. His average speed for the sixty minutes was 121.23mph – over two miles a minute for the first time in motor cycling history.

TT notes and news in the technical journals carried details of new Velocettes with large, square-finned cylinder heads, but with single-camshaft valve gear. After the blow-up of Stanley Woods' dohc mount in the previous year, Velo's race chief Harold Willis abandoned the twin-cam experiment. On the other hand, Joe Craig had copied the idea for his Nortons and double-knocker engines were taken to the Island. Contrary to what the papers said, however, the Bracebridge Street teamsters used single-cam machines in the races.

Another experiment was the introduction of an evening practice session, aimed to give the tuning experts a chance to ply their skills under atmospheric conditions more akin to those obtaining on race days than on cold, damp early mornings.

In the Junior, the Nortons of Guthrie, Frith and White were supreme and the lap record was frequently broken, ultimately being shared by Jimmy and Freddie at 85.18mph. For the first time, the Lightweight race saw a foreign victory, Omobono Tenni taking his Guzzi to the flag with a record average of 74.72mph and a record lap at 77.72mph.

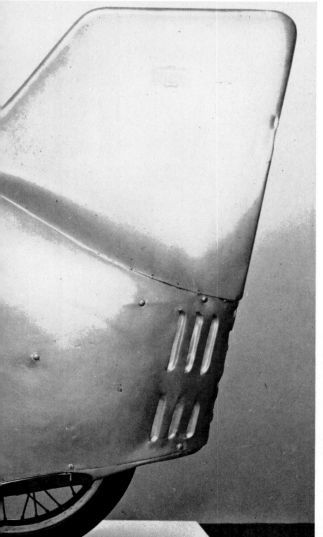

Bottom right: Norton's 1937 TT team, with Frith, White and Guthrie. They shone brightest of all in the Junior event with a Guthrie, Frith, White 1-2-3. They are seen on their senior bikes which achieved a first and third, with Frith taking the honours and White again not far behind in third place

Although there were only a meagre 23 starters, the Senior was an exciting race. The fourth lap leaders were Guthrie (Norton), Woods (Velocette), Frith (Norton), Jock West (BMW), White (Norton) and Tenni (Guzzi). On the next round Guthrie's engine went dead at the Cutting on the Mountain climb and Woods took the lead. Frith got an 'all-out' signal and on the sixth lap he was level-pegging with Stanley. Then, in a muck-or-nettles final fling, Frith shot the lap record for the first time above the 90mph mark and won from the Dubliner by fifteen seconds. White was third, Ted Mellors (Velocette) and Harold Daniell (Norton) fourth and fifth. West, afflicted with a leaking petrol tank, had to push in to finish sixth. Tenni had retired with a broken throttle cable.

Freddie Frith's great victory gave the Senior Tourist Trophy to Nortons for the sixth time in seven years and in that period the marque had filled seventeen of the 21 first, second and third places in the 500cc race.

TT echoes had hardly died away when an event that was to have long-lasting repercussions occurred quietly, almost casually, on a summer's day at Brooklands. The occasion, on Wednesday, 30 June 1937, was just another run-of-the-mill, mid-week handicap meeting, organised by the BMCRC and staged purely for members' enjoyment. Except for the usual little band of helpers, friends and officials, there were no spectators. So what was special about it? Simply that the programme included an entry, by BSA Cycles Limited of W. L. Handley (500 BSA).

Walter Handley had retired from motor cycle racing two years earlier; he had never previously competed with BSA machines; and the company had not made an entry in a race since 1921, when its six ohv 'specials' all blew up disastrously. The credit for persuading Handley to resume his leathers goes to BSA competitions manager Bert Perrigo. Who persuaded the Small Heath management to revoke its anti-racing policy is not certain. The machine was an iron-engined ohv Empire Star, designed by David Munro as a sports-tourer without any track aspirations whatsoever.

Nevertheless, the handicapper put Wal on the scratch mark in the three-lap Allcomers' Handicap. He should have been put way behind it, for he swept through the field at an average of 102.27mph, with a fastest lap at 107.57mph.

So W. L. Handley, TT ace (retired), joined the elite coterie of Brooklands Gold Star holders and when BSA, later in the season, introduced a machine based on Wal's mount, but with an alloy engine, it naturally called it the Gold Star model; and for the next 25 years BSA Gold Stars shone brightly wherever motor cycles were ridden, in the Isle of Man, in motocross, in trials and in the hands of hundreds of thousands of enthusiastic private owners, whose lament was loud and long when production came to an end after 1962.

Earlier than usual, the ISDT was held in July and after five days of bashing over Welsh mountain tracks and moorland byways, the British and German Trophy teams were dead-heating when they reached Donington for the final speed test. Vic Brittain (350 Norton), George Rowley (350 AJS) and Stuart Waycott (495 Velocette and sidecar) beat the 494cc BMW trio of J. Stelzer, G. Meier and L. Krauss by the cliff-hanging margin of ten seconds. Stelzer and Krauss were veteran BMW competitors; Georg ('Schorsch') Meier was a young Bavarian newcomer, soon to share with Ernst Henne the distinction of *meisterfahrer* (master rider) in the Munich company's impressive hall of fame.

At the Belgian Grand Prix, also in July, FN had a machine

164

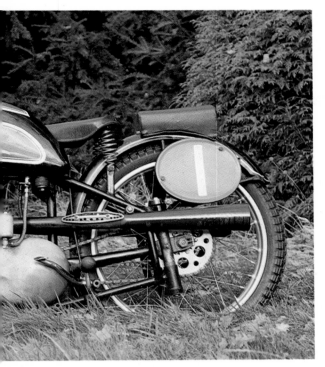

Top: a 1938 DKW 250 Rennsport, which was used for record breaking, in streamlined form, and also Grand Prix racing, as shown. Top speeds were approximately 170mph and 120mph, respectively. The engine of this bike is a split-single-cylinder, water-cooled, supercharged two-stroke

Left: a competitor negotiates the Devil's Staircase during the 1937 Scottish Six Days Trial

Above: Spanish rider Miguel Simo raced 250 and 350 Terrot machines at the TT every year between 1935 and 1939. He is seen here with his 1937 250 bike and mechanic. Unfortunately, Miguel was a non-starter, having crashed in the Junior event earlier in the week

described by one of the English journals as 'a most interesting motor cycle'. It was a 500cc vertical-twin, unit-construction job with chain-driven overhead camshaft gear. After close inspection, Joe Craig remarked that it appeared to have potentialities. In fact, its rider, René Milhoux, was well able to keep up with the Nortons of Guthrie and Frith until, near the race's end, a piston cracked; thereafter no more was heard of it, but just a month later came first accounts of another vertical-twin about which there was much to be heard . . . for years to come.

This was Edward Turner's Triumph Speed Twin, in the opinion of many the most successful motor cycle ever constructed. Not only has its basic engine layout been continued – with the same marque name – to the present day, but it was universally copied and it set a fashion that seems likely to persist so long as motor cycles are made.

Turner's arrangement of vertical cylinders paired across the frame was nothing new. Scott, Peugeot and the Val Page 650cc Triumph of 1933 were but three earlier examples. The 500 ohv Speed Twin, however, embodied all the latest techniques so cleverly and compactly that, on the engineers' dictum 'to be right, it must look right', it could not fail to succeed.

The pistons rose and fell side by side, there being a single, central flywheel in a barrel-shaped crankcase. Con-rods with split big-ends and shell bearings were used. Transverse camshafts fore and aft of the block operated pushrods in tubes extending up between the cylinders to fully enclosing, positively lubricated rocker-boxes. Cylinder dimensions were 63mm by 80mm, 498cc and, on a 7:1 compression ratio, 26bhp was developed at 6000rpm, representing a top speed near 90mph. Catalogued as the model 5T, it was priced at £75.

Throughout the summer, Norton had been collecting its customary laurel garlands and in the Swiss GP, that year's European championship, Guthrie and Frith were first and second in the 350 and 500cc races. It was the seventh successive time that Joe Craig's machines had achieved the 'double' in this event and from it Guthrie emerged as the Junior and Senior Champion of Europe.

Last fixture in the continental calendar of *grandes épreuves* was the German Grand Prix, scheduled for Sunday 8 August on the tricky Hohenstein-Ernstthall circuit, near Chemnitz in southern Saxony.

Harold Daniell and Crasher White were first and second in the Junior race. In the Senior, Frith's Norton misfired persistently and it was left to his partner, Guthrie, to fight it out with Germany's leading men, headed by Karl Gall (BMW). After a poor start Jimmy was soon in the lead, and his third consecutive German Grand Prix victory was in sight when, on the last corner of the last lap, not a mile from the finish where the Union Jack was ready for hoisting, he crashed heavily. The Norton's rear axle had snapped.

Gallant Jimmy Guthrie was taken to a local hospital where he died a few hours later. The shock of his death reverberated around the world, for this 41-year-old Scot, six times a TT winner, had won the admiration of sportsmen everywhere. On a racing motor cycle no rival could surpass his determined 'will to win', yet, out of the saddle, he was a quiet, gentle, unassuming family man who shared with his brother, Archie, the running of their motor business in their Lowland home town, Hawick.

As a mark of respect for Jim's memory, Norton withdrew its entries from the next week's Ulster GP, won by Jock West (BMW) after Stanley Woods (Guzzi) had retired from the lead with engine trouble. Ted Mellors (Velocette) won the 350cc class and Ernie Thomas (DKW) took the 250cc prize.

In the autumn of 1937, the Triumph company undertook a tough demonstration of the Tiger types. At Donington a 250 model 70, a 350 model 80 and a 500 model 90 were each subjected to a three-hour thrashing at maximum revs in each of the four gears. Then, under ACU seal, they were taken to Brooklands, where they returned the following speeds over a flying lap: Tiger 70, 66.39mph; Tiger 80, 74.68mph; Tiger 90, 82.31mph. The riders were Ted Thacker, Freddie Clarke and Allan Jeffries; their reward was the Maudes Trophy.

Another feather in Triumphs' cap was the winning by Ivan Wickstead of the Prestwich Cup for the year's fastest Brooklands lap on a 500cc machine. His 494cc mount lapped at 110.68mph.

A big dispute arose when Piero Taruffi attacked Eric Fernihough's world's fastest record of 169.8mph. The Italian's torpedo-like 500cc blown Gilera reached 170.373mph, but his actual improvement in time was 0.04 of a second, and the FICM record rules book said that anything under 0.05 seconds didn't count. They were still arguing about it when Ernst Henne settled the matter by retaking the title with his blown 500cc BMW. On the Frankfurt autobahn on 28 November he averaged 173.675mph, and for good measure added the 500, 750 and 1000cc class, one-mile, five-miles and five-kilos flying start records to his score. Having done that, he announced his retirement from competitive motor cycling, taking with him a world's fastest title that stood in his name for fourteen years.

At the 1938 Berlin Show, BMW exhibited its shaft-drive models with plunger rear suspension, and on the NSU stand was a hefty-looking parallel-twin racer with individual drives to the twin overhead camshafts. The Neckarsulm firm, TT supporters, on and off, since 1907, had never before been noteworthy for originality in its racing designs. Since the mid-1930s, when ex-Norton development chief Walter Moore had joined the company, its orthodox single-cylinder ohc machines had looked very much like Bracebridge Street products. Now it was evident

Above and below: Ernst Henne's streamlined record-breaking BMW seen in 1937. On the Frankfurt autobahn on 28 November, Ernst took the record at 173.675mph

166

that fresh talent was at work and that NSU meant business.

About this time there was an upheaval in Crow Lane, Coventry, since bicycle boom days the home of Rudge-Whitworth. The firm's financial structure had for some time been wavering, and now the directors sold the motor cycle business, which was transferred to Hayes, Middlesex, where production of some of the models, particularly the famous Ulster type, was continued by the Gramophone Company, better known as HMV and later as EMI. George Hack moved into the world of aero-engines, Tyrell Smith joined Excelsior and, in March, Graham Walker took over the editorship of the weekly *Motor Cycling* publication.

April saw Eric Fernihough back in Hungary, waiting for suitable weather to wrest his record back from Henne. Meanwhile, on 13 April, with a sidecar attached to his Brough-Superior, Noel Pope raised the Outer Circuit three-wheel record to 106.6mph.

Conditions on the Gyon road were considered, on Saturday 23 April, to be favourable for Fernihough to make his solo attempt. It was a tragic decision. The big Brough-Superior was thundering up to peak revs when a sudden side-wind gusted the machine clear off the road into a shallow drainage ditch. Courageous, clever, try-and-try-again Eric was killed instantly and the Scalded Cat was reduced to write-off wreckage. No praise can be too high for those gallant forays by Fernihough and his little band of helpers. Without any back-up from the resources of a wealthy factory, they were conducted on a strictly shoe-string budget, most of the preparation, organisation and expense being undertaken by Eric himself, motivated by a burning spirit of patriotism. With his death it seemed likely that any hope of Britain regaining the world's fastest title had expired with him . . . until it was learned that Noel Pope and Francis Beart, sponsored by George Brough, were at work on another challenge. Unfortunately, a World War had to be fought before that enterprise could be put to the test.

Above: Eric Fernihough, the gallant privateer who tried to wrest the bike speed record from Henne in 1938

Below: a 1937 500cc Rudge Ulster, a model now regarded as a classic

For the TT, AJS added a Zoller supercharger to its vee-four, blowing at 6lb above atmospheric pressure. Norton had the 350 and 500 double-knocker engines in frames with much improved plunger rear suspension and telescopic front forks that had no damping, hydraulic or friction. Excelsior had reverted to its single-ohc Manxman layout and OK-Supreme had an entirely new 250 ohc engine with a single 'double-ended-hairpin' spring controlling both valves.

For the first time in seven years, Norton failed to win the Junior, Frith, Johnny Lockett and Daniell being unable to cope with the flying Velocettes of Woods and Mellors. In winning, Woods put the lap record up to 84.75mph.

Records went again in the Lightweight which Ewald Kluge (DKW) won at 78.48mph, sending the lap speed over 80mph.

There was nothing amiss with Nortons' Senior double-knockers, but its trio of Frith, Daniell and White were up against Stanley Woods, by far the most experienced man in the business and on the fastest Velocette ever raced in the TT. Apart from these two Birmingham firms, the only other makes in the 25-strong field consisted of BMWs in the hands of Georg Meier and Jock West, an AJS four for Bob Foster and a Vincent-HRD for Dubliner Manliff Barrington.

The battle opened with Frith leading Woods fractionally for two laps. White was third and Daniell fourth. Foster, Barrington and Meier had all already retired. For the next three laps Woods kept just ahead of Frith, but the bulky Londoner, Daniell, was stoking up the pressure and on the fifth lap he dead-heated with Frith in second position, having equalled Fred's 1937 lap record of 90.27mph. Then, on the sixth round, Harold broke through the 25-minute barrier, his 24min 57sec time putting him at the head of a race in which Frith and Woods were now level-pegging in second berth and only placed five seconds behind.

Above: the German entry for the 1938 ISDT arrives at Southampton before going on to Wales for the event

Calling on every rev from his Velocette, Woods shook free from Frith, but he was still actually losing ground to Daniell, who was tearing records to shreds. Harold covered the last lap in 24 minutes 52.6 seconds – exactly 91mph, a figure that was to stand unscathed for twelve years. His race average was 89.11mph and he beat Woods by 15.2 seconds. Frith was only 1.6 seconds behind the Irishman and, with under seventeen seconds separating the first three, it was 'a damn close run thing!' It was also Nortons' nineteenth TT victory and it won the manufacturers team prize for the fifth time in six years.

The continental circus events were carried through, but with somewhat limited British support for the international situation was becoming increasingly tense. Civil Defence training had been started; a part-time militia force, the Local Defence Volunteers (later the Home Guard), was being recruited; private flying clubs were organised into a Civil Air Guard. Evidence of the War Office's recognition of the military value of motor cycles was emphasised when the Army staged an impressive inter-command reliability trial. Organised by Eastern Command, it attracted an entry of ten officers and 65 other ranks. They rode standard WD machines, mostly side-valvers, and carried full kit, including tin hats and gas masks. The winner, on a 500 BSA, was Lt B. D. S. Ginn (RAOC), already well known and successful in civilian trials.

Again in July, and again in Wales, the ISDT was different in that Trophy teams – there were three, Great Britain, Germany and Czechoslovakia – comprised three solos and one sidecar outfit, and there was a new prize, presented by Germany's motor sport leader, General Hühnlein, for the best military team. Britain's Trophy team was the same as in 1937 with the addition of Jack Williams (350 Norton). The Germans mounted their soloists on 175 DKWs, old-timer Krauss reappearing with his 597 BMW outfit. The Czech solo men were all on Jawa-CZs.

Below: three competitors wind their way through the valleys of Wales in the 1938 International Six Days Trial event

Germany was out of the running on the second day when two DKWs retired. The Czechs finished intact, but with a loss of 504 marks, and the British boys cleaned up, with a deficit of only nine points.

The Ulster GP regained its 'fastest road race' title (lost to the Dutch TT in 1937) when Jock West (BMW) had another win, this time at 93.98mph with a lap at 98.93mph. Ted Mellors (Velocette) was first in the 350 class and Ewald Kluge (DKW) headed the 250 field.

In the Manx GP, which had never seen a foreign machine in the first three (until 1947, when Austin Munks had a 250 Guzzi win), Norton rang up its third 'double-treble' in a long row of such feats. London optician Kenneth Bills won both the Junior and Senior with record averages and laps. Yorkshire's Denis Parkinson, who had ridden in MGPs since 1932, was a third-time Lightweight winner on an Excelsior.

At the end of September Prime Minister Neville Chamberlain returned from a Munich meeting with Hitler, bearing a pledge for 'peace in our time'. Britain and France redoubled their precautions against war. For motor cyclists a significant reminder of the seriousness of the situation came when Norton Motors' Managing Director, Bill Mansell, announced his firm's intention to withdraw from participation in competitive events, especially racing. The company was heavily committed to WD contracts, which for the time being had to take top priority. With the shut-down of Bracebridge Street's celebrated race shop, Joe Craig moved to AJS at the company's Woolwich factory.

Another side effect of the national 'be prepared' mood was the launching by the motor cycle industry and press of a drive to popularise autocycles. Mostly powered by 98cc Villiers two-

Left: by 1939, BMWs were already identifiable by their classic style with a flat-twin engine; this Super Sport R51 is no exception

Below: the little Raynal autocycle of 1938 does not seem to be far removed from the powered bikes of the early part of the century

Bottom: a 249cc Francis-Barnett J45 of 1939

Overleaf: two happy young sailors arrive by Ariel at Waterloo after being called up for the Reserve Fleet in July 1939

stroke engines, with auxiliary pedalling gear, their extreme economy of fuel was their chief selling point, and demonstrations and rallies were organised to prove their capabilities. They became known as 'Wilfreds'. Older readers may remember a strip cartoon telling the adventures of three little creatures, Pip, Squeak and Wilfred. Small motor cycles had for long been termed 'pip-squeaks', so it was natural that the littlest member of the newspaper trio should give his name to the new breed of tiddlers.

Forty-one motor cycle manufacturers announced their ranges for the 1939 season and as these were the last of the pre-war models it is not without interest to list the makes then available on the British market. They were:- AJS, AJW, Ariel, BMW, Cotton, Coventry-Eagle, Cyc-Auto, DKW, Dayton, Douglas, Excelsior, Francis-Barnett, Harley-Davidson, HEC, James, Levis, Matchless, Montgomery, Morgan, New Imperial, Norton, OEC, OK-Supreme, P & M, Raynall, Royal Enfield, Rudge, Scott, SOS, Sun, Sunbeam, Triumph, Velocette, Vincent, Wolf, Zenith and Zündapp.

During the year Sunbeam had been acquired by the Collier brothers and Sunbeams redesigned by the Woolwich firm – now restructured as Associated Motor Cycles Ltd, – were replacing John Marston's Wolverhampton types. One of the industry's 'oldest inhabitants', Calthorpe, was missing from the list. It had become the property of Bruce Douglas (Bristol) Motors but the west country had not got around to implementing its plan to make Douglas machines with Matchless engines.

The exhibit that took the 1938 Show by storm was George Brough's magnificent concept, the Golden Dream. Glistening with gilt enamel, it was an air-cooled, transverse, flat-four, with one pair of cylinders sited above the other. Single-throw crankshafts were directly geared at the rear of the engine and the pistons moved inwards and outwards in unison. On each crankpin, one of the big-ends was forked around the other, so there was no staggering of the cylinders. Drive was taken from the lower crankshaft in a straight line through a car-type clutch and a four-speed gearbox via an enclosed prop shaft to a worm-and-wheel unit on the plunger-sprung rear axle. The magdyno was coupled to the top crankshaft which also drove, by 2:1 chain reduction, a gear-type oil pump in the sump. Alongside the lower sprocket was another, which chain-drove the two camshafts running crosswise between the upper and lower cylinder blocks. The all-enclosed overhead valves were designed to be pushrod operated.

Cylinder dimensions were 71mm by 63mm, 996cc, and each cylinder head was a separate casting. With a wealth of typical Brough refinements, including a four and a half gallon tank with a rain-drainer, an eight-inch diameter headlamp, Castle fork and a 120mph speedometer, the Earls Court prototype was ticketed at £185 – a dream many would have liked to translate into reality but, before production could begin, the Nottingham factory was switched to war work and never built another motor cycle.

The uneasy peace continued into 1939. Everyone, including infants, was issued with a gas mask, and throughout Britain back gardens sprouted corrugated-iron air-raid shelters. 'Work of national importance' found its way into almost every kind of occupation and activity. BSA, Norton, Matchless and Triumph painted most of their output either khaki or blue and other companies had to rejig their workshops to make all sorts of unfamiliar bits and pieces that came under the general heading of munitions and military equipment.

Nevertheless, motor cycle sport went blithely forward

through the customary calendar of events, to which were added numerous trials for servicemen. The international racing season opened for business as usual with the TT in which, curiously, in view of the ominous atmosphere, there was strong competition from the state-backed continental factories. Germany entered a trio of blown BMWs for the Senior; NSU had Junior and Senior teams riding its new, dohc, supercharged, parallel-twins; and there were DKWs for all three classes. Italy's usual contribution of 250 and 500cc Guzzis was supplemented by a pair of Benellis.

With Norton absent, British works support was reduced to three makes, AJS, Velocette and CTS. The Woolwich firm had applied water-cooling to its fearsome blown vee-fours, to be ridden by Bob Foster and Walter Rusk. Velocette produced a challenging 500cc, supercharged, dohc, in-line vertical-twin, with shaft drive, for use by Stanley Woods. It was named the Roarer. CTS machines were made by Chris Tattersall, who specialised in building Rudge-engined lightweight racers.

Frith and Daniell had made arrangements to ride standard Manx Nortons, but Bill Mansell later allowed them to 'borrow' their 1938 mounts on the strict understanding that there would be no works back-up. Crasher White, who was engaged by NSU for the Junior, was also eventually able to use his previous year's Senior Norton. 'No sense in letting it gather dust', said Mansell.

After leading the Junior for three laps, Frith dropped behind and the race became a duel between Daniell and Woods (Velocette), who won, by eight seconds, his tenth Tourist Trophy. Ted Mellors (Benelli) got his well-deserved Lightweight Trophy after Woods (Guzzi) had packed up.

On the day following the Lightweight race a large crowd attended the unveiling, by the Lieutenant Governor, of the Jimmy Guthrie memorial, a greystone cairn erected at the Cutting, where the great Scots rider had retired in his last TT, the 1937 Senior. The epitaph on the monument reads: 'James Guthrie, 1897–1937. Erected to the memory of Jimmy Guthrie, of Hawick, a brilliant motor cycle rider, famous on the Isle of Man Tourist Trophy course for his wonderful riding and great sportsmanship. He won the race six times, beat many world records and was first in numerous foreign races. He died while upholding the honour of his country in the German Grand Prix, August, 1937'.

There were 47 starters in the Senior race and the BMWs of George Meier and Jock West went straight into the lead, followed by the unblown singles of Frith (Norton) and Woods (Velocette), and that was the order at the finish. It was Stanley Woods' last TT. He had taken part in every meeting for seventeen successive years, had ridden 37 races, won ten of them, used nine different makes of machine and never once finished off the leader board. It was also the Roarer's one and only Island appearance. After Stanley had tried it in practising, it was considered to be not sufficiently developed for racing and, indeed, it never did contest a race in earnest.

Georg Meier raised the race speed slightly, but Harold Daniell's epic 91mph lap record of the previous year was never in danger; in fact, it was to stand for the next twelve years.

Never before, in one week, had the machines of three nations each secured a Tourist Trophy – one for Britain, one for Germany and one for Italy.

British successes in the following round of continental circus races were minimal, but by the time the Ulster Grand Prix was looming up in August, the AJS people had really got their vee-four moving, and their head jockey, Walter Rusk, set patriotic hopes soaring when he became the first man ever to lap

the Clady Course at a three-figure speed – bang on 100mph. But then his front fork broke, and Italy's Dorino Serafini (one-time chauffeur to Mussolini) cut the 'Blond Bombshell's' time by one-fifth of a second, setting the all-time record at 100.3mph on the Gilera four. His average speed for the race was 97.85mph.

So, at the end of the season, the threatened 'foreign menace' had really come to pass. A German on a German machine had won the supreme event, the TT; an Italian on an Italian machine had won the world's fastest motor cycle road race; and, to rub it in, Taruffi had raised the hour record to 127.53mph with a 500 Gilera four that developed 90bhp.

While the speedsters were hard at it, the trials men were faced with a dilemma. The ACU had declined its right to run the 1939 ISDT and the FICM had accepted Germany's offer to stage the event, celebrating its twenty-first birthday, in their newly over-run territory, Austria. Mistrustful of assurances from the Fatherland that they would be welcome, many potential British entrants hung back – until the War Office declared that it would send three Army teams to contest the Hühnlein Trophy.

If Whitehall said it was okay, fair enough, and in splendid August weather a large contingent of Britons crossed the Channel . . . to be considerably disturbed when they found French troops mobilising along the much-vaunted Maginot Line. Doubts increased when even greater activity was encountered on the Siegfried Line, and there was a shortage of petrol that grew more acute the further they penetrated into the territory of the Reich.

However, at the headquarters town of Salzburg there appeared to be no special problems, except that the organisers had chosen for the final speed test a course more like a motocross set-up than the traditional concrete or black-top road circuit. For the first three days things went smoothly. The British Trophy team, the Army's BSA-mounted trio, one of the British Silver Vase teams and several factory squads were all unpenalised and confidently looking forward to the speed test, in which it was thought that scrambles' experience might stand 'our men' in good stead. Then came the news that Germany and Russia had signed a non-aggression pact, and that German troops were massing on the Polish frontier.

That did it. The ACU representatives called a midnight meeting at the headquarters, from which emerged a decision to withdraw immediately all the official British teams. Others could please themselves if they wished to carry on. In fact, the majority joined the great retreat through Switzerland and France to Dieppe, the only Channel port then still open to civilians.

The Germans carried the trial through to the end and claimed both the Trophy and the Silver Vase, but the FICM promptly declared all the results null and void. After the war, officers of the Allied Occupation Commission recovered the Trophy and returned it to the governing body to be competed for when the time was ripe, which did not happen until 1947.

In the last year of racing at Brooklands, soon to be built over by the Vickers company, Theresa Wallach became a Gold Star holder for a lap at 101.64mph on a 350 Norton while Noel Pope took his Brough-Superior round at 125mph, so becoming both solo and sidecar Outer Circuit record holder in perpetuity.

When the Isle of Man packet boats should have been ferrying Manx Grand Prix fans, Stukas were preparing the way for the Wehrmacht's invasion of Poland and, on Sunday 3 September 1939, Premier Chamberlain told the nation that Britain and France were at war with the axis. The blackout went up and the lights over Europe went out.

Chapter 9
War and Peace (1940-1949)

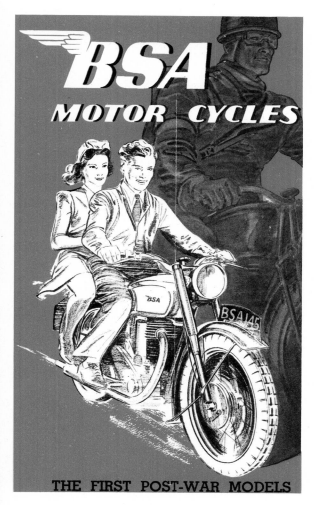

THE FIRST POST-WAR MODELS

Left: the parallel-twin, shaft-drive, 500cc Sunbeam S7 of 1947. This ohc bike featured a unit-construction clutch and gearbox and plunger rear suspension

Above: BSA proudly announce their first post-war models in 1946

To give just credit to the part played by allied forces' motor cyclists and the British motor cycle industry throughout World War II would be a task far beyond the compass of this history. One company alone, BSA, needed a full-length book (*The Other Battle*, by Donovan M. Ward) to describe, even in condensed form, its incredible feats in the production of 'articles of war' which, of course, included a continuous stream of motor cycles, mostly that soldier's friend, the ever-reliable 500cc sv Model M20. From Bracebridge Street came 16H and Big Four machines in such quantities that at the end the company was able to claim that of all the motor cycles supplied to the allies, one in four was a Norton.

Matchless especially endeared itself to DRs when it fitted the WD models with its excellent Teledraulic, oil-damped front fork. Triumph made not only military motor cycles but also thousands of stationary engines for powering generators, fire pumps, fans and similar equipment. One of the many odd incidents thrown up by the war was the discovery, after the bombing of a French town, of a cellar-full of Triumphs, all built during the 1914–18 conflict and never ridden.

With the increasing employment of airborne troops came a need for ultra-light, collapsible machines for parachutists' use after they had landed. For this purpose Royal Enfield produced its folding Flying Flea model and Excelsior provided an ingenious, soup-plate-wheeled mount, the Welbike, that could be fitted into an air-drop container scarcely bigger than a bolster case. Marketed later in civilian form as the Corgi, it inspired the great postwar scooter movement. On its formation the Royal Flying Corps had adopted P & M motor cycles for its two-wheeled transport. The Cleckheaton factory was not big enough to supply the needs of the RAF but the tradition held, and at the outset of hostilities, Ministry of Supply officials scoured dealers' showrooms, impressing every P & M they could find so that there was hardly an airfield in the land that did not have at least one Panther in its MT section.

In the 1930s a Gloucestershire trials man, W. E. Hayward, had devised a clever method of providing positive drive for his sidecar wheel. It was so successful that Norton Motors obtained the right to copy it and for a time, until the ACU put a ban on sidecar wheel drive, Hayward and Nortons' expert, Dennis Mansell, were virtually unbeatable in the three-wheeled class. When the North African campaign began, Norton resuscitated the idea and supplied the Eighth Army with machines that could go through deep sand on equal terms with the big German BMW and Zündapp gun-carrying outfits.

Throughout the war the training of service motor cyclists was given a high priority and instruction centres were set up in many parts of the country. One of the most celebrated was the Lakeland MT School at Keswick where Captain 'Dickie' Wilkins, later to become a keen TT supporter and road-racing sponsor, had on his staff some of the finest all-round riders in the game. Much invaluable tuition was also given by civilians, such as ACU officials, factory executives, technical journalists, professional competition riders and others who, for some reason, often *anno domini*, were not in uniform.

Towards the end of the war, particularly in the period following Germany's surrender, the Services encouraged motor cycle competitions as a useful form of keep-fit entertainment and many of the lads who were to be among the industry's first postwar customers learned their riding and caught the motor cycling bug in events run by units wherever British troops were stationed.

Meantime, AMC had sold the Sunbeam trademark to BSA, and Jack Sangster had also sold his Ariel interests to the Small Heath Group, leaving himself free to concentrate on building up his other motor cycle business, Triumph Engineering, where Edward Turner was now the Managing Director. Ariel production continued from its old home in Selly Oak, Birmingham, on a virtually independent basis.

In six years of strife, 420,000 motor cycles had been supplied to the allies, BSA and Norton each claiming that a quarter of the total had come from their factories.

VE Day, 8 March 1945, brought the end of the blackout and, although the capitulation of Japan was still to come, the British Government launched the basic petrol rationing scheme. From 1 June coupons were available permitting the purchase of limited amounts of commercial-grade, unbranded, 'pool' petrol. Motor cyclists were allowed two gallons a month for machines under 250cc and three gallons for bigger models, and would-be buyers of new machines no longer needed a licence to acquire them.

Meagre though it was, the basic ration brought an immediate revival of the sport. On 17 June the MCC held its first postwar meeting at Wrotham Park and in the same month the Ulster MCC staged a grand reunion grass-track race where 'old-timers' such as Artie Bell, Ernie Lyons and Rex McCandless were the winners. In August the MCC ran a road race over a circuit at Bangor, County Down, home of a hard-riding young man, Bill Nicholson, who was to become one of Britain's premier trials and scrambles aces. More than 25,000 Londoners welcomed the return of speedway racing by packing the New Cross Stadium on 27 June.

At the year's end Tom Loughborough relinquished his thirty years of ACU Secretaryship, handing over to his assistant, Sam Huggett. For the time being, Loughborough continued as Secretary-General of the FICM.

A race among the manufacturers to be first with a postwar programme was won by Triumph, who in March 1945, listed a range of Speed Twins and Tiger types. AMC followed quickly and in August BSA produced the first genuinely new, never-before-marketed model, the B31 ohv 350 with a telescopic fork and a prestigious future.

Thus did the motor cycling movement enter a new era of popularity. From a then-record high of three-quarters of a million machines on British roads in 1929, the annual

Below: three triumphant RAF mechanics at the Gates of Tripoli take the opportunity to try a bike captured from the enemy. The machine is a 750cc, side-valve, two-wheel-drive BMW

Right: Allied troops get the hang of riding and packing the ingenious little Excelsior Welbike. Its power unit was a 98cc, two-stroke engine with single gear

registrations had declined steadily to around a quarter million ten years later, but within twelve months of the end of World War II there were nearly half a million machines in use and in the next decade the total would mount to one and a half millions.

The rapid rate at which the motor cycle makers returned to peace-time production was remarkable in view of the problems they had to meet. There were shortages and bottlenecks in the supply of materials; worn-out machine tools needed to be replaced; run-down plants and premises had to be refurbished; there were business staffs to be recruited and sales outlets to be reorganised. Severe restrictions on overseas travel and the urgent need to earn foreign currency meant that a big proportion of output had to be earmarked 'For Export Only'. This put a brake on the development of the home market and disappointed thousands of would-be customers eager to get their hands on the latest models. Furthermore, there was Purchase Tax to be added to basic costs. This levy, imposed during the war, affected almost all goods and commodities and raised motor cycle prices by approximately 25 per cent.

For those firms with racing aspirations the position was even more difficult, for not only had they to adapt their engines to run on low-octane petrol, but the FICM had decreed that henceforth superchargers were barred. The object of this ban was to reduce production costs, but it upset the plans of many companies which had already achieved experience with blowers – Gilera, BMW, Guzzi, Velocette, AJS, NSU and Vincent being some of them.

Although there had earlier been a happy reunion of trials men in the Stroud Team Trial, the Comore Cup Trial in February 1946 actually reopened the customary calendar of classic one-day open events and, in an entry of 150, ex-sergeant Freddie Rist was the winner on a competitions version of the new B31 BSA. On a similar machine, Irishman Bill Nicholson was the runner-up.

A few weeks later BSA announced its 'new kind of motor

Left: David Whitworth and Velocette await the start of the first Continental bike race after the war. The venue is Le Zoute near the Belgian-Dutch border and the date is June 1946

Above: C.E. 'Titch' Allen, BEM, founder member of the Vintage Motor Cycle Club, seen at Stanford Hall Museum in 1977

cycle', the Sunbeam model S7. Designed by Erling Poppe, member of a distinguished family of engineers, and built in BSA's wartime shadow factory at Redditch, Worcester, this 500cc ohc, in-line, vertical-twin was a clever combination of car and motor cycle practices, embodying a unit-construction clutch and gearbox, with shaft drive, plunger rear springing and 4.75 by 16-inch balloon tyres among its numerous unusual features. The basic price of this luxury mount was £175. By contrast, the strictly utilitarian Corgi scooter, made for Excelsior by the Brockhouse Engineering Company at Southport, Lancashire, went on sale at £50, less tax.

While news of new models was hitting the headlines there came a movement aimed at preserving antique machines, and on 28 April some 45 enthusiasts, gathered together by the enthusiastic C. E. 'Tich' Allen, BEM, met at a café on the Hog's Back in Surrey to form the Vintage MCC. They decided that a motor cycle should be classed as a vintage model if it was made between 31 December 1914 and 31 December 1930. Veteran machines would be those constructed before that period, and this formula still applies among the Club's present day four-thousand membership.

An opportunity to resume continental racing came in June when the Sunbeam MCC combined with the Belgian Motorcycle Federation to run an 'international' event on a pocket-handkerchief course at Le Zoute, near the Belgian-Dutch frontier. A dozen Britons joined riders from Belgium, Holland and Finland and the classes were won by Jack Brett (250 Excelsior), Peter Goodman, grandson of the founder of Veloce Limited (350 Velocette) and Maurice Cann (500 Guzzi).

Then, in July, came the well remembered Anglo-Irish match race, staged before a crowd of 15,000 by the Bermondsey MCC on the Brands Hatch grass track. Ernie Lyons, Artie Bell, Rex McCandless and Bill Nicholson were in the Irish side and English teamsters included Jock West, Eric Oliver, Harry Ditchburn, Arthur Wheeler and Jack Surtees, father of future World Champion, John.

England beat Ireland by nineteen points to seventeen but the most memorable feature of the meeting was the debut of the McCandless swinging rear-fork frame, prototype of a design that was to gain world fame as the 'Featherbed'.

Rear suspension with a difference, prewar product of Edward Turner's ingenious brain but never before seen in public, was the spring-hub fitted to a special Triumph twin raced by Ernie Lyons in the Ulster Road Race. Aldergrove aerodrome had been built over part of the original Clady Course, shortening the circuit to sixteen miles. Because of this, and a meagre entry of 35, mostly local riders, it had been decided not to dignify the event with a Grand Prix title.

Apart from the spring-hub, Lyons's machine was virtually a Speed Twin with an engine based on an AAPP (Airborne Auxiliary Power Plant) portable generator unit as used in bomber aircraft. The cylinder block and heads were of silicon-aluminium alloy, had square fins and a twin-carburettor induction system. Les Martin (Excelsior) won the 250 class, Vic Willoughby (Velocette) the 350 and local man B. M. Graham (Norton) was the only finisher from fourteen 500cc entrants. Lyons had plug trouble, Artie Bell (Norton) went out with a burst tyre – synthetic rubber covers were all that were then available. Ex-RAF Pathfinder pilot R. L. 'Les' Graham, DFC (Norton) was stopped with piston seizure – castor-based racing oil was unobtainable in Ireland.

The IoM Government had been able to make available

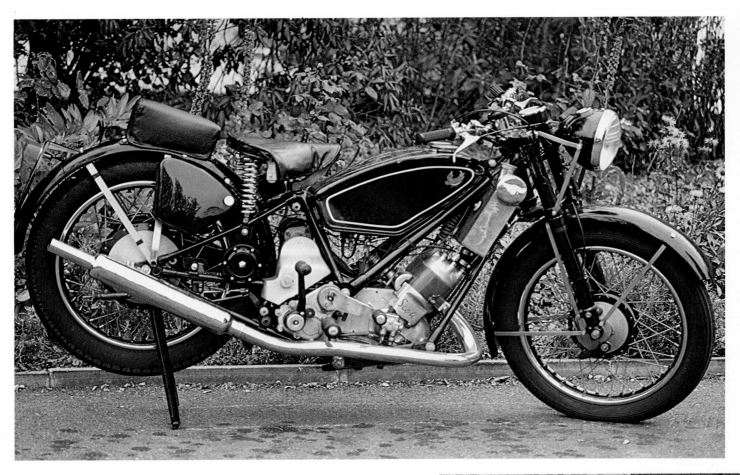

sufficient petrol for the Manx MCC to run a full-scale MGP and the September races afforded the first real opportunity for the fans to get together in a grand and glorious reunion. Of the 133 entrants a high proportion were men who had ridden in the 1938 races and their mounts were mostly veterans retrieved from six idle years of storage, with compression ratios rigged to suit the poor quality pool petrol.

Expectedly, Ken Bills (Norton) won the Junior. Unexpectedly, L. W. Parsons was the Lightweight victor on the last Rudge ever to win an Island race. On his spring-hub, alloy-engined Triumph twin, Eire's jolly farmer Ernie Lyons sprang the biggest surprise when he beat Bills (Norton) by over two minutes to take the Senior prize, averaging 76.73mph in pouring rain and with a broken front down tube. His fastest lap was 78.80mph as against Ken Bills's 1938 record of 86.31mph.

The distinction of organising the first postwar international car and motor cycle show went to France where, in October, at the Paris Salon, there was a brave but not very exciting display of either old or hastily conceived new models. FN featured an unusual type of front fork using a system of coil tension springs and rubber bands.

At the end of the year BSA added a rigid-frame 500cc vertical-twin to its range. Listed as the A7, with an engine not unlike the 1935 Triumph 6T, it fathered a dynasty of Small Heath mounts based on the same layout.

Norton put its roadster international models back in production, together with racing versions classified as the Manx 30 and 40 types. Scott Squirrels (596cc) reappeared; a newcomer in the Lightweight class was the Villiers-engined Norman, made in Ashford, Kent, and the first machine to look like a proper scooter was the Swallow Gadabout, with 4.00 by 8.00-inch tyres and made by Helliwells Ltd at Walsall Airport.

Top: a 1947 two-stroke, water-cooled, 596cc Scott Squirrel roadster

Above: the 1946 Villiers-powered Ambassador

That great leveller of trials men, the British Experts Trial came back to life in November, producing Bob Ray (Ariel) and Harold Tozer (BSA) as the solo and sidecar champions.

Highlights in January 1947 were the return to motor cycle production by the Austrian Puch concern, with its twin-piston two-strokes, and the arrival of a new British marque, Ambassador – Villiers-powered lightweights launched by former car and motor boat world record breaker Kaye Don, from premises near Ascot, Berkshire.

The Milan Show in March held such a wealth of well-engineered, sophisticated machinery that British visitors returned with long faces, muttering prophesies of a revival of the dreaded 'foreign menace'. A centre of interest at Milan was a new 500cc horizontal-cylinder Guzzi, the *Gambalungha* (long leg). Gilera showed its transverse four, shorn of its supercharger but otherwise ready for racing.

The new year also brought news of three important decisions: Bill and Dennis Mansell announced their departure from Norton Motors; the Manufacturers Union declared its intention to hold a show at Earls Court in October; the ACU would reinstate the Tourist Trophy races in June together with a

Below: this is a 1947 example of the Gadabout, a scooter built at the Swallow sidecar factory. Their 123cc Villiers-engined machine attempted to take a large part of the scooter market from the foreign opposition in England, but it did not really succeed

Clubman's TT for sports machines. Entries for the latter would be accepted from affiliated clubs nominating riders who had not entered for any of the 1947 International TT races. Machines were to be as per catalogue and fully equipped except for lighting sets and silencers.

Within three months, the proposed Earls Court show was cancelled. Bottlenecks in supplies and a severe shortage of coal were affecting industry generally and it was more important, said the Union, to maintain output than to develop new models. That did not stop Austrian-born, long-time British citizen, Dr Josef Ehrlich from going ahead with his 350cc EMC twin-piston, split-single, two-stroke machine which he marketed at £191, tax included.

Petrol rationing inevitably shortened the traditional long-distance events. The London-Land's End trial started at Taunton and finished at Perranporth, a route of barely one hundred miles. Instead of starting from Edinburgh, the revived Scottish Six Days Trial was centred on the Highlands town of

Fort William, and Hugh Viney (AJS) began his three-year 'best solo' succession. One-legged Harold Taylor made his best sidecar performance with an Ariel outfit.

The FICM 'no superchargers' rule had put paid to the Velocette Roarer, reckoned to be non-competitive without its blower. For the same reason the AJS V4 was also out, but to replace it the Woolwich firm had an entirely new concept, a 500 dohc, horizontal parallel-twin which, because of its spiky finning, was quickly nicknamed the Porcupine. Initially intended for supercharging and developed by former Triumph expert Freddie Clarke, with Les Graham as chief test pilot, it proved to be a fine, fast machine but, unblown, it never had a chance to reveal its true as-designed potential.

Entries for the first postwar TT closed with a list of 33 Seniors, fifty Juniors and 22 Lightweights. The corresponding

Above: an Ehrlich 348cc bike which was manufactured in 1947 and, top, its engine. The engine is of the twin-piston, single-combustion-chamber type which has the advantage of providing a uni-directional flow of gases from the inlet ports of one cylinder to the exhaust ports in the other. Doctor Josef Ehrlich later dabbled with racing cars

Right: competitors on the shortened London-to-Land's End Trial of 1947, which actually took place between Taunton and Perranporth

182

figures for the new Clubman's series were 33, 23 and eight. There was only one foreign machine in the Senior TT, Freddie Frith's Guzzi twin, and that was soon put out of the picture by an early practice accident. All the Junior riders were on British mounts, including Czechoslovakia's Frans Juhan (Velocette). The Lightweights included Sven Sorensen (Excelsior) from Copenhagen, and three Guzzis in British hands.

Although World War II had been more merciful than World War I in its casualty toll among the racing fraternity, there were some TT riders who would never visit the Island again, among them Walter Rusk, Walter Handley and Harry Lamacraft, all flying men. Civilian victims of the Luftwaffe's vengeance raids on south coast towns were F. W. 'Freddie' Barnes, of Zenith Gradua fame, whose first Isle of Man race was in the 1905 eliminating trials for the International Cup race, and Phil Pike, who rode Levis and Velocette machines from 1914 to 1926 and was a key man in Norton's succession of Maudes Trophy achievements through the early 1920s.

The 1947 Junior TT was a resounding Velocette one-two-three-four victory, led by Bob Foster. Manliff Barrington and Maurice Cann were first and second on Lightweight Guzzis and on the same day the three classes of the Clubman's TT were run concurrently, Eric Briggs and Denis Parkinson on International Nortons being the Senior and Junior winners. After a protest, Bill McVeigh (Triumph) was declared the Lightweight winner.

In the Senior, the old Norton/Velo rivalry was resumed and Harold Daniell had to ride hard to keep ahead of two men making their TT debuts – Artie Bell (Norton) and Peter Goodman (Velocette) who had the fastest lap at 84.07mph. There were 27 starters and among the fourteen finishers were Les Graham (ninth) and Jock West (fourteenth) on the new AJS Porcupines.

Because of a mix-up by the FICM, the Swiss GP, that year's European Championship, was held at Berne while the TT was taking place in the Isle of Man, which accounts for the absence of British works riders in the Grand Prix and of Guzzi

and Gilera in the Island. The Swiss event was a mixture of cars and motor cycles and careless behaviour by members of the eighty-thousand crowd caused many accidents, including the death of Gilera's number one rider, P. Ruggieri, during practising. The Arcore firm withdrew its entries and Tenni (Guzzi) was the 500 class winner. A regular prewar continental circus performer, Fergus Anderson (Velocette) stepped into the limelight by becoming 350 European Champion, and he was also third in an all-Guzzi one-two-three in the Lightweight race.

The FICM's first international rough-riding event, the Motocross des Nations, was a three-cornered fight between Britain, Holland and Belgium, run in July in Holland. Bill Nicholson and Fred Rist (both on BSAs) and Bob Ray (Ariel) narrowly won from the Belgians, whose team leader Auguste Mingels made the best individual performance on an FN.

Reinstated, with its proper title, to the international fixture list, the Ulster GP was run over the shortened Clady course and in the Senior event Artie Bell and Ernie Lyons, on Nortons,

Left: the Isle of Man in 1947 and the start of the Clubman's TT races

Above: one of the first batch of postwar Manx Nortons, this being the example ridden in the 1947 TT by Eric Oliver. He finished ninth at an average speed of 73mph. When its racing career was over this bike was used as a roadster

were first and second ahead of Jock West (AJS Porcupine). Johnny Lockett's Norton led the Velocettes of Les Dear and Bertram Goodman (Peter's cousin) in the Junior, and the 250 Guzzis of Cann and Barrington headed Les Martin's Excelsior.

Back in the Isle of Man, Yorkshire woollen merchant Eric Briggs achieved the remarkable distinction of winning three Mountain Course races in three months, for he added to his Senior Clubman's success a Manx GP 'double' – again on his ultra-reliable Nortons.

While British riders and British machines were upholding British prestige in motor cycling sport, however, the British nation was heading for more trouble. The coal shortage had turned into a general energy crisis and the Government was threatening to withdraw the basic petrol ration. Austerity was back with a vengeance.

The ACU decided it could not afford to support the ISDT, which was being organised by Czechoslovakia, and for the first time since the inception of the trial in 1920 there were no British teams for the Trophy and Silver Vase competitions which were both won by Czech riders.

Thankful that there was no Earls Court show to prepare for, British manufacturers mostly confined their new season's programmes to 'as before' ranges, Ariel being about the only company to introduce new models – the KH Red Hunter and KG deluxe vertical twins.

In October the RAC-ACU Learner Training Scheme was introduced to teach young motor cyclists how to be knowledgeable and safe riders. Financed jointly by RAC and government money, operated by ACU clubs and assisted by gifts of machines from the industry, this very practical scheme had barely started when the blow fell. As from 30 November the basic petrol ration was withdrawn completely and vehicle owners were back where they had been during the war, with empty tanks unless they could justify an entitlement to hard-to-get 'Essential Use' coupons.

For the motor cycle movement the position was critical. There was valuable foreign currency to be earned from an expanding export field, but to obtain overseas orders it was essential to maintain and develop a sound, progressive domestic market. Demonstrating the worth of British motor cycles through competitive events had always been the industry's way of 'improving the breed' and winning respect for its products. Without petrol, home sales dwindled and, without the spur of on-going competition, development would perish.

Eventually the authorities acknowledged the validity of at least a part of these arguments and relented so far as to allow sufficient petrol to be available for the open trials of 1948. There was no mention of fuel for racing. Nevertheless, AMC made a New Year announcement of its over-the-counter 350cc ohc model 7R, the popular Boy Racer, a best-seller from birth and through a long life. At the same time came Triumph Grand Prix models, replicas of Ernie Lyons's Senior MGP-winning machine. The price was £342 18s including the spring hub and the hated purchase tax.

With a fine disregard for petrol problems, Vincent produced the Series B Black Shadow, a 1000cc 110mph roadburner with ebony-anodised crankcase, cylinder barrels and heads, costing £500 plus £81 purchase tax. At the other end of the scale, BSA came out with a 123cc, two-stroke, the pretty, practical little Bantam. At a basic £60 it began a career that many believe ought never to have ended.

Every March since 1937, the American Motorcycle Association had staged important races on the sands of Daytona Beach, Florida. The meeting consisted of two events, a 200-miler for Experts and a 100-miler for Amateurs. A few British machines had appeared in past years, but Harley-Davidson and Indian mounts had always dominated. With an eye to future business in North America, Edward Turner and Gilbert Smith, who had become Norton's chief executive, sent machines to the States for use by American riders – International models from Norton and Grand Prix and Tiger 100 types from Triumph. Harold Daniell's brother-in-law, tuning expert Steve Lancefield, went along to look after Norton interests. The Experts race was won by Floyd Emde on an Indian; a Canadian, Billy Mathews, was second on a Norton, Woody Simmons (Harley-Davidson) was third and a GP Triumph finished sixth. Norton scored a one-two Amateur

Left: Ariel was one of the few manufacturers to introduce new models for the 1948 season, their Red Hunter parallel-twin being one of two shown by the company.

Above: Eric Briggs won three races on the Island in 1947, and is seen here with his Norton, which was victorious in the Junior Manx Grand Prix.

Below: an example of the Vincent-HRD Series C Black Shadow of 1949 – light, low and lean and very fast

success, the riders being Don Evans and Dick Klamfoth.

In the UK, the Easter bank holiday was renamed 'bankrupt holiday' – with no petrol, it was a stay-at-home weekend, but abroad there were no such problems and at the Circuit de Pau race in southern France Fergus Anderson won the 500 class on a Guzzi *Gambalungha*. In the 350 event, he was doing well on the first AJS 7R to come off the production line when the clutch eventually gave up.

Italian champion Tenni was on the TT scene again in 1948 and he easily led the Senior for four laps, one at 88.06mph, but his Guzzi wide-angle twin, not liking pool petrol, turned itself into a single and the outcome was a Norton hat-trick for Bell, Bill Doran and Jock Weddell. Fourth place went to Geoff Murdoch on a 350 AJS 7R, a higher placing than the type had achieved in the Junior, wherein the Velocettes of Frith and Foster beat the Nortons of Bell and Lockett.

In July, the Indian company introduced new models, all of which had a distinctly 'English' look about them. There were two 217cc ohv singles, the Silver and Gold Arrows, and two 490cc vertical twins, the Sport Scout and Super Scout.

Gilera fielded a trio of Italian riders on their new air-cooled, unblown fours in the Dutch TT and their best man, Nello Pagani, finished second to Artie Bell (Norton) with Jock West third on an AJS Porcupine. In the Lightweight class, some Spanish-built Montesa two-strokes made their international racing bow. While practicing for the Swiss Circuit de Berne, Omobono Tenni was killed. Aged 43, he was at the height of a brilliant racing career. He had joined the Guzzi squad in 1934.

In Britain, two new race circuits came into use. On Army land at Blandford, Dorset, the Blackmore Vale club had laid out a 3.2-mile course and the first event there saw Bob Foster the Senior winner on a GP Triumph, with lap speeds exceeding 80mph. In mid Wales, the Eppynt Mountain course (5.2 miles) was set up by local clubs and here the fastest man was Les Graham on an AJS 7R. A Yorkshireman, Don Crossley, who owned a bakery in Ramsey, Isle of Man, was the Senior Manx GP winner on a GP Triumph. On a Velocette he was placed third in the Junior, won by Denis Parkinson (Norton).

It fell to Italy to run the ISDT, over a Riviera course centred on San Remo. It was an exceptionally tough event and only 25 of the 150 starters kept clean sheets. Britain won both the Trophy and the Silver Vase, the team men being, respectively, Allan Jefferies (Triumph), Charlie Rogers (Royal Enfield), Jack Williams (Norton), Hugh Viney (AJS), Vic Brittain (Royal Enfield), Jim Alves (Triumph), Bob Ray (Ariel) and Jack Stocker (Royal Enfield). A feature of the trial was the excellent showing made by the riders of Lambretta and Vespa scooters, machines which by this time were being built in huge quantities by the former aircraft constructors from Italy, Innocenti and Piaggio.

On the Bonneville Salt Flats in Utah, a Hollywood garage mechanic, Roland Free, rode a Vincent Black Lightning at 150.313mph, setting a US national record. Almost concurrently, on the Ostend motorway, Belgium's René Milhoux used another Black Lightning to capture a clutch of world sidecar records, including the standing-start mile which had long been held by Ernst Henne. Milhoux's speed was 94mph. Without the third wheel he covered the flying-start kilometre at 143mph, a Belgian national record. The Series C Black Lightning, with Vincent's patent Girdraulic front fork, cost £508 including tax.

As showtime came around, manufacturers announced their new models. Sunbeam had a cheaper version of the ohc twin, the model S8. Royal Enfield, AMC and Norton all had vertical twins, the Norton Dominator being designed by the much respected Herbert Hopwood.

The show stopper, however, was Velocette's 'Everyman Machine', the LE model, a 150cc water-cooled, side-valve, horizontally opposed-transverse twin. The engine and gearbox unit was contained in a pressed steel frame, with shaft drive and swing-fork rear suspension. Although it never attained its makers' planned output target, it won great respect and affection. Used by many police forces for beat-work, it will always be remembered as the 'Noddy-bike'. Including tax, its price was £126.

The Earls Court show, the first since 1938, ran from 10am to 10pm for six days and drew immense crowds – admittance cost 2s 6d. Two notable absentees among the exhibitors were Brough-Superior and Rudge, both gone forever from the ranks of motor cycle manufacturers.

'And now what about the new year? Petrol . . . the position is less promising than it was twelve months ago. We shall probably get a slight all-round increase in our supplies, but the end of rationing looks to be farther away than ever!' So wrote *Motor Cycling's* commentator 'Carbon' in his New Year review of 1949 prospects. Britain's annual taxation rates were now: under 150cc, 17s 6d; 150–250cc, £1 17s 6d; over 250cc, £3 15s; sidecar, £1 5s extra; threewheeler, £5.

The FICM shortened its name to FIM – Fédèration Internationale Motocycliste – and launched a new points-scoring road-racing World Championship scheme covering 125, 250, 350 and 500cc solo and 600cc sidecar classes. There would be separate titles for the most successful riders and manufacturers in each class, in the Isle of Man TT and in the Grands Prix of Switzerland, Holland, Belgium, Ulster and Italy.

The British Manufacturers Union approved trade support for fifteen open trials and four scrambles, and Norton came out with its first purpose-built trials mount, the 500T model. At Daytona Beach, Norton, under the charge of Francis Beart, had sweeping successes – one-two-three in the Experts race and one-two in the Amateur while, at the Easter Blandford meeting, a young trials and scrambles rider, Geoff Duke, was mixing it with the old hands, Foster, Daniell and Graham, with speeds now up in the nineties. Hugh Viney (AJS) won the Scottish Six Days Trial for the third successive year.

For the TT, Velocette built dohc engines, basically to the same design which had been abandoned after the 1935 breakdown of Stanley Woods's prototype. Two 500s and two 350s were prepared for Nigel Spring's jockeys, Frith and Bills; 350s were issued to Bob Foster (Dickie Wilkins's entry), Ernie Thomas (entered by Ron Harris) and David Whitworth (sponsored by Ted Pink). The new models performed well in the Junior. Frith won the race (for the second successive year), Ernie Lyons, deputising for Bills, was second and Foster was sixth, Bell and Daniell put Norton into third and fourth places and Dubliner Reg Armstrong was fifth on an AJS 7R.

Watched by ACU patron, the Duke of Edinburgh, Harold Daniell (Norton) won the Senior at 86.93mph. Bob Foster (Guzzi twin) made the fastest lap at 89.75mph. Ill luck again hit the AJS Porcupines. Midway through the sixth lap, they were lying first and second. Then, first for Doran and next Graham, came troubles that tumbled them to eighth and tenth finishing places. Their team-mate Reg Armstrong was seventh. The Clubman's TT witnessed a sensational debut for the 350 Gold Star BSAs, Harold Clark scoring the first of eight Junior

Left: Britain took the ISDT Trophy again in 1949, with the same team as in the year before. Here, the Triumph works riders are seen before the event

Below: the unusual LE Velocette of 1949 was powered by a horizontally opposed, twin-cylinder, water-cooled, four-stroke engine of 149cc. It drove through a hand-change, three-speed gearbox and shaft drive. The bike was finished off with enclosed bodywork, leg shields, panniers and a glove box

victories gained by riders of this popular machine. In the Senior Clubman's, Geoff Duke (Norton) began his brilliant reign with an 82.97mph win from Allan Jefferies (Triumph).

By July, Freddie Frith, with his speedy Velocette, had made himself the unbeatable 350cc World Champion. Nevertheless, he went on to score more points in the Ulster GP in which Les Graham gained a thoroughly deserved win on the Porcupine. With wins and fastest laps in the Swiss and Belgian GPs, Eric Oliver (Norton) headed the Sidecar Championship table and at the season's end, league leaders were Les Graham (AJS) in the 500 class, Freddie Frith (Velocette), 350cc, and Eric Oliver (Norton), sidecar. British competition in the 125 and 250cc classes was non-existent. For his clear-cut supremacy and for his contribution to the sport of motor cycling, Freddie Frith became the first rider to be Royally honoured, by admission to the Order of the British Empire.

Wales was once again to host the ISDT and Britain won the Trophy with the same team as in the previous year, except that Fred Rist (BSA) took the place of Jack Stocker; they lost only one mark. A Czechoslovakian team of 125cc CZ riders sacrificed no points to take the Silver Vase.

In the Isle of Man, Geoff Duke (Norton) had his second Mountain Course victory when he won the Senior Manx GP at an average speed of 86.063mph, only 0.865mph outside the 1948 Senior TT winning speed of 86.928mph.

The British vertical-twin was getting bigger. Triumph brought out its 650cc Thunderbird and demonstrated it with an impressive high-speed test at Montlhéry where three machines were subjected to 500 miles of lappery at speeds up in the nineties, with a final burst in which each Thunderbird did a circuit at over 100mph. BSA's 646cc Golden Flash was an immediate success on both sides of the Atlantic.

Montlhéry was in use again when Norton sent Artie Bell, Geoff Duke and Eric Oliver on a speed spree in which they collected 21 world records, the best of which was Bell's 111.88mph for two hours.

The BMCRC, no longer able to use its postwar circuit at Dunholme airfield, ran the first motor cycle race at Silverstone, Northants, in October. Fastest man of the day was Les Graham, who sent his AJS Porcupine round at 90.05mph.

Noel Pope's attempt to take the world's speed record with his all-enclosed Brough-Superior, on the Bonneville Salt Flats, came to grief when the machine went off course, struck some rough ground and capsized, casting Noel out through the roof, fortunately unharmed. The Brough was badly damaged, however, and this gallant attempt had to be abandoned.

At the Silver Jubilee Show – the Manufacturers Union's twenty-fifth since the first at Olympia in 1910 – new marques seen included the Tandon, a London-built product of an Indian designer. First-time visitors to Earls Court were the Jawa company. After a long absence, OEC returned, while Excelsior showed a 250 parallel-twin two-stroke, the Talisman. The exhibition was officially opened by Mr J. L. Callaghan, MP, Parliamentary Secretary to the Ministry of Transport. Although he complimented the industry on its cock-of-the-walk position in the world of sport, he offered no comfort for those who were unfortunately without petrol.

Indeed, as the first half of the twentieth century closed, Britain's roadfarers had their New Year goodwill thoughts soured when they were warned that, although there was a surplus of oil accumulating in sterling area countries, there would be no extra petrol ration for private use.

Chapter 10
The Second Golden Age (1950-1954)

Left: 1954 was the year that the Ariel Square Four was given a redesigned cylinder head with four separate exhaust ports and pipes in a bid to overcome the overheating and consequent distortion which had plagued earlier models

Above: a lightweight CZ of the early 1950s with its tiny two-stroke engine of 125cc. This machine was really of prewar design but was used to get the company on its feet again after the hostilities

Two decades on, the 1950s are described as a golden age for motor cycling, and sometimes, by pedants with memories stretching back to the 'twenties or with a taste for relevant reading, as the *second* golden age – which phrase may not trip so lightly off the tongue but undoubtedly has strict accuracy on its side. There are, in motor cycling terms, parallels and important differences between the 'twenties and the 'fifties. Both were postwar decades, but much of the 1930s had been shadowed by international hostilities. The political tensions and localised conflicts of Europe which led to World War II had pre-empted thoughts and actions for much of two decades. However, 1950 held no threat of war for western Europe, although World War II's after-effects were still in evidence – ironically, in many ways more noticeably in Britain than in those countries which had suffered invasion and occupation.

Britain started the 1950s still with petrol rationing and remnants of other wartime restrictions on food, clothing and confectionery, providing lush conditions for the black marketeers who prosper in over-regulated economies. It was particularly galling for British road-users – enjoined by their betters in government to exercise thrift and discrimination in the use of a meagre fuel ration, while being aware that France, Belgium, Norway, Holland, Russia and Italy were free of all restraint – to learn that Germany had declared its intention of abandoning, in February, any form of petrol rationing.

As the 'fifties began, Britain was almost certainly the largest motor cycle producer in the world ('almost' is inserted in deference to the undisclosed output of the mighty Jawa-CZ combine in Czechoslovakia). The early postwar years had seen major – and, as it was to turn out, in a sense virtually final – changes to the British motor cycle. Putting the matter in *very* broad, terms, it might be said that in the late 1940s the British motor cycle, at around its traditional 500cc displacement, became a parallel-twin, on the Triumph pattern and thereafter, like the dodo, would not change until it became extinct. In 1950, however, that fate was a long way off and the parallel – more often termed vertical-twin, despite a thirteen-year history in familiar Triumph form, seemed fresh and new with 'Royal Enfield', 'Norton', 'AJS' and 'Matchless' on the tank. It was, anyhow, generally agreed to be a great improvement on the industry-old single.

So satisfied were manufacturers with their bulging order books at the time that they did not propose to organise a show at Earls Court. Not that that particular reason was put forward, of course, it being held in motor cycle manufacturing circles, as in other forms of big business, that any such hint of complacency was not the sort of face to present to the public.

If there was to be no motor cycle show in London there were plenty of exhibitions on the continent of Europe, however, and British manufacturers, with financial incentive from the Board of Trade, usually went to the trouble of attending these. At the Paris Salon, the sharp division in design thinking was made clear between the continental makers (particularly the French) who favoured small two-strokes, with almost nothing over 200cc on show, and the British, with their continued emphasis on 350 and over, high-performance machines. In France, the motor-assisted bicycle, finally by consent labelled the cyclemotor, was appearing on the roads in enormous numbers, aided by the absence of insurance and taxation requirements. It should be explained that the term cyclemotor, although by no means as felicitous as the later 'moped', was in fact the right word for the times. In 1950, the typical 50cc two-wheeler was essentially a bicycle, strengthened – or in some cases *not* strengthened – above pedal-cycle standards, and with the tiny engine, usually a two-stroke, attached to front or rear wheel, or to the bottom bracket, and providing scarcely more power than would be available from a pair of reasonably muscular legs.

At the Brussels Show, the home country, its economy in better shape than that of France, was displaying a growing interest in bigger motor cycles. Germany was represented by four concerns, a modest enough showing but significant as a barometer of the Belgians' now dwindling prejudices which had previously insisted on German participation being tucked away in the form of unnamed component parts of Belgian-made models. Now Sachs was showing under its own name, as were DKW, NSU and Bauer. Britain had a little island of sixteen makes at the show.

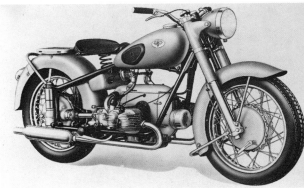

It was the German effort that captured the attention of thoughtful observers of the motor cycle scene. Germany, its industries in ruins not more than four years before, was displaying the qualities that were to push the country to the forefront of Europe, and of most of the world. The Federal Republic had made full use of the 'European Recovery Plan' – a portentous title for aid by way of millions of US dollars – and had negotiated a substantial increase in the number of motor cycles it was allowed to produce (originally pegged at a ludicrously low 10,000 a year, none of which was to be over 250cc). As 1950 began, Germany had achieved an annual output of 82,844 machines, with familiar names like BMW, Horex, Zündapp and NSU settling down to volume production. NSU, in particular, already involved in a profitable arrangement with Lambretta to sell German-made chassis fitted with the Italian scooter engine, demonstrated the formidable dedication of German industry by building and equipping a factory from scratch in just six months, to turn out in March 1950 an initial twenty scooters a day – a prelude to a grandiose but by now quite believable plan to reach 70,000 in the year, which would put the company ahead of any competitor, of any nation. The regeneration of Germany's motor cycling power was evident, too, at the Swiss and, later, the Frankfurt Shows.

If the British had reason to be apprehensive about Germany, nobody in western Europe attached much importance to the far-off activities of Japan, whose sole incursion into the

headlines in 1950 was to receive a mild ticking-off for pirating designs from BSA and Lucas to slip into world markets.

A further parallel with the 1920s was to be seen, admittedly in somewhat diminished form and from beyond Britain's shores. Thirty years before, following World War I, British factories had produced a rash of open-frame scooters, for the most part ill-conceived, badly made and underpowered, which lasted a few years. Now, in 1950, Britain had just one scooter in production, the Villiers-powered Swallow Gadabout. The continentals were showing great interest in the form, turning out thousands of Vespas, Lambrettas and NSU-Lambrettas. The Italians even pre-empted what might have been a typically British compromise between motor cycle and scooter with the Guzzi Galletto, a machine with bigger-than-scooter wheels, enclosure for engine and transmission and an open frame giving protection for the rider's legs. The British manufacturers were not impressed by scooters – some with long memories cited the post-World War I 'bubble' – and refused to take them seriously until the late 'fifties, by which time foreign imports were too firmly established to be dislodged by the home industry's efforts to turn out a comparable product.

On the sporting side, the road-race World Championships, introduced the previous year, were to be held over seven meetings, beginning as before with the Isle of Man TT and continuing over the French, Belgian, Swiss, Ulster, Dutch and Italian Grands Prix. The 1950 series remains notable for the international debut of Geoff Duke on a new motor cycle frame, usually a faintly mundane item but this one was designed by the McCandless brothers, Rex and Cromie, and dubbed 'Featherbed'. By realistic standards it was not a very apt nickname, but 'Featherbed' still rings a bell with motor cyclists

Above left: Les Graham seen in 1950, a year after becoming World Champion

Above: Geoff Duke with Norton in the Swiss GP at Berne in 1950

Left: the 598cc K 601 Zündapp of 1950, with Earles-type fork

Below: Les Graham, No 62, heads for victory as seven competitors come to grief in the 350cc race at Berne, Switzerland, in 1950

of all ages many years after the last Norton frame of this type was built. What the Featherbed did, with some little help from Duke *et al*, was to inject a further winning streak into the fortunes of Norton Motors just when the pundits were writing off the racing chances of that great concern. Its venerable double-knocker single, housed in the tall, vibratory, accident-prone frame had in the later years of its long life acquired a soubriquet as striking as 'Featherbed', although rather less complimentary: the 'Garden Gate' Norton, after its 'lucky' win in the 1949 Isle of Man Senior TT, had evidently come to the end of the road.

British race followers, however, hoping for new machines from Norton, cherished ideas of radical developments in engine technology . . . multi-cylinders, rare and complicated valve mechanisms, convoluted carburation: something like the other British contender, the AJS Porcupine, but successful this time because, after all Norton, and Joe Craig, would be making it; something to outshine the exotica from MV, Gilera

and Guzzi. Instead, here were the same (well, almost the same) old engines – much loved, but tame stuff compared with the foreign multis – set in an oddly named frame which appeared to be the only really new part of the bikes. The combination was to work wonderfully well, though. The behaviour of the Featherbed chassis in the hands of riders of the calibre of Duke, Lockett, Bell and, later, Commonwealth stars like Ken Kavanagh and Ray Amm, permitted the last vestige of power from the still formidable single (regularly uprated, year by year, through meticulous detail modifications) to get to the road. So, the Nortons fought off the Italian fours till almost the middle of the decade, and nowhere was the Norton better able to hold its own than on the narrow, bumpy $37\frac{3}{4}$ miles of the Mountain circuit of the Isle of Man.

There Norton achieved a tremendous double: a double treble you could call it, with the 1950 machines coming home first, second and third in both Junior and Senior events. The 'new boy', Duke, took the 500 race at 92.27mph and made the

Top left: Umberto Masetti, who was twice 500cc World Champion with the Gilera four-cylinder racers

Left: another Gilera racer of the early years of the World Championship series was Nello Pagani, who was runner-up to Les Graham in 1949. Nello had the consolation of riding a Mondial to the 125cc title of that same year

Above: the start of an era – Geoff Duke pilots a Featherbed Norton in its debut event at Blandford Camp in 1950

fastest lap at 93.33mph, nearly $2\frac{1}{2}$mph over the longstanding 1938 record of Harold Daniell (who was to announce his retirement, after sixteen years of racing, at the end of TT week with a 1950 tally of third place in the Junior and fifth in the Senior). The 350 race went to Artie Bell, with Duke second. Again, race and lap records were established. In the Lightweight, another sort of record was set . . . after seven laps, $264\frac{1}{4}$ miles, the time difference between the winner, Dario Ambrosini on a dohc Benelli single, and second man Maurice Cann (Guzzi) amounted to just one-fifth of a second!

Then, in the second round of the World Championship series, things began to go wrong; mainly for Norton. At the Belgian Grand Prix, on the very fast Spa-Francorchamps circuit, Duke seemed a certain winner, although early on it had become apparent that on such an open course the merits of the Featherbed allied to the single's ever-usable torque were simply not enough to overcome the sheer power of the Gilera fours. Only Duke's extraordinary skills were keeping him ahead, but then his rear tyre let him down, the tread flailing along the road in long ribbons. The Italian riders Mello Pagani and Umberto Masetti on the Gileras, were unaffected and carried on to finish first and second. New-mix tyres were made available for the next meeting, the Dutch TT, but on this occasion *all* the British 500 factory racers were sidelined by disintegrating treads, with Duke suffering a 100mph crash as his tyre shredded on a fast bend. For the next event, Norton used another make of tyre and there was no repetition of the trouble.

At this stage in the season, it became clear that Norton was going to be very lucky to take the 500 rider's title in the championship (it was not to be: Duke ended one point behind Masetti with the Gilera). The firm's initial walkover with the 'new' 350 in the Island, if not a fluke, was definitely not to be taken as a portent of its chances against the spindly, girder-forked, but amazingly fast, Velocette of Bob Foster, now Hall Green's number one (teamed with Bill Lomas and Cecil Sandford). Foster went on to beat Duke and the Norton by thirty points to 24, with the separate manufacturers' title going to Veloce Ltd.

As 1950 ended, the statisticians recorded four million cars registered in Britain and something over 700,000 motor cycles. Demand was unabated in both categories, but only motor bikes could be supplied in anything like a reasonable time. Now, a typical 500cc single cost around £160, a twin about £50 more, with the most expensive British roadster, the 120mph Vincent Black Shadow, rising to £400. Appearing on the British market for the first time since prewar days, BMW comfortably topped anybody else's price with the £450 demanded for their R67 flat-twin. No English maker having the prospect of apparently unlimited sales was going to put himself to the expense of designing and developing radically new motor cycles. Long experience – the top men in the industry were, in the main, those who had been in charge or coming up fast in the 1930s – had shown that the motor cyclist in the street was eminently conservative in his tastes, reluctant to put down money on luxuries like shaft drive or enclosure or, come to that, on multis with cylinders adding up to more than two (and those two had preferably to look, Triumph-style, like one).

The Earls Court Show of 1951 did not reveal any spectacular fruits from the makers' two-year seclusion. Everything appeared to be much as before except that everything was a little duller on account of a shortage of nickel for use in the chromium-plating process. To see new motor cycles in full glitter-glory it was necessary to go to continental shows like that at Frankfurt where the organisers had filled twelve large halls with their own and other nations' offerings.

At the Show, opened by the Minister of Transport for the new Conservative Government that in one form or another was to lead the country throughout the 1950s, an impartial observer might have noted that the only big change was in the cyclemotor representation, up from nil two years before to over a dozen makes, some of them British – including one comprising an engine built into a rear wheel and marketed by EMI. Price for these attachments was around £25, going up to £50-plus when a bicycle was thrown in with the engine.

Attracting very little notice among British motor cyclists,

Top: Ivor Arber leaps Ballaugh Bridge with his International model Norton on his way to victory in the 1951 Senior Clubman's TT at the Isle of Man

Above: Carlo Ubbiali gets his 125cc Mondial under way in the Ultra-Lightweight TT of 1951. Carlo came second in the race to team-mate Cromie McCandless, but went on to take the World Championship of that year

Right: one of a crop of cyclemotors which appeared at Earls Court in 1951 was the British Cyclemaster

who when they wanted a small machine thought almost exclusively in terms of a small motor cycle, was the launching of of the British-made Vespa scooter and its compatriot from Italy, the Lambretta. The Vespa was made under licence in Bristol by Douglas. Soon these bulbous, curvy machines were seen in increasing numbers. Not ridden by the 'traditional' motor cyclist, who might be identified by enveloping 'storm coat', waders, goggles and cap, but by people who were (to judge by their lightweight clothing, often light-coloured too which would have been an anathema to any seasoned rider used to the grubbiness implicit in motor cycle ownership, and by their sometimes shaky riding) refugees from bus and tube travel.

The scooter, with small wheels, open chassis, rear-mounted engine – for the Vespa, the Lambretta's was further amidships – did not give the accurate steering of the best motor cycles, but the modest speeds it attained did not demand high standards. More important, the people attracted to scooters did not have other two-wheeler experience to throw up odious comparisons. By 1952 Douglas was selling so many of its £100 models – 150 to 200 a week were the figures quoted – that it was able to introduce a special sidecar for attachment to the scooter.

As Douglas-Vespa and the concessioned Lambretta began to explore the potential of the UK market, with almost predictable timing the Swallow Gadabout, sole home-grown example of the breed, was withdrawn from circulation. Possibly it was a case of fine judgment on the part of the makers, fearful for the Gadabout's fate in competition with the newcomers, but this is doubtful for there have been few instances of modesty in the history of the British motor cycle industry.

Before proceeding, reference must be made to the sidecars shown at Earls Court in single-seater, child-adult and double-adult form: dozens of them, all basically unsociable so far as relations with the driver were concerned and most of them distinctly uninviting for anybody who had not recently graduated from pillion-riding and might be assumed to be grateful for protection from wind and rain. Yet the sidecar outfit had charms, especially for the enthusiast, in inverse ratio to its looks and practicality. In certain – usually bad – conditions the manner in which it could be hustled through corners was rewarding beyond rational explanation. They were cheap, and special terms were available from insurance companies which (inexplicably to any novice driver) classed the sidecar outfit as extra-safe; perhaps it was because most sidecar drivers were *not* novices, were middle-aged or older, had family responsibilities, and did not drive at all quickly. Money was not plentiful, and the Issigonis Mini was eight years away. Sober, decent, hard-up motor cyclists, with a family and a loyalty to two wheels, attached sidecars to their long-suffering motor bikes, briefly bemoaned the consequent loss of performance (about twenty per cent) and thereafter happily endured worsening steering as the all-important alignment of 'chair' and bike deteriorated.

The sidecar carried on through the 1950s, a few single-seater examples attaining a sort of beauty, but more often suffering appalling exaggeration as manufacturers threw reason to the winds and expanded bodywork to grotesque size, overshadowing the biggest motor bike and depressing performance almost to scooter level. Near the end of the decade this weird mutation met the hot breath of the £500 Mini and overnight – for all practical sales purposes – took to innumerable back gardens and died.

In racing it was Geoff Duke's year. His Nortons, modified

197

from the previous season towards 'square' bore and stroke, with better braking and ignition, carried him to victory in the Isle of Man Senior and Junior TTs and finally to the head of the World Championship tables, with Norton taking the manufacturers' class. Eric Oliver and Norton again carried off the sidecar awards. An addition to the TT programme was the Ultra-Lightweight (125) TT, run over two laps of the Mountain course and won by Cromie McCandless (Mondial). The extent of Norton's reliance on Duke's talents may be gauged from the presence of three riders of four-cylinder machines among the first six finishers in the championship and the lowly sixth place of the next best Norton, ridden by Reg Armstrong. At the Italian Grand Prix, on the ultra-fast Monza autodrome, the first three men, on Gileras, were obviously much faster than fourth man Duke. A year later the highest-ranking Norton 500 in the World Championship was ridden by third placed Armstrong behind the Italian multis of Masetti and Les Graham. The latter had left AJS for MV Agusta where in his role of development engineer-rider he persuaded the factory to replace the original telescopic forks with the pivoted-fork system designed by brilliant Ernie Earles of Birmingham.

If some British race followers had reservations about national fortunes on the international scene, there was plenty to enthuse about at home, with over-subscribed entry lists for a vast spread of short-circuit meetings. In rough-riding too, Britain's prestige was high. At this time 'scrambles' was the English word and 'motocross' the term favoured by continentals. A few English riders regularly competed in motocross events across the Channel, enjoying little of the renown of a later generation of motocross men and rather less of their considerable financial rewards. In 1952 the Belgians persuaded the FIM to introduce a season-long motocross competition on the lines of the road-race championships, with the British to transform the old-established Cotswold Scramble into the 'British Grand Prix de Moto-Cross' in 1953. For the moment, though, at the Moto-Cross des Nations, the main team event of the year, the British team, including such excellent riders as Geoff Ward, John Avery, Jack Stocker, Bill Nicholson, Brian Stonebridge and Les Archer, had to be content with second place to Belgium.

Held around Varese, the 1951 ISDT was, despite the best efforts of the Italian organisers to throw everything into confusion, another victory for British riders in the main

Top: Geoff Duke working hard at Monza in 1951 found that the handling of his Norton was no match for the sheer power of the Gileras of Milani, Masetti and Pagani. Geoff had the consolation of taking that year's world title

Above: 39-year-old Wilhelm Herz gets ready to take the bike speed record with his 500cc NSU in April 1951. He reached his goal with a speed of 180mph

Right: the Excelsior Talisman as it appeared in late 1952, featuring a 250cc, two-stroke, twin-cylinder engine

Trophy competition, with a second place in the Silver Vase.

Record-breaking was the medium which Germany, recently admitted to the FIM, chose for its return to the world stage in motor cycling. On 12 April the NSU company had run a magnificently organised, utterly confident attack on various world records over a stretch of the Munich-Ingoldstadt autobahn. Wilhelm Herz took a supercharged dohc 500 NSU, encased in a long, graceful, wind-tunnel-tested 'shell', over the course to push the world's maximum up to 180mph, and then with a change of engine put the 350 solo figure up to 173.3mph and the 350 sidecar to 116.1mph. Culmination of months of in-depth planning, and reflecting the no-expense-spared methods of the German industry in matters of international prestige, this demonstration further pointed up the contrast with the gallant but essentially amateur approach of English sportsmen interested in world records who had to rely on out of date and mainly untested machinery and limited financial backing.

At the Brussels Salon, Britain was level-pegging with Germany at around seventeen makes each, but a few weeks later, at the influential Swiss Show, the Germans were in the ascendency with 25 makers showing their latest wares against twenty from Italy and thirteen from Britain. Never short of ready money to gratify transport/pleasure whims, the Swiss had, for several of the postwar years, been good customers for British imports. Now they had switched allegiance to Germany and Italy, with the UK trailing a poor third. Part of the reason was undoubtedly the continental concentration on scooters. Further new models in the genre at Geneva were German Goggo, Austrian Puch and French Terrot. Britain had nothing to show. *Motor Cycling* was prompted to devote a short leading article to the matter, headed 'Scooter sales abroad cannot be ignored', which sounded the right note but fell on deaf ears.

Later in the year, at the Earls Court Show opened by the Duke of Edinburgh, English reaction to the worldwide demand for small capacity two-wheelers was seen in Edward Turner's new design for an overhead-valve 150, the first under-350cc Triumph to be made for many years and a clear indication as to the thinking of the most successful English designer of the day. The Terrier was in effect a scaled-down big motor cycle which, whether or not its designer acknowledged the fact, was likely to appeal exclusively to the motor cycle enthusiast forced, for financial reasons, to trade down from a bigger machine, and to new riders who would eventually graduate to 350s and 500s.

The British manufacturer could not be blamed for ignoring scooters. His products, meeting resistance in foreign markets because of State-imposed restrictions allied to a wavering in customer loyalty in favour of emerging continental designs, were largely diverted to the home market where there was no shortage of buyers for excellent, well engineered – if a little dated – models. They varied from the odd-looking 98cc Auto-cycle, a throw-back to a type popular in prewar days and still listed by many makers, through 125 two-strokes, a 250 twin two-stroke (Excelsior Talisman), 500 ohv singles (Norton, AJS, BSA, Ariel, Royal Enfield), 500 and 650 ohv twins, ohc 'race bred' singles and ohc twins (the refined, elegant Sunbeam), a 600 water-cooled two-stroke twin, the Scott, which could not be said to be freely available to anyone, at home or abroad, but *might* be obtained by dint of pleading or the promise of lots of ready money from the idiosyncratic manufacturers in Birmingham) up to the latest, all-alloy, four-port Ariel Square Four and the magnificent 150mph vee-twin Vincent Black Lightning selling at £504. In all, there were around forty makers, some of them having only tenuous connections with 'pure' motor cycling but through tax/insurance affinities or immemorial custom accepted under the 'motor cycle' heading,

Throughout the 'fifties there was no shortage of press reports about brave new designs, some of extraordinary complexity. Some indeed, like the brainchild of talented John Wooler – he of the Wooler family whose 'Flying Banana' model was still remembered from the 1920s – were said to be poised for deliveries on such and such a date: April 1953 was the appointed time for Mr Wooler's shaft-drive four which, in its several developing forms, had tantalised an expectant public for more than four years. No deliveries were made in April that year, or, indeed ever, but it was a beautiful, clever design years ahead of anything on the market, at home or abroad.

Bottom: Wooler spent many years enticing the public with their four-cylinder, shaft-drive superbikes, this being their 1953 flat-four design. Below, is a close-up of the camshaft layout of the similar engine of 1950, which differed in that its cylinders were in pairs mounted vertically

In the 1952 road-race series, Italian fours, as indicated earlier, proved too good for English singles and twins – at least, in the 500 class. Duke, after being sidelined by clutch trouble when leading the Senior TT (which Norton won anyway with Reg Armstrong coming home a fraction ahead of Graham), lost by yards to Masetti on the Gilera in the succeeding Dutch and Belgian events; then he crashed in a minor German event and was out of action for the season.

Italy in fact had a very successful year in all classes of the eight event championships other than the 350 and the sidecar. Among the 350s, AJS and Norton made all the running, with Duke collecting four wins straight off, before his crash, and finishing the season well clear of Armstrong, the runner-up, with Ray Amm (Norton) third. Among the three-wheelers England had found a new champion – a World Champion, as it turned out – during the temporary eclipse of Eric Oliver, long master of the class. Surviving on the minimum of factory support, Cyril Smith took his Norton-Watsonian through in close company with Alfredo Milani (Gilera), making up for his lack of speed with a blend of skill and doggedness.

While the Italian factories conducted internecine war in the smaller capacity classes, on the periphery, watching the Latins – and English – desport, were the riders of one or two distinctly promising German machines, of which more later.
MV Agusta had abandoned shaft drive in favour of chain for its big four and this, with the adoption of the Earles fork, helped to turn the 150mph monster into a much more predictable handler on all types of course. All the main contenders in the 250 and over classes were equipped with pivoted-fork rear suspension, including the latest BMW which picked up a solitary point at the German Grand Prix but appeared at very few other meetings; already the horizontally opposed power plant and shaft-drive transmission were proving more suited to the demands of sidecar racing. The 500 AJS twin had lost its 'Porcupine' finning and had been developed in a number of minor ways which did not appear to be giving much practical benefit, for the best New Zealand rider Rod Coleman could achieve was fourth place in the championships. He repeated this placing, incidentally, in the 350 table, but on a more radically modified AJS, the new three-valver (with one large inlet valve and two smaller exhausts) which, though only marginally faster than its two-valve predecessor, was very reliable, and ripe for a great deal of further development.

The Italian models dominating the 125 and 250cc classes – MV, Mondial and Guzzi – were all singles with valves (except on the 248 Guzzi) actuated by twin camshafts. Only NSU of Germany fielded a four-stroke twin, the dohc 250, but this was arguably the fastest in its class, and DKW had a two-stroke twin. Despite DKW's adherence to the form – in addition to the 250 twin it entered very accelerative, and noisy, 350 threes in some championship events – two-strokes were largely discounted at this time in racing circles, and on the showing of the 125 Spanish Montesas they deserved to be.

In 1953 the build-up of the British industry continued, with big firms going on to notch up respectable trading profits which were the more notable for occurring during a period when British industry generally was beginning to feel the weight of overseas competition. AMC Limited were to finish the year with £234,540 in hand (though in fact this was a drop from the previous year's figure) and Royal Enfield with £79,000.

Road-racing was especially interesting in 1953, with the long-postponed takeover by the continental constructors no

Above: Geoff Duke leads Sigi Wuensche's three-cylinder, two-stroke DKW at a minor 350cc race at Schottenring in July 1952. A broken transmission chain caused Duke's Norton to crash and it effectively put him out of racing for that season. The race was won by Ray Amm, who can just be seen at the top of the picture, on another Norton (No. 85)

Overleaf: the 1952 Ariel HT5 of trials ace Sammy Miller. This 260lb machine was one of the most successful competition machines of all, winning, among other things, every major trial between 1961 and 1964

longer to be denied, except by Eric Oliver and Cyril Smith who finished first and second among the sidecars on their Nortons. Geoff Duke had announced that he was to continue with Norton, thereby moving no less than *The Times* to write, 'The decision of this superlative rider to continue to race British machines will be widely applauded . . . that he has put his country's prestige to the forefront is wholly to his credit. Sadly, Duke made an eleventh hour switch to Gilera, just before the opening round of the nine-event championships, and thereafter rode the four to such purpose that he finished the season as 500 World Champion, ahead of Armstrong, who had accompanied Duke to Gilera, and Milani on the third-place 'four'. In the TT, however, Norton was magnificently served by Australian Ken Kavanagh and Rhodesia's Ray Amm. The latter, riding conventional 'naked' models instead of the streamlined 'kneeler' he had appeared on in practice, won both the Senior (after Duke had crashed) and Junior TTs at record speeds. Future TT winner and World Champion, 19-year-old John Surtees, due to make an appearance as a Norton works rider, was sidelined by a practice accident. In the line-up on the Island there were, apart from Gilera and Norton, 125 and 250 NSUs, which were second in their TT races and then carried off both championships, in the hands of Werner Haas. There were three-cylinder 350 DKWs, even noisier than before but not significantly faster. There was the in-line four-cylinder Guzzi, technically interesting, with fuel injection and varying degrees of streamlining. On occasion this displayed enormous speed but more often struck trouble, finishing no higher than fourth in the manufacturer's table. There were fuel-injected BMWs which thereafter appeared only infrequently while development proceeded at Munich, and there was the MV Agusta, vastly improved over previous seasons but, following the death of Les Graham, on the second lap of the Senior TT, seldom to be seen on European circuits during 1953. One other, very successful, design must be mentioned: the 350 Guzzi single, which was in essence the 250 (itself pretty long in the tooth) bored out, operating on sohc, and somehow proving devastatingly fast. It was altogether too much for the British entries which had, hitherto, considered the 350cc class a national prerogative. Comfort of a sort could be derived from the fact that the Italian factory had the good sense to choose an English rider, the veteran Fergus Anderson, as its racing *chef d'equipe*, and that it was he who ended the season as 350cc World Champion.

Apart from advances in engine technology, the 1953 series marked the makers' deepening interest in streamlining as a source of vital miles per hour. If Norton preferred not to persevere with its streamliner in the Grands Prix, it was ready to use it when all-out speed was the main consideration. At Montlhéry (just before the Earls Court Show, for maximum publicity) Joe Craig, Eric Oliver and Ray Amm, appeared with several streamliners and a few changes of engine, eventually to depart after setting records as various as the One Hour (350) at 124.3mph and 100 Miles (500) at 133mph. The final tally amounted to 61 records. The Nortons were standard factory racers, plus streamlining, running on alcohol-compatible compression ratios. After the scares and disappointments with tyres in the 1952 series and instances of chain breakages – the most notable being Armstrong's as he crossed the line to win the Senior TT – great satisfaction was felt at the impeccable performance of the latest Avon tyres and Perry chains.

After several years of dominating the event, Britain suffered a severe setback in the International Six Days Trial.

with a new Trophy team captain, the vastly experienced Hugh Viney, and a new team member in Bob Manns. There was a great deal of well organised competition among the entry of 262 which gathered at Bad Aussee in Austria, but what beat the British team was a run of mechanical breakdowns (ignition and gearboxes being the main culprits) which helped to reduce the UK effort from 55 starters to about 27 finishers, of whom seventeen won gold medals. The only bright spot was the performance of three standard 500 A7 BSA Star Twins in the hands of Norman Vanhouse, Fred Rist and Brian Martin who took in the ISDT as part of a long, ACU-observed attempt to gain the Maudes Trophy. They were deservedly successful and finished the trial with no loss of marks.

The Czechoslovak-run Trial the following year was a wonder of efficient organisation, with a 1500-mile course centred on Gottwaldov being ridden by 247 competitors from eighteen nations, the British accounting for 23, the host country for 48 and South Africa for one. Britain's Trophy team of Jack

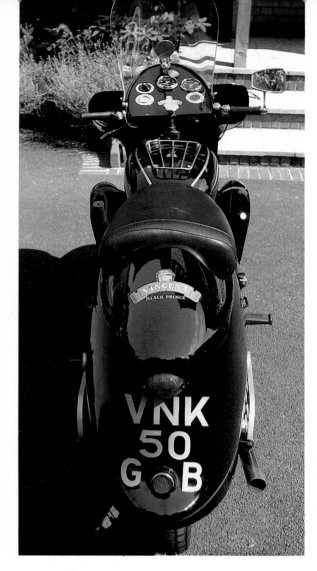

Top left: Eric Oliver and Stanley Dibben
with their Norton-Watsonian outfit just before
the start of the 1953 Belgian GP

Left: a 1956 BSA A7 500cc Shooting Star

Above: the faired Series D version of the
Black Shadow Vincent was called the Black
Prince. This is a 1955 example

Below: an Indian Big Chief 80 of 1953

Stocker and Johnny Brittain (500 Royal Enfields), Jim Alves
(650 Triumph), Manns (500 Matchless) and Viney (500 AJS)
lost not a single mark and won from Czechoslovakia, although
that country's riders were able to demonstrate that their small
capacity machines were much better placed to gain bonus
marks at the final speed tests than were the big twins of the
English. A similar situation prevailed in the Silver Vase, except
that Czechoslovakia's showing with her 150 CZs, and
Poland's with her 250 Jawas, during the speed test did in fact
push Britain out of the lead, down to third position.

In general, British manufacturers had little to worry about
and, as in previous years, small incentive to alter their products
beyond a judicious face-lifting to justify another appearance at
Earls Court, pages of detailed description in the two British
weekly journals, and – possibly – another modest price rise. Two
British-made scooters were announced: the Dayton Albatross,
a large-bodied 250 with a pivoted front fork, and the Harper
Scootamobile, powered by a Villiers 197, which was on the big
side too, but marginally less awkwardly styled than the Dayton.
Neither, however, was the work of a big motor cycle concern
(Harper's interests were in aviation, Dayton was famous for
pedal cycles) and it was clear that the industry still did not
consider scooters as worthy of its attention.

It is of course easy, and thus inviting, to dwell on the
complacency displayed by the manufacturers during this decade
of big sales. A reluctance to face a charge of being wise after
the event should not, however, deter a reviewer from pursuing
the matter a little further, at least to the extent of listing some of
the continental designs that graced overseas exhibitions during
1954 – and these not, in the main let it be noted, for scooters.
At Milan, for instance, there was the beautifully styled 304cc
ohv twin Gilera, a 175 ohc Ferrari twin, the SIM Ariete – a
150 two-stroke with shaft drive and rear wheel suspended on a
massive, light-alloy swing arm, the Capriole Cento with
horizontally-opposed 150 twin power unit, the 98cc Ducati
Sport (with oil cooler), a Sessa two-stroke, its rear suspension
controlled by torsion bar, the superbly practical 98cc Guzzi
Zigolo, Rumi's two-stroke twin and, of course, plenty of
relatively conventional, high-quality machinery like the 175
ohc Mondial and the MV Agusta. Rear-chain enclosure was
common and gearboxes were invariably in unit with the engine.

There was at least one parallel between developments
among road machines and racers in 1954, and that concerned
streamlining, which began to take over in earnest in the racing
world (as will be shown) and filtered through to the 'world's
fastest production motor cycle', the big-twin Vincent, which
ended the year with glassfibre bodywork and name of
Black Prince. Victor was the title for the 500 single, but because
of the fairly complete nature of the coachwork, there was little
to distinguish the two externally. With an integral windscreen
and built-in leg-shielding to complete the new look, the Black
Prince provided high-speed transport with freedom from the
strain ordinarily imposed by wind and temperature. The year
saw much activity in the Stevenage concern for these all-Vincent
models followed a tie-up, some months earlier, between the
English company and NSU of Germany in which the German
machines were 'anglicised' by Vincent – mainly by the fitting of
short, straight handlebars, dual seat and mudguards – for sale
on the British market. Another variation on Vincent enclosure,
for a very different purpose, was designed by expatriate Scot
Robert Burns, a resident of New Zealand, and fitted to his
secondhand 1951 big-twin. With the bike thus adorned, a third

'sidecar' wheel on the left, and a few telling improvements to engine tune, Burns thundered along to a new world's fastest record of 155mph, 1mph over the existing NSU figure and a marvellous effort for an under-financed, private venture. His friend, Russell Wright, set national solo records with another Vincent, in unstreamlined form.

The most notable record-breaking attempt, however, was undertaken by NSU, again on the Munich–Ubgoldstadt autobahn where, in April, Gustav Baumm, lying almost flat on his back in a nine feet long, thirty-inch wide, 'cigar' took various records with engines ranging from 50 to 98cc. Baumm demonstrated the wind-cheating properties of a properly designed streamlined shell which could be nursed along by modest power to sensational speeds. With the biggest of his engines installed, he achieved 111.2mph for the flying mile, and with the fifty he achieved 79.4mph over the same distance.

It was almost an anti-climax for BMW to trundle along from Munich to Ingoldstadt, about a month after NSU, and turn in eight and nine-hour figures of 103.3mph and 102.7mph. Much later in the year, BMW's sidecar champion, Wilhelm Noll, came to the same stretch of road for record-breaking sessions culminating in the ten kilometres at 132.6mph. One wonders what the Fatherland's businessmen, constantly re-routed, thought of all this disruption to normal traffic.

Streamlining began to be the rage among the race camps. Geoff Duke was reported as saying (apropos what was not made clear, but an educated guess would suggest Moto Guzzi), 'When a standard machine allegedly producing only 45bhp can hold and even pass an unstreamlined machine turning out 65bhp, only a fool would refuse to bow to the inevitable'. Duke was no fool; he, and Gilera, bowed but only, in 1954, to a limited extent. The Gilera usually carried only vestigial streamlining – side panels, no more; not until late in the season, at the Italian Grand Prix, did it appear in anything nearing full enclosure. Duke won at an average of 111.46mph.

Moto Guzzi was setting the pace with all enveloping streamlining developed at the company's wind tunnel at Mandello. It was, as Duke had indicated rather bitterly, so effective that the horizontal single-cylinder engine, as old as the Manx Norton and producing by current race standards only moderate power in any of its 250, 350 or 500cc forms, was retained by Guzzi throughout the season. In the 500 class that was at the expense of the more powerful, but temperamental, in-line four and in 350 form it proved good enough to give Fergus Anderson his second championship title. In the 125 and 250 classes, however, NSU were too fast for the Italians; indeed these remarkable dohc machines, turning out 33bhp in 250 twin-cylinder form, or 17bhp as a 125 single, were so powerful that they might have won the day without benefit of streamlining, but the Germans were taking no chances anyway and continued to experiment with fairings throughout the year, appearing with successive versions ranging from side panels plus a beak-like projection over the front wheel, through a blunt, stepped enclosure that covered most of the front wheel, and finishing with a smoother, more comprehensive version of form number two. The young Rupert Hollaus on the NSU won the Isle of Man Ultra Lightweight race, over ten laps of the new 10.79-mile Clypse circuit, by just four seconds from Ubbiali on the MV. He went on to score four Grand Prix wins, enough to give him the maximum count of 32 points and the championship title, before he died in a crash at the Italian Grand Prix at Monza. Haas again took the 250cc title.

The factory Nortons were almost as outlandish-looking as the previous year's 'kneelers' had been, though in reality the latest models, with high nose-fairing protruding beyond the wheel's circumference, were less of a departure from conventional practice. In his annual quest for more horses, Joe Craig had moved the flywheel to the great outdoors – like Guzzi many years before – which allowed the crankcase to be narrower and more rigid, in support of Norton's ever-shortening stroke, now down to 90mm for the 500 and to 78mm for the 350. Against logical expectation, but aided by an incalculable boost in the never-say-die riding style of Ray Amm, Norton very nearly pulled off another Senior/Junior double. A broken cam-follower took Amm out of the lead at the 13th Milestone on the final lap of the Junior, which let Rod Coleman – riding a three-valve AJS, unstreamlined beyond the effect given by a deep pannier tank – into the lead. It was the first Junior win for AJS since 1922, and another three-valver, ridden by Derek Farrant, was second.

The Senior, on the Friday of race week, though it provided a win for Norton and Ray Amm, was not a happy occasion. It began in rain, and was run in rain throughout, the first Senior to be so affected since 1934. On Stewards' orders it was stopped after 1¾ hours and four laps, one lap over half-distance. At this point Amm had taken the lead from Duke who had paused to refuel after his third circuit. The Rhodesian was declared the winner, with Duke as second man; Jack Brett (Norton) was third and Armstrong fourth. All of which was unsatisfactory to the principals and to their thousands of fans – to Duke partisans, in particular, who were by no means convinced that 'their' man would have been down at number two after a full seven laps. Protests were handed in to the ACU, but it appeared that race regulations had been complied with in the decision to allow the fourth-lap order to stand. So Amm was confirmed as winner, the fourth man (after Charlie Dodson, Stanley Woods and Duke) to take two consecutive Senior TTs.

Another – much happier – novelty marked the 1954 TT programme. This was the re-introduction, after thirty years, of the Sidecar TT, held over ten leps of the Clypse course and won, appropriately, by evergreen Eric Oliver who, with a fully streamlined Norton-Watsonian, outdrove his German rivals on BMW outfits. Oliver went on to win the Ulster and Belgian Grands Prix but, in taking only a further two points from the remaining three events catering for sidecars, dropped his end-of-season total to 26, four behind Noll who had notched wins in the German, Swiss and Italian Grands Prix and a next-best second place to Oliver in the Belgian. This was the beginning of a foreign, mainly German, domination of world-class sidecar racing, that was not to be interrupted for 23 years. Duke carried on winning after his Isle of Man hiccough and took no fewer than five Grands Prix by the end of the season to give himself his fifth World Championship, Amm managed two second places later in the year and ended as runner up, with Kavanagh, on the Guzzi, four points further down, third. At home, a rival to Duke as a crowd-puller was the young Londoner, John Surtees who, at meeting after meeting, at Brands Hatch, Castle Coombe, Ibsley, Aberdare and Cadwell Park, proved unbeatable with his over-the-counter Manx Norton. Perhaps his most notable races were two that he did not win: the 350 Ulster, which he led for four laps against top 'factory' opposition, and the 500 class of the Hutchinson 100, held at a rain-washed Silverstone, where he convincingly outrode Duke on the Gilera before having to retire.

Left: this Rumi of 1955 shows a very compact engine layout with both parallel cylinders, laid down and pointing forwards. The unit is of two-stroke design. This 125cc model was known as the Junior Gentleman

Below: Fergus Anderson on his way to the 1954 world title for 350cc bikes. The machine Fergus is riding is a Guzzi – he became a director of their competition department after his 'retirement' in '54

The rain at Silverstone was not an exception. It had rained. as one commentator remarked, seemingly from the TT right up to the International Six Days Trial, taking in the Senior Manx Grand Prix won by G.R. Costain (Norton) but relenting, briefly, for the Junior, which went to another Manxman, Derek Ennett on an AJS. Just as the Manx opened a link with AJS, and through AJS with Matchless, all was lost when C.R. Collier, Joint Managing Director of Associated Motor Cycles. died at his office in south east London: Mr Charlie, as he was known, had been with the industry for more than half a century and had ridden in the first Isle of Man TT in 1907 when he won the single-cylinder class on a 3½hp Matchless. Another loss sustained by AMC occurred with the death of H.J. Hatch, designer of the three-valve engine.

While the big factories were devoting competition-department time to fettling special models for the forthcoming ISDT, their Press Officers were releasing details of the 1955 models which would be shown at Earls Court. Triumph, it was

learned, were standardising pivoted-fork rear springing; Villiers were bringing out a 150 (a canny move, not merely for use in lightweight motor cycles but for the scooters now being planned by several makers); the once-famous Cotton marque was rehabilitated at Gloucester; Amal took a look at their ageing carburettors and came up with a new instrument, the Monobloc, with integral float chamber.

Just before the Show a new 350 Douglas was announced. The Dragonfly was, like its predecessors, a flat-twin but was far more 'styled', with a nacelle around the steering head and Earles-type front forks. It was to be produced side by side with the Vespa scooter which had been claiming most of the company's attentions during the past three years. At the Show itself, newcomers – apart from the Dragonfly and the enclosed Vincents – were mainly confined to a distaff side of motor cycling, the three-wheelers. The little Bond with its 180 degree steering lock and extraordinary kickstarting – commonplace on a 197 motor bike but demanding rare patience and some gymnastic ability when transferred to a three-wheeler – the AC Petite (350 two-stroke) and the Reliant Regal (a water-cooled 750, and distant relative of the prewar Austin 7) had been joined by the 197 Gordon and the 350 Allard.

As 1954 ended there were signs that road-racing was entering a 'difficult' phase. Having been urged to put the Fatherland back on the motor cycling map, NSU was facing criticism at home for having done the job almost too well; other German firms had complained of the near-impossibility of breaking NSU's stranglehold on the 125 and 250 classes. Most of the trouble, however, came from a clash between the constructors and the FIM over the World Championship series which, said the makers, took in too many events and involved enormous expenses which could not be justified by their showing – even if successful – in countries where sales were likely to remain minute or non-existent. The FIM, however, in its December deliberations in Paris, remained adamant that the nine event set-up (later reduced to eight) must be retained, and they explained, somewhat speciously, that there was no call for manufacturers to support more than the four meetings at which maximum points could be amassed. Although strictly true, this ignored the practical aspect of points-seeking which forced manufacturers to travel the length and breadth of Europe to boost their final scores from second and third places. All this, together with the costs involved in developing the streamlining deemed necessary to keep in touch with the Italian factories, suggested that the British, and probably the Germans, would be pulling out of full-time racing; and this was how it turned out, with Nortons and AMC entering instead what they called 'production prototype' models, equipped with features that might figure in next year's production racers for sale to the public. Such a description effectively ruled out the 500 AJS parallel twin. The AMC candidate in the Senior class became the G45 Matchless, a race-developed version of the G9 roadster twin and a far cry from being a purpose-built racing machine. The three-valve AJS was dropped. All the 'official' machines – in the case of Norton to be ridden by Jack Brett, John Hartle and John Surtees – would appear without streamlining. Ray Amm, realising his World Championship chances were slim if he continued with Norton, made a deal with MV Augusta, but the contest everybody hoped to see – Duke versus Amm, 'four' against 'four' over the Mountain course – was not to be: in his first outing for the Italian firm, at Imola, the Rhodesian slid off, hit an iron post, and was killed.

Chapter 11
An Indian Summer (1955-1959)

Left: a 1959 example of the Norton 88 Dominator, which had a 497cc, ohv, twin-cylinder engine. Probably more important is that the bike had a Featherbed frame, which gave this sports tourer excellent handling qualities

The only news to cheer Norton fans in the early months of 1955 was of tuning wizard Steve Lancefield's return to the fold after years attending to the needs of Norton 500 car racers like Stirling Moss. Not that Lancefield, speaking with the authority of half a dozen TT wins, was anxious to foster hopes for the current British effort in road racing. The Italian multis, he declared from behind a battery of Norton engines in his London sitting room/workshop, had been nine years in the making and were not going to bend the knee to anything less than a full-scale effort from the British . . . and by 'British' he did not mean Norton and AMC alone; 'other firms should chip in with brains and money to help restore the international position which we held up to two or three seasons ago'.

In the event, the TT was an all-continental benefit, with every one of the international trophies going abroad. Bill Lomas had a wonderful week, winning the Clypse circuit 250 Lightweight on a new 202 MV single, and the Junior, in which he rode a Guzzi. His involvement with Moto Guzzi – he was to ride for them, on 500s as well, throughout the season – came late in the day after he fell out with AMC who had previously engaged him for the 350 and 500 events and took exception to his riding for MV Agusta in the Lightweight.

It was Duke's Senior. His average speed over the seven laps was 97.93mph, higher than the previous lap record, which he hoisted to just 0.03mph short of 100mph despite a lurid full-lock slide at 135mph. The finishing order after him was Armstrong and Kavanagh, second and third, with Brett bringing the leading official Norton into fourth place and Bob McIntyre on a private Joe Potts-tuned Norton little more than a minute slower, fifth. Sometime Manx Grand Prix winner, a rider of the highest calibre, McIntyre earlier in the week had led the Junior for three laps on a Norton fitted with enclosure designed and built by the resourceful Potts. The Sidecar Race went to BMW in the person of Walter Schneider, but only after the rest of the German entries on carburettored twins had retired; after Schneider the finishing order was all-British.

The only *wins* for British machines were in the Clubman's events, held on the Clypse circuit, and, because of this, poorly supported by clubmen who had been brought up in the belief that Island racing meant only one thing, the traditional Mountain Circuit. Both races were won by BSA Gold Star riders, Jimmy Buchan in the 350 and Eddie Dow in the 500. They, like the rest of the entry, had to put up with the inconvenience of carrying the lighting equipment and 'efficient' silencers decreed by the ACU in its latest efforts to bring uniformity into the Clubman's TT. Previously, it was compulsory for the lighting equipment to be removed; and silencers, and a host of other items, could be removed or modified at rider's discretion.

The Clubman's TT was to be held only once more, the following year, when the races returned to the full course for further wins by Gold Star riders. The very success of these remarkably fast, reliable ohv singles – 'a specialist model for the clubman' – was in some degree responsible for the run down of the series which in the immediate postwar years, when there was a fair spread of more or less evenly matched machinery from which the clubman-racer might make his choice, had been a distinct attraction in the TT programme. Falling entries, plus BSA's near monopoly – seven wins in the seven Junior events of the 'fifties and three Seniors in the last three meetings – were frightening off other makers, and the Clubman's was an expendable item.

After the Isle of Man TT, World Championship racing carried on in relatively calm fashion, Duke and Lomas doing most of the big-class winning, until the advent on 16 July of Grand Prix number five, the Grote Prijs van Nederland – the Dutch 'TT' – at Assen, which became notorious in racing circles for the riders' 'strike' and the suspension of fourteen riders, including Duke and Armstrong, for 'conduct prejudicial to the sport'. Briefly . . . a group of riders, mainly private owners, had raced for one lap only, then pulled in to demonstrate their feelings about the low start money paid by the organisers who, despite the 100,000 paying customers annually attracted to Assen, had become a byword for penny pinching. The attitude extended even to factory entries like Gilera, anxious to maintain its placing in the championship and thus reluctant to leap-frog the 'Dutch', which would have been the sensible thing to do, financially. The 'one-lappers' appealed to Duke and Armstrong, but the factory riders had little success in presenting a case until they too threatened to withdraw, when the organisers capitulated, increasing fees but promising disciplinary action which materialised later as a six months ban, to be effective from 1 January 1956. The long-term effect of the 'strike' – more important than the ban – was the formation of the Professional Riders Association and a new, ever-soaring valuation of their own worth by riders. This was to reach a peak in the fees demanded, and paid, in the Hailwood-Sheene years. It marked the beginning of a new appreciation of racing motor cyclists as professional showmen with enormous money-making potential for both organisers and manufacturers.

The Gileras were now so fast . . . Duke had been privately timed at over 160mph . . . that they could afford to dispense with full streamlining, but even their race speeds were tame compared with the figures thrown up in an orgy of record-breaking that began in the summer and went on to Earls Court Show time. In New Zealand in July the record breakers, Burns and Wright, had pooled resources – Wright contributing a Black Lightning Vincent, Burns his painstaking copy, from photographs, of the shell used for the 1951 NSU record breaker and the result was a new world's fastest title for Wright, at 185mph, and a three-wheeler record of 163mph for Burns. It was some compensation for Britain, now getting used to a new second-class status in road-racing; it was a throw-back to the 1930s and Fernihough's balmy days. BMW returned to the attack and deposed Burns without much difficulty, upping the figure to

Left: Johnny Allen who attempted to wrest the world land speed record for bikes from Russell Wright's Vincent with his 650 Triumph at Bonneville in 1955. Wranglings from the FIM prevented him from acquiring the blue riband, however, due to a technicality over the timing equipment used

Below: messrs Wright and Burns load their Vincent Black Lightning into a crate, ready to be shipped out to New Zealand for a bike land speed record attempt

174mph with a fuel-injected streamlined 500 outfit, but though the German firm collected innumerable other records along the way its solo rider, Zeller, was unable to touch Wright's figure.

Then NSU put Baumm to work on the good old dependable Munich-Ingoldstadt highway. He made twenty or more records ranging from 91 to 135.5mph with 50cc and 125cc power for his 'Flying Deckchair' – amazing speeds which, judged by any relevance to engine capacity, were more striking than 185mph achieved with the brute power of a vee-twin thousand but were quite lacking in the impact, the glamour, the publicity value, that went with the title, 'world's fastest'. Tall, bearded Baumm, one of the best engineers of his generation, was killed at the Nürburgring a few weeks later. Before the end of the year Italy got into the act. Moto Guzzi despatched Lomas, Anderson and Dickie Dale to Montlhéry where they made a fastest-ever 350 lap at 133.18mph and picked up a grand total of 128 records. It was left to an American to depose Russell Wright. Johnny Allen of Texas took a nitro-methane-burning 650 Triumph, encased in a glass-fibre shell, along the Bonneville Salt Flats, and after the requisite back-and-forth runs was credited with 193.7mph, unquestionably an accurate figure because nobody would doubt American expertise in this sort of technology, but disallowed by the FIM on the ground that the timing apparatus had not been seen and approved by the European body. So it was still officially Wright's title when he and Burns met Allen at the London Show, a few weeks after 28 disconsolate Britons had returned empty handed from the thirtieth International Six Days Trial – 'the biggest publicity stunt in the world of motor cycling', as one of the weekly journals described it – held in Czechoslovakia and dominated by German riders of 175 and 250cc machines.

Gloom deepened with P.C. Vincent's September announcement, less than twelve months after the introduction of the all-enclosed D models, that Vincent motor cycles were to go out of production 'almost immediately'. The manufacture by a small, under-capitalised company of a low-volume-production specialist motor cycle had become uneconomic. After a 28-year history the marque would not be showing at Earls Court.

In 1955 the British manufacturer had acknowledged, in the words of *Motor Cycling's* Year Book, that 'there may be markets for machines which do not follow the traditional English pattern'. A small concession, it might be thought, when he was confronted with evidence of the contracting market for 'bigger bangers', coupled with the appearance of more and more foreign lightweights and scooters.

On the continent the trend, as revealed by registration figures, was towards scooters. In 1951, a mere 18,846 scooters were registered in Germany, against an output of 318,916 motor cycles. In 1952 the figures were 69,658 scooters to 369,225 motor cycles. Three years later scooter production had soared to 134,159 and motor cycles had dropped to 170,549. In another couple of years the positions would be reversed, both categories falling, but the motor cycle sensationally so – to 52,860 as compared with the scooter total of 90,411.

So around the mid 'fifties there was a general, if reluctant, acceptance by British manufacturers of the scooter phenomenon that was sweeping the continent and filtering, in ever-increasing volume, over the Channel to invade what appeared to be the final crumbling, bastion of the *real* motor cycle. Coming to England during the year were the 175cc ohv Heinkel, and the Contessa, both with electric starting, with the automatic-gear Hobby joining Moby, Zündapp, Bella and the Italian pair. The

British contribution was growing too, the most significant being the neatly styled BSA Beeza with horizontal 200cc sv engine, and its sidekick, the 70cc Dandy (in retrospect uncannily like the best-selling Honda 50 step-thru of the '60s). Both appeared at Earls Court where they were described as 'probably the biggest production venture ever to emanate from the Small Heath factory'. 'Carbon' of *Motor Cycling*, his scooter phobia a thing of the past, was moved to write . . . 'How typically British it is, both in war and peace, to let one's adversaries get so far ahead that the race seems to be lost and then to put on a spurt and leave them all standing'. The Beeza was to be Britain's spurt and 'with all the vast resources of Small Heath behind it, it should form the spearhead of a formidable continental D-Day'. But no Beezas, except a couple for showing at continental salons, ever crossed the Channel. Production was postponed, and finally abandoned in late 1956, following the departure of the Beeza's designer, Herbert Hopwood, from BSA to Norton. Nevertheless it could be claimed that at the end of 1955 fifteen makes of scooter were listed as available, or to be available shortly, on the English market.

In 1956 western Europe was to taste something of the almost forgotten austerity of wartime living, with the imposition of fuel rationing in the aftermath of England's (and France's) 'mad imperialist gamble' of a Suez War against Nasser's Egypt that had the practical effect of closing the Suez Canal and reducing oil supplies to Europe to a dilatory trickle. Nobody welcomed petrol rationing and a top price of over thirty pence a gallon but publicists for the industry lost no time in pointing out the enhanced standing of cheap-to-run two-wheelers in straightened times. All this was in November, but the year had opened in good heart with Geoff Duke expressing hopes of an early remission of his 'sentence' and John Surtees reported as going great guns in practice runs on the new four he was to ride for MV. Even were Duke's ban to drag out its full time (as it did) he would still be able to ride in four of the classic meetings, and in any case Surtees would have stiff competition from the new Guzzi V8, to be ridden by Lomas. This magnificent 70bhp water-cooled device, the work of Ing Carcano, appeared at Imola in April and thereafter sporadically through the season, dogged with teething troubles – some, like a broken crankshaft, not so 'teething' – but having a performance that was, in the laconic words of Duke, who was passed by one in the German Grand Prix at Solitude, 'really something'.

Surtees gave notice of *his* plans for the year in early-season appearances at Crystal Palace and Silverstone where he flattened all opposition with beautifully judged rides on the big MV. With the TT a month away, the racing world was saddened by Fergus Anderson's untimely death at Floreffe. 47-year-old Anderson, racing since 1932, winner of two TTs, two World Championships and innumerable continental Grands Prix had left Moto Guzzi because of 'personality differences' and was riding a factory BMW when he died. Apart from the Italians' continued support, road-racing was being progressively phased out of top manufacturers' plans. In England, Norton and AMC adhered to their production-prototype policy, wheeling out for their 'official' riders models having detail modifications – to combustion chamber and valves, or even, in the case of the 7R, to bore and stroke measurements – that were said, and later seen, to be worth a few extra horses. In Germany only DKW (Auto Union) was involved in a full-scale race effort with 135/140mph, three-cylinder two-strokes that were patently unable to match,

214

except in acceleration, the Italian fours and were due to be retired, probably at the end of the season. NSU was selling only standard race-kit 250s and in June gave notice that service for these machines would be ended very shortly. BMW had made little change to its machines used by semi-official entries in the sidecar class and by Walter Zeller in some 500 solo events.

The German industry was feeling the effects of a downturn in two-wheeler sales. NSU had relinquished its partnership with Lambretta and was producing instead an all-German scooter, the Prima, which was a de luxe version of the old model. BMW was selling comparatively few of its big, fast (and very expensive) R series twins and hardly any of the 250 singles, and the Isetta 'bubble car' was not exactly in the big league either. The results of this business depression were evident in July in enforced redundancy for several hundred NSU workers, followed by similar action a few weeks later at the BMW works in Munich.

With Carlo Ubbiali, one of the most consistently successful of all Grand Prix riders, aboard them, 125 and 250 MV singles won their classes in the World Championships, starting off with a double at the TT. Surtees did the same in the 500 class, in the process making himself individual champion too, with consecutive wins in the TT, the Dutch and the Belgian. At his next meeting, the German Grand Prix, at that point leading the 350 class with the new 48bhp four, Surtees crashed while chasing Lomas and was out of racing for the remainder of 1956.

Duke, when he got back to the championship round, had very little luck. His first Grand Prix, the Belgian in July, was going well for him until a piston broke up while he was leading Surtees; in the German he had electrical trouble while battling with Lomas on the V8 and had to retire (as did Lomas); and in the Ulster he overdid things trying to keep a safe distance ahead of John Hartle on a 'works' Norton and came off, letting Hartle through for his first Grand Prix win of 1956. Duke's first, and only, victory of the year was at the Italian, which did not give him enough points to join the first five in the end-of-season championship points table.

Top: the magnificent 500cc V8 Moto Guzzi of 1956, which, although incredibly fast, never held together long enough to make a lasting impression

Above: John Surtees and MV on their way to victory in the 1956 Senior TT and that year's World Championship

Left: not only did MV have Surtees winning a championship for them in 1956, but Carlo Ubbiali, too, who was victorious in the 125 and 250cc classes

Right: the NSU Prima of 1956 was that company's attempt to break into the Italian-dominated scooter market

215

In the record-breaking arena the situation, as previously recounted, was that the 'big one' – the world's fastest – was still technically in the hands of Russell Wright, though nobody doubted that Allen in the USA had actually gone faster. The other privateer, Burns, had seen his sidecar world's fastest beaten by BMW; obviously it was now the turn of NSU to do its bit for Germany by bringing home the solo record. This it duly did, but not for very long, by taking its 500 streamliner to Utah and, with Herz as rider, pushing the figure up to 211mph. A few weeks later Burns and Wright turned up at Utah, where Burns got his sidecar record back, at 176mph, and Wright on the solo found that he could not quite reach 200mph. The record-breaking 'season' ended with the world's fastest title back with a British machine – Allen's Triumph, which in September averaged 214mph over both runs of the kilometre and prompted the proud makers in Meriden to order thousands of little stickers proclaiming 'World's Fastest' for adornment of Triumph petrol tanks.

'Mopeds, mopeds, mopeds – and precious little else' was the summing up of the Brussels Salon, early in the year, by one experienced reporter. Nobody said anything like that about Earls Court which, alone of all the European exhibitions, could claim to remain a showplace for orthodox motor cycles, including the products of no fewer than nine 'over-500cc' manufacturers. Continental Europe had indicated conclusively that all it wanted from two-wheelers was low-cost, low-speed transport, preferably with the minimum of registration formalities and official interference.

Figures from the Paris Salon in October serve to reinforce this picture of continental tastes. France, largest user and producer of 'motor cycles' in the world, had 4½ million two-wheeler users on its roads in 1955, of whom more than half were mounted on mopeds. In 1955, 1,145,750 motor cycles were produced (830,575 of them mopeds, 135,657 scooters, 179,519 over 50cc). More significantly, in corresponding nine month periods of 1955 and '56, moped production had increased by 125,000, scooters by 6000 – and motor cycles over 50cc had dropped by 50,000.

In Britain the traditional motor cycle still ruled, though scooters were coming up fast with no fewer than 28 different makes listed by the end of the year. Most of these were imported – at least one, the French Terrot, by an old-established English motor cycle manufacturer, Phelon and Moore. Maico of Germany had joined Dayton with a 250cc scooter, the Maicoletta (also available in 277 form) with electric starting. This machine was more to the English way of thinking, having performance fully the equal of the typical 250 motor cycle – with the added refinement of course of weather protection.

For 'proper' motor cycles there were new 250 two-stroke engines. From Villiers came the 2T twin, to be used by the half dozen or more independent makers in the lightweight field, and from AMC came a new single, the first two-stroke to be made by the company, it appeared in machines marketed by the James and Francis Barnett offshoots of the AMC empire. Royal Enfield came out with an all new 250, the Crusader, a four-stroke with cast-in oil reservoir and enclosure for the rear chain, the latter a feature seen on some of the latest Ariels who with BSA – following Norton's dropping a couple of years earlier of its 16H and Big Four models – were the only makers producing big-capacity side-valve machines.

Velocette, possibly the smallest of the 'big-name' manufacturers, continued to show inventive resource and this

Left: this is probably the most complicated racing engine ever, the 499cc V8 Moto Guzzi of 1957. This engine featured water cooling, four camshafts and no less than eight Dell'Orto carburettors. By the end of its racing life, this engine was producing 80bhp

Below: the bikes line up for the start of the 1957 350cc Belgian GP. The front row is, from left to right, Campbell (Moto Guzzi, winner of the race and that year's champion), Liberati (Gilera), Brown (Gilera), Montana (Moto Guzzi), Surtees (MV) and Wheeler (Moto Guzzi)

Right: what was regarded by some as a 'British BMW', the Velocette Valiant 200, which was announced in 1956

year introduced the 200 Valiant, an air-cooled, horizontally-opposed-overhead-valve twin – sporting cousin of the LE or a small-scale BMW, according to taste.

There was no Earls Court Show in 1957 – it was the first of the 'off' years following the decision, towards the end of 1956, to make the show an every-other-year-event. Some of the incentive for annual change was thus removed, and little of startling novelty appeared. Another three-wheeler was introduced, the Coronet with 328cc Anzani twin two-stroke power, and having two wheels at the front like the Powerdrive, a Villiers-engined newcomer backed by Blue Star Garages that had appeared during the previous year. Neither of these new models sold in any number.

It was Golden Jubilee year for the TT, and for the second year Geoff Duke was not to ride on the Island. At Imola in April, chasing his new Gilera team mate, Bob McIntyre – Reg Armstrong having retired to business interests in Ireland – Duke cast himself off the 500 and damaged a shoulder bone so badly that he, in company with Lomas who crashed at the same meeting, was out of racing for several months. McIntyre won both the Senior, lengthened to eight laps for the Jubilee, and Junior on his Gilera fours. Without Duke, he had Bob Brown to back him; they faced Dickie Dale on Lomas's V8 Guzzi, Keith Campbell on a Guzzi single and World Champion Surtees on an MV four. McIntyre's speed for the Senior was 98.9mph, and he broke the '100' barrier on four circuits, his best figure being 100.12mph. Surtees was second and Brown, on Gilera number two, third. In the Junior the 29-year-old Scotsman came home ahead of Campbell (Guzzi), with Brown again third and Surtees fourth; again it was a record-speed race, on average and for the lap, for McIntyre.

The Clypse circuit 250 Lightweight went to Cecil Sandford on a Mondial, but only after a last-lap fall for his team mate, the young Sammy Miller, at that early stage in his career torn between road-racing and trials riding and displaying amazing facility in both. Another Mondial rider, Provini, won the 125, and in what had become accepted practice the Sidecar race went to a BMW exponent, the previous year's winner, Fritz Hillebrand. By the end of the week record laps and race averages had been set in all five TT events. There was little of new technical interest – apart from the appearance of a disc brake, then *very* new, on a British sidecar – during a season which ended with Italian machines winning the four solo classes: Mondials won the 125 and 250, Guzzi the 350 and Gilera the 500, in the hands of the Italian Liberati, for McIntyre had lost a little fire following a crash in the Dutch TT (meeting number three) enough to drop him to second in both Junior 350 and Senior 500 classes.

By the autumn the racing scene had altered dramatically with Gilera, Guzzi and Mondial announcing their withdrawal from active racing. High costs in race development were showing no appreciable effect in countering falling sales for roadsters and could be justified no longer. This left MV Agusta, with outside engineering interests to cushion race expenses, to rule the roost. Then, in the end-of-year congress of the FIM, full frontal streamlining was banned for future racing, a salutary move in view of the distinctly odd handling, on occasion, of even the best of the 'dustbin-equipped' machines from the top factories.

In March 1958, Associated Motor Cycles appeared at the Swiss Show with Matchless and AJS 250 four-stroke singles,

whose engines were in unit with the gearbox, with integral oil reservoir and AC generator. They were smoothly styled, rather 'continental' in fact, and stood up well to the competition provided by the Swiss-made Condor and Universal 250s. These latter two were shaft driven, by no means uncommon across the Channel, but in England still reserved for oddities like the LE Velocette and the 500 Sunbeam. They were the first 250 machines to carry AMC's 'big' brand names since 1939. In the lightweight field AMC were represented by attractive, if not especially memorable, machines such as the Francis Barnett Plover and the James Cavalier with two-stroke power from the Villiers factory in Wolverhampton.

Royal Enfield, who had been ahead of the trend with the 250 Crusader of the previous year, were out to keep their lead and produced the Crusader Airflow, which was the 250 adorned with a comprehensive glass-fibre fairing plus windscreen. In a way it epitomised English thinking. It was to be a paragon on wheels that would offer the current 'darling' of the industry, the speedy, economical 250, plus scooter protection, plus a 'racer' look that even the racers couldn't legally aspire to, after the 1957 FIM ruling on streamlining. It happened, too, to be a motor cycle, and was to outlast most, if not all, of its contemporaries. At the same time, to show they could satisfy traditional tastes, Enfield brought out a sporting 700 which became the biggest vertical-twin on the market and was, despite a tendency to disintegrate under sustained stress, an occasional contender in long-distance race outings. In June, for instance, a 700 in the hands of Bob McIntyre and Derek Powell battled through to second place in the Thruxton 500 Miler behind the Tiger 110 of Mike Hailwood and Dan Shorey.

In July came the Ariel Leader, the work of Val Page, three years in the making and a brilliantly clever design that would not have been noticeably outdated on today's roads. A 250 twin two-stroke (the engine type chosen by a big majority of potential owners quizzed by Ariel) was slung under a box frame, with leading-link forks, the whole enclosed in pressed-steel panelwork, with in-built panniers, legshields, and windscreen. The Leader was an adventurous yet practical solution to the problem of making a *civilised* motor cycle. Its price, in basic trim, was around £210, but this figure could be upped considerably if the host of available extras, like winking indicators, panniers, and electric clock, were included. A few weeks after the Leader had astonished the motor cycle world, Ariel's parent company, BSA, brought out surprises of their own, in the shape of a nicely styled scooter powered by a 175cc two-stroke single or 250 ohv twin. The body was identical for both; the price varied between £165 and £185. The BSAs were duplicated by Triumph versions, and in fact the Triumph 250, the Tigress, became the best known. The design was Edward Turner's, and in 250 form (there was little opportunity to assess the two-stroke for it was virtually still-born), the chief characteristics were high performance, especially good acceleration, and above-average handling. It was, in fact, a motor cyclist's idea of what a scooter . . . a two-wheeler . . . should be, and thus was undoubtedly a speedier device than the average Italian 150 job on that oft-quoted high speed dash from point A to point B.

After 'leaking' news of the scooters, BSA brought out a new 250 motor cycle, the C15 Star, to replace the old C12. This 67 by 70mm ohv single was almost spartan, with its unadorned framework standing out against the trend towards full or partial enclosure that was sweeping the market, exemplified by BSA's most famous subsidiary, Triumph, with their new rear panelling. While being ready to introduce new models, BSA could also perform a gentle hatchet job, and this is what happened in the case of their sidecars, which were dropped from production, and of Sunbeam motor cycles – the rubber-mounted ohv twins which had for so long set the highest standards in the British industry for (reasonably) quick, and comfortable travel. The name Sunbeam was switched to the 250 scooter.

There could be no complaint that the British industry, once it was in a mind to innovate, was slow or timid. The twin themes for 1958 were 250cc (or thereabouts) and/or enclosure. Other firms to come out with variations were Velocette, who extensively dressed up the 200 Valiant in plastics and called it the Vee Line, and then, warming to their task, carried on a trifle less fully, with 350 and 500 singles, Panther, with a 325 Villiers-powered job; Francis Barnett, with the Cruiser 84, a 250 two-stroke single with rear enclosure and valanced front mudguard; and Ambassador's enclosed Super S. Finally, in November, Norton announced their first 250, the work of the new managing director, Bert Hopwood. This was called the Jubilee and was an ohv twin engine tipping forward a little, with

Below left: a 1957 example of the Royal Enfield 700, a machine which set the trend for large parallel twins. Although sometimes very unreliable, they were nevertheless sporty and had occasional success on the race tracks

Below: by 1958, the Mondial 125 was not that competitive in grand prix racing, especially with the might of MV now in full swing. This is a 1958 example which was once raced by Mike Hailwood

gearbox in unit and rear panelling on the lines of an inverted
bath tub, with a casing for the rear chain. It was a nice-looking
bike, keenly priced at £215 or so.

Several factories had been busy on the scooter front. Most
of them – apart from Panther – had no particular claim to a
motor cycle tradition. They were not intent on showing the
continentals how to go about the job of building a scooter that
would steer and accelerate like a motor bike: they wanted to get
some of the money that seemed to be pouring into the coffers of
the scooter concessionaires. With Villiers to provide the engine,
the job was half-way done . . . or so it appeared. Thus there
were scooters like the Sun Geni, a 98cc job, followed by 150 and
175 models. Ex-racer Ernie Barrett's Phoenix line-up (with
eight models, reputedly the biggest scooter *range* of any
English maker), the DKR, which was a product of a Willenhall
Radiator subsidiary in Wolverhampton, and quite a few others,
all used the ubiquitous Villiers engine/gear unit. At Marston
Road, Wolverhampton, home of Villiers, this new activity with
small bikes, scooters, and three-wheelers was manna, enabling
them to resume full five-day working, in expectation that the
previous record of 15,386 mopeds and 26,658 scooters produced
by English factories would shortly be beaten. All these new
machines, amounting to some 240 different models, were shown
at Earls Court.

Scooters even invaded the racing world. After a timid start
in 1957, the Isle of Man Scooter Rally received more than 200
entries for the second annual event, which included reliability
runs during a 'night of chilly mist and rain in which nearly 100
scooters buzzed round the Mountain course, all but ten
surviving to complete the tests and prove the reliability of the
scooter and the hardiness of its riders'. However admirable their
riders, scooters seemed pallid performers to those few TT
spectators who had stayed on after watching Surtees get his first
double of the season, in Senior and Junior events. He went on
to 350/500 wins on the MV in five subsequent GPs, and was
unbeaten in any race until the end of the season when, at
Brands Hatch, he capitulated to twin misfortunes of plug
trouble on the MV and opposition from Derek Minter, on a
very fast Norton. Surtees was backed by John Hartle, on
another four, who managed good second places, except when he
tangled with Keith Campbell (Norton), in the Belgian Grand
Prix, and a very determined Bob McIntyre (Norton), in
the Ulster Grand Prix.

*Top: one of the neat little Sun scooters of
1958 being put through its paces for a road
test in a popular weekly newspaper. This is
the Villiers-engined Wasp*

*Above: Tarquinio Provini with his 250
MV Agusta heads for victory in the 1958
Ulster Grand Prix. Tarquinio took four out of
the six races in that year to take the World
Championship*

Above: John Surtees winning the 500cc race at the Isle of Man in 1958 and, right, Carlo Ubbiali who was also MV mounted, taking the Ultra-Lightweight 125 race. Both John and Carlo went on to take world titles that year and helped MV embark on an incredible run of success: they took every solo World Championship class for three consecutive years

MV Agusta won the 125 and 250 championships too, but with a shade more difficulty, for the 250 six-speed Morinis turned out to be exceptionally fast, as did 'desmo' Ducatis among the ultra-lightweights. However, from the Ulster GP on, Provini's 32bhp, 250cc MV and the 125 ridden by Ubbiali went ahead of the opposition consistently

The English 'prototype' racers were changed somewhat, the G45 Matchless twin giving way to an enlarged 7R single, the 496 G50 Matchless, which was claimed to develop 48bhp at 6800rpm, and pulled a very high gear, while the Manx Nortons benefited from the attentions of Hopwood and Doug Hele in combustion chamber design, bore and stroke, crankshafts and bearings, in the quest for higher revs. Several versions were tried in the season, and the best of them were fast and reliable: Surtees said his MV was not more than 3mph faster, but agreed that he had more than an edge in acceleration.

Duke's much publicised tie-up with BMW fizzled out fairly early as it became apparent that his dohc twin was not much

faster than ordinary BMWs available to riders like Dickie Dale, and was certainly deficient in handling and braking. Finally the factory withdrew from the solo class, leaving Schneider to win the sidecar and Duke to go racing on Nortons, which he did with evident enjoyment and no particular success, apart from a 350/500 double at the Swedish GP, in the absence of Surtees and MV, who were simply too powerful for the old Norton.

Mike Hailwood began to figure prominently in race results in 1958. It was his second year of racing and by the end of it he had acquired four TT replicas, three of the new ACU Road Race Stars, eight trophies from Bemsee meetings, and the Pinhard Prize. Derek Minter was competing regularly in the Continental GPs in close company with other Norton riders like Duke, Hailwood and Campbell, and a little to the rear of John Hartle on MV number two. Another rider beginning to make his name was Gary Hocking, a 20-year-old Rhodesian who took over an unfamiliar Norton and rode it over the difficult Nürburgring to such purpose that he split the MV one-two for a while, and eventually finished within a minute of Hartle after 127 miles of German GP. Somewhat further down the lists was another German champion to be, Jim Redman.

In the USA, in the last of the Daytona 200-mile events to be run on the original 4.1-mile beach course, Harley-Davidson riders took most of the leading positions, with Joe Leonard as the winner. Riders of British machines – once kingpins in this race – could do no better than eighth and ninth.

Throughout 1958 recriminations were exchanged between Triumph and the FIM, concerning the latter's persistent refusal to endorse the Johnny Allen 214mph world speed record. The affair dragged on, with the manufacturers finally entering a civil court action against the FIM.

The FIM were pressing ahead with plans for a Formula One class for over-the-counter racing machines and getting a somewhat tepid reception from the ACU, who were concerned about the upheaval extra racing might cause in the Isle of Man Tourist Trophy programme.

In February, the Japanese Honda factory said it would be sending a team of three to the TT, to ride in the 125cc race. They were to be the first Japanese to do so since 1930, when one K. Tada had taken a Velocette through the Junior to finish fifteenth. A month later the Japanese – Honda again – restated their interest in the European market by appearing at the

*Below: an example of the 496cc, 48bhp G50
Matchless of 1958, which was a great rival
of the Manx Norton. This machine has been
slightly modified and is still seen in clubman
racing events*

Amsterdam Show with the 250 Dream, priced, for Holland, on a
par with the British 250s, like the Ariel Leader, on display there.
Nobody took much notice as the winter was still oppressive.
There was no point in idle conjecture about unlikely looking
motor cycles from Japan, especially with talk of the 250's
8500rpm: it was clear they'd soon wear out, or blow up, under
such stress.

On 19 February, one of the weekly journals, in
announcing a regular scooter section, declared that well over
250,000 scooters were in use in Britain, in a two-wheeler
population which had now passed 1½ millions, to put motor
cycles at one to every three cars. Registrations showed that
Britain was following the continental lead, with mopeds well
ahead, and over-250cc machines at the bottom of the list – apart
from sidecars, whose sales were miniscule. Three-wheelers were
selling reasonably well, with new models appearing, like the
Frisky, the Nobel (this one with impressive Bristol Aeroplane
pedigree and Sachs engine) and the 328 Excelsior-engined
Berkeley. A non-show year, 1959 still had its share of new or
modified motor cycles, such as the 250 AMC-powered James
Commodore, which served as a fair example of English thinking
in the matter of 250 two-strokes, with slick lines, all-chain
transmission, kick-starting, unexceptional performance and
modest price. Royal Enfield brought out a 'sports' Crusader
(unfaired) and a high-performance 500 twin; Triumph a duplex-
tube frame, unit-construction for the Tiger 100, and further
rear-wheel enclosure; and Norton covered the rear of their 88
and 99 models and called them De Luxe. AMC enlarged the
250s of the previous year, and called them 'Light 350s' to
distinguish them from the continuing 350s with separate
gearbox and a few more pounds to carry.

Although a scrambles expert like Derek Rickman might
take his 500 hybrid Metisse to wins in the top motocross
meetings, it was plain that the day of the big single (or twin) on
the rough was coming to an end. Jeff Smith, equally at home in
motocross and scrambles, was delighted when trials and
scrambles versions of the C15 250 Star were introduced, and
appeared on one at the Scottish Six Days Trial in May. His
team mates, Brian Martin, Johnny Draper and Arthur Lampkin,
were also equipped with 250s. At the Scottish, the move
towards lightweights was very marked – this in an event where
the terrain had always been thought to favour the 350-and-over
single with its famed capacity for infinite 'plonking' on
impossible gradients. Now the 250s, many of them two-strokes,
totalled a quarter of the entry with the 350s/500s comprising
only 72 among 172 entrants. Brian Stonebridge, an
outstanding scrambler on Greeves two-strokes, was there with a
250 sidecar outfit. Alan Kimber, who much later helped to put
Japanese two-strokes on the British map, had the effrontery to
enter on a Lambretta scooter. Most convincing of all, the Trial
was won by Roy Peplow on a 200 Triumph Cub, a 'stretched'
and competition-modified version of Edward Turner's original
single cylinder, 150cc Terrier.

Broad conclusions about 1959 road-racing could be, in no
particularly significant order . . . that works-prepared racers,
like the MVs, would outclass non-works machinery. Walkover
demonstrations by riders of works-prepared motor cycles were
boring for spectators and counter-productive for the
manufacturers, whose standing was not enhanced by such
hollow victories. Furthermore, two-strokes could make very
powerful racers: a trite comment now, but the fact was
surprising in 1959 when it was still generally considered,

and demonstrated, that a good four-stroke was too quick for any two-stroke. The East German MZ, with rotary-valve controlled induction and a tuned exhaust system, challenged that view in 1959. MZs, ridden by Ernst Degner and H. Fuegner and, on occasion, by Hocking, Minter and Luigi Taveri, proved to be almost a match for the overhead-camshaft four-strokes of Italy.

Norton 'semi-official' entries in the World Championship races were, as in 1958, through the dealer Reg Dearden, who

Left: a 1954 works 350cc Norton with special outside-flywheel engine. This bike was later fitted with a Doug Hele engine, which was originally intended to be used in a Domiracer frame

Top: John Surtees, 350 MV has a long lead over the opposition at the 1959 Ulster Grand Prix

Above: a young Mike Hailwood heading for third place in the 1958 250 TT with his leading-link-forked NSU

nominated Hocking and Terry Shepherd to ride models with the camshaft drive modified to run on splines and needle rollers; also available, and tested (but not raced) by Shepherd in the Island, was a desmodromic 500. In the Junior TT it was Surtees all the way, with Hartle second and Alastair King, on a Potts-tuned Norton, third. Duke was fourth. The Clypse course, in use that year for the last time, catered for 125, 250 and sidecar races, the 125 having the distinction at the finish of having five nations represented in the marques on the leaderboard, with two vertical four-stroke singles, a pair of two-stroke singles, a 'desmo' single, and a four-stroke twin. This last was a Honda, ridden by N. Taniguchi, who with his team mates carried off the manufacturer's prize. The Senior, postponed from Friday to the following day because of bad weather, started under a reasonable sky, but within a lap was being fought out in incessant rain and low scudding mist, and ended with a shivering, exhausted Surtees winning at 87.94mph.

In the Formula One 350 and 500 events, run concurrently on the Saturday before race week, the Potts Norton-mounted entries of McIntyre (Senior) and King (Junior) were successful. The series carried on through the season, imposing a confusing pattern on the usual structure of the Grand Prix meetings with – for example – the Senior race of the Swedish GP and the 350 races in the Dutch and Belgian GPs becoming F1 events. Formula One was dropped at the end of the year and the 500 World Championship was allowed to continue.

Surtees ended the season as 350 and 500 champion, with wins in all meetings contested. Hailwood, his eventual successor as team leader for MV, had notched up his first classic win, at the 125 Ulster GP on a desmodromic Ducati, ahead of Hocking and Degner (MZs).

At Gottwaldov in Czechoslovakia teams from sixteen nations contested the ISDT, including a rather shake-me-down selection of riders from Britain financed by donations from 500 ACU clubs in the absence of more solid support from the manufacturers. The English riders were reduced to three early on, and the Czechs came through for a clean sweep in both Trophy and Vase contests.

As 1959 ended, motor cycling in Europe was in an Indian summer. It was to be short-lived, but there were still remnants of great energy, enthusiasm and invention, if not of good management, to keep European motor cycling rolling over the hump of the decade.

Chapter 12
The Rising Sun (1960-1966)

Left: this racing version of the Ariel Arrow Super Sports came seventh in the Junior TT at the Isle of Man in 1960, ridden by O'Rourke. The Arrow was a twin-cylinder, two-stroke 250 of square 54 × 54mm dimensions, with unusual oval-section con-rods

When the sun rose on 1 January 1960, it heralded not only the start of a new decade but a new era in motor cycling history. Ironically, the symbol that represented that new era was the rising sun, the official flag of the islands of Japan. In the years that were to follow, Japan would dominate the motor cycle industry in a way that not even the British had managed to do.

The rise of the Japanese industry was nothing short of spectacular. Defeat at the hands of the Allies during World War II had left the country shattered, and her top industrialists soon realised that the only way to drag the country back to its feet was to get its people back to work. So began a fascinating experiment. The men of power decided to invest heavily in industry and, aided to a certain extent by American capital, Japanese bankers were soon offering businessmen large sums of money for investment purposes. Many Japanese companies invested heavily in the future of Japan but they soon realised that, having borrowed large sums of money and taken on large numbers of staff, their product turnover would have to be large as well. This meant exporting, and the more they borrowed the more they needed to sell abroad. It was a vicious circle and one that would have disastrous consequences for the motor cycling industries of other countries, particularly Great Britain. By the mid 1970s, just fifteen years after their arrival in Europe, the Japanese companies could have destroyed the British industry – although cynics would say it didn't need the Japanese to destroy the British, the British were doing a perfectly good job of doing it themselves. Be that as it may, it was also interesting to note that in establishing themselves as the industry's top dogs, the Japanese big four – Honda, Yamaha, Suzuki and Kawasaki – also destroyed much of the rest of the Japanese motor cycle industry as they rose to dominance.

It seems strange now, but by the mid 1950s there were more than eighty Japanese motor cycle companies all vying for a place in the market. Today, the names of companies like Marusho, Hosk, Tohatsu, Rikuo, Tsubasa, Cabton and Showa mean precisely nothing to the average motor cycle enthusiast, yet once upon a time they were actively competing in one of the toughest markets in the world, that of Japan. One by one these companies went out of business. Some, like Meguro who were swallowed by Kawasaki in 1964, were taken over, and slowly their numbers were whittled away until, by the early 1960s, only a handful of companies had survived the onslaught of the giants like the powerful Honda company.

Honda, obviously, wasn't always a giant. Indeed, the company's origins were exceedingly humble, but by 1960 it was ready to fight for a place in the American and European markets. Honda's arrival in Europe was marked by the 1959 Isle of Man TT where their machines were met with interest but not a great deal of success. In 1960, however, Honda arrived on the Island meaning business. They had learned a lot from their exploratory venture the year before and, whereas their arrival then had been marked principally by some patronising interest from European observers, it was soon obvious that 1960's TT effort by the Japanese was in deadly earnest. For the TT, Honda arrived with a formidable twelve man team and some equally formidable machines. The 125cc twin, debuted the previous year, had now been improved. The camel-backed tank had been replaced and the cylinders were now inclined steeply forward. In addition, the old trailing-link front forks had been jettisoned in favour of new telescopic forks. Even more interesting, however, was the introduction of Honda's new 250cc racer, a four-cylinder, overhead-camshaft machine of impressive construction. Honda now also included among their team two non-Japanese riders, the experienced Australians Tom Phillis and Bob Brown.

By the end of TT week, it was obvious that Honda had come to stay. In the 125cc race, Honda machines finished in sixth, seventh, eighth, ninth and tenth places, beaten only by the mighty MV Agusta machines from Italy, while in the 250cc TT Honda scored an even more impressive result with Bob Brown bringing his bike home in fourth place, with Moto Kitano fifth and Tom Phillis sixth.

Having established themselves as a force to be reckoned with, Honda then decided to contest the rest of that year's World Championship events. At the following meeting, the Dutch TT at Assen, fate was to take an interesting turn. Tom Phillis crashed during practice and broke a collar bone, effectively putting him out of action for some months. On Phillis's recommendation, a young Rhodesian, Jim Redman, was taken in as a replacement. In years to come, Redman would play a vital part in establishing Honda as the team to beat in Grand Prix racing. Jim Redman was an unusual man. Born in London and orphaned at a fairly early age, he eventually emigrated to Rhodesia to avoid being conscripted into the army and to take care of his younger brothers and sisters. His never ending battle with the bureaucrats had developed him into a highly individual personality, a loner with a self sufficient character few people could understand. Ironically, Redman was to become a superb team man and one on whom Honda came to rely very heavily.

For the Dutch TT then, Redman was signed to ride the 125 machine as well as the 250, and a fourth place in the 125 race plus an eighth in the 250cc event got his career off to a promising start. In the following Grand Prix, in Belgium, Redman and Bob Brown had to be content with the 125cc machines as the 250s had been withdrawn for modification. In West Germany, Brown and Redman switched to the newly modified 250s but during practice Bob Brown was killed and so Honda lost a valuable ally. Fortunately, Tom Phillis's injuries soon healed and he joined Redman to contest the remainder of the season. Indeed, Phillis and Redman finished second and third, behind Italy's Carlo Ubbiali, in the 250cc Ulster Grand Prix and Redman ended the season with a fighting second place in the Italian 250cc Grand Prix at Monza.

For Honda, it had been a satisfying season. True, they had been beaten in both the 125 and 250 categories by the MV Agusta of Carlo Ubbiali but they had learned a lot. For their

Above: 1960 was the year that Honda made a serious assault on the European road racing scene after checking out the opposition at the TT the year before. Here, Tom Phillis, with 125, heads toward Quarter Bridge

part, the famous MV company, having taken all four solo world titles in 1960 (John Surtees had swept all before him in the 350 and 500cc categories), announced at the end of the season that they would quit the smaller classes to concentrate on the larger capacity events. There was now nothing to prevent Honda from conquering Europe.

Honda's successes on the race tracks ensured that the company's road bikes attracted a lot of attention. Honda's marketing debut in Europe had come at the 1959 Dutch Show where it exhibited the new 250cc Dream roadster. Although, to European eyes, the Dream was unusually styled, it was obviously well engineered and it also had the unusual asset of being fitted with a self starter. Its engine was a jewel-like, overhead-camshaft, all-aluminium unit and the introduction of the Dream into Britain during 1959 and 1960 was to present a serious challenge to the British Norton company which had just marketed a new 250cc model, the overhead-valve Juvilee. As time would prove, this wasn't the last challenge a British

Above right: although British manufacturers were not short of ideas for exotic bikes in the early 1960s, they stayed with their original formulae; this is a 1960 AJS 500 single with a modified G80 Matchless engine

company would face from a Japanese manufacturer.

At this stage, however, the British industry was not particularly worried. Indeed, at the end of 1960 the powerful BSA/Triumph group (which had merged in 1951 and which included the Ariel company) announced profits of £3½ million. The group had also celebrated the year by introducing the Ariel Arrow, a sleeker and sportier version of the company's little two-stroke, 250cc Leader model. Like the Leader, however, the Arrow would not prove a huge sales success and this in some ways was a foretaste of problems to come for the British industry. The Arrow and the Leader were both reasonably sophisticated machines but the public just did not want them. The innate conservatism of the British buying public rejected the Ariel models just as it had other innovative models, such as Matchless's 600cc, four-cylinder Silver Hawk of the 1930s. For some reason, technical innovations which fascinated the crowds at motor shows could seldom be translated into hard cash in the dealer showrooms. So, in 1960, the sales catalogues in Britain were full of manufacturers like AJS, BSA, Matchless, Triumph, Norton, Royal Enfield and Velocette, all making conventional four-stroke, single or twin-cylinder machines. Others like Francis-Barnett, James, DMW, Cotton, Excelsior and Greeves were taking the small two-stroke route, with engines usually being supplied by Wolverhampton's Villiers concern.

Another interesting development in 1960 was the establishment of an assembly plant at Kobe in Japan by the giant Kawasaki Aircraft Company, designed to develop and mass produce motor cycles. Kawasaki's history, in fact, goes back to 1878 when the Kawasaki Dockland Company was established. The company prospered, grew and diversified into all kinds of industrial development – ships, locomotives and bridge trusses to name but three. In 1949, the company entered the field of motor cycle engine production, supplying motors to a number of companies. In 1961, the first all Kawasaki motor cycle was built and the following year it went into production as the Kawasaki B8 model. The B8 was a small, 125cc, single-cylinder, two-stroke machine and it laid the foundations for better things to come. By this time, the Kawasaki conglomerate had established the Kawasaki Auto Sales Company as a sales outlet for its bikes and had also signed a technical and sales agreement with the Meguro Manufacturing Company – then Japan's oldest motor cycle manufacturer – to produce a full range of motor cycles from 50cc right through to 500cc. Kawasaki had become a major manufacturer in its own right.

To the motor cycle enthusiast in Europe, however, the dreams of companies like Kawasaki were still pie in the sky. All he was interested in was to see what the 1961 Grand Prix racing season would bring, as it had all the makings of being an interesting one. Those two great MV Agusta riders Carlo Ubbiali and John Surtees had retired, as, indeed, had the MV Agusta company itself. This so-called retirement, however, was a farce because Gary Hocking turned up on 350 and 500cc MVs which, although entered by the MV Privat team, were anything but privately prepared machines. The Rhodesian Hocking swept all before him, winning four 350cc Grands Prix and seven 500cc events to clinch a double 350 and 500cc World Championship.

In the smaller 125 and 250cc classes, Honda, taking full advantage of MV's absence, scored their first World Championship victories. In the 250cc class, the company fielded regulars Tom Phillis and Jim Redman plus newcomer Luigi Taveri; they also lent works bikes to British aces Mike Hailwood and Bob McIntyre. This powerful team was unbeatable and at the end of the season Honda riders filled the first five places in the 250cc world title table with the Championship itself going to the brilliant young Mike Hailwood: his first world title.

In the 125cc class, Honda were again unbeatable, this time

Top left: Rhodesian Gary Hocking, with his 350 MV, heading for victory in Ulster in 1961

Above: Hailwood and Honda try to pull out a lead over Hocking and his MV twin at Sulby Bridge during the 1961 250 TT

Top right: Yamaha test rider Fumio Ito on his RD48 racer in the 1961 250 TT

Above right: a Honda Benly of 1961

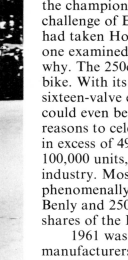

the championship title going to Tom Phillis who fought off the challenge of Ernst Degner and the East German MZ team. It had taken Honda only two years to conquer Europe and, when one examined Honda's racing machines, it was not hard to see why. The 250cc racer, for example, was a superbly engineered bike. With its four cylinders set in-line across the frame, the sixteen-valve engine produced around 42bhp at 13,000rpm and could even be revved safely to 14,000rpm. Honda also had other reasons to celebrate 1961. Their total exports for the year were in excess of 49,000 and, during August, monthly sales topped 100,000 units, an unprecedented record in the motor cycle industry. Most of the sales were accounted for by the phenomenally popular 50cc Super Cub moped; but the 125cc Benly and 250cc Dream models were beginning to capture shares of the British and European markets for themselves.

1961 was also a good year for the other major Japanese manufacturers, Yamaha and Suzuki. Yamaha had introduced the YD3 250cc roadster as well as the little YA5 125cc model

and both were proving popular. There had been two black blots on Yamaha's copybook, however, and they were the failure of the MF1 moped and the SC1 scooter introduced in 1960. Yamaha had been keen to crack both the scooter and moped markets and had embarked on an ambitious development of a new 50cc moped plus a 175cc scooter with blower-cooled two-stroke motor. Unfortunately, heavy styling and unforeseen technical problems meant that neither project was fully realised and Yamaha took a financial hammering from which they took several years to recover.

Suzuki, which had begun life in 1952 as an off-shoot of a textile and engineering company and had spent the latter half of the 1950s and early '60s developing its range of small two-stroke machines, now decided that they would follow Honda's lead and go Grand Prix racing. The publicity that Honda had accrued as a result of their race victories was enormous and Suzuki wanted a share. Like Honda, Suzuki had sent a works team to the Isle of Man in 1960 to contest the 125cc TT but their little two-strokes had been comprehensively outpaced.

In spite of their failure the previous year, Suzuki were back on the Isle of Man in 1961 by which time they had added a 250cc machine to their stable. Once again, their machines were outpaced by the Hondas and the MZs. Also outpaced were the new Yamaha 125 and 250cc two-strokes which were making their European racing debut in the hands of the spectacular Japanese ace Fumio Ito.

The TT races themselves were notable for a hat trick of victories by Mike Hailwood. Riding the works Hondas, he scored victories in the 125 and 250 events and followed this up with a sensational victory in the 500cc Senior TT riding a Bill Lacey tuned Norton – the first time a Norton had won the Senior since 1954. Norton also secured victory in the 350cc Junior TT when Phil Read raced home at an average of 95.1mph, beating Gary Hocking and the magical MV in the process. Apart from these two Norton victories, however, it was a fairly lean year for British achievements. Dave Bickers, the motocross ace, managed to salvage some honour for the UK by riding his Greeves to victory in the European Moto Cross Championship (forerunner of the present World Championship), while at the Montlhéry circuit in France, a modified Velocette Venom set a new world record for a continuous 24-hour run, at a speed of 100.05mph.

Over the winter of 1961/62, it was announced that Ernst Degner, the brilliant East German rider, had defected from the

Left: Mike Hailwood rounds Signpost Corner on his way to winning the Senior TT in 1961 with his single-cylinder Ecurie Sportive Norton. Mike became the first man to average 100mph in a TT race with a single

Below: a Velocette Venom Veeline of 1960, powered by a 499cc, single-cylinder, overhead-valve engine

east and gone to live in West Germany. His defection immediately caused a stir in the racing world because, apart from his abilities as a rider, Degner was also a superb engineer, having learned his trade at the elbow of MZ's Walter Kaaden. Suzuki immediately beat a path to his door and the East German was persuaded to spend the winter in Japan developing a new generation of Suzuki racing machines. He soon proved his worth, for when the racing season commenced Degner took his Suzuki to victory in the newly introduced 50cc World Championship. Degner's influence on the Suzuki's design could clearly be seen. Like the MZ, the little Suzuki had a disc valve to control the induction on the single-cylinder, two-stroke engine, which produced about 10bhp at 11,000rpm and gave the tiny bike a top speed of over 95 mph. Degner won four Grand Prix events that year and, in spite of having to fight off a challenge from Honda who had also built a new 50cc machine, he gave Suzuki their first World Championship title.

Honda gained their revenge in the larger classes, however. They had stepped up their challenge to include the 350cc championship, and the highlight of the 1962 season was the battle in the 350 class between Honda and the reigning champions MV Agusta. The MVs were scaled down versions of the fabulously successful four-cylinder 'fire-engine' 500s, while the 285cc Honda was an enlarged version of the 250cc four (with 49×45mm bore and stroke) which gave the bikes a power output of over 50bhp at 12,500rpm.

Unfortunately, the season started disastrously for Honda. Racing in the 350cc TT on the Isle of Man, Tom Phillis crashed the new Honda and was killed. Many critics believe that Phillis's death came because the Honda lacked the power of the MVs and that Phillis was trying to make up the deficiency by sheer riding skill and daring. Whatever the reason, it was a blow to Honda and to two of Phillis's close friends, the Rhodesians Redman and Hocking. So upset was Hocking, in fact, that after winning the 500cc TT for MV Agusta he announced his retirement and went back home. Ironically, he later decided to try car racing and was killed when his Lotus skidded off the track and crashed during practice for the Natal Grand Prix in South Africa. Normally, the loss of a rider of Hocking's ability to a team like MV would have been a major blow but MV had an eminently suitable replacement in Mike Hailwood who had quit Honda for a place in the Italian team. So the scene was set for the rest of the 1962 season – it would be Jim Redman on the Honda versus Mike Hailwood on the MV. In the end, it was Redman who eclipsed the 350cc class. He won four Grands Prix on the trot, in Holland, Ulster, East Germany and Italy, to take the title in fine style. Just to make it a season to remember, he also annexed the 250cc class, winning no less than six of the year's major events. Hailwood salvaged some pride for the MV concern by winning the 500cc World Championship and achieving five outright wins.

In the 125cc World Championship, Honda made it a hat trick of world titles with Luigi Taveri of Switzerland eventually taking the title after scoring no less than six consecutive Grand Prix wins. Honda had somehow done what seemed to be impossible: they had eclipsed their sensational record of 1961 and made their mark on motor cycle history in no uncertain manner. Honda had other reasons to celebrate as well. Total production for the year had exceeded one million units, 142,000 of those being exported, and the total sales figure for 1962 exceeded £59 million. In addition, they had also constructed a test and development circuit at Suzuka, a track which is now used regularly for motor cycle and motor racing events.

Back in Britain, BSA had been hogging much of the limelight. 1962 wasn't a week old before they announced two new additions to their twin-cylinder range. These were the A50 and A65 Star twins. Of new design, they differed from the long standing A7, Shooting Star and Golden Flash models (which, incidentally, they soon replaced) in having engine-gearbox unit construction and Lucas AC/DC 12-volt electrical equipment instead of the usual separate magneto and dynamo layout. Another design feature was the use of a one-piece, die-cast, light-alloy cylinder head with integral lugs to make a very rigid rocker assembly. The two engines shared a common stroke measurement of 74mm, the bores being of 65.5 and 75mm, producing capacities of 499 and 654cc, respectively. These two models were followed a month later by a high-performance hybrid, the Rocket Gold Star. This was a marriage of the 46bhp engine from the Super Rocket and the frame of the race bred Gold Star. Both the parent models remained unchanged, although the Gold Stars were offered in limited quantities only, either to scrambles specification or in clubmans' road-racing trim. This was the year that the famed Gold Star was eventually to be dropped from the catalogues, although it was in fact possible to obtain DBD type 34s on special order for a couple of years after 1962.

BSA also enjoyed some much needed publicity when Chris Vincent raced his BSA-powered sidecar outfit to victory in that year's Sidecar TT, beating the might of the BMWs in the process. It was a one-off victory, however, because Max Deubel went on to win the world sidecar title, as he had done the previous year. It was BMW's ninth world sidecar title in a row and, indeed, they were destined to rule the sidecar roost for quite a few years yet.

1962 was also a notable year for another continental manufacturer – Husqvarna of Sweden. This little factory was to prepare the winning motocross machines of Rolf Tibblin and Torsten Hallman in the 500cc and 250cc European Moto Cross Championships and, like BMW in the sidecar class, would still play an active part in international and World Championship motocross events for many years to come.

In November 1962, the motor cycling world, having completed its racing season, focused its attention on the bi-annual London Motor Cycle Show held in the echoing halls of Earls Court. As usual, the crowds flocked to the Show in their thousands and as usual the weekly magazines trumped on about 'showtime magic', but in all honesty there wasn't that much to get excited about. BSA took the opportunity to introduce their 75cc Beagle lightweight runabout but it was hardly a show-stopper. Triumph showed their new 349cc sports model Tiger 90 while Velocette produced their all-enclosed LE Vogue powered by their 192cc side-valve engine and on which the shaft final drive was suspended from a single-tube, backbone frame. The all enveloping bodywork was in glassfibre and featured a twin headlight assembly. It attracted a lot of attention but, as was so often the case, when the time came for talking terms, customers were sadly lacking. Royal Enfield also used the Show to introduce their big new 736cc twin-cylinder Interceptor model, a 350cc Bullet – derived from the successful Crusader 250 – and their new five-speed Continental sportster. And that was about it. Enthusiasts could still ogle at AJS's 650 Hurricane, BSA's 650 Super Rocket, Matchless's 650 Monarch, Norton's Dominator 650SS and Triumph's 650 Bonneville, but these were not new, nor was there too much sign of them being replaced or

Top: Luigi Taveri, who was three times 125cc world champion with Honda, the first title coming in 1962

Above: Chris Vincent and Eric Bliss caused an upset at the 1962 Sidecar TT when they took their BSA-Watsonian outfit to victory in front of the much-favoured BMW opposition. The German company had the consolation of seeing their machines win the five other rounds of the sidecar championship that year, however

Right: the BSA Gold Star 500cc single was the archetypal British sports thumper – hard to start, uncomfortable to ride far, but exhilarating on twisty roads

updated. The Japanese stands provided some interest, with Suzuki making a last-minute appearance. Honda showing their 125cc Benly and 250cc Dream models and Yamaha displaying the 125cc YA5, the standard YD3 250cc roadster and the more exciting YDS2 sports 250cc machine. Even more interesting, however, was the appearance of Yamaha's production racer TD1 250 model. This was a development of the twin-cylinder, two-stroke 250 racers which had been appearing on the race tracks of Europe earlier in the season. The TD1, in time, would be developed into the TR and TZ production racing models, the most successful production-built racers the world had ever seen – and that taking into account the Norton Featherbed and AJS 7R machines.

If 1962 had been an exciting year for racing, 1963 promised to be even more so. Honda were committed to four classes – 50, 125, 250 and 350cc – and Suzuki and Yamaha were becoming steadily more competitive. In addition, there was the return to racing of Tarquinio Provini of Italy racing a works 250cc

Morini, while rumours were flying that Gilera would return to racing, albeit in the form of a private team to be run by Geoff Duke and using the old 500cc, four-cylinder screamers of 1957. The championship battles were certainly intense. In the 50cc class, Suzuki again took the honours with New Zealander Hugh Anderson triumphing after a season long battle with Hans-Georg Anscheidt on the German Kreidler, both riders eclipsing the works Honda effort. The works Hondas were also beaten in the 125cc class, where Hugh Anderson, riding a Degner-inspired, disc-valve, air-cooled, twin-cylinder Suzuki, soundly thrashed them, winning six World Championship events. Honda gained some revenge in the 250cc class with Jim Redman winning the title, but not without some fright because Provini, riding the single-cylinder Morini, took him to the final round and then only lost the title by two points. The Morini was a single-cylinder, four-stroke machine and the near success for the little Italian company proved that clever design and light weight could be an able substitute for vast sums of money and masses

of cylinders. Yamaha were also making some progress in their racing development. Taking a leaf out of MZ's and Suzuki's books, they abandoned their usual piston-port design for the disc-valve option and produced a very competitive 250cc, air-cooled twin on which Fumio Ito won in Belgium, and finally finished third in the end of season championship tables.

The 350cc class was, however, a complete Honda benefit. Hailwood's heavier MV beat Redman on two occasions but in the end Redman, with six wins to his credit, claimed the title. It was the second consecutive year in which Redman and Honda had achieved a 250 and 350cc championship double.

The 500cc class was given something of a lift by the reappearance of the Gilera team, managed by Geoff Duke and carrying the Scuderia Duke banner. The machines, however, looked similar to those of 1957 – not surprising, for they were the same machines just taken out of mothballs! – and the five year lack of development proved too much for riders Phil Read, John Hartle and Derek Minter. John Hartle did manage to win the Dutch TT, where Hailwood's MV dropped out, but in the end they were no match for the flying MV, and Hailwood

Top: the horizontal in-line, four-cylinder, 600cc Ariel prototype which was designed for army use. This bike used a Leader frame, but underneath was quite different. It also featured shaft drive and electric start

Above left: Hugh Anderson pilots his 125 Suzuki to victory in the Isle of Man in 1963; in so doing, he took the World Championship

Above: Tarquinio Provini and his Morini 250 single head for victory in Spain in 1963

Right: after the demise of the Gilera works team, Geoff Duke formed his own team. Here Scuderia Duke rider Hartle is seen in Ulster heading for second place in 1963

finished the season with seven wins (out of a possible eight) to his credit. A final indignity was handed to Gilera when Alan Shepherd on a Matchless outscored them by a single point to take second place in the championship. At the end of the season, Gilera retired again, which was sad, because motor cycle enthusiasts had a genuine affection for the famed Italian company and would have liked nothing more than to see them return competitively to motor cycle sport.

In the sidecar class, Max Deubel took the title yet again for BMW, while in the world of motocross, Rolf Tibblin and Torsten Hallman repeated their 500 and 250cc European Moto Cross Championship victories as they had done the year before.

Over in Japan, Honda were once again announcing record profits. Their annual production had risen to $1\frac{1}{4}$ million units, 338,000 being exported, of which 114,000 had been taken by the United States. Yamaha too were looking healthier. After the SC1 and MF1 debacle they had staged something of a comeback and their newly introduced 75cc YG1 lightweight motor cycle was proving a popular seller. Suzuki's range of small two-strokes was also proving popular, while Kawasaki introduced a motocross version of their B8, the 125cc B8M, which took the first six places in the Japanese championship.

Back in Britain, alas, things were not looking quite so rosy. In mid July 1962 had come the shattering news that Associated Motor Cycles Limited (who had absorbed Norton in 1953) were to close the famous Norton works at Bracebridge Street in Birmingham and that Norton was to be merged with the Matchless company, both makes now to be built at the Matchless factory in Plumstead Road, Woolwich, London. To Norton enthusiasts it was like saying the Queen would be moving out of Buckingham Palace into a back street hotel. This 'rationalisation', as it had been called, was done mainly for economic reasons, because at the end of 1961 AMC were forced to announce that their previous year's profits of £219,000 had been turned into a deficit of £350,000. The move to Woolwich was completed in 1963, by which time Norton had created the Atlas model. It was intended primarily for export and featured a 73 × 89mm, 745cc engine, which developed nearly 50bhp. Basically, it was an uprated Dominator, but it did prove particularly popular with British riders who, unlike the Americans, were not obsessed with size, and were quite happy with their 650s, thank you very much.

1963 also saw the beginning of the end for another popular British make, the Ariel. Ariel, who had become part of the BSA group in the early 1950s, were in financial trouble, as were BSA, and so the decision was taken to move Ariel production from its famous Selly Oak home to BSA's huge factory at Small Heath in Birmingham where production of the 250cc Arrow model was continued alongside the development of a 200cc version and the building of the lightweight 50cc Pixie. Prior to the move, work was being undertaken on a four-cylinder, in-line, 600cc prototype, designed for army use, but when the Government announced spending cuts, this Ariel project was allowed to die a natural death. Had this project been successful, it may well have saved both Ariel and the Selly Oak factory, but with its failure any hope of an independent Ariel existence faded and the move to Small Heath became inevitable.

The following year, 1964, saw the beginning of another 'golden age' in motor cycle racing. It was eventually to become known as the era of 'the race for cylinders' and it would last for three glorious and very expensive years. During this time, more exotic machinery appeared on the racing circuits than had ever

been seen before – or since. By now, Honda had established themselves as top dogs in the world of racing but found Suzuki and Yamaha snapping at their heels. Indeed, Suzuki had already claimed three world titles for themselves.

Honda faced a crisis. For policy reasons – all of their production road machines were four-strokes – Honda was committed to the four-stroke principle. Suzuki and Yamaha, however, were in the two-stroke camp and by this time had developed really competitive machines based on the disc-valve and expansion chamber exhaust arrangement developed initially by Walter Kaaden of MZ in East Germany. The only way Honda could combat the rise of the two-strokes was to increase the efficiency of their engines and the only way to do this, they believed, was to increase the number of cylinders. This they did to such brilliant effect that Yamaha and Suzuki were forced to reply in kind, by creating complex multi-cylinder engine layouts. Needless to say, development of this kind was costly.

So, in 1964, Honda returned to racing with a big challenge. They replaced their single-cylinder 50cc racer with a twin, their twin-cylinder 125cc machine with an eight-speed, four-cylinder model and, towards the end of the season, even replaced their trusty four-cylinder 250cc with an incredible six-cylinder bike. Ironically, the complicated six was introduced only as a result of the enormous success of Yamaha's fairly simple RD56 twin-cylinder 250 model.

Honda's machines bear closer examination. For example, the little 50cc racer with its tiny twin cylinders (33×29.2mm bore and stroke) produced 13bhp at an incredible 19,700rpm, enough to give the machine a top speed of over 100mph. The little 125cc four (35×32mm) revved to 16,000rpm, produced 25bhp and had a top speed of 120mph (and these were the days, remember, when even a road going 650cc Norton could barely reach 110mph). The pride of Honda's pack, the six-cylinder 250 drove through an eight-speed gearbox and the engine, which produced a spine-tingling, howling sound, punched out 53bhp at 16,500rpm giving the bike a top speed in the region of 150mph.

The season itself produced some epic battles. In the 50cc class, in spite of their new machine, Honda were forced to take a back seat by the Suzuki of Hugh Anderson. Nevertheless, Ralph Bryans, with four Grand Prix victories to his credit, served warning that Honda were now a force to be reckoned with in this category. Honda were successful in the 125cc class, however, and beat off the Suzuki challenge. Luigi Taveri was

Left: Jim Redman won each round of the 350cc class Grands Prix in 1964, and he is seen here with his four-cylinder Honda on his winning way in Ulster

Below: Max Deubel and Emil Horner round Governor's Bridge hairpin with their BMW in the 1964 Sidecar TT, which they won

Bottom left: Jeff Smith with his 500 BSA, hard at work in 1964 winning his Moto Cross World Championship

Bottom right: Jeff Smith's main rival in 1964 was Rolf Tibblin, seen here with his Hedlund at that year's Moto Cross des Nations at Hawkstone Park

the man who eventually took the title, having piloted his red and silver Honda to wins in five of the championship rounds.

It was in the 250cc class that the major upset of the year occurred. Here, the main protagonists were Honda's Jim Redman and Yamaha's young Briton, Phil Read. After two quite surprising results in the first two rounds, at Daytona and Barcelona – Alan Shepherd on an MZ won the former race and Tarquinio Provini on a works Benelli the latter – Read and Redman got to grips. All season long they battled but, even though Honda introduced their six-cylinder racer towards the end of the year, it was Read who took the title for Yamaha by 46 points to Redman's 42. The victory gave Yamaha their first world title, Read his first and it was also the first time a two-stroke machine had ever won the 250cc championship.

In the 350cc class, Jim Redman managed to salvage some honour for himself and Honda by winning the world title in fine style from his protégé and fellow Rhodesian Bruce Beale, a newcomer to the Honda team. The 500cc class, almost overlooked amidst the blood and thunder of the lightweight classes, went quite predictably to Mike Hailwood and the MV Agusta. With no works opposition to threaten him, Hailwood cruised to seven wins out of a possible nine. The sidecar class went to Max Deubel and Emil Horner on the inevitable BMW. For once, however, Deubel did not have things all his own way because he was beaten several times during the season, twice by Fritz Scheidegger (BMW), once by Florian Camathias on a Gilera powered outfit and once by Britain's Colin Seeley on a BMW outfit. In later years, Seeley would go on to become a well known frame manufacturer with his own thriving business.

For British fans, 1964 was memorable for another reason. It was the year in which a Briton won the 500cc World Moto Cross Championship on a British bike. The man was Jeff Smith and the machine was a thundering 500cc BSA four-stroke. Smith therefore joined Les Archer (Norton) and Dave Bickers (Greeves) as the only British men on British machines to make a mark on the otherwise continental dominated world of motocross. Smith had had to fight very hard for his title, however, and the championship had to go to the final round in Spain before Smith could stamp his authority over Sweden's Rolf Tibblin and his Hedlund machine.

1964 also saw the running of the first 250cc World Moto Cross Championship, the series until then being known as the

European Championship, and this also provided an interesting result. The eventual World Champion was a young, burly and aggressive Belgian by the name of Joël Robert. Riding a Czechoslovakian CZ machine, he stamped his authority on the championship in no uncertain manner and in years to come Robert would become the most controversial motocross rider – and the most successful – that the world has ever seen.

Apart from Jeff Smith's success, there wasn't too much for British fans to enthuse about. If anything, it was a time for mourning because yet another independent British manufacturing company had gone to the wall. This time it was the Excelsior firm, which for some years had been building lightweight machines but were in the end simply swamped by the Japanese. The Excelsior name did not die altogether, however, because in later years the title was bought by the giant Britax concern and used to help market that company's motor cycling accessories.

These were gloomy years for the British motor cycle industry and worse was to follow. Honda, Yamaha and Suzuki had not only taken control of the race circuits but had also taken control of the production market and, just to add insult to injury, Kawasaki were now in a strong enough position to open an office in Chicago from where they could control sales to the American market. The office was opened in early 1965, by which time Kawasaki had also announced their new 50cc M10 model, a lightweight designed to compete directly with the other Japanese models of that type.

The 1965 racing season got under way with the promise of some spectacular race action. This time, Honda faced not only a challenge from Yamaha and Suzuki in the smaller classes but a threat from MV Agusta in the normally Honda dominated 350cc category. MV had decided to go the opposite route to Honda and, instead of adding cylinders, they produced a new slimline three-cylinder 350 to replace the old heavyweight four. The bike was lighter, handled better and, with reduced frontal area, was also faster. In addition, MV produced a new trump card in the form of a new rider to back up Mike Hailwood. He was a young, talented, good looking Italian by the name of Giacomo Agostini whom MV had signed up from Morini. Agostini, born in Brescia, Italy, in 1942 of fairly wealthy parents, had made his name in Italian national events on the small racing Morini models and was now being given a chance by the powerful MV concern to prove himself outside of Italy.

Top left: Hugh Anderson at Oulton Park in April 1965 with his 125 Suzuki. In that year, Hugh took the world title with this bike

Top right: Joël Robert with his CZ at a special TV meeting in early 1965. Joël went on to take six world titles

Above: the legendary Count Domenico Agusta with his equally legendary riders, Giamoco Agostini, left, and Mike Hailwood, right. They are seen at Monza in 1965

MV Agusta was not the only company that had been busy over the winter. For 1965, Suzuki also produced a completely redesigned 125cc twin. It was a water-cooled, disc-valve machine that was to tear the heart out of Honda's 125cc challenge. Suzuki also brought back the 250cc four-cylinder machine that they had introduced the previous season. It too was a water-cooled, disc-valve machine, this time with its four cylinders placed in a square; its gearbox was a six-speed unit. Unfortunately, it hadn't worked the previous year in the hands of riders like Hugh Anderson, and it failed again in 1965. Overheating was the main problem and it proved to Suzuki that simply adding another pair of cylinders to the otherwise successful 125cc twin was no way to go about making a successful 250cc four. They did not give up, however, and continued to develop the theme, so it was no coincidence that many years later, during the mid 1970s, Suzuki were reigning supreme in the 500cc class with a disc-valve, square-four model.

Yamaha also continued to develop their machines and, by

Above: Mike Hailwood, with his MV Agusta, on his winning way in the Senior TT of 1965. Earlier on in the race, Mike had dropped his bike at Sarah's Cottage smashing the windscreen and damaging the carburettors. Mike got going again and called at the pits to have a throttle slide taken off. He went out again with his twistgrip working just three of the four carburettors, and carried on to win perhaps his hardest ever race

this time, the little RD56 250cc racer was capable of producing 50bhp at 13,000rpm, although its rider, Phil Read, needed to manipulate the seven-speed gearbox furiously to keep it in its narrow power band.

When the season actually started, it soon became apparent that a few surprises were in store. For one thing, Suzuki were no longer dominant in the 50cc class, and the twin-cylinder Hondas had been developed to perfection. Suzuki's Degner and Anderson did manage to grab three wins on the little blue and silver machines but by the end of the season Irishman Ralph Bryans had taken control of the class for Honda. He finished up with three wins and took the title from team-mate Luigi Taveri who pushed the previous year's champion, Hugh Anderson, down into third spot. Anderson, however, exacted his revenge on Honda in the 125cc class in a determined manner with Suzuki's new twin proving more than a match for the four-cylinder Hondas. He won at Daytona, Nürburgring, Barcelona, Rouen, Imatra, Monza and Suzuka to emerge a clear victor. Honda, however, were not going to take defeat without fighting back, and at Suzuka, the last round of that year's championship, they wheeled out their new secret weapon, and great white hope for the following season, in typically flamboyant and extravagant Honda style. It was nothing less than a five-cylinder model, being literally two and a half 50cc models joined end to end. The first of these five-cylinder models revved to an incredible 18,000rpm and produced 30bhp but, with constant development, later models were to push out 35bhp at over 20,000rpm. The designer of this amazing machine was a young engineer named Soichiro Irimajiri who in later years would become known to motor cycle enthusiasts for his part in designing the CB400 twins and the remarkable six-cylinder CBX1000. Indeed, the fact that the CBX could be designed so quickly was largely due to the grounding in multi-cylinder development that Irimajiri had undergone during those golden years of the mid '60s. As an aside, Irimajiri was also the man who designed the V12 engine of the Honda racing car which John Surtees drove in the late '60s.

In the 250cc class, the battle royal was once again between Jim Redman and Phil Read. Redman, unfortunately, was forced to miss some of the earlier rounds due to an injury and Read took the first five races in a row. Redman made a splendid comeback at the TT, finishing second, and then went on to win the next three races on the trot. Alas for Redman, Read had done enough to win the title again. Once more, the lightweight twin-cylinder, two-stroke had beaten its more complicated and heavier four-stroke rival.

Redman was also given a hard fight in the 350cc class, this time by the new three-cylinder MV of Giacomo Agostini. In fact, this was his toughest season in this class for years. Redman managed to win the rounds in the Isle of Man, Holland, East Germany and Czechoslovakia but Agostini replied by winning in Germany, Finland and Italy. The championship was therefore decided at the final round, held at Suzuka in Japan, and the MV ace almost shook the might of Honda by leading during the early stages of the race. Then, with the race his for the taking, the MV broke a contact-breaker spring and Ago dropped back to fifth. Hailwood on his MV swept by to win the race but second place was all Redman needed to take the championship title, albeit by only six points.

In the 500cc class, the MVs of Hailwood and Agostini were invincible and Hailwood went on to clinch yet another world title, his fourth 500cc championship in as many years. In the sidecar category, Fritz Scheidegger and his English passenger John Robinson took the title, thereby ending the stranglehold that Max Deubel had held on it for the past three years. Scheidegger was mounted on a BMW, however, so there was no change in the winning marque.

At the end of the season, Honda announced some of their plans for the following year. A large sum of money was being offered to Mike Hailwood to tempt him away from MV and work was being undertaken on a new four-cylinder 500cc machine with which MV's supremacy in the 500cc class was to be challenged. In addition, there were rumours of a new 50cc racer. It was a three-cylinder machine capable of 25,000rpm and the prototype was said to have been completed before the Japanese Grand Prix in October but kept under wraps because the existing twins proved fast enough.

Jim Redman, after a disappointing season, found himself at

Below: Dave Degens of Triton fame track tests the 'black bomber' CB450 Honda for a motor cycle newspaper at Brands Hatch. Although a very popular machine with many enthusiasts, the bike was never accepted by the general bike-buying public

Right: at the end of 1965, Honda shocked the world with its five-cylinder, 125cc racer. However, the company was having enough success with its twin-cylinder bikes, so it did not need to use its other 'ace' card. It was this bike which ultimately caused the FIM to ban bikes with more than two cylinders in the smaller classes.

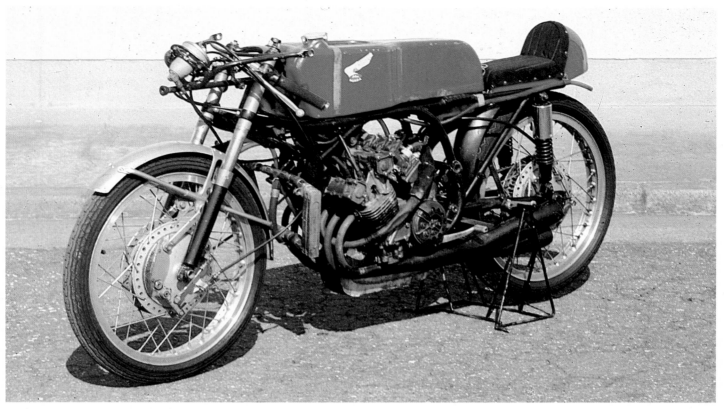

odds with the Honda management over his future and had to fly to Japan and undergo some hard talking to keep his place in the team. With Hailwood secured for 1966, and Redman's career in its twilight, Honda wanted Redman to continue with them in a sort of non-riding team captain capacity but Redman was having none of it. His persuasive powers won the day and he took his place in the team for 1966.

The other major news item from Honda during 1965 was the introduction of the CB450 model, a twin-overhead-camshaft machine which soon came to be known as the 'black bomber'. This was their new top of the range model, a genuine 100mph roadster with an all-alloy twin-cylinder motor. It failed to capture the American imagination, however, and there were also rumours that badly spaced gear ratios and troublesome fuel delivery were being blamed for its failure. Nevertheless, the CB450's failure wasn't too painful for Honda to bear because by this time they were the ninth major exporter in the whole of Japan, earning the Japanese economy well over one hundred million dollars in foreign exchange.

In Britain, there was little in the way of real development. AJS were marketing their new 745cc Atlas-engined Model 33, while BSA announced they would be marketing a production version of the 420cc BSA scrambler on which Jeff Smith had just scored his second world motocross title. Panther were still struggling on with their lightweight two-strokes and big singles while Velocette had introduced what was to prove the last of their classic machines, the 500cc Thruxton. The Thruxton represented the ultimate in the development of the 'M' series of singles and in many respects it could be likened to a latter day Mk VIII KTT model because its performance was quite astonishing for a pushrod-engined machine. Triumph were marketing a range of scooters, the 100cc Tina and the 173cc Tigress, but these were hardly the stuff that financial fortunes were made of. So, as the motor cycling world prepared itself for 1966, it looked to be a pretty grim year for Britain.

Chapter 13
End of an Era (1966-1979)

Left: an 850cc Electric Start Norton Commando of 1976, which ended an era of vertical-twin bikes for the NVT company. After the demise of the Commando, the public eagerly awaited the arrival of the new-generation Norton, the 1200cc twin-rotor Wankel bike, which was due to be launched in mid 1979

By 1966, just seven years after the Japanese had made their first appearance on the Isle of Man, the British industry seemed to be in a sorry state. Few people, however, realised that it was dying. Indeed, the British motor cycle industry took a long time to die, and like any wounded animal its convoluted thrashing to stay alive left chaos and confusion in its wake. The old industry didn't go down without a fight but it made a dreadful mess.

In fact, there are those who would say that the industry has not died at all, and point to Meriden, Rickman and the new NVT as living proof. These companies do survive, it is true, but they are isolated cases, and most people would agree that the industry, as those enthusiasts of the 1940s and '50s knew it, has gone – perhaps forever.

It was in August 1966 that the first really important nail was driven into the coffin of Britain's bike building industry. The Associated Motor Cycle group (which comprised AJS, Francis-Barnett, James, Norton and Matchless) found itself unable to carry on financially, and a Receiver was appointed by its bank. At this stage, AMC had rationalised its range to a great extent. For example, Norton were marketing only six machines, two of which – the Mk II and ES Mk II – were virtually 350 and 500cc AJS/Matchless machines with Norton tank badges. By September, however, AMC had found itself what appeared to be a saviour in the form of the Manganese Bronze Holdings company, whose chairman was Dennis Poore, a motoring enthusiast whose earlier activities had even included being a member of the famed Aston Martin car racing team.

A year earlier, Manganese Bronze Holdings had taken over the Villiers Engineering Company and a plan was now formulated to merge the AMC group with Villiers. By way of explanation, Dennis Poore later wrote: 'By 1961, Associated Motor Cycles Ltd, the once proud home of so many famous marques, was languishing under a heavy burden of debt. The Villiers Engineering Company Ltd, which had been the foremost supplier of small petrol engines for industrial and motor cycle use since most people could remember, was facing severe competition from American and Japanese imports; its profit and loss account was telling the inevitable tale. What was to be done to rejuvenate this vital industry so that it could resume its proper place on the British scene? The answer proposed by my colleagues on the Manganese Bronze Holdings group board was a marriage of these two companies within our group. The financial implications were studied, obstacles overcome and the bold concept of this plan was started in 1962. By 1966 it had been consumated and Norton Villiers Limited was born'.

The fact that the name Norton appeared in the new Norton Villiers logo, and not AMC, was indicative of the way that Poore and his group were thinking. Norton was by far the most famous name in the group's armoury. It represented success, both on the race track and the road, and it would be their passport, hopefully, to new glory. As with all mergers of this nature, however, there had to be some casualties, and the first to suffer were Francis-Barnett and James. Both had spent the last few years marketing Villiers-engined lightweights. Francis-Barnett were making the Falcon, Cruiser and Fulmar models while James were trying to sell their Cadet model, neither company achieving a great deal of success. Consequently, the two once-famous names were allowed to die, the James factory being sold off to a pump manufacturer. Only a few months later, even the outline of the James shield which had once graced the gates of the factory had vanished into the pages of history.

Shortly after the demise of Francis-Barnett and James came the next couple of casualties, AJS and Matchless, two grand and glorious old names famous throughout the world for their racing exploits. At that stage, AJS were marketing a number of machines using 650 and even 750cc twin-cylinder engines as well as the 31CSR and other single-cylinder models, while Matchless's range also contained a number of Norton/Matchless hybrids such as the 745cc Atlas powered G15 roadster. Norton Villiers Limited quickly dropped the last Matchless 250, the Monitor, and it was followed a few months later by the 650cc Monarch vertical-twin. Shortly afterwards, in early 1967, the last machine to bear the once proud Matchless tank badge, the 750 G15 CSR, was condemned to the great motor cycle scrapyard in the sky and the Matchless marque was no more. AJS had likewise been closed but in time it would re-emerge as the manufacturer of potent 250 and 370cc scrambles machines. The AJS name, in fact, still exists today, its destinies being guided by 'Fluff' Brown, an enthusiastic businessman from the county of Hampshire.

AJS and Matchless were not the only manufacturers to come under Norton Villiers' knife because even the Norton range of models was severely pruned. All the single-cylinder models were dropped and only the big twins continued in production. In addition, all of AMC's racing equipment was sold off to help recoup the company's debts. Thus, by drastic rationalisation, did Norton Villiers bring its product line within reasonable bounds.

Having reshaped the company, Norton Villiers then set about planning for the future. In early 1967, it recruited from Rolls-Royce a talented engineer by the name of Dr Stephen Bauer. He was to head a design team briefed to produce an entirely new Norton model – to be known as the Commando. Working alongside Dr Bauer in this project were two motor cycle development engineers, Bernard Hooper and Bob Trigg, whose concept of a new form of engine mounting – which is now known throughout the world as the Isolastic system – later won them the 1969 Ferodo award for the most meritorious contribution to motor cycle development.

The first Commando model appeared in 1968 and was given the name Fastback because of its unusual all-enveloping rear end styling. Years later, almost all the Japanese models would incorporate rear end styling not dissimilar from that of the Fastback. The Commando was powered by the 73 × 89mm bore and stroke, 750cc Atlas engine which was inclined and mounted

Top: a G5 Matchless 350 of 1962, which used a single-cylinder engine of conventional design

Above: Malcolm Davis with his 250cc, two-stroke AJS, seen at a special TV motocross event in 1968

Right: an early example of the Isolastic-framed, separate-gearbox 750 Norton Commando

in an entirely new frame featuring the Isolastic principle wherein the engine, separate gearbox and pivot bearings for the swinging arm suspension were all carried in a sub-frame, rubber mounted within the main duplex frame, thus securing a high degree of frame rigidity with a minimum of vibration. Roadholder-type front forks were used in conjunction with Girling rear suspension units to give the powerful new 120mph roadster quite immaculate handling. The Commando, it was hoped, would be Norton Villiers' salvation.

Meanwhile, back in the Midlands, the BSA/Triumph group was busy getting itself into financial difficulties as well. Unlike AMC of Woolwich, this group had entered the 1960s in a reasonable strong position, thanks mainly to the various business interests within the group. In 1961, for example, BSA had acquired the Churchill Machine Tool Company which, with other connections, made it the largest machine tool company in Britain. So diversified were they that no less than thirty separate companies operated within the group from twenty different

factories, making everything from coal cleaning plant to taxis.

Somewhere along the line, however, a few expensive mistakes had been made. In 1959, in an attempt to cash in on the scooter craze, BSA launched its 250cc, vertical twin, four-stroke Sunbeam scooter. It flopped and even an attempt in 1963 to fit electric self starting couldn't save the project. Triumph also dabbled with the scooter, notably with its 100cc Tina and 175cc Tigress models, and these were a little more successful but an attempt to market the 250cc Tigress, which was simply a Sunbeam under another name, proved disastrous.

In addition, in February 1967, a new research and development centre was created at Umberside Hall and, while the staff there produced some interesting designs, the venture had cost £750,000, a sum the group could not afford to add to its already heavy annual overheads.

It seemed that nothing BSA/Triumph did during the 1960s could go right. Their model range mainstays owed much to designs created during previous decades – the trusty Triumph Bonneville could trace its ancestry back to the Speed Twin models of 1937 – and every new introduction just seemed to bring failure. The 90cc Dandy step-through model had seemed a good idea but it had failed. The 75cc Beagle was plagued by teething troubles while the three-wheeler Ariel 50cc moped project was an embarrasing disaster which not only cost huge sums of money, but killed off the once famous Ariel name just for good measure.

In the main, there was some justification in these recriminations. For some time, BSA's management had been preoccupied with diversifying the company's interests into fields that had absolutely nothing to do with the motor cycle market. Consequently, by the late 1960s, BSA's model range had been reduced to a handful of machines. The old four-speed D10 Bantam model had been discontinued in favour of the 175cc D14 Bantam Super, the only two-stroke model left on BSAs books. A high-performance 250 called either the Starfire or the Barracuda, according to specification, had been evolved from the successful Victor World Championship winning motocross model while a roadgoing Victor, the 441cc B44 Shooting Star was also available. Completing the model range were the 500cc, twin-cylinder A50 Royal Star, and the single and dual carburettor 650cc A65T Thunderbolt and A65L Lightning twins.

It wasn't all black clouds and disaster for BSA/Triumph in the late '60s, however, because in 1967 and '68 both companies were to receive the Queen's Award for Industry for their successful sales and contribution to the motor cycle industry during preceeding years. Indeed, as 1968 dawned it looked as though better days were ahead for the group with the announcement of two brand new machines.

These two new machines, to be known as the Triumph Trident and the BSA Rocket III, were the first really new machines to come out of the BSA group for years and they were welcomed with open arms, initially, by the public. Both machines were powered by new three-cylinder, 750cc engines and were theoretically the first of what later came to be known as the 'superbikes'. Although the two bikes used the same engine, the BSA differed in that it used a full-loop duplex tube frame in which the engine's cylinders were inclined forward at a slight angle, while the Trident had the engine block upright in a single front-down-tube frame. The engines, designed by Bert Hopwood, Doug Hele and Jack Wicks at Triumph's Meriden factory, had a bore and stroke of 67 × 70mm giving a cubic capacity of 740cc.

Initially, the Rocket III and Trident models were intended for export to the US and it was not until April of 1969 that deliveries on the home market took place. The idea of introducing two models which were otherwise similar, however, was not universally popular and one of the men who spoke out loudest against what he called 'badge engineering' was Jack Sangster, a former BSA chairman who had retired in 1960. He argued that it would undermine pride of ownership among riders and that it was questionable whether two names would sell more of a first class product. In addition, he said, the cost of

Below: the BSA Rocket 3, which was arguably the first of the modern generation of 'superbikes', having been launched in 1968. Stablemate to the Rocket was the Triumph Trident, early versions of which had a vertical (as opposed to inclined) engine and a different frame

Right: the American team members pose at Brands Hatch for the 1971 GB v US Match races with their BSA and Triumph machines

effective advertising and distribution would obviously be very much higher while the spare parts service had to be duplicated, all of which added to the overall cost. In time his prophetic words would prove to be right.

The triples spawned a new racing machine which in turn spawned a new racing formula now known as Formula 750. This came about with the increase of interest by the BSA group in the prestigious Daytona 200 race in America. BSA/Triumph knew the benefits to be had from winning such a major American race and set about developing a new racer based on the Trident and Rocket triples. In time, these new racers would also create a new racing series known as the Anglo-American Transatlantic challenge, which would become immensely popular with racing fans in Britain.

So, with BSA and Triumph having launched their new triples and the new Norton Villiers group having introduced its new Commando, the British industry approached the beginning of the 1970s with some hope for the future.

The same couldn't be said for the other motor cycle manufacturing companies in Britain, however. Already two famous names, Panther and Royal Enfield, had died in 1967 while another, Velocette, was only to last until 1971.

Panther, a direct descendant of the famous old P & M concern, had spent the earlier part of the 1960s marketing a range of small Villiers-engined two-strokes plus a big 645cc single which owed its origins to the 1930s. This was the Model 120 machine: it was a motor cycle from a different era and sales were dropping. Even an attempt in 1966 to revive the famous old Red Panther name, this time in the guise of a 250cc Villiers-powered machine painted in an all-over coat of red, failed to attract the customers and in 1967 the tired old Panther was finally put to sleep.

Royal Enfield were in much the same position during the 1960s. They had introduced several interesting models during the early '60s but none was a huge sales success and without the necessary finance Enfield couldn't alter their product line to fight off the Japanese invasion. At the end of 1962, Royal Enfield had introduced their powerful 736cc Interceptor twin and this was followed by the racy little 250cc Continental GT in 1965. The Continental, with its bright red tank and sporty lines, had a top speed of 90mph and appealed mostly to the youngster who, alas, did not buy it in sufficient numbers to save Enfield. The company also dabbled with a 250cc production racer which used a two-stroke Alpha/Enfield engine, but the project had to be curtailed. In 1967, the long history of Royal Enfield ground to a halt and the machinery and stock were sold off while the company's famed Redditch factory was eventually sold to the local Development Corporation.

The Velocette company of Birmingham managed to last a little longer. Several marketing mistakes during the 1960s had also cost this famous old company dearly. Like so many others, Velocette had burned their fingers when, in 1960, they had ventured into the scooter market with the Viceroy model. The scooter in itself was an interesting little machine of clever design and featured a horizontally opposed, twin-cylinder, two-stroke engine, but it did not sell. The venture cost the company money it could ill afford and it never wholly recovered from it. In 1963 came another interesting creation and another financial hammering. This time the model was the all-enclosed glassfibre bodied 200cc LE Vogue. Less than 500 were made. In 1964 came the last of the great Velocettes, the 500cc single-cylinder Thruxton model. The Thruxton, however, was also a throwback to an earlier generation of machines and it alone could not stave off impending bankruptcy. During the early part of 1971 the company went into voluntary liquidation and another famous name was lost to the winds of time. Viewed in retrospect it is surprising that Velocette had even managed to last that long, for it was never a large company and had almost always had to work to a tight budget and against tough competition.

With Harold MacMillan's 'you never had it so good' speech ringing in its ears, the British motor cycle industry turned its back on the 1960s to face the 1970s. AJS had gone, so too had Matchless, Ariel, Francis-Barnett, James, Excelsior, Panther, Royal Enfield and Velocette. Who, motor cycle enthusiasts wondered, was next?

Back at Norton Villiers and BSA/Triumph, it was very much business as usual, but their hoped-for revival with their newly introduced Commando and Trident/Rocket models ran into a problem during the middle of 1969. This was the year in which Honda decided to launch its new 'superbike', the CB750, and the introduction of this model, aimed specifically at the US market, hurt Norton and BSA very badly. The CB750 was a master stroke by the Japanese. It was a four-cylinder machine with a chain-driven single-overhead-camshaft, 736cc engine producing 67bhp at 8000rpm. It had four carburettors, five gears and an electric starter. If ever a motor cycle could be described as an iron fist in a velvet glove this was it. In addition, it was marketed at a price that dealt Norton and BSA a severe blow to the solar plexus. The CB750 Four had a top speed of over 120mph, massive front disc brake and, although it didn't handle as well as the British triples, it sold in huge quantities all around the world. It was a superb sports tourer and, of course, it had the advantages of an extra cylinder and extra power over the triples. Just to add to the problems of the British

Left: the Velocette Viceroy was yet another attempt by a British company to break into the lucrative scooter market. However, it proved to be little more than another nail in the coffin for Velocette

Below: one of the last ever Royal Enfields was this production-racing two-stroke 250, seen with Percy Tait in late 1965

Right: although the BSA/Triumph triples were in production before it, the Honda 750 Four was regarded as the first important superbike. Indeed, it set the style for others

Left: after the failures Velocette had with the LE and the Viceroy, they marketed this Thruxton, a 500cc, single-cylinder racer. Regarded by many as the last of the great Velos, it was no saviour for the company, which was already too deep in trouble to survive for much longer

manufacturers, another Japanese giant was rumoured to be building a triple of its own. This was the Suzuki company but its machine was not a four-stroke triple, it was a two-stroke of 750cc featuring water cooling. Suzuki's new GT750, as the bike was eventually to be known, did not have the impact that Honda's CB750 had on the world market but it was enough to take even more sales from the now desperate British manufacturers and that was the last thing they could afford. The introduction of the Triumph and BSA triples had been a last ditch attempt by the BSA group to survive. There was no more money with which to build a new superbike to counter the Honda and Suzuki threats and, at the end of 1971, came the shattering news from BSA that the group had sustained a loss of over £8 million. At that stage BSA's chairman, Eric Turner, resigned and was succeeded by Lord Shawcross. One of the most immediate effects of the announcement was the closure of the competition works which had been preparing the by now famous three-cylinder Formula 750 racers plus the successful motocross team. Sadly, the closure of the competitions department also killed off the development of a new and supposedly revolutionary lightweight motocross machine with which BSA hoped to conquer the world.

Although Lord Shawcross and a reconstituted board of directors tried gamely to save the failing fortunes of BSA, the balance sheet at the end of the 1972 financial year showed a further loss – some £3.3 million. Clearly something had to be done if the group was not to go bankrupt. Serious discussions now began with the Government's Department of Trade and Industry in an attempt to save the industry, and eventually a new scheme was hatched. Basically the idea was that Britain's big two manufacturers, Norton Villiers and BSA/Triumph, would merge to form one viable group. The new company, to be called Norton Villiers Triumph Limited, would be formed with a capital of £10 million, almost half of which would be subscribed by the government and the remainder by the Manganese Bronze Holdings firm, the parent company of Norton Villiers Ltd. MBH would make a bid for the whole of the BSA group which, of course, included Triumph. Norton Villiers Triumph would then acquire from MBH the Norton Villiers company while MBH would retain the whole of the non-motor cycling interests of the group. The effect was to create a combined organisation of the two major British manufacturers with a board of directors and management which could concentrate wholly on motor cycle manufacture. The new company's brief was to evolve, with the help of this substantial new investment, a sound enterprise capable of competing with the Japanese in world markets, and to make a profit. This brief – to ensure a viable commercial future – was to have enormous importance in the future history of the company. The scheme was subsequently accepted by the BSA shareholders – they hadn't much option – and the net result was that the old BSA group was no more. Sadly, amongst all the financial jiggery pokery, the BSA name had been allowed to die and so another famous scalp was added to the Japanese belt. From amidst all this chaos was born Norton Villiers Triumph in July 1973.

Before the merger was completed, however, there had been one or two interesting developments from both Norton and BSA. For Norton's part these included the formation of a new racing team in 1972 which was sponsored by the giant John Player cigarette company. The team was to be led by Peter Williams and would be under the management of former racing ace Frank Perris. The bikes themselves were lightweight

Right: in 1971, the Triumph/BSA conglomerate announced plans to build a new medium capacity machine, using a twin-cam, twin-cylinder engine of 350cc. Unfortunately, the Triumph Bandit and BSA Fury models, as the machines were to be known, never went into production. Our picture shows the ill-fated BSA Fury prototype

Below left: Dennis Poore, chairman of Norton Villiers Triumph, poses with the company's 'last chance' models, the Triumph Trident and Norton Commando machines, in 1975; sadly, these machines were not a great success

Below right: Peter Williams in action on the works twin-cylinder, 750cc John Player Norton at Mallory Park in 1975

machines designed to compete in the Formula 750 category and had four-stroke, twin-cylinder engines developed from the production Commando models.

BSA's new project, which was never to see the light of day, was the announcement, in 1971, of a new range of twin-cylinder, twin overhead camshaft BSA and Triumph 350cc models. To be known as the BSA Fury and the Triumph Bandit, the little newcomers had been designed by Edward Turner and were aimed directly at the Japanese opposition. Unfortunately, they were prematurely publicised and a huge investment in tooling up was lost when major faults were discovered, only a few prototypes having been made. This was just one more of the calamities which had brought about the downfall of BSA.

The new NVT company, as it soon became known, then set about reorganising itself for the forthcoming battle but it ran

into trouble almost immediately. It was proving impossible for NVT to run all their existing factories, and so they decided to rationalise by moving Triumph production to the former BSA factory at Small Heath in Birmingham. At this stage, the Small Heath factory was building Triumph Trident engines which were then transported to the Meriden factory where the complete bikes were built. This arrangement had existed since 1971 when BSA had stopped making the Rocket III to concentrate on one superbike only, the Trident. Unfortunately for NVT, the closure of the Meriden plant did not quite fit in with the plans of the Meriden plant workers and they refused to co-operate. Some 1750 workers operated from Meriden, and when faced with redundancy, they threatened a sit-in.

So began the famous Meriden affair, one which resulted in the newly established NVT company being unable to operate as it wished. Because of NVT's insistence that Meriden be closed, a sit-in did take place, and for over eighteen months the sides remained deadlocked. As a result, NVT could not get at its

stocks of Trident parts and so the model, which all had hoped would be the salvation of Triumph, came to a sticky end. The Small Heath factory did manage to make some Trident models but because new drawings and tools were needed, at a cost of £500,000, it was not until April of 1974 that Trident production could start, by which time it was too late anyway. Production continued into 1977, at a steadily declining rate, whereafter the model was discontinued.

The Norton side of NVT was not without its difficulties as well. In 1973, the capacity of the Commando was upped to 830cc in an attempt to give it more power and prestige. Gradually, however, production of the Commando at NVT's Wolverhampton factory dwindled and by 1976 the Commando too was virtually extinct. In place of the big capacity machines which had once been its forte, NVT now turned its attention to the ultra lightweight market and in the mid 1970s was concentrating on the production of its tiny Easy Rider mopeds. These were built in Britain from parts bought out from various parts of the world.

Ironically, the only major Norton Villiers Triumph factory to survive the troubled 1970s was the Meriden factory in Warwickshire. The Meriden men's sit-in became one of the major industrial news issues of the day and attracted attention from both press and television alike. In the end, Meriden got its way, and, with heavy subsidies from the government, the Meriden Co-operative was formed in 1975 to build a range of 750cc Triumph Tiger TR7 and Bonneville models which, initially, were actually marketed through NVT.

Although NVT's history during the 1970s was one of turbulent decline, the company did experiment with one or two unusual developments which may yet see the light of day. One of the most interesting was the creation of the Challenge project. This involved the commissioning of Keith Duckworth, the genius behind the Formula One car racing Cosworth engine, to create a new engine which would be used initially in a racing machine and, if plans worked out, eventually in a road bike. Duckworth based his design on two cylinders sliced off the 3-litre V8 Cosworth, with their fuel injection and water cooling, plus contra-rotating counter balance shafts for added smoothness. The Cosworth engine was then fitted to the newly designed monocoque John Player Norton racer but, in spite of power figures quoting 115bhp, the bike's first few racing appearances were distinctly disappointing and the Challenge programme was quietly shelved. Whether the Challenge could have been developed into a world beater, had sufficient time and capital been available, will remain one of motor cycling's more frustrating mysteries.

The other unusual NVT project was centred around the building of a Wankel type rotary-engined bike. It used a German Fichtel & Sachs twin-rotor motor and a prototype was built and shown to the press in 1974. The bike's performance was impressive (the engine was reputed to develop some 65bhp at 8000rpm) as was the handling and overall smoothness. Economy, however, proved a bugbear and, in any case, NVT soon became embroiled in a legal case with NSU who claimed to have the patent rights sewn up, thereby leaving NVT out in the cold should it decide to produce the rotary-engined model. In 1978, however, NVT and the NSU company settled their differences and NVT were given the go-ahead to produce their exciting rotary-engined speedster.

By 1978, the NVT concern was operating mainly from a new factory at Shenstone in Staffordshire from where it

Top left: Derek (left) and Don Rickman pose with two of the home-prepared machines, on which they made their name in the world of motocross

Top right: a close-up of the Wankel-type rotary engine built by Norton Villiers Triumph during the mid 1970s and intended for use in a new generation of British-built superbikes

Above: a view of Derek Rickman's immaculate 500cc Matchless Metisse of the early 1960s

Right: by 1978, the once legendary Norton Villiers Triumph company was a pale shadow of its former self. This is a 125cc NVT Ranger, a hybrid assembled by NVT from parts supplied by a number of manufacturers around the world

concentrated on marketing Easy Rider mopeds and a range of little off-road machines, perhaps the most notable being the 125cc Yamaha-engined Ranger. The company was also co-operating with Yamaha to produce a police bike, based mainly on the Japanese company's three-cylinder 750cc model. Yamaha also supplied the 500cc single-cylinder engines which appeared in a limited production motocross model built by NVT, the Bengt Aberg replica. By this time, NVT had also withdrawn from its arrangement to market the Meriden models – relations between the two companies had always been severely strained – and Meriden was left to face the big bad outside world all alone. In August 1978, however, Meriden announced that it had been given a substantial grant to help develop new models to replace the ageing Tiger and Bonneville models. The grant had been made by the Wolfson Foundation to Manchester University's Simon Engineering Department with whom the Meriden men had been collaborating in the design of a new engine.

The dismal tale of the decline of the British motor cycle industry is not, however, entirely without relief. Although the major companies had either died or lapsed into a state of terminal decay, there were a few rays of hope. These last outposts of British two-wheeled engineering did not have the same production capacity as their forebearers, but tended to cater for a more limited market; those discerning few who opted for quality.

One firm that has managed to survive the adversity that has afflicted the rest of its counterparts, is the concern started by the Rickman brothers, Don and Derek. So successfully did they weather the storm, that they managed to attract one million pounds worth of business in a single year, and as a result were presented with the Queen's Award for Industry, and by 1978 they were rated as the second largest motor cycle manufacturer in the United Kingdom, ranking only behind Meriden. Their history began with the brothers' interest in motocross, where they first experimented with frame building. The first Rickman framed machine was christened the 'Metisse', which was a rather deprecatory title derived from a Gallic phrase meaning 'mongrel bitch'. However, the frame proved to be one which was remarkably effective in operation, and led to a number of enquiries from various parties, who felt that they could benefit from such a design. This brought about the production of the first Rickman-framed motocross bikes.

As business progressed, the Rickman brothers began to expand into other spheres of the motor cycle market. The early frames had been designed to accommodate the pre-unit construction Triumph twin engine and the Matchless single-cylinder motor for motocross purposes. However, it became apparent that there was scope for their expertise in the field of motor cycle racing, and they built a number of machines to this end. Utilising the Triumph twin, they commissioned the engineering firm of Harry Weslake to produce a top-end conversion which would substantially increase the motor's performance. This was achieved by evolving an eight port head for the Bonneville engine. Machines thus equipped with both Rickman frames and Weslake top ends were successfully campaigned around the British and continental circuits, until the advent of more sophisticated and powerful bikes rendered them uncompetitive. At much the same time, the company was producing a highly competitive off-road bike powered by a 125cc motor made by the German company, Zündapp. This little bike was very successful, both empirically and commercially, and contributed to a large degree in the expansion of the Rickman concern. The company also produced a quantity of Triumph-engined police bikes, which were manufactured with a number of accessories including glassfibre fairings, tailpieces and side panels.

As their other lines began to decline in commercial viability, the Rickmans experimented with the new wave of Nipponese superbike engines in their frames. The first Rickman with a Honda CB 750 Four motor was not as good a handler as it should have been. However, some modifications to the swinging arm bushes and the tyres resulted in a vast improvement. At the time, there were no suitable tyres available, but the company approached Dunlop, and the KR84 road tyre was developed. In 1974, the first of the so-called CRs (café racers) rolled off the production line. Initially, the only motor available for the CR was the Honda CB750, but more recently the option of a Kawasaki 900 or 1000cc could be had. In 1978, despite all the development that had gone into the manufacture of rolling chassis, the Rickman company derived 85 per cent of its income from the accessories it made. Thus, what was then Britain's second largest motor bike company turned out to be a business which made the vast bulk of its profits from mere accessories, rather than actual motor cycles.

Another name which comes to mind when contemplating British frame-builders is that of Colin Seeley. This particular bender of Reynolds 531 tubing was also involved in racing in the early stages of his career, but not on solo machines. He was in fact the British sidecar Champion in 1962. However, he was inspired to form the company of Colin Seeley Racing Developments Ltd and began designing and building solo frames in 1966. Initially, he utilised the AJS 7R and Matchless G50 engines, principally for club racers. Unfortunately, financial difficulties arose with AMC, who supplied the motors, and Seeley bought their racing department. Subsequently, a road-going version of the G50-engined Seeley was produced, which bore the name 'Condor'. Despite the efforts of the factory, the AJS and Matchless motors were being surpassed by technologically superior machines, and these dated old campaigners had to be dropped.

In the years which followed, a number of Japanese engines were graced by Seeley frames, notably John Cooper's Yamsel and Barry Sheene's Seeley-based Suzukis. Although mainly concerned with racing bikes, the firm had been experimenting with the Honda CB750 four-cylinder engine, and rolling chassis had been manufactured since 1973 to incorporate this motor. A new company entitled Colin Seeley International Ltd was formed, which was solely concerned with producing Honda-engined Seeleys and related accessories.

Another British company which tended to concentrate its attentions on the engineering aspects of motor cycling, was that of Harry Weslake. This name has been around motor engineering for over fifty years, starting in the early 1920s with Weslake's interest in fuel induction and carburation. His experiments in this field led to extensive development of gas-flowing as a method of improving porting in internal combustion engines. His early career as a development engineer began with the RAF, but shortly thereafter he branched out on his own, forming the firm of Weslake and Co Ltd, Research Engineers. His theories of induction were put into practice in the Weslake V12 car engine, which incorporated the narrow included valve angle, pent-roof chamber and flat topped piston. A vehicle with this motor won the Belgian GP in 1967, which

conclusively proved its efficacy. Commissioned by Rickman, they designed cylinder head, barrel and piston conversions for the BSA Victor and Bonneville engines. This conversion, for the Bonneville motor, had an eight-valve head using valve rockers and pushrods off the existing cam followers. By utilising the pent-roof combustion chamber they were able to fit flat topped pistons. However, the Triumph con-rods were unable to withstand consistent revving in the upper ranges, and Weslake designed replacement items for these.

In 1973, the Jawa-engined singles dominated speedway almost totally, but the following two years saw this stranglehold broken by the emergence of Weslake's four-valve single, which ultimately ousted all its competitors in this sport. Only after 1977 did the Weslake see any real threat to its dominance, with the advent of more powerful opposition. By 1978, Weslake also had a fifty degree vee-twin of 1000cc in the pipeline, but had only manufactured a methanol-fuelled model, although there were plans for petrol versions of varying capacities.

Left: Harry Weslake, the brilliant master of motor engineering and driving force behind the company which bore his name. He died in 1978 after spending more than fifty years in the engineering industry

Below: by the late 1970s, the Rickman company had become one of Britain's major motor cycle manufacturers – at a production total of fifteen bikes a week. This is the stylish Rickman Kawasaki 900 Café Racer model from the 1977 range

So far, only partly British vehicles have been discussed; that is, vehicles comprising an amalgamation of local and foreign components. There have been, however, certain two-wheeled machines manufactured in their entirety within the UK. One of these totally British bikes is a twin-cylinder, water-cooled revival of the old Scott. Named after its maker George Silk, it embodies those concepts of motor cycling that most enthusiasts find lacking in the mass produced bikes built by the Japanese in the late 'seventies.

The Silk is a tribute to one man's faith in a motor design which time had threatened to render obsolete. The Scott water-cooled twin was remarkable in its ability to produce low speed torque from a two-stroke. Initially, George Silk negotiated for the rights to produce the two-stroke engine under the original Scott licence. He was unsuccessful, however, and had to manufacture the machine under his own patent. After some

Top: the shape of the 1990s? This is the Quasar of 1978, a hand built machine using a Reliant 850cc engine

Above: the Silk 700S is perhaps the rarest of that rare breed, the modern day British superbike. The Silk is built in Derby by George Silk and uses a water-cooled, twin-cylinder, two-stroke, 682cc engine, based on the famed old Scott design

Left: the Seeley Honda of 1978 featured the best of both worlds. It used a frame made in Britain by ace frame builder Colin Seeley and a four-cylinder, 750cc engine from the giant Japanese concern Honda

consultation with his colleagues, he designed an engine with a capacity of 682cc which weighed a mere 64lbs.

Another machine which showed that British motor cycle design had not stagnated with Edward Turner's twin, was the revolutionary Quasar. This fully faired and enclosed two-wheeler was certainly an innovative creation in the conservative world of bike design. Utilising an 850cc, four-cylinder Reliant engine, with water-cooling, final drive was by shaft. Malcolm Newell, the designer, also incorporated such peripheral items as a hand warmer, which channelled hot air from the cooling system on to the hands of the driver. With twin headlights, three discs, windscreen wipers and total weather protection, the Quasar had obvious advantages over its more conventional brethren when it came to wet weather touring. The bike's single carburettor, abetted by the aerodynamics of the glassfibre superstructure gave the whole plot a frugal appetite, which resulted in the extraordinary consumption figure of 68mpg.

Chapter 14
European Growth (1960-1979)

Left: by 1978, the four-cylinder MV Agusta was available in several forms, ranging from the 'ordinary' 788cc America, through the 837cc Monza to the 861cc Arturo Magni Special, which was named after the company's famed engine tuner. Common to all bikes were a race-bred engine, with gear-driven overhead camshafts, an excellent shaft drive, relatively low weight and superb road manners. These details justified the prices, which were at the very top of the production bike scale

Above: the Moto-Guzzi Stornello Regolarità of 1968 was a 125cc single of not very inspired design, but nevertheless helped to get the company into its stride in the late 1960s

The saga of the collapse of the British industry is a sad one. Mistakes were made, opportunities were lost and a lot of good money and talent were wasted. Ironically, Britain's industry in the late 1970s was in the same sorry position that the European industry found itself in after World War II, down but not out.

The revival of the Italian industry is a particularly interesting story. Following World War II, Italy had dragged itself back to work. Slowly her industries began to grow stronger, and the motor cycle industry was aided by the fact that for much of the postwar period the Italian Government imposed restrictions on the import of foreign machines, thereby leaving the local market wholly open to Italian influence. By the 1950s and early '60s, Italy was marketing a whole range of different machines, mostly small capacity models, and was even enjoying impressive dominance in the racing field. Names like Mondial, MV Agusta, Gilera and Moto Guzzi were quite familiar to the racing enthusiast of the early 1960s.

Slowly, a variety of Italian manufacturers began to make their presence felt on the world motor cycling scene. Perhaps the best known of these is the Moto Guzzi company of Mandello del Lario on the shores of the beautiful Lake Como. For most of the 1960s, Guzzi marketed a range of rather uninspired small-capacity models like the 125cc Stornello singles and made most of its money by supplying machines to the Italian army and police forces. Then, in the late 1960s, came the breakthrough that set Moto Guzzi on its way, if not to fortune, certainly to fame. The new machine was known as the V7, basically because it was a vee-twin of 703cc. This later grew to 757 and, in 1971, even to 850cc by which time the engine gave 64bhp; the bike weighed 510lb and the top speed was around 110mph. This model, the V850GT, was also joined in 1971 by a delightful looking sports model known as the V7 Sport. Much of the engine development on the bike had been done by the talented Lino Tonti and the most visible change to the engine had been the substitution of an alternator for the dynamo, this modification allowing the engine to be built lower, enhancing the sleek lines of the bike. The engine capacity was 748cc and the steering and handling were of extraordinarily high standards. Final drive was by shaft which made for smooth performance as the rider wound his way towards the impressive 125mph top speed.

In time, the Guzzi range of vee-twins was extended to include the 850cc T3 and T3 California models, as well as the

remarkable V1000 Convert, the world's first automatic transmission large capacity tourer. The T3 and T3 California models were aimed mainly at the touring market, the California model differing only in its appearance by the addition of panniers and screen because, as the name suggested, it was aimed at the American touring market. The Convert was a fascinating machine. It used a 949cc vee-twin motor which developed 71bhp at 6500rpm and which was coupled to a torque converter and semi-automatic two-speed gearbox. It too was aimed at the touring market, so much so that in place of foot rests the Convert used foot boards. Another interesting aspect of the Convert was its use of a braking system which linked the foot pedal to the left hand front disc (the Guzzis being fitted with two front discs) and to the rear brake in a ratio of about 70/30. In other words, the braking system was balanced in such a way that it was not necessary to use the normal front brake handlebar lever coupled to the other front disc except in an emergency. Many road testers have since gone on record as saying that the Guzzi integral braking system is the best in modern motor cycling.

In the mid 1970s, the S3 Sport, which replaced the V7 Sports Guzzi, was itself replaced by the sleek 850 Le Mans model, a full-blown 850cc model with racy lines and a tiny, but effective, windscreen/fairing unit. The 850 Le Mans also used the familiar vee-twin, shaft-drive layout and by now the engine had been coaxed to give 81bhp at 7600rpm, enough to give the machine a top speed close to 135mph. By this time, Guzzi had also entered a number of other markets. It had produced two new smaller capacity models, both on the tried and trusted vee-twin theme. These new models were the 350cc V35 and 500cc V50 machines and, typically Guzzi, they were sleek, fast and a joy to ride. In addition, late in 1977, Moto Guzzi launched its new top-of-the-range model, the SP1000 Spada. It featured a stylish two-piece fairing, the vee-twin engine was bored out to 949cc and it was a strictly up-market device aimed to compete directly with BMW's luxurious R100RS model. At a price considerably below that of BMW's road burner, the SP1000 Spada represented effective competition.

For much of the 1970s, Moto Guzzi had been influenced by the business involvement of a mysterious Argentinian, named Alejandro De Tomaso, who spent much of his time trying to make the Italian motor cycle industry his personal property. De Tomaso was well connected and had already made something

Above left: one of the first Moto Guzzis to use the company's patented integral braking system was the 750 S3 of 1975. It was developed into one of Guzzi's most popular models, the 850cc Le Mans café racer

Left: an 850GT Guzzi of the early 1970s

Below left: a Moto Guzzi V50 engine. Although like the larger vee-twins in the Guzzi range from the outside, the V50 differed in that it utilised a Heron head design

Above: a 703cc V7 as used by the Italian police

Right: a 1978 Moto Guzzi T3 Californian, with bodywork like that of the V1000 Convert

Below: Benelli's fabulous 750 Sei, which was based on a Honda design

of a name for himself in the car world with his expensive and high-speed Mangusta and Pantera models. It was also De Tomaso who had a large influence on another famous Italian name, that of Benelli.

Benelli had entered the 1960s preceded by an interesting racing reputation. They had been fairly successful during the late 1950s, particularly in the 250cc class, but with the arrival of Honda had withdrawn, aware that they had neither the money nor the facilities with which to tackle the invader from the East. With the subsequent withdrawal of Honda in 1966, however, Benelli made a racing comeback in 1967 with four-cylinder 250 and 500cc machines. The 500cc machine was never a serious threat to the MVs, however, and Benelli decided to concentrate on the 250cc category. This they did to such good effect that by 1969 the 250cc Benelli four was a force to be reckoned with. For the 1969 racing season, Benelli signed an Australian, Kel Carruthers, to ride their machines, and from that point on Benelli featured strongly in the results. Carruthers

took the Benelli to victory in the Lightweight TT and also won the Ulster and Yugoslavian Grands Prix to clinch the world 250cc title for the little Italian factory. The glory was to be short-lived, however, because at the end of 1969 the FIM announced that from then on the 125 and 250cc classes would be restricted to machines with a maximum of two cylinders only. For several years, Benelli soldiered on in the 350 and 500cc classes but without too much success.

It was in 1972 that De Tomaso made his appearance. Financed by his Ford-backed company, he took over Benelli's Pesaro based factory, and later that same year he annexed the part of the Moto Guzzi concern which was not state owned, thereby bringing the two rival names under his control. Benelli's efforts were now turned away from the race tracks and towards the production of road machines. At that stage, Benelli were building mostly small bikes, 125cc trail bikes plus 125 and 250cc two-stroke, twin-cylinder roadsters, but then along came a big four-stroke, the majestic twin-cylinder, overhead-valve, 650cc Tornado model. The Tornado was a fine example of Italian engineering and was typical of the kind of big, impressive machine that De Tomaso liked so much. The Tornado's engine pushed out 52bhp at 7200rpm.

In 1974, however, De Tomaso revealed a machine even more impressive than the Tornado. This was the new 750cc Benelli Sei, a spectacular six-cylinder, overhead-camshaft machine capable of almost 120mph. On closer inspection, the Sei's engine bore a remarkable similarity to that of Honda's CB500, except of course, that it had two more cylinders. It was obvious that the Sei had been inspired by the Japanese masterpiece and even De Tomaso did not attempt to deny the allegation. As far as he was concerned, the allegation didn't bother him. Indeed, he was probably quite pleased, as the Honda association would not hurt the Sei's image at all. Nor did Honda mind, in fact. Another interesting aspect of the Sei's image was its astonishingly low price, and sales were initially quite spectacular. At the time of its production, the Benelli 750 was the world's only six-cylinder series production roadster. De Tomaso also introduced a 500cc model but this was a four-cylinder machine and was really just a 500 Honda in different, and better handling, form. In time, the 750 Sei was stretched to 900cc and at the 1977 Milan Show, Benelli showed a 900cc model encased in a sleek body, which was destined to go into production during 1979. By this time, also, Benelli had introduced a remarkable little four-cylinder, four-stroke 250cc model, the 250/4. Unlike the 750 Sei, however, the 250/4 was anything but cheap and sales, outside of Italy at any rate, were not exactly encouraging.

Another company which came very close to falling into De Tomaso's clutches was the famous old Ducati company of Bologna. By 1977, Ducati had sustained heavy financial losses for several years, and was offered to De Tomaso. However, he was reluctant to include it in his plans for the renaissance of the Italian industry until the company's debts were cleared up, and so Ducati remained independent.

Ducati had entered the 1960s, like Benelli, with a reputation for racing success. By this stage, their production range was centred around a single-cylinder 250cc engine available in various forms. Perhaps the best known of these was the Ducati Daytona, a sporty little roadster capable of seeing off just about anything its size. In 1962, Ducati brought out two new two-two-stroke machines, of 48 and 80cc, anticipating a buoyant moped market, only to find that the customers preferred the kind of machine the Japanese were making. Production of the Daytona 250 model, and its five-speed Mach 1 variant, continued into 1966, however, when they were abandoned for the new 250cc Monza and 340cc Sebring models. During this time, Ducati also announced details of its fascinating new project, the Apollo police bike. The Apollo, which would also have been marketed in the USA, was a 1260cc wide-angle vee-four, but somehow it never got beyond the development stage. As it happened, the work that did go into the Apollo was not wholly wasted because in later years Ducati would market a range of vee-twins which owed their origins to the Apollo.

In 1969, Ducati announced a range of 250, 350 and 450cc models, all of which featured the desmodromic valvegear for which Ducati would later become world famous. The models sold reasonably well both in Europe and America, but they were still not the kind of product which could compete favourably with those of Honda or Yamaha. It was during 1970 that Ducati made an announcement that startled the motor cycling world. They had decided to enter the large capacity production class with a 750cc vee-twin model. The original design had a 750cc valve spring engine and was exported to America initially, where it had a remarkable effect on the motor cycling enthusiast. The

Top left: Fabio Taglioni's vee-twin engine in conventional valve-spring form, as used in the 1976 Ducati 860GTS

Top right: this is the stylish 500 Twin Desmo of 1976, with styling by Leo Tartarini. This was used before a 500cc version of the Taglioni twin was ready for 1979

Above: the famous desmodromic-valve 900SS Ducati of 1977. This bike was the fastest in the company's range, with a top speed in excess of 130mph. Also, in slightly modified form it took the Formula One World Championship title in 1978 on the Isle of Man. The bike was prepared by Sports Motorcycles of Manchester and was piloted by Mike Hailwood

joys of vee-twin riding, which had all but disappeared, were rediscovered by the dyed-in-the-wool enthusiasts who took the the new 'Duke' to their hearts.

At the Imola 200 event of 1972, Paul Smart and Bruno Spaggiari proved the worth of Ducati's new vee-twin design by piloting their machines to a spectacular one-two result. In due course, an improved version of the 750cc Desmo Ducati engine was installed in the new 750SS model and this eventually replaced the original 750V model and its two later variants, the GT750 and 750 Sport. In time, the vee-twin engine, designed by the fabled Dr Fabio Taglioni, would be uprated to 860cc and used in both desmo and ordinary valve spring guises. The valve spring engine found its way into the 860GTS model while the desmo version was used in the super sporting 900SS model and the attractive 900 Darmah model. The Darmah was part of a new range of bikes, which included 350 and 500cc vertical twins, the styling of which was undertaken by Leo Tartarini, himself the head of the company which created the tiny Italjet machines. By 1978, Ducati's range of machines was impressive and there were great hopes that the financial disaster, which at one time had seemed so close, would now be staved off. By this time, both the 900SS and 900 Darmah models were being exported to the USA and it only remained to be seen whether or not the Americans would accept the intricacies of the desmodromic valvegear.

Another Italian manufacturer which made huge strides during the 1960s and '70s was Laverda. This company, run by Francisco Laverda and his two sons, Massimo and Piero, was an off-shoot of the highly successful Laverda combine harvester and caravan company, and first began manufacturing motor cycles in 1949. It was all very low key in those days and Laverda's first machine was a little single-cylinder 75cc machine. During the 1950s, the little bike was gradually modified. By 1954, a 100cc racer had been added to the range, and then in 1958, came a small two-stroke moped of 50cc. In spite of the fact that these were all small bikes, one fact quickly emerged: the Laverda machines were well engineered and a lot of thought went into their design.

During the early 1960s, Laverda flirted briefly with scooter production but without too much success. Then, in 1962, Laverda introduced a new 200cc twin which was to be the mainstay of their production for nearly a decade. The little 200 had a frame that was conventionally tubular and telescopic at the front but with a pressed-steel backbone and hips. By 1966, however, the company had decided to change its image somewhat and head for the choppy waters of the sporting market. They introduced a little 125cc single, with completely new overhead-valve engine, and clothed in very sporting bodywork. It proved popular with the Italian boy racers, and so Laverda decided to break into the big capacity sporting bike market.

Laverda's first large capacity machine was shown to the world during 1968 but its introduction was met with some odd looks from public and press alike. The reason was that the new machine, a four-stroke, twin-cylinder of 650cc, looked remarkably similar to Honda's sporting CB77 although, of course, it was nearly twice the capacity of the Japanese machine. Then, when the critics looked more closely, they noticed that while Honda may have inspired some of the Laverda design, the Italian machine certainly had some interesting features of its own. The engine castings were quite magnificent and the finish superb. There could be little doubt that Laverda's new machine had been a labour of love.

Only 100 of Laverda's 650 model were made before the designers decided to uprate the engine to 750cc, and soon afterwards all accusations of 'Honda copy' design were forgotten as Laverda machines swept to a convincing one-two result in the Giro d'Italia road race. Laverda had arrived in no uncertain manner. Quite suddenly, they had become accepted among the elite of motor cycling, and not without good reason. Their bikes were superbly engineered and Laverda soon became to motor cycling what Lamborghini had become to car manufacturing – a small company capable of turning out the most breathtaking machinery. In 1971, the Laverda 750GT model gained a new stable mate in the even more sporting 750SF and the SF in turn was gradually modified until it was developed into the rorty 750 SFC model. In fact, the SFC was really too much for the road. With its single seat and clip-on handlebars it looked and sounded like a demented road racer. The power output was around 65bhp and a top speed of 120mph was possible. The SF model, apart from spawning the tearaway

Top: the four-cylinder Moto Guzzi 400GTS bears more than a passing resemblance to its larger Italian cousin, the Benelli 500, and indeed they are both made at the same factory

Above: the 1970 Laverda 750SF is a vertical twin which embodies all the desirable traits of such an engine configuration, although it is prone to high-speed vibration

Left: the 1978 double-overhead-camshaft, 500cc Laverda Alpino 'S' is another fine twin in the great Italian tradition. Its impeccable handling and torquey performance make it one of the most competitive machines in its class

SFC, was also developed into the more manageable SF2 (with two disc brakes) and later the SF3 (with three discs). These superbly engineered machines soon became popular throughout Europe.

In the early 1970s, Laverda began experimenting with a machine even more exciting than the 750s. The new project was a three-cylinder bike of 1000cc, but it was to be some time before all the production bugs were ironed out of this particular beast. For a start, the conical couple developed by a crankshaft with three crankpins set 120 degrees apart created serious vibration problems. This meant that the engine had to be rebalanced with the outer pins spaced 180 degrees from the inner. The new machine, known as the 3C, also suffered from ignition problems in its early development but with steady and patient development these problems were overcome. Gradually, the big 3C developed a reputation for spectacular performance combined with steady handling and the Laverda company's image was firmly set. In Britain, Roger Slater, the Laverda concessionaire, produced a modified version of the 3C, solely for the British market, which became known as the Jota. The stunningly fast Jota soon became a motor cycling status symbol and, just to prove it went as well as it looked and sounded, became the machine to beat in UK production racing events.

Ironically, having established themselves as manufacturers of fast, expensive and exotic machines, Laverda, in the mid 1970s, then began to look downmarket and decided to build a new twin-cylinder 500cc machine, the delightful Alpino. The little 500 was a typically well engineered machine and produced 44bhp at 10,300rpm. Top speed was in the region of 120mph and fuel consumption figures of fifty miles per gallon were most impressive. In addition, the company began marketing 125cc and 175cc machines, using two-stroke Zündapp engines in place of normal four-stroke Laverda units.

In spite of occasional forays into the smaller capacity markets, however, Laverda did not forget or neglect large capacity machines and, in mid 1978, a new range of 1200cc three-cylinder models was launched. Top of the range, in Britain at least, was the mighty Mirage 1200 model and its performance specifications made for interesting reading. With around 90bhp at its disposal, the 1200 Mirage scorched up to 100mph in under ten seconds. A more sedate 1200 model was also available, which was intended more as a high speed tourer than as a road burning street racer. One thing that both the 1200 and the Mirage had in common, though, was a rather hefty price tag.

Bearing in mind that the first large capacity engined Laverda only made its debut in 1968, Laverda's growth during the following ten years was particularly impressive. By 1978, the company's range extended from the little single-cylinder, two-stroke 125 through an eight-valve, twin-cylinder 350 model (introduced at the 1977 Milan Show) to the 500 Alpino and on to the big twin-cylinder SF 750s. Then came the fabulous 1000cc 3C models and the massive 1200, plus the British Jota 1000 and Mirage 1200 variants. By this time, Laverda were also exporting several of their models to America where the big 1200 was, rather confusingly, marketed as the Jota America.

In spite of their already impressive history, the best of Laverda may still lie in the future because, in November 1977, Laverda unveiled a machine which, ostensibly, was the prototype of production models for the 1980s. The bike, launched at the 1977 Milan Show, was an endurance racer using a magnificently engineered V6 engine of 1000cc capacity. The engine, designed by Laverda's Lucciano Zen in collaboration with Guilio Alfiero of Maserati car fame, had its crankshaft in line with the frame, and cylinder banks 90 degrees apart. Each bank of cylinders utilised twin overhead camshafts and each cylinder had four valves. In addition, the engine was water-cooled and the estimated power output was in the region of 140bhp at 10,500rpm. Top speed was believed to be about 190mph and the engine breathed through no less than six Dell' Orto carburettors. Final drive was by shaft, the gearbox was a five-speed unit and, quite astonishingly, the whole thing was said to weigh only 385lb. Although it was intended to be used initially as a long-distance endurance road racer, the two Laverda brothers, Massimo and Piero, who now ran the company, planned to use the machine as a test bed for a projected production model, scheduled to appear during the early 1980s.

The success of Laverda, however, is in sharp contrast to the troubled times faced during the 1960s and '70s by another famous Italian manufacturer, MV Agusta. Like Laverda, the MV company was an off-shoot of a powerful industrial empire, in this case the Agusta helicopter company. The MV Agusta concern, however, was really set up at the whim of the wealthy Count Domenico Agusta, and was at first interested only in racing. MV's success in the world of Grand Prix racing is now, of course, legendary. With an incredible list of 37 world championships to their credit, MV Agusta are the most successful company in the history of racing, but it is not their racing history with which we are now concerned, rather the more troubled story of MV's production road bikes. The original idea was that MV's road bike sales would pay for the racing, but this plan never really worked, and MV production proved more of a hobby than a serious commercial venture for the Agusta family.

The first production MV Agustas to be announced arrived during the mid 1940s and were small capacity machines. Indeed, the first ever MV was the Vespa 98 model, a tiny two-stroke, single-cylinder roadster. By 1960, the range included a 175cc overhead-valve single, the model EL, plus two 250cc overhead-valve machines, the Tavare and the Raid. Like many other companies during the early 1960s, MV also dabbled with a scooter and, like so many of the others, got their fingers burned.

Right through the 1960s, MV continued production of their small capacity machines which, if the truth be told, weren't particularly inspiring machines and sold mainly on the reputation of the all-conquering 350 and 500cc 'fire engine' Grand Prix racing machines. Then, towards the end of the 1960s, MV decided to take the plunge into the large capacity road bike market and produced a four-cylinder 750cc machine. It had all the right ingredients for success except one – the price. Looking, sounding and even behaving like one of MV's fabulous racers, the bike had a twin-overhead-camshaft engine and shaft final drive. The 750 model continued through the early 1970s, first as the 750S and later as the restyled 750S America. In 1977, the British concessionaires began to offer an 850cc version first known as the Boxer, then later as the Monza. The Monza was a breathtaking piece of equipment. Its four-cylinder engine had an output in excess of 90bhp and a top speed, depending on the gearing, of anything up to 140mph. It weighed only 500lb and the handling was everything that a race developed machine of its heritage could be. There was one problem, however. The big four-cylinder MVs were limited production machines and their price was high – in Britain, in 1978, a Monza cost in excess of £4000. Consequently, sales were never very high and by 1978 MV Agusta were in serious

Above: apart from building mouth-watering four-cylinder roadsters, MV have produced some less elaborate bikes like the single-cylinder pushrod 125S, seen in 1976. Not quite as sophisticated as its larger stablemates, the little MV handled and performed at least as well as the other machines in its class.

Right: an example of the Laverda 3CL, dating from 1977. Although there were a few quicker superbikes around with smoother and quieter power delivery, the Laverda was the archetypal muscle bike, and for many was the ultimate machine for sports riding

financial trouble. By this time, they were also marketing a twin-cylinder sportster, the 350 Sport, but it too was highly priced and, in any case, was particularly disappointing in terms of reliability and performance. Attempts have been made to market the MV in America, hence the America designation on the 750S model, but the idiosyncratic nature of the MV never allowed it to become a best seller. With a limited production range, MV's future remained at best uncertain and not helped by the fact that its one time guiding light, Count Domenico Agusta, died in 1971, leaving behind him a great reputation but precious little else which MV might use to steer their way to financial safety. Whether MV Agusta could survive the financial crisis they found themselves in during the late 1970s, only time would tell but it would be very sad if such a famous name were lost to the motor cycling world.

Another company which, by the late 1970s, had also seen better days was Gilera, a firm which, like MV, had made its reputation on the Grand Prix race circuits of the world. During the 1950s, the four-cylinder 500cc Gileras were the bikes to beat and they had taken men like Geoff Duke to racing immortality. At the end of 1957, the Gilera Grand Prix racing team was shelved and the company settled down to meeting its production commitments. Because the 1960s saw a boom in scooter production in Italy, Gilera also entered this particular market. To some extent, they were forced to since sales of small capacity motor cycles – which Gilera at the time specialised in – were being hit hard by the advent of the scooter and they could either move with the trend or go bankrupt. Unfortunately, the scooter boom did not last very long and by 1969 Gilera were in terrible trouble. Sales had fallen drastically and they were ready to throw in the towel. A saviour was found, however, in the form of the Piaggio company, manufacturers of the fantastically successful Vespa scooter, and it was Piaggio who eventually bought out the ailing Gilera concern. Piaggio's move, needless to say, was not purely philanthropic. They had forseen that there would be a boom in small capacity motor cycles during the 1970s and quickly realised that Gilera's expertise in this field could be put to good use.

Money was poured into development work and soon Gilera had developed two new small capacity machines, the 125cc single-cylinder Arcore and a similar 150cc model. They had pleasing lines and plenty of performance and were exactly suited to the needs of the local Italian market. By 1973, the upsurge in interest in 50cc machines had also resulted in Gilera producing a new lightweight 50cc model and in the first ten months of that year Gilera sold 14,000 machines, 9000 of them to the Italian market alone. Shortly afterwards Gilera expanded their model range into the 75, 100 and 125cc capacity classes and were also quick to spot the potential of off-road machinery. Quickly they developed a range of off-road enduro machines and by 1977 Gilera's top of the range off-road machine was a delightfully quick single-cylinder two-stroke 125cc machine capable of producing 23bhp at 9500rpm. The cylinder barrel was of light alloy and incorporated three transfer ports, with generous finning for efficient cooling. In addition it had a six-speed gearbox and the machine was a credit to the Italian company's creative abilities. It also supported Gilera's claim that they had lost none of their ability to produce competitive machinery. It may not have been a four-cylinder 500cc Grand Prix racer but it certainly came from the same stable. In 1978, whether Gilera, like MV and Laverda, would graduate from small capacity machinery into the larger classes remained to be

Top: a 1977 50cc Gilera 'Trial', which, despite its title, was more suited to trail riding

Above: the 350cc MV Agusta vertical twin has a massive crankcase, which was designed to house two counter-rotating balance shafts; these were never actually fitted

seen. It would certainly be pleasing to motor cycle enthusiasts to see the famed Gilera name on something a little more powerful than a 50cc two-stroke moped!

If the survival of Gilera can be described as a success of sorts, then the growth of the little Morini company was little short of sensational. Like so many Italian motor cycle companies, Morini is a family concern, being originally founded by Alphonso Morini in 1937. World War II put a stop to any serious plans for motor cycle production, and it was not until the middle of the 1940s that Morini could get back to building them. Initially, they concentrated on small capacity models and by the time the 1960s arrived the firm had a small range of rather impressively built machines. During the early 1960's, Morini produced an overhead camshaft 250cc machine which was used for racing. Some of the better known riders who used Morini's little 250 to good effect included Tarquinio Provini and the young Giacomo Agostini, later destined for greater things.

By the mid 1960s, Morini had dropped most of the overhead camshaft models which had made up so much of their production during the 1950s and concentrated on a range of 50, 100, 125 and 150cc machines, all of which used overhead-valve engines. In addition, a range of off-road machines had been developed and, together with the road bikes, these models were in production until the early 1970s. It was not until 1971 that Morini really began to be noticed outside Italy, however. By this time, Alphonso Morini had died, leaving his business in the hands of his daughter Gabrielli. Morini's designers at this stage were Gianni Marchetti, who was also General Manager, and Franco Lambertini Junior. It was these two men who planned and created a new range of machines, a range which would secure Morini's future in the troubled times of the 1970s. The first prototypes were built in 1971 and by 1973 the first production models of the now famous 3½ range of 350cc vee-twins rolled off the lines. It was around this brilliant little engine that the Morini company planned its future. Like the Laverda family, the Morini company believed in good solid engineering and the new 3½ engine was indeed a superb piece of engineering. It was an overhead-valve vee-twin, which pushed out nearly 40bhp and was installed in a frame that would have made the Norton Featherbed designers smile in appreciation. Two versions of the new 3½ model were available, the Strada – a touring version – and the more racy Sports model.

The 3½ models were met with great favour both in America and Europe and, in time, 125 and 250cc single-cylinder

Right: another 350cc Italian motor cycle, the Morini 3½. The novelty of such a small-capacity vee-twin did not detract from its efficiency as a roadburner; by using Heron combustion chambers the manufacturers succeeded in extracting a surprising amount of power from it

derivatives of the 350 were also added to the range. By 1978, however, Morini had become even more ambitious and launched a 500cc version of the vee-twin. The 500 had a top speed in the region of 110mph and could cover the quarter-mile in 14½ seconds. Its engine punched out 43bhp and, like the 3½ model, the handling was a revelation. So, as the 1980s approached, the tightly knit Morini company could face the future knowing it had as good a chance of survival as any of its perhaps better known rivals.

Of the other Italian companies in existence during the 1970s, perhaps the best known is FB Mondial. This company had known great success during the late 1950s with its 250cc racing machines, but by the time the 1960s arrived Mondial had quit the race circuits to concentrate on building production machines. Their production range was always modest and by the start of 1977 had been condensed to just three machines, a 50cc two-stroke moped, a 125cc two-stroke single and a 125cc four-stroke single. Mondial's can hardly be described as a success story, but at least the famous old name survives.

Mondial, in fact, was typical of dozens of small companies operating in Italy during the late 1970s. Because the Italians just cannot seem to get enough of the small lightweight type of motor cycle, there exists a whole battery of manufacturers who specialise in the building of small capacity machines. They include Fantic, who build a quite amazing range of lightweights, Garelli, Itom, Testi, Italjet, Tecnomoto and Malaguti, plus a whole host of names which mean precisely nothing outside of Italy.

Of the remaining Italian companies, only one is of any real importance. It is the Aermacchi company of Varese which, in 1960, was taken over by the Harley-Davidson company of America. From then on, although the Aermacchi factory continued to build the bikes, they were marketed as Harley-Davidsons. The Harley-Davidson company gained a great deal of publicity from its deal with Aermacchi because during the 1970s a number of world road racing championships were won by Italian ace Walter Villa riding 250 and 350cc Italian-built Harley-Davidsons. On the production side, however, the Harley-Davidson/Aermacchi company did not fare so well. Their range of 125, 175, 250 and 350 single-cylinder two-stroke machines never sold in very large numbers and by 1978 the company was in serious financial trouble, so much so that the American AMF concern pulled out, leaving Cagiva to pick up the pieces. For a while, the bikes were called H-Ds before they took over the new company's identity completely.

No mention of the Italian motor cycle industry would be complete, however, without a mention of the Italian scooter industry and, in particular, the two giants of that industry, Lambretta and Vespa. Strictly speaking, scooters are not motor cycles in the accepted sense of the word but they are a vital part of the world of two wheels and only the most die-hard of anti-scooterists would dispute that.

The scooter has been primarily a creature of fashion and as such is subject to marked fluctuations of fortune. During the 1950s and early '60s it was very much in fashion but then went into a decline until the late 1960s when it began to experience a slight upsurge in interest. During those heady years of the 1950s, many European manufacturers tried to climb aboard the bandwagon, but few succeeded. Throughout the whole of the scooter industry's history, however, two companies remained relatively unscathed. They were Innocenti and Piaggio, the founders of the scooter industry.

Above: by the 1970s, the once great Mondial concern had been reduced to producing lightweight machines only. This is their Sachs-engined 125cc off-roader of 1975

Above right: in the mid 1970s, the scooter industry enjoyed a revival and once again these machines were to be seen on the roads of Europe in great numbers. This is a Lambretta GP150 of 1977

Right: Aermacchi were bought out by Harley-Davidson in 1960 and some time later the famous American name appeared on the Italian bikes. This is an SS125 of 1977, which had a perky performance and good handling characteristics. In 1978, however, AMF, the new owners of Harley-Davidson, decided to sell the project and the offer was taken up by Cagiva, who marketed the bikes as H-Ds for a while

Both Innocenti, who made the Lambretta, and Piaggio, builders of the Vespa, had their origins in the mid 1940s. Both built their empires out of the ruins of World War II and both were strong enough to withstand the challenge of would-be imitators during the thirty years that followed. Indeed, in 1978 Piaggio could claim to be the fourth largest producer of two-wheeled motorised vehicles in the world, beaten only by Honda, Yamaha and Suzuki.

The similarity of design between Lambretta and Vespa products is noticeable. Both ranges consist of single-cylinder, two-stroke models of various sizes and power outputs. Improvements are made year by year but the basic formula remains the same. Such is their popularity that Lambrettas are now built not only in Italy, but in Spain and even India, while the Vespa, for many years, was also assembled in the Bristol workshops of the once famous and powerful Douglas company.

It is difficult to understand why Innocenti and Piaggio continued to succeed where so many other failed. Perhaps it was

because they were the founders of the industry and established a firm grip on it right from the start, or maybe it is because a potential scooter purchaser invariably thinks of the names Lambretta and Vespa when he thinks of a scooter. Whatever the reason, Lambretta and Vespa models continued to proliferate while the two companies concerned patiently waited for the scooter to come back into fashion. Indeed, the entire Italian motor cycle industry waits to see what the future brings. The 1980s will surely prove a watershed for the industry. Many famous names like Ducati and MV Agusta stand a step away from the brink of disaster, while others like Morini and Laverda hope the 1980s will bring them prosperity and growth.

Another European country which had to pick itself up off the floor after World War II was Germany. In typical Teutonic fashion, the German motor cycle industry has been reformed carefully rather than spectacularly. Unlike Italy, which has a multitude of manufacturers scratching for a living, the German industry settled round a small handful of names and was nurtured slowly back to health.

Typical of the companies whose progress has been slow but steady is Germany's best known manufacturer, BMW. Following World War II, it was not until 1948 that this company resumed production, and then it was only with the little 250cc R24. Then, with the German economy slowly strengthening, the company was permitted in 1950 to start work again on the big twins. Right through the 1950s BMW battled on and it was not until the beginning of the following decade that the company began to enjoy the fruits of its labour. Indeed, there were times during the 1950s when it seemed that the BMW company would never survive at all. Nevertheless, the BMW engineers plugged on, continuing to refine their machines and refusing to compromise their product. Their persistence paid off in 1961 when BMW's new range of motor cars began to capture the

Right: in 1978 BMW launched a new range of middleweight models, the R45 and R65 machines. Our picture shows the 450cc R45 horizontally opposed twin

Below right: a view of the wind-tunnel-developed fairing on the BMW R100RS. It improved high-speed handling and prevented the front-end becoming light through the passage of air over the wedge-shaped screen and the lateral air-dams

Below: the precursor of the 'new generation' BMWs, the 750cc R75/5, which had Bing constant-vacuum carburettors, electric starting and a three-phase alternator. These features were all innovative on the Bavarian twins at that time.

attention of the motoring world. Gradually some of the gloss and financial gain began to rub off on the motor cycle division. By 1963, the BMW company, under its new and very astute boss, Karl-Heinz Sonne, announced to its shareholders the first dividend they had enjoyed in twenty years.

The motor cycle engineers were still somewhat unhappy, however. It was the car division which kept BMW solvent, most of the motor cycle division's money coming from sales to various police forces. Nevertheless, the company continued to have faith in its product and began to plan for a new and revitalised future for the motor cycle division. Thus, in 1969, BMW opened a new motor cycle factory at Spandau and, simultaneously, launched their new /5 range of models. Typically BMW, most of the changes on the /5 machines were not immediately obvious. Instead of built-up crankshafts flexing inside rolling-element bearings, there was a sturdy new one-piece affair carrying the split big ends of con-rods from the six-cylinder car engines. There was a new electric starter and a refined exhaust system and the bike featured a diaphragm clutch, three-shaft, four-speed gearbox and redesigned shaft drive. BMW had timed the new range to a nicety. By 1969 the world was experiencing a revival of interest in motor cycling – especially in big capacity machines. By this time BMW had dropped the 250cc model and the range now consisted of 500, 600 and 750cc machines. As the years went by, the /5 range was supplanted by the /6 and eventually the /7 ranges, all employing the traditional, horizontally opposed, twin-cylinder formula. Every new range, however, incorporated new refinements, new ideas and greater success for the BMW company. The 750cc machines grew into 800s and even into 1000s. The company's sales policy was clearly defined. BMW bikes were aimed at the upper end of the price bracket. Exclusiveness was the key word. Remarkably, the idea worked. Sold at quite astonishing prices, the twin-cylinder bikes built for themselves a reputation of reliability and trustworthiness. They became the tourers' delight, the bike for the individualist. By 1977, the range comprised the 600cc R60, the 800cc R80, the touring 100/7 model and its more sporty sister the R100S, and the top of the range R100RS, a fully faired high-speed tourer with a price in the 'super executive' bracket.

Ironically, in 1978 BMW branched away from the big bikes which had made their reputation and headed downmarket. They felt certain that if a market for quality products existed in the upper ranges, one also existed in the middle price bracket. Consequently the new R45 and R65 models were launched. The R45, as the designation suggested was a 450cc machine while the R65 was a 650. The two new machines still used the boxer-twin engine but had stylish, up to date lines aimed at the middleweight market. They embodied all the engineering technique that BMW had learned over the past two decades and there was no doubt that these were serious machines aimed at taking a chunk out of a market which had, until then, been dominated by the Japanese.

Although BMW is the best known of the German companies, it is not Germany's biggest manufacturer. This honour belongs to the Zweirad Union AG group which comprises such famous names as DKW, Hercules, Victoria and Express. The company's history is a complicated business and is the result of a number of mergers carried out within the German industry since World War II. By 1978, the company was making most of its money by producing a range of lightweight machines aimed mostly at the local market. A little badge engineering also went on, with DKWs being sold in some countries as Hercules and vice versa. Most of the machines were fitted with small Sachs two-stroke engines, the Sachs concern also having a financial interest in the Union. Perhaps the most interesting machine to have come out of this conglomerate was one of the least successful. It was the Wankel-type rotary engined Hercules W2000 which caused a great deal of discussion when it was launched in 1974. The W2000 had a single-rotor snowmobile engine, built by Sachs and producing 32bhp at 6500rpm. The machine had a six-speed gearbox and top speed was in the region of 100mph. This rotary engine application, however, was never wholly accepted by the public and the W2000 was not a sales success. Consequently, Hercules and DKW went back to the production of their highly popular and efficient lightweight roadster and off-road machines.

In Germany and Austria, there also existed a number of companies who, like the massive Zweirad Union AG, made most of their money marketing small capacity machines. Some, like the Zündapp company, a famed name of old, concentrated on the moped market while others, like Maico, concentrated on the highly specialised field of off-road competition. Another well known off-road bike manufacturer was Austria's KTM concern which, by the late 1970s, had several 250cc motocross world championships under its belt. Another Austrian company which won itself a world motocross title was Puch who, in 1975, supplied Belgian ace Harry Everts with a 250cc machine on which he won the world title. Puch's main claim to fame was not their motocross bikes, however, but the large range of mopeds and lightweight motor cycles which they marketed to the four corners of the earth.

The German industry, like the Italian industry, relied very heavily on the production of the commuter-type motor cycle for its existence. Many of the German companies made use of the Sachs engine, rather than build their own, and the Sachs unit became to Germany what the Villiers engine was to the British industry in days gone by. Some of the small German companies are virtually unknown outside of their native borders. Were it not for Kreidler's spectacular successes in the field of 50cc Grand Prix racing, it is doubtful if the average British or American motor cycle enthusiast would even know the name. Yet in Germany, the Kreidler range of lightweight motor cycles and mopeds is very popular and the streets are full of young men on Kreidlers which inevitably act as stepping stones to machines of a larger capacity.

Of the remaining European countries, only France, Sweden and Spain are in the motor cycle manufacturing business. France, in fact, has a moped industry rather than a motor cycle industry. The moped in France has become as popular as the bicycle in Holland, and millions of them can now be found on French streets. Consequently, companies like Motobecane and Velosolex concentrate almost solely on the manufacture of mopeds to the near total exclusion of actual motor cycles. Those Frenchmen who want something more powerful than a moped invariably turn to the Japanese, and French enthusiasts can often be seen at race meetings with the most incredibly modified Hondas and Kawasakis, many sporting the distinctive fairings of the Japauto company which specialises in making the Frenchman's motor cycling fantasies a reality. Some companies, like Motobécane, do make proper motor cycles but not in any great number. Another famous French manufacturer is Peugeot, sister to the famous car building company, but it it too specialises in the making of mopeds.

Top: the 294cc, rotary-engined DKW W2000. The Wankel-type motor produced 32bhp at 6500rpm. However, the conservative buying public did not readily accept the Wankel and the line was discontinued

Above: a rear view of the Bultaco Pursang showing the long-travel rear suspension

Top right: an Ossa 250 two-stroke single. This purpose-built trials machine is entitled the 'Super Pioneer'

Above right: a 348cc 'Malcolm Rathmell replica' Montesa 'Cota' from Spain

Right: a 390cc, automatic transmission motocross Husqvarna, manufactured in Sweden

Just as the French industry specialises in a single type of motorised two-wheel vehicle, so does the Swedish. The Swedish industry's forte, however, is the off-road vehicle, and in this field Husqvarna and Monark lead. Husqvarna's history goes right back to the turn of the century, but it wasn't until the 1960s that the company really began to be noticed outside of Sweden. In 1961, Husqvarna's total annual production was only 423 machines and it was at this stage that Husqvarna decided to drop their road going machines and concentrate wholly on off-road machinery. A year earlier, in 1960, Bill Nilsson had taken Husqvarna's new 500cc motocross machine to victory in the World Championship and this was the foundation on which Husqvarna hoped to build their future. Fielding new 250 and 500cc machines for the 1962 season, Husqvarna found themselves victors in two more World Championships when Rolf Tibblin took the senior title, and Torsten Hallman the 250cc Championship. Just to prove it was no fluke, the same two riders took the same titles during the following year. By now.

Husqvarna had begun to market their new range of motocross machines and it was with these single-cylinder, two-stroke machines that the Swedish manufacturer tackled the world. At first, two models were marketed, a 250cc machine and a 360cc model which was later uprated to 390cc. In time, Husqvarna extended the range to include new enduro type machines designed specially for the American market. These were also supplemented during the 1970s by a fully automatic version of the 390 which featured a simple infinitely variable DAF car-type automatic transmission unit. The Automatic also found its way into military service with the Swedish army.

By the mid 1970s, however, Husqvarna's grip on the motocross world had been loosened, particularly by the Japanese. Although still popular in America, Husqvarna, in

277

1978, faced an uncertain future unless their bikes developed more power with which to combat the marauders from the East.

Two other Swedish companies which earned most of their income from the local market, much of it from the Swedish armed forces, were Monark and Hagglund, of which Monark are perhaps the better known. Monark's machines were also off-road specials although in their case they were generally powered by the ubiquitous German Sachs engine. The company's successes included the manufacture of machines which were used to good effect in various International Six Days Trials events. Hagglund is a name little known outside of Sweden and their main contribution to the Swedish motor cycling industry was the creation of an all-purpose, all-terrain machine designed specifically for military use.

Probably the most surprising motor cycle industry in all of Europe is that of Spain, which boasts no fewer than four serious manufacturers – Bultaco, Montesa, Ossa and Derbi. Spain is not exactly famous for its industrial output and it is a credit to the men concerned with these four factories that they exist at all. The Spanish industry does not produce machines in any great number but it does specialise in one particular field, off-road machinery, and in one particular branch of this market, specifically trials bikes, it has yet to meet its master.

Bultaco are possibly the best known Spanish manufacturers although Montesa are not far behind. In fact it was the Montesa company which helped to spawn the Bultaco factory, although it would possibly prefer not to be remembered that way. Bultaco was formed as the result of an argument, in 1958, between members of Montesa's management and one of the company's employees, Francisco Xavier Bulto. Bulto was convinced of the need for Montesa to branch out into the sporting aspect of motor cycling but Montesa wanted none of it. Consequently, Bulto resigned in a huff and went off to form his own company, taking sixteen former Montesa staff members with him. The new Bultaco factory was built in Barcelona and it was from here that the first Bultaco models emerged. Right from the start Bultaco machines were sport orientated. Bulto offered a range of trials and motocross machines which, over the years, have been refined or redesigned as the need arose. Eventually, enduro and long-distance off-road machines were added to the range. It was in the field of trials riding, however, that Bultaco machines really made their mark and championship after championship fell to the men from Barcelona. Even in 1976 and '77, the world champion, Yrjo Vesterinen of Finland, was Bultaco mounted. The motocross machines were never quite so successful, however, perhaps because they had such stiff competition from the Japanese. Trials and trials riding, however, is a specialised art and one in which Bultaco had a head start.

Indeed, most of Bultaco's opposition during the 1960s and '70s was to come from their compatriots, Montesa. This little Spanish company had been founded in 1944 and at first concentrated on road and racing machinery, but after the bust-up with Francisco Bulto, the Montesa boss, Pedro Permanyer, also decided to concentrate on off-road motor cycling. Like Bultaco, Montesa also marketed a range of trials, enduro and scrambles machines and it is for these machines that Montesa are best known today.

The other two lesser known Spanish factories are Ossa and Derbi. Ossa was founded in 1951 and, like Bultaco and Montesa, took the off-road route. Unfortunately, however, they never enjoyed quite the same success and although Ossa and English trials rider Mick Andrews achieved some notable victories in the

Below: an MZ TS250 Supa of 1978, which, although not as excitingly styled as its European and Japanese opposition, was nonetheless good value for money, and offered an exceptional amount of standard equipment in its basic price. It was powered by a single-cylinder, two-stroke engine

278

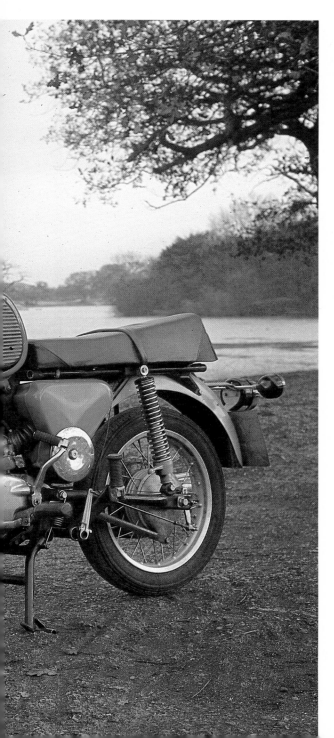

trials world, the little Ossa company, by late 1978, was in such financial trouble as to need assistance from the Government.

The sole remaining Spanish company is Derbi which, unlike Bultaco, Montesa and Ossa, specialises in road bikes of small capacity and markets an impressive range of 50cc mopeds and lightweight motor cycles. Derbi has also had some impressive victories in the world of Grand Prix racing. Spanish ace Angel Nieto won the 50cc World Championship for Derbi in 1969 and 1970 and added the 125cc title to his collection in 1971. To prove Derbi's superiority, he took both the 50 and the 125cc titles in 1972. Since that time, however, the company has withdrawn from motor cycle racing to concentrate on production requirements.

Derbi was not the only Spanish factory to achieve success in Grand Prix racing, however, because Bultaco too gained some spectacular results, also in the small capacity classes. Having quit Derbi, Angel Nieto was later to join Bultaco and helped to develop their 50cc racer to such good effect that he won the 1976 and '77 World Championship Grand Prix titles on it.

Of the other motor cycle factories dotted around Europe, only a handful are really worth mentioning. In Holland, the Batavus company produces a range of well made lightweights, while Holland was, in 1978, also the home of the world's most expensive motor cycle, the Van Veen OCR 1000. The Van Veen was practically hand made and used a rotary engine, with twin rotors, that pushed out some 100bhp at 6000rpm.

The eastern European bloc also produces a number of motor cycles, most of which conform to the austere utilitarian mould which has been the hallmark of products emanating from behind the Iron Curtain. The East Germans produce the MZ, from the company's factory in Zschopau. The factory started production in 1953 under the MZ banner, although the origin of the company dates back to the 1920s. It produced a number of racing machines in the early years, which were successfully campaigned around the European circuits.

CZ is another little firm which produces a range of middleweight utility machines, where production is state-controlled, and a large number of parts are designed to be common to the other Czechoslovakian bike, the Jawa. The CZs are all two-strokes, ranging from 125cc to 350cc in the road bike selection. There are also two motocross models, designated the CZ MX250RV and the MX400RV. Jawa produce a selection of sport orientated two-stroke machines, which include a very competitive enduro/trials machine, the ISDT Jawa. In addition, Jawa's four-stroke, single-cylinder, 500cc engine has been a major force in speedway racing for many years.

On the other side of the Atlantic, motor cycle production was enjoying a new lease of life, having faltered rather badly in the face of Japanese competition. Harley-Davidson rejuvenated their sales, not as one might imagine by some innovative technology, but through a tremendous marketing campaign appealing to public sentiment, patriotism and machismo.

Two other manufacturers producing bikes, mainly for off-road purposes, are the Canadian based Can-Am, and the American based Hodaka. The former are built by the Bombadier snowmobile company, and the machines feature 125, 175 and 250cc engines. Jeff Smith, formerly with BSA, was instrumental in their design, and he incorporated an adjustable rake in the steering head, as well as other unusual items. The Hodaka was the result of financial disaster on the part of a Japanese company, which resulted in the American importers developing the bike in Oregon, then having it built in Japan.

279

Chapter 15
Back on the Japanese Trail (1966-1979)

Left: Yamaha's three-cylinder XS750 was criticised by some, when it was announced, for being somewhat slower than its superbike opposition, although undoubtedly quick for a 750. However, this machine turned out to be just a taste of things to come, for it was not long before the company added an extra cylinder and produced the awesome XS1100, an incredibly fast and very heavy high-speed tourer, with its comfortable riding position and reliable shaft final drive

If the years between the mid 1960s and the mid 1970s were turbulent ones for the British and European industries, they were less so for the Japanese. This was a period of intense growth for them, a period of consolidation. Having destroyed the British opposition, Japan was ready to conquer the motor cycling world.

By 1966, Honda was ready to try and win the most prestigious title in motor cycle sport, the 500cc World Championship. In October of the previous year, they had succeeded in luring Mike Hailwood away from the MV Agusta team and for 1966 the company promised him a brand new 500cc four-cylinder machine. Unfortunately for Honda, a combination of team politics and the 500 machine's poor handling meant that they were not to be rewarded with yet another world title. The political problem arose when team captain Jim Redman decided he also wanted a crack at the prestigious 500cc world title. Having given Honda a total of six world titles, and approaching the end of his career, Redman felt he should be allowed to win the big one. In exchange for the 500 title, he would allow newcomer Hailwood to win the 250 and 350 titles! Alas for Honda and Redman, neither had reckoned on the old warhorse MV Agusta. Knowing they faced a serious challenge from the Japanese, they began to develop a three-cylinder 420cc machine for their number one rider, Giacomo Agostini, and in the end it was this machine that won the day.

At the first Grand Prix of the season, the German Grand Prix at Hockenheim, Honda produced two new 500cc machines for Hailwood and Redman but during practice Redman damaged one bike's gearbox. As team captain, he commandeered the sole remaining machine and charged to an impressive win. Impressive as it was, however, Honda soon realised that something was very wrong with their machine. It was certainly powerful enough and in a straight line it was shatteringly fast, but it just would not handle. The power was too much for the frame and try as Honda might they could not iron out the handling bugs.

At the following event, the Dutch TT at Assen, MV wheeled out their new three-cylinder machine and the bike immediately proved a sensation. It was as quick as the Hondas and its handling was superior. During the race, Redman and Agostini staged a fierce duel and it was only through some spectacular riding that Redman eventually clinched victory. His joy was short-lived, however, because he crashed during the following Grand Prix, at Spa in Belgium, breaking his arm. The accident meant that he would miss a number of vital championship rounds but it also meant that Hailwood now became the undisputed Honda number one and that the Honda mechanics could give him their undivided attention. Unfortunately, he was by now a long way behind in the world championship points table.

Following the East German Grand Prix, where neither Hailwood nor Agostini finished in the 500cc points, the Grand Prix circus moved on to Czechoslovakia and it was here that Hailwood began to assert his challenge. He won the event, but Agostini was not far behind. In Finland, Agostini fought back and this time it was he who led Hailwood home. The season had become a see-saw battle between Hailwood and Agostini, Honda and MV Agusta.

The scene then moved to Dunrod in Ulster, home of the Ulster TT. By now, Redman was ready to return to racing but during practice his arm began to stiffen and he withdrew from the race. Shortly afterwards he announced his retirement and eventually returned to southern Africa where he set up a successful motor cycle dealership – selling Yamahas. The Ulster Grand Prix itself was a major triumph for Mike Hailwood, and he won in superb style. He followed this up with another great win, this time at the Isle of Man. The TT races had been postponed from their normal June date because of a seaman's strike and now became the penultimate round of the year's world championship series.

Hailwood's win in the 1966 Senior TT was a marvellous achievement. His big 500cc Honda was totally unsuited to the twisty course and reports from spectators of Hailwood having to stand on the footpegs in order to wrestle the bucking Honda back into a straight line abounded. No one doubted that he had earned his victory.

For Honda and MV Agusta, the final testing ground would be at Monza. Theoretically, it was still possible for Hailwood to win the title, although Agostini held a points advantage. For Hailwood, however, Monza was an anti-climax. His Honda failed to finish and Agostini stormed through to victory and the World Championship.

For Honda and Hailwood, defeat in the 500cc class was a bitter disappointment. In the 250 and 350cc classes, however, it was a different story. Riding the new six-cylinder 250 machine, Hailwood streaked to victory in no fewer than nine Grands Prix, taking the title with almost contemptuous ease. Victory in the 350cc class was less easy because here he had to fight off the MV of Agostini, but in the end Hailwood took six wins to Ago's three to clinch the title.

To some extent, Hailwood's win in the 250cc class was aided by the fact that Yamaha had decided to withdraw their highly successful two-stroke, twin-cylinder RD56 machines and replace them with new and complicated vee-fours. These machines were water-cooled and, to retain the favoured disc-valve arrangement, the engine was virtually one 125cc twin atop another with the crankshafts geared together. Like the big Honda 500, however, the vee-four engines were too powerful for their frames, and riders Phil Read and Bill Ivy struggled to achieve any sort of reasonable result.

In the smaller 125 and 50cc classes, Japanese machines were again dominant. The 50cc category was won by German Hans-Georg Anscheidt on a Suzuki, while Luigi Taveri took the incredible five-cylinder 125cc Honda to victory in the ultra-lightweight World Championship. Indeed, the only category not

dominated by the Japanese or the Italian MVs was that of the sidecar and here, as usual, victory went to a BMW, this time in the hands of Swiss ace Fritz Scheidegger.

In some ways, the 1966 racing season marked a turning point in the history of Grand Prix racing. Never before had there been such intense activity in this field. Never before had so much money been spent on the development of new and exotic machinery. Honda had spent a fortune on the new 500cc four only to see it fail. Yamaha's highly complicated vee-fours were also proving troublesome. The Japanese, it seemed, could make the most remarkable engines but could not match them with suitable frames. The whole Grand Prix scene was beginning to smack of overkill on the part of the men from the east.

At the end of 1966, Honda took a serious look at their Grand Prix challenge. The company had spent several hundred thousand pounds to develop its complex multi-cylinder creations, but still the simple two-stroke designs were proving competitively troublesome. In the 50cc class, Suzuki had beaten

Left: in 1966, Honda enlarged their six-cylinder, 250cc engine so that it could be used in bikes for the larger, 350cc, class. So confident were they that it would be successful, that they only enlarged it to 297cc. Mike Hailwood took the 350cc class in that year, beating arch-rival Agostini

Below: Mike Hailwood winning the 1966 Senior TT with his Honda 500cc four. Spectators on the Island will never forget the sight of Hailwood wrestling the powerful but unwieldy bike around the tortuous course

Honda quite comprehensively and by now Yamaha were beginning to master their bothersome vee-four machines. In addition, it was becoming obvious to the big Japanese companies that America was the place to market their machines and that this market did not give two hoots who won such esoteric events as 50 and 125cc Grand Prix races. Consequently, Honda decided to pull out of the 50 and 125 categories to concentrate on the larger classes and that elusive 500cc title in particular. With Redman gone, Hailwood became the undisputed number one. Little was he to know that the following year would be the toughest racing season of his career.

1966 was also a notable year for another Japanese company, Kawasaki. The company had opened an office in Los Angeles from where they would launch new products on to an unsuspecting American public. Included in the new product range was the recently introduced 250cc A1 Samurai model plus the new 90cc G1, 125cc B1L and 100cc D1 machines, while of interest to road racing enthusiasts was the announcement of the

Top: a YR3 Yamaha 350cc, two-stroke twin of 1969, which was subsequently developed into the RD350 and thence the RD400. By the late 1960s, Japanese roadsters were renowned for their sparkling performance

Left: Bill Ivy and Phil Read bank their 125cc, V4 Yamahas on their way to a one-two finish in the Ulster Grand Prix of 1967. In the following season, their team tussle turned into something more of a feud

Above: Mike Hailwood and his six-cylinder, 250cc Honda at Whitegates, in the 1967 Lightweight TT

A1R model, a modified version of the twin-cylinder, two-stroke Samurai. From these humble beginnings would grow a company which in the course of time would become recognised as one of Japan's big four.

The year 1966 was an interesting one for another Japanese manufacturer, Bridgestone. This company was a subsidiary of the massive Bridgestone tyre company and in the mid 1960s was marketing a range of small to middleweight machines. From beginnings in the early '60s, the Bridgestone motor cycle company grew to the stage where, by 1966, they were making over 50,000 machines a year, many of which were being marketed in America. Top of Bridgestone's range was the stylish 350GTR, a racy 350cc twin-cylinder machine with disc valves and a six-speed gearbox. The engine produced 40bhp and the machine was quite capable of out running opposition machines of the time, such as Yamaha's 350cc YR3 model and Honda's CB350. Unfortunately for Bridgestone, however, the pollution conscious Americans were demanding ever more stringent emission controls and the Bridgestone company, reluctant to become involved in expensive test and development expenditure, decided to cut their losses and withdraw from the market. By 1967, sales had dropped to 36,000 and shortly afterwards the company stopped production. The Bridgestone history was proof that not even Japanese companies could jump on the motor cycle bandwagon and become immediately successful.

Back in Europe the Grand Prix season of 1967 was about to start. Honda had cut back on its teams as had Suzuki. In spite of cutting expenditure. Suzuki once again managed to win the 50cc class with Hans-Georg Anscheidt taking the world title. In fact, Suzuki took the first three places in the championship table, but it was a fairly hollow victory without serious opposition from the Honda team.

In the 125cc class it was the turn of Yamaha to dominate. They produced a scaled down version of the 250cc vee-four for this class and, with little Bill Ivy in the saddle, the Yamaha was uncatchable. Towards the end of the season Suzuki unveiled a new four-cylinder 125cc rival but it was only raced once, at the Japanese Grand Prix. In taking the 125cc title, Ivy managed to win eight out of a possible twelve events.

The 250cc championship of 1967 was a much more closely contested series, however. Yamaha had stepped up their challenge to Honda and the new four-cylinder Yamahas were much lighter, lower and faster than the machines of the previous year. The battle between Yamaha's Phil Read and Mike Hailwood on the six-cylinder Honda was intense and continued right until the last round, held in Japan. Even then few were certain who had won the title because both men finished with a total of fifty points. Fortunately for Hailwood, he had five overall wins to Read's four and so the title was awarded to him.

In the 350cc class, Hailwood triumphed again. He was just too good for Agostini and the MV, winning six out of the eight championship rounds to take the title quite easily. Agostini got his revenge in the 500cc class, however, and the season-long duel between the two men has now gone down in motor cycling legend as one of the most exciting ever. Typical of the fierce contests between the two was the Isle of Man Senior TT, a race which saw the two men nose to tail for almost the whole event. Time and time again the lap record was smashed, with both riders eventually bettering the 108mph mark. Then, on the fifth lap of a seven lap race, with Agostini a mere two seconds ahead, the rear chain on the Italian MV jumped its sprocket and broke, leaving a relieved Hailwood to sprint home for victory.

After the event, Hailwood was critical of the big Honda's handling. It was still not right and even on the straights it would weave from side to side. Right through the season, Hailwood tried everything he knew to get the beast to handle. Honda strengthened the frame but all to no avail and in the end it was left to Hailwood's amazing courage and riding ability to keep the company in contention. The battle between Hailwood and Ago raged on all season. After his TT victory, Hailwood took the Dutch TT only to be beaten in the Belgian and East German events. He fought back to win the Czechoslovakian Grand Prix but was immediately answered by Agostini who won the next race, in Finland. Hailwood followed up with a win in the Ulster Grand Prix and Agostini retaliated by winning the Italian Grand Prix. The season finally closed in Canada where Hailwood screamed to victory closely followed by Agostini. The points were quickly tallied up and both men were found to have 46. As before it was decided to give the championship to the man with the most wins, but here again each rider was level with the other – five wins apiece. Finally, it was decided to award the the title to the man with the most second places and so, after much controversy and calculation, the title was awarded to MV Agusta's Giacomo Agostini. Once again, Honda had failed to win the much sought after 500cc crown.

There was no surprise in the sidecar class, however. Once again, the title went to the seemingly invincible BMW, the rider in this instance being the talented German Klaus Enders. With passenger Ralf Englehardt in the chair, he swept to five championship race victories and won the world sidecar championship title more or less as he pleased.

Away from the race track, 1967 was also an interesting year for a number of reasons. It was the year in which Norton launched the Commando model and it was also a year which saw the deaths of the Panther and Royal Enfield companies. If it was a bad year for the British, the same could not be said of the Japanese. Kawasaki, in conjunction with the Meguro company, had launched their new W1 model, a 650cc four-stroke machine, while Honda announced that total production of their little Super Club model had reached a staggering five million. Yamaha and Suzuki also had little cause for complaint because their two-stroke light and middleweight machines were selling like hot cakes, especially in America.

It was at the end of 1967, however, when Honda made an announcement that was to send shock waves around the race circuits of the world. They had decided to withdraw from Grand Prix racing. Speaking from Paris, at a specially arranged press conference, Soichiro Honda himself said that racing had been abandoned because all design and technical staff were required to work on a new Formula One racing car that Honda had decided to develop. But there were other reasons as well. Racing had become a hugely expensive business and the publicity that Honda had gained from it was now academic. Shortly after Honda's withdrawal came the news that Suzuki was also to stage a major cutback and so, as the 1968 season approached, only Yamaha would field pukka works bikes for Grand Prix world championship events.

Not surprisingly, after the glorious no-holds-barred days of the mid sixties, the 1968 racing season fell a bit flat and it was only a fierce feud between Yamaha team-mates Phil Read and Bill Ivy that did anything to liven it up. Despite his successes for Yamaha in seasons past, Phil Read found himself out of favour with the Japanese, who decided that Bill Ivy should win both the 125 and 250cc world titles. Read objected strongly and

286

Left: Soichiro Honda in 1961 on the Isle of Man, where Mike Hailwood and Tom Phillis got their successful assaults on the world championships under way – the first of many victories for Honda

Below: Giacomo Agostini, with his 500 MV, winning the 1968 Senior TT, the first of five wins in a row in this event for 'Ago'

Below right: there was a break in the BMW stranglehold of the sidecar World Championship in 1968, when Helmut Fath and Walter Kalauch took their URS to the title

eventually Yamaha said Read could win the 125cc title but that Ivy must have the 250 championship. As the season wore on, the rivalry between the two became more bitter. At the Isle of Man, Bill Ivy set a fantastic pace in the 125cc race, smashing the lap record and establishing a new one of 100.32mph, the first ever 100mph lap by a 125cc machine. This record, in fact, was to survive for years to come. On the last lap he slowed, having made his point to Yamaha and Read, and allowed Read to win the race. By mid-season, Read had safely tucked up the 125cc title and now he set about winning the 250cc Championship as well. Yamaha were in a real predicament. The FIM had warned them that it would not tolerate them stage managing races and that Read and Ivy must be allowed to dispute any race in which they competed. Yamaha could, of course, have withdrawn Read from the team but this was sure to result in bad publicity. Eventually, the team's management just shrugged the problem off and left the two feuding team-mates to get on with it. After all, they decided, a Yamaha would win the title anyway, what did it matter who rode it? Eventually, after a season long battle, the two protagonists finished the season level pegging on 52 points each. Both had five wins and two second places and the tie was eventually resolved by adding up the total times of the races in which they had competed. Read was adjudged to have had the quicker race times and was declared the new champion, much to the disgust of Ivy and, let it be said, the Yamaha management, who hadn't cared for the way Read had gone about winning the title in direct opposition to team orders.

Without any opposition from Honda, the 350 and 500cc classes were a benefit for Giacomo Agostini and the howling MV Agusta, and he finished up winning both titles with contemptuous ease. The winner of the remaining solo category, the 50cc class, was Hans-Georg Anscheidt, riding a Suzuki borrowed from the factory but without much in the way of official support.

In the sidecar class, there was a sensation: for once, a BMW did not win. Ever since Wilhelm Noll's victory in 1954, a BMW had been the title winner but on this occasion the title went to Helmut Fath on his home-brewed URS. Fath, who won the title on a BMW in 1960, had been injured in an accident in 1961 and had spent the intervening years developing the new four-cylinder machine at a small workshop in his home town of Ursenbach, from whence came the initials URS.

Away from the race track, 1968 will be remembered as the year in which the BSA/Triumph group launched its new Rocket and Trident three-cylinder, 750cc machines. It was also the year in which Honda production reached a total of ten million machines, one million of which had been sold in America.

By 1969, the Japanese factories had completely faded from the European racing scene because Yamaha had decided to withdraw following the embarrassing antics of its riders the year before. In fact, only one Japanese team was represented and this was the newcomer Kawasaki who supplied Dave Simmonds with a new 125cc machine. By this time, the FIM had also restricted the 50cc class to machines with single-cylinders and a maximum of six gears. In this way, they hoped to attract new manufacturers back to racing. To some extent, the ploy succeeded because with no Suzuki or Honda to worry about, the Spanish Derbi company fielded a new machine for countryman Angel Nieto who promptly swept all before him to win the 50cc title. The 125cc title also went to a newcomer, in this case the little Kawasaki of Dave Simmonds. This was to be Kawasaki's first world title and it would be a long time before they were to win another.

It was in the 250 and 350cc classes in which most interest was focussed, however. The Yamaha company had launched a new range of production built racers, the 250 TD2 and 350 TR2 models, which had been developed in America for races such as the prestigious Daytona meeting. They were remarkably simple devices with twin cylinders featuring four transfer ports and one exhaust port. No longer were there any disc valves to worry about. The little machines were incredibly competitive, with the

Top: probably the most ferocious roadster ever built was the Kawasaki 500, seen here in 1970 Mach III form. It was quite a few years before 750cc bikes were able to approach its performance standards, while other 500s have never done so

Above: Australian Kel Carruthers heads for victory in the 1969 250cc TT. Kel went on to take the World Championship of that year, with his Benelli, and then left to become Yamaha team leader in America. After retiring from racing, he became team manager for the American ace Kenny Roberts

little 250 pushing out 44bhp at 10,000rpm and the larger machine producing 54bhp at 9500rpm. Even more important, they weren't particularly expensive and, with the works bikes gone, the privateer at last stood a chance of finishing in the world championship Grand Prix results.

As it happened, both the 250 and 350 classes were still won by works machines, but the Yamahas were not far behind. In the 250cc class there was a monumental battle between the four-cylinder Benellis of Australian Kel Carruthers and his team-mate Gilberto Parlotti, the incredibly fast monocoque framed single-cylinder, two-stroke Ossa of Spaniard Santiago Herrero and the new Yamaha of Sweden's Kent Andersson. The title was eventually won by Carruthers but only after he had been forced to fight every inch of the way.

The 350cc category again went to Agostini but it might have been more closely fought had Bill Ivy not been killed at the East German Grand Prix, when the engine of his new four-cylinder Jawa seized during a practice session, resulting in a

Top: Ago winning the Senior TT again. This time he is seen at Governor's Bridge hairpin during the 1969 event

Above: in 1969, Dave Simmonds took the 125 Championship, winning eight out of eleven rounds in that year's title race. It was nine years before Kawasaki won another World Championship

terrible crash. Ironically, Ivy was only riding the Jawa to supplement his finances as he had already embarked on a career in car racing. The 500cc title was also a foregone conclusion, and Agostini romped home an easy winner, finishing up with a total number of points three times that of his nearest rival. In the sidecar class, things were back to normal and the title went back to BMW, this time in the hands of Germany's remarkable sidecar ace Klaus Enders.

Although the racing season had proved predictable and even a little dull at times, the same could not be said for the world's production industries. During 1969, Kawasaki had gathered their various groups together to form a new and powerful company, Kawasaki Heavy Industries Limited. They celebrated the creation of this conglomerate by launching the new Mach III model, a road-burning, three-cylinder, two-stroke machine of 500cc. It was a monster of a machine: in a straight line, its performance was shattering and the front wheel would reach for the sky at every possible opportunity. Handling was atrocious but it didn't seem to matter, particularly to the Americans who took the howling thunder-and-lightning machine to their hearts. The Mach III would be the first in a series of high performance machines on which Kawasaki would build its future success and in time the two-stroke, three-cylinder concept was developed to include an even quicker 750cc model, as well as 350 and even 250cc versions.

1969 was also a memorable year because it heralded the introduction of the now legendary Honda CB750 four-cylinder model. This was the world's first mass-produced four-cylinder superbike, and its introduction ripped the heart out of the challenge that the British had been mounting in the form of their Norton Commando and Triumph/BSA triples. The Honda was a superbly engineered, single-overhead-camshaft, four-cylinder,

Left: Roger De Coster, with his Suzuki, at the British Moto Cross 500 Grand Prix of 1971. Roger went on to be one of the most successful motocross riders ever, with only fellow countryman Joël Robert winning more championship titles

Below: 125cc action at Jarama in September 1971, with Barry Sheene (Suzuki) leading Dieter Braun (Maico), Angel Nieto (Derbi) and Borje Jansson (Maico). Spaniard Nieto won the race from Barry Sheene and in so doing took that year's 125cc World Championship title

four-stroke machine with a five-speed gearbox and a turbine smooth performance. It had near faultless electrics and a top speed in the region of 120mph. Moreover, it sold for a price that was highly competitive against its British rivals. Needless to say, the Americans bought them by the bagful and the age of the superbike had truly dawned.

At the beginning of the 1970 racing season, the FIM announced even more restrictions on racing machinery. Both the 125 and 250cc categories were now limited to twin-cylinder bikes with a maximum of six ratios in the gearboxes. The only company really affected by this ruling, however, was Benelli who had to put their faithful old four-cylinder 250s out to grass. This ruling left the smaller classes wide open to the production-racing Yamaha machines. Consequently, it came as no surprise to see the talented Rod Gould storm to victory in the 250cc World Championship, his main opposition coming from fellow Yamaha rider Kel Carruthers.

In fact, none of the Championships was particularly closely fought in 1970. Angel Nieto retained his 50cc title, while West German Dieter Braun, riding an ex-works Suzuki twin, won the 125cc class with relative ease. In the 350 and 500cc classes, it was the same old story – Ago and the MV. Even the sidecars produced the same result as before, the title going once again to Klaus Enders and the BMW. The only real talking point of the year came at Daytona in America where AMA star Dick Mann rode a modified CB750 Honda to victory in the Daytona 200 Formula 750 event.

1970 was also significant in that it was the year in which the Japanese started taking a serious interest in the world of motocross. Suzuki began to field a works 250cc team and their star rider, Joël Robert of Belgium, obliged them with their first World Moto Cross Championship. In the 500cc class, Bengt Aberg managed to win for Husqvarna but it would not be long before Suzuki dominated that class as well. In fact, it took the company only one year because, by the end of 1971, Roger De Coster had taken his first 500cc title for Suzuki, the first of many to follow in the years ahead.

The 1971 racing season was not a particularly notable one. Agostini and the MV dominated the 350 and 500 classes with monotonous regularity, while Phil Read took the 250cc class on his privately entered and developed Yamaha twin. The 50cc category was won by Dutchman Jan de Vries on his Van Veen modified Kreidler, while the 125cc class was won by Angel Nieto on his new 125cc Derbi, the major interest in this category being supplied by the emergence of a young and talented rider from London named Barry Sheene. Indeed, the sidecar class supplied the major upset of the year when young German motor mechanic Horst Owesle rode his URS to victory, beating the might of the BMW riders in the process.

The 1972 racing season saw a slight upsurge in the sport's fortunes, supplied mainly by the arrival of a new water-cooled 350cc Yamaha model, the TZ350, and a brilliant young Finnish rider by the name of Jarno Saarinen. Saarinen started the season in spectacular fashion by winning in Germany and France. It was the first time Agostini and the 350 MV had been beaten in a World Championship event since 1967, and the Italian company countered by introducing a new four-cylinder model to replace the existing triple. It also added Briton Phil Read to their riding staff. MV's efforts finally bore fruit, for although Saarinen actually won more Grands Prix, Agostini eventually clinched the 350cc world championship title through more consistent points scoring.

291

Saarinen was not to be denied a championship, however, and he took the 250cc title in typically stylish fashion, beating former champion Rod Gould into second place. Angel Nieto also finished the season in impressive style by winning both the 50 and 125cc titles on his Spanish built Derbi machines. Agostini, as usual, won the 500cc title, while the sidecar class again returned to BMW and the German ace Klaus Enders.

If the 1972 season proved anything, however, it was that the days of the four-stroke racer were numbered. The little Yamahas were proving indecently quick, and only the might of MV could hold them off. Even in the 500cc class, two-stroke machines were beginning to emerge. Various riders were using 500cc twin-cylinder Suzuki engines, as fitted to the 500cc Suzuki Titan roadsters, to good effect, while Kawasaki's 500cc H1R racer, developed from the Mach III roadster, was proving very fast if a little unpredictable round the bends. Also, a number of overbored 354cc Yamaha twins had found their way into the 500cc class and were showing surprisingly fast form.

Several new developments were also taking place in the newly introduced Formula 750 category. This formula had been designed specially for the Americans and was originally based around production 750cc machines such as the Triumph and BSA three-cylinder models. Since the introduction of the formula, however, Suzuki had introduced their water-cooled GT750 three-cylinder roadster and this engine soon found itself, albeit in modified form, installed in an F750 racer. By 1972, Kawasaki had also joined the bandwagon with the introduction of the 750cc H2R three-cylinder F750 racer as had the Norton factory with the formation of the John Player Norton team. As the years went by, the popularity of F750 grew and then waned. This was largely due to the withdrawal of the British teams in the early and mid 1970s and the arrival of the phenomenally fast Yamaha TZ700 production machines. The TZ700s, which later grew into full-blooded 750s, could be bought by anyone with the necessary cash, and by the late 1970s the Yamahas totally dominated the formula. Although Suzuki developed a 650cc racer for Barry Sheene to use in the British Superbike series during 1977 and '78, they refused to homologate the bike for use in the F750, and with only Kawasaki offering any sort of token resistance, Yamaha took over total control of the formula. Ironically, F750 became a World Championship class in 1977, a year in which interest in the class was already beginning to fade, the title being won by American Steve Baker. One of the better by-products of the F750 category, however, was the introduction of the Anglo-American Transatlantic Trophy series. This series, held in Britain every year over the Easter weekend, is a contest between two teams drawn from the best riders in Britain and America. Over the years, the Transatlantic series has produced some fascinating racing and has proved very popular with the paying public. By 1978, the results were very much in Britain's favour but perhaps the most important part played by the series was in the road racing development of a number of talented Americans. Men like Kenny Roberts, Pat Hennen, Steve Baker and Skip Aksland owed much of their initial road racing experience to the Transatlantic series.

Shortly after Kawasaki announced the H2R racer in 1972 came the news that they were developing a new superbike, and in September of that year the new machine was launched. Known as the Z1, the bike was a breathtakingly quick 903cc twin-overhead-camshaft machine. The power output was a staggering 82bhp at 8500rpm and top speed was in the region of

Right: those people who thought that the environmentalists who killed off the fast-thirsty and dirty high-performance two-strokes had killed off fast roadsters for ever were quite wrong, for in September 1972 Kawasaki launched the Z1. This 903cc, twin-cam bike was at least as quick as anything before it, but being a four-stroke, was also clean and frugal

Below: Kenny Roberts with his TZ700 Yamaha at Brands Hatch in 1974. The Yamaha range was the first in racing to be made available on the mass market, so that, in theory, anyone with sufficient skill could go out and win a Grand Prix.

130mph. The bike was originally meant to have been a 750cc model but when Honda released the CB750 first, the Kawasaki engineers were forced to indulge in a little one upmanship. Not surprisingly, the Americans took to the big Z1 in large numbers and before long the bike had been nicknamed 'the king'.

Meanwhile, back on the racing circuits of Europe, the 1973 racing season was about to get under way. There were high hopes that this season would see a revival in racing's flagging fortunes, particularly as Yamaha had decided to contest the 500cc class with new works four-cylinder, two-stroke machines to be ridden by Jarno Saarinen and his fellow countryman Tepi Lansivuori. Saarinen, who had started the season in spectacular form by winning both the Daytona 200 and Imola 200 races on his 350cc Yamaha, also started the Grand Prix season in sensational fashion winning the opening 500cc rounds at Paul Ricard in France and at Salzburg in Austria. Phil Read

fought back to take the German Grand Prix for MV Agusta and then the circus moved on to Monza for the Italian Grand Prix. This event, however, will go down in the motor cycling history books as one of racing's blackets days. Soon after the start of the 250cc race there was a massive pile-up at the Curva Grande and in the accident Jarno Saarinen and the Italian ace Renzo Pasolini lost their lives. For Yamaha, this was a tragic blow and as a tribute to Saarinen they withdrew their machines for the rest of the season. No one will ever know whether Saarinen and Yamaha could have beaten the MV Agusta, but in the end it was MV who once again triumphed, although this time the rider was Phil Read and not Giacomo Agostini. The Italian Agostini got his revenge in the 350cc class, however, winning the title from Read, while in the 250cc category, victory went to the German Dieter Braun on a privately entered Yamaha twin. Yamaha also won the 125cc class, with Kent Andersson doing the honours, while the 50cc world title went to Jan de Vries, riding the works Kreidler. The sidecar class again went to a BMW machine, the rider being that most successful of all sidecar competitors, Klaus Enders of Germany. What had started as a most promising season had become one of the most frustrating. The world had lost one of its brightest new stars in Saarinen, and the 350 and 500cc classes were still being ruled by MV, although these two classes were at least being livened up by the rivalry between team-mates Read and Agostini, both on the track and in various newspaper columns around the world!

The year of 1973 will also be remembered as a bad one for British enthusiasts, because it was the year in which the BSA name died due to the merger of Norton and Triumph into the Norton Villiers Triumph company. There was some consolation, however, because this was the year in which Norton factory rider Peter Williams rode his John Player Norton to a superb victory in the Isle of Man Formula 750 TT. For Kawasaki, it was also good news because total production had now passed the one million mark, and to celebrate, they launched their new KX250 motocross machine on to the market as a direct competitor to Honda's Elsinore 250 model, which was proving so popular at that time. 1973 was also the year in which the famed TZ700 Yamaha was first produced. This bike, in various stages of development, would go on making headlines in motor-cycle racing for years to come.

Left: Peter Williams accelerates his John Player Norton 750 at Bungalow during the 1973 750TT. Peter piloted this handsome machine to victory, but it spelt the end of an era for the great British four-stroke twins in world-class bike racing

Above: Klaus Enders came out of his 'retirement' after only a year, and at 35 he partnered Ralf Engelhardt to another World Championship with a BMW in 1972 – they are seen at that year's TT. In fact, Klaus went on to take the title for the following two years

In 1974, however, most of the headlines revolved around the MV Agusta and Yamaha teams and the renewed rivalry between Phil Read and Giacomo Agostini. All season long, these two aces battled for supremacy in the 350 and 500cc classes, their duel being spiced up by some juicy off-track broadsides at each other in the motor cycling press. To add fuel to the fire, Agostini had quit the MV team at the beginning of the season and had now signed for Yamaha, leaving Read and new team-mate Gianfranco Bonera to uphold the MV honour. Agostini had not cared much for the way that MV had allowed Read to come into the team and usurp his number one position, and so he retaliated by signing up with a Japanese team.

In the end, however, neither Read nor Agostini could claim the season as his alone. In the 350cc class, it was Agostini and Yamaha who dominated, so much so that MV withdrew halfway through the season to concentrate, so they said, on the 500cc class. The truth was, however, that at long last the MV had met its match, in the 350cc class at least. Agostini stormed on to win five of that year's Championship rounds and ended up the season as 350cc World Champion, his fourteenth world title.

In the 500cc class, Agostini did not fare so well. Although the Yamaha was spectacularly fast, it suffered some frustrating mechanical faults, added to which Agostini broke his shoulder at the Swedish Grand Prix and so missed two Championship rounds. While all this was going on, Phil Read was riding his MV quickly and steadily to some impressive results. He won the French and Finnish Grands Prix at the beginning of the season and followed these up later with wins in Czechoslovakia and Belgium to take the 1974 500cc world title. This win gave MV Agusta their 37th World Championship but little did the motor cycling world realise that this would be its last ever world title.

There were a few surprise results in the smaller capacity classes as well. For once, the 250cc class did not fall to the Japanese Yamaha but to an outsider in the form of Walter Villa and his two-stroke, twin-cylinder Harley-Davidson (née Aermacchi). In spite of strong opposition, the little Italian won four Championship rounds to clinch the title for the delighted Harley-Davidson team. Yamaha were not to be denied a title, however, and their works 125cc rider Kent Andersson took the honours in this class in most convincing style. The sidecar class again went to Klaus Enders and the BMW. Ironically, this year would also see the last world title that BMW, like MV Agusta, would win. The sole remaining solo championship, the 50cc category, was again dominated by the Kreidler team, Dutch rider Henk van Kessel winning the title.

Away from all the hustle and bustle of the racing world, Honda were getting on with the business of making motor cycles, and 1974 saw the building of the ten millionth Super Cub model. Not content to rest on their laurels, Honda launched a new top of the range machine, the GL1000 Gold Wing. The Gold Wing was a four-cylinder machine, but unlike the CB750 it had its cylinders horizontally-opposed and water-cooled. In addition, the big machine was fitted with shaft drive in an attempt to compete directly with the big tourers being marketed by BMW and Moto Guzzi. Once again, Honda had a hit on their hands and the Americans bought Gold Wings in their thousands. Elsewhere, particularly in Britain, the Gold Wing got a cooler reception. It was a big, heavy machine not suited to the more crowded European roads and the Europeans were getting a little tired of having their taste dictated by the Americans in the eyes of the Japanese. To some extent, they were mollified with the introduction that same year of Honda's little CB400 Four machine. Now this was a motor cycle the Europeans could identify with, for it was a slim, nimble lightweight that handled like a racer and was fitted with a jewel-like 400cc, four-cylinder, overhead-camshaft engine that gave the bike a genuine top speed of over 100mph.

It was around this time, however, that a new world crisis emerged which would have serious consequences for the motor cycling world. This was the so-called Arab petrol crisis in which the Arabs refused to supply oil unless the western powers paid greatly increased prices. The net result of the crisis was that the world became more 'energy conscious' than it had ever been before. Manufacturers sought ways to improve fuel economy and this soon resulted in a rash of new economy machines being launched onto the market. Typical of these was the Kawasaki Z400, a twin-cylinder, four-stroke machine from a company which had previously made its reputation as a builder of such fire-eating monsters as the Mach III and Z1 900 models. Honda also introduced a new economy machine, the twin-cylinder CB500T, while those traditional two-stroke manufacturers Yamaha and Suzuki also began to give serious thought to the

Top: by 1975, the MV was coming to the end of its reign, although it was not eclipsed totally. Here, Phil Read leads Barry Sheene's RG500 in one of their epic scraps of that year

Above: the Honda super tourer GL1000 Gold Wing, a bike that Honda hoped would take many sales from BMW. This is a 1978 American spec bike

production of new four-stroke machines. Although Yamaha had already dabbled in the manufacture of four-stroke engines with the XS650 and TX750 twins of the early 1970s, most of the production was taken up with single and twin-cylinder, two-stroke bikes, while Suzuki's production was concentrated round a range of two and three-cylinder, two-stroke models. In fact, the top of the range model at Suzuki was still the water-cooled GT750 triple. In time, Suzuki tried to break away from the two-stroke mould in quite spectacular fashion with its rotary-engined RE5, but by this time the public's mind had been poisoned towards the petrol-guzzling rotary engine concept and the RE5 died a premature and rather lonely death, which it did not wholly deserve because the bike certainly had some attractive features, not the least of which was a very smooth ride.

By now, the tide was beginning to turn against the two-stroke, high-performance machine, ironically at a time in which the two-stroke was beginning to dominate the world of road racing in a way in which it had never been able to previously. Added to this was the ever increasing problem of exhaust emission controls being foisted upon the Japanese manufacturers by the American and Japanese governments. Very soon, it became obvious that the day of the two-stroke had passed and that the era of the Japanese four-stroke had begun.

One battleground where the two-stroke still reigned supreme, however, was that of the motocross course. The 1974 championship year saw some surprising results as, for once, the Suzuki team was vanquished in both the 250 and 500cc categories. Roger De Coster's normally unbeatable Suzuki had to take second place to Heikki Mikkola's Husqvarna in the senior class, while Russian Gennady Moisseev gained the 250cc title for the KTM company.

In spite of all their problems elsewhere, two-stroke motor cycles were now ready to dominate the world of Grand Prix racing completely and, by the end of 1975, the two-stroke revolution had succeeded comprehensively. For the first time in history, every racing class, including the sidecar category, was won by a machine working on the two-stroke principle.

In the 500cc class, MV Agusta for once could find no answer to the speed of the Yamahas, although Phil Read tried everything he knew to keep Agostini's screaming Japanese machine at bay. Indeed, the contest went right to the last round before the popular Italian stamped his authority on the class. Agostini won four Grand Prix races to Read's two, while much interest was supplied by the arrival of a new four-cylinder Suzuki racer in the hands of Barry Sheene, who managed to snap up two wins, in Holland and in Sweden.

The 1975 350cc racing season also managed to provide a spectacular surprise in that it was won by a rider who until that season was totally unheard of outside of his native Venezuela. His name was Johnny Cecotto, and he started the season in magnificent form by winning the first event on the calendar, the French Grand Prix. Young Cecotto was mounted on a Yamaha supplied by the Venezuelan importer Andres flash in the pan. As the months went by, he added the Italian and German Grands Prix to his tally and finished off the season by winning the Finnish Grand Prix to become the 350cc World Champion. At the time, he was only nineteen years of age, the youngest World Champion in the history of the sport.

Another rider who proved that his previous year's victory was no fluke was Walter Villa who again took his little Harley-Davidson to victory in the 250cc class. Villa had to fight off a tough challenge from Yamaha's Johnny Cecotto and his own team-mate Michel Rougerie, but in the end, with five victories to his credit, Villa was declared the champion. Another surprise came in the 125cc class which was won by the relatively unknown Italian Paolo Pileri on his new Morbidelli machine. There was no great surprise in the 50cc class, however, where Angel Nieto again triumphed.

There was a major upset in the sidecar class, however, with the BMWs totally vanquished; indeed, after the 1975 season, BMW machines ceased to play any significant part in the sidecar category, as they could no longer match the power of the new generation of two-stroke sidecar engines. The man who finally buried BMW was the German Rolf Steinhausen who piloted his König-engined machine to victory in the sidecar championship, winning three of that year's seven sidecar Grands Prix.

Apart from the fact that the two-strokes totally dominated the 1975 season, the year was also significant in that it was only the second time in 27 years that a British rider had not scored a championship victory, the first occasion being 1972.

For Kawasaki, 1975 was also a year of which to be proud. Kawasaki 750cc racers in the hands of Mick Grant and Barry Ditchburn had scored an impressive one-two in the British Superbike Championship, while Grant had also won that year's Isle of Man Senior TT on the ill-handling Kawasaki H1R 500cc machine. In addition, Kawasaki machines had finished first and second in the prestigious Bol d'Or endurance event for the second consecutive year. For Suzuki, it was also a good year. Their new square-four, disc-valve RG500 racer had proved very impressive in the hands of Barry Sheene and would go on to achieve even greater things, while in the 500cc motocross class Roger De Coster had once again become champion.

By 1976, the four-stroke challenge in Grand Prix racing had faded completely. Although Giacomo Agostini ran a privately entered MV Agusta during the early rounds of the 500cc championship, he soon switched to the more competitive Yamaha 500 for the remainder of the year. By this stage, even Phil Read had taken the Suzuki route and the legend of MV Agusta became a thing of the past. The year belonged wholly to Suzuki, at least in the 500cc class. Through their British team, Texaco Heron, Suzuki swept to a superb championship victory, the title going to the highly talented Barry Sheene. Sheene had brought a new sparkle to Grand Prix racing and his good looks and tremendous talent soon added a glamorous new dimension to racing. It became respectable, with sponsors pouring money in as they had never done before.

The smaller classes also attracted a lot of attention, but it was the quiet and shy Walter Villa who emerged from all the ballyhoo to collect the honours. By this time, Harley-Davidson had stretched its 250cc racer into a 350cc machine to such good effect that Villa won both the 250 and 350cc titles for the Italian-American company. The 50cc category again went to Angel Nieto, this time on a new Bultaco machine, while Morbidelli again won the 125cc title, with Pierpaolo Bianchi in the saddle. The sidecar class provided no surprises either, the victor being the previous year's champion, Rolf Steinhausen. One of the saddest aspects of 1976, however, was that the Isle of Man TT races had been stripped of their World Championship status, many leading riders now refusing to race on the circuit on the grounds that it was too dangerous.

At the end of the season, Suzuki, flushed with their racing success, launched a new top of the range road machine, the GS750 model. It was a four-cylinder, four-stroke machine using a twin-overhead-camshaft engine of 750cc, and with it Suzuki

Top: the superstar of the 1970s, Barry Sheene, with his works Suzuki RG500 in 1977

Left: the nimble and quick Suzuki GS750 of 1977, a four-stroke, four-cylinder bike

Above: the state of the art in 1978: the 105bhp, six-cylinder Honda CBX engine

broke away from their traditional image as wholly two-stroke bike makers. The GS750 was also unusual in that it gained rave reviews in the motor cycling press for its good handling, something that Japanese machines, particularly the big ones, were not exactly noted for. The GS750 was also supplemented by the little GS400, a twin-cylinder, four-stroke model aimed at the economy commuter market, and it was further proof that the Japanese were now firmly committed to the four-stroke principle. To combat the success of the Suzuki, Yamaha launched their new XS750 model, a three-cylinder, 750cc machine which featured shaft drive. They also produced a new 400cc twin-cylinder, four-stroke model, the XS400. Honda countered in early 1977 by announcing the new 750F2 model, a sports version of the trusty CB750. Honda followed this up with the launch of the new CB400T range of twin-cylinder, four-strokes and, just to twist the knife a little, also announced an automatic transmission version to join the 750 Hondamatic launched a year earlier. By this time, Kawasaki had also got into the act. They launched a 1000cc version of the 900, the Z1000, and followed this up with the announcement of a new four-cylinder sports machine, the Z650. By this time, there wasn't a hole in the market that the Japanese had not plugged in some way or other. Honda had also become interested in European long-distance endurance racing and had introduced the new twin-cam, 1000cc RCB racers which quickly became the machines to beat in this category.

By the start of the 1977 racing season, Japanese domination of the world motor cycling scene was total. Japan had won every racing honour there was to win and even the sidecar racers were now fitting the four-cylinder TZ750 Yamaha motors to their machines in an effort to go even faster. In the smaller racing classes, only the Italians were offering any sort of resistance, and in the 125 and 250cc classes the World Championship honours went to the lively Morbidelli company with Pierpaolo Bianchi winning the 125 class and Mario Lega the 250 category. Yamaha clinched the 350cc title with works rider Takazumi Katayama, while Suzuki again took the 500cc class, Barry Sheen proving himself the man to beat. The sidecar championship went to George O'Dell of Britain, the first time a Briton had won the title since Eric Oliver clinched it in 1953.

The Japanese were not content to rest, however, and over the winter of 1977 the big four manufacturers engaged in as spectacular a piece of vicious in-fighting as had ever been seen before. Kawasaki started the ball rolling by announcing the new Z1R model, a sleek and streamlined version of the Z1000 machine. Suzuki and Yamaha were quick to retaliate, however. Soon, Suzuki had announced their new GS1000 model, a four-cylinder, twin-overhead-camshaft machine capable of 135mph. Yamaha, not to be outdone, launched their new XS1100 model. This featured a four-cylinder engine, pushing out 95bhp, allied to shaft final drive, all in an awesome package weighing well over 600lb. Meanwhile, Honda were waiting in the wings and eventually upstaged them all when they announced the new CBX1000 model, a six-cylinder, twin-overhead-camshaft machine with a power output of 105bhp.

The Japanese teams continued their winning ways during the 1978 Grand Prix racing season as well. Kawasaki had developed new disc-valve twin-cylinder 250 and 350cc machines and these proved unbeatable. Works rider Kork Ballington of South Africa swept to a double World Championship, his only real opposition coming from his Australian team-mate Gregg Hansford. In the 500cc class, Kenny Roberts of America took the title from Barry Sheene, the British rider's challenge being hampered by an early season virus contracted at the opening meeting in Venezuela. The off-form Sheene was never really able to get to grips with mercurial Yamaha rider, and in the end was forced to concede. The season was marred somewhat by an incident at the non-championship Isle of Man TT meeting when Pat Hennen, Sheene's Suzuki team-mate, was involved in a serious accident which kept him out of racing for the rest of the season, thus preventing Suzuki from staging any serious threat to the Yamaha team. In the 750 category, the honours went to Venezuelan Johnny Cecotto, but only after a season long battle with Roberts. The sidecar title went to Swiss ace Rolf Biland and his controversial Beo outfit, a machine with two driven wheels which more closely resembled a racing car than a traditional sidecar outfit. Riccardo Tormo rode his Bultaco to win the 50cc class, while Eugenio Lazzarini of Italy scooped the 125cc honours. Perhaps the most interesting occurrence during the year was the successful return to the Isle of Man by Mike

Hailwood, the great ace winning the Formula One event.

With the 1970s drawing to a close, motor cycle enthusiasts looked back on a decade which had seen some remarkable developments. It was a decade which had seen the virtual destruction of the British industry and the enormous growth of the Japanese industry. On the race track, the two-stroke reigned supreme, while on the road it was being bludgeoned into extinction by the bureaucrats. And then, at the Cologne Show in Germany at the end of 1978, came an announcement that typified the competitive and sometimes chaotic nature of motor cycling in the 1970s. Kawasaki launched its new Z1300 machine, a six-cylinder, water-cooled model, with shaft drive, and a power output of 120bhp. The onlooking public could only gape in awe and wonder where on earth it would all end.

Top: after years of TZ Yamaha domination in the 250 and 350 classes of World Championship racing, Kawasaki broke the stranglehold with their machines, which had longitudinally mounted, parallel-twin engines. In 1978, South African Kork Ballington took both classes, this being his 250 machine

Above: in 1978, Kawasaki announced what they believed would be the superbike to beat all superbikes, the Z1300 model. This machine featured a water-cooled, twin-camshaft, six-cylinder engine capable of developing 120bhp. Final drive was by shaft

In many ways, the 1978 Cologne Show marked a watershed for motor cycle production. While the bike-buying public was still reeling from the sight of the gargantuan six-cylinder Kawasaki Z1300, those behind the scenes began to realise that this sort of one-upmanship couldn't go on for much longer. For one thing governmental authorities were beginning to make threatening noises about motor cycling safety. Even while the Cologne Show was still running the West German transport authorities announced a 100bhp limit on all large-capacity machines. Still cock-a-hoop over their Cologne triumph, Kawasaki were suddenly forced to lose 20bhp from their monster or risk being unable to sell it in Germany. For a while it looked as though other countries might follow suit and the Japanese were forced to act quickly. They formed a 'gentlemen's agreement' to restrict any future superbikes to power outputs of less than 100bhp. In years to come this agreement was flagrantly violated, but at the time it served to take the sting out of further possible bureaucratic intervention. In fact, the bureaucrats never quite left the scene, and in time they began to exercise more and more influence over the industry. This was particularly true in Britain, where the appalling road accident figures caused any number of politicians to jump on the 'road safety' bandwagon.

In spite of their continual indulgence in muscle flexing, however, the Japanese factories were acutely aware of the need for more practical motor cycles and this trend was also in evidence at Cologne. Although totally overshadowed by the Z1300, Kawasaki's new Z1000ST was launched at the show. This was a shaft-driven touring machine powered by a derivative of the punchy Z900 motor that had once terrified motor cyclists. With its subtle, almost bland, styling and its smooth, sophisticated engine it was hard to believe that the big ST was in any way related to the old Z900. The Z1000ST's introduction was an indication that the Japanese would go to any lengths to cover all possible holes in the market. It was also proof, if any were needed, that the Japanese had complete control of the motor cycle industry. When a company like Kawasaki, the smallest of the four Japanese manufacturers, could allow itself the luxury of introducing two new large-capacity tourers – the Z1300 and the Z1000ST – there could hardly be any doubt about the health of the Japanese economy.

Nevertheless, the European manufacturers weren't totally daunted by this show of strength and continued to do the things they did best. The Moto Guzzi company of Italy also unveiled a new tourer at Cologne – the SP1000 Spada. Basically this was a sports/touring version of the 1000cc vee-twin, fitted with a rather attractive fairing. If anything, it was aimed more at the BMW buyer, being a direct competitor to that company's R100RS model, but the Spada was considerably cheaper than the BMW, which must have caused BMW officials some anxious moments. The BMW people had other worries, however, as the Japanese companies of Yamaha and Suzuki had also launched new tourers at Cologne, models that would compete directly with the German company's own machines. From Yamaha came the new XS850. Shaft-driven, and with an air-cooled, three-cylinder, four-stroke motor, it was merely a larger and more sophisticated version of their XS750 triple. Suzuki had adopted the same tactics, too, with the launch of their new GS850. It was basically an overblown 750, but with shaft drive as opposed to the 750's chain final drive. The worrying part, from the points of view of Moto Guzzi and BMW, was that both these new tourers sported

Below: the 1979 Moto Guzzi SP1000 showed that the Japanese still didn't quite have it all their own way in the field of innovation. In 1975, Moto Guzzi patented its integral brake system, in which the foot pedal operated one front and the rear disc, with automatic balance to prevent premature locking. The handlebar lever operated the second front disc, for emergency stops. The system, claimed to allow shorter, safer stops, was used on the 120mph SP1000 tourer with a fairing designed in the Guzzi wind tunnel, around the rider, for protection and aerodynamic stability

prices that undercut their European rivals considerably. In the past, the Japanese had been content to let the Europeans dominate certain sectors of the market, but that now seemed to be a thing of the past. In their all-consuming war with each other, the Japanese were now preparing to fight for every place on the market, irrespective of who got hurt along the way.

The one area where the Japanese were still lacking, however, was in the middleweight sports bike market. To exploit this gap the Italian Ducati company launched its new generation of machines, the most important of which was the Pantah 500. Like its bigger brother, the 900SS, the Pantah used a 90-degree vee-twin motor with desmodromic valve operation. However, instead of shaft drive for the camshafts, as on the 900SS, the little Pantah substituted inverted-tooth rubber belts. They were cheaper and lighter, and their overall effect was to make the motor both smooth and easy to operate. Together with the superb handling afforded by the Pantah's chassis, this made Ducati's new entry into the middleweight sports league a formidable one. Unfortunately, production costs meant that the Pantah's price was way above that of any corresponding Japanese rival, so once again the Japanese had lost the battle only to win the war.

With the Cologne Show behind it, the motor cycling world settled itself in for a long winter of inevitable rumour and counter-rumour before the final season of the decade. Most of the attention centred around the intentions of Barry Sheene, who was planning to move to the world of four wheels, as riders like Giacomo Agostini and Mike Hailwood had done before him. Sheene's heart didn't seem totally lost to the car-racing scene, however, so when sufficient sponsorship failed to materialise he returned to his first love and once again signed for the Texaco-Heron Suzuki team. Meanwhile, his great rival, Kenny Roberts, experienced an even more unfortunate off season. While testing his new '79 machines at Yamaha's test track in Japan he was involved in a serious accident, which left him with numerous broken bones. As is so often the case with great racing champions, Roberts's misfortune made him even more determined to return to racing, and within weeks he was on the mend and preparing for the forthcoming season. He was forced to miss a number of early events, however, including the Daytona 200 in his native America.

For years the prestige of the 200 had been declining and by 1979 the race entry was almost entirely made up of privateers on Yamaha 750s. The eventual winner of the event

Top left: having steamrolled the performance and commuter markets, the Japanese industry turned to touring with bikes such as the shaft-drive Yamaha XS850, heftily undercutting the likes of BMW

Top: the 1979 Ducati 500SL Pantah was every inch a thoroughbred, combining near faultless handling with the wonderfully smooth desmo V-twin, now with belt-driven cams

Above: Kenny Roberts missed the American season openers in 1979 while he was recovering from serious injuries after a testing crash in Japan, but, in the end, the determined American clinched his second world 500 championship in fine style

was Dale Singleton from Georgia. The amiable American will always be remembered within the sport as 'the pig farmer from Georgia', although he was a professional racer and never a pig farmer. He had simply turned up at Daytona with his pet pig Elmer in tow and somehow the tag had stuck. In years to come Singleton's name was to crop up a number of times with regard to success in the Daytona 200.

Although Daytona marked the opening of the 1979 racing season, the world championship series proper didn't start until mid-March, with the universally unpopular Venezuelan Grand Prix. The Venezuelan event owed its existence to the influence of Johnny Cecotto and his sponsor, Andres Ippolito, the Venezuelan Yamaha importer, but it was disliked by most of the European competitors. Not only was it hugely expensive to travel to Venezuela, but the racing conditions were often far from ideal. Nevertheless, with points at stake the European circus was forced to take its act to South America, where Barry Sheene emerged as the top performer. He won the 500cc event in style, but his victory was somewhat overshadowed when young Carlos Lavado won the 300cc event. Lavado was yet another Ippolito protégé and a Venezuelan and his victory gave the local population a worthy excuse to celebrate well into the night.

Although Kenny Roberts was making a good recovery he was still not strong enough to take his place in the American team for the traditional Transatlantic match races at Easter. Indeed, with Pat Hennen also unavailable through injury (in fact, Hennen would never return to racing) it looked as though the strong British team would triumph; but it wasn't to be. America produced yet another ace from its sleeve in the form of Mike Baldwin, who went on to become top scorer in the series and help the USA to trounce the UK by 448 points to 352. He was assisted to a great degree by supporting performances from those old pros Dave Aldana and Gene Romero, while yet another young American, Randy Mamola, left his mark on a European audience by finishing the series as the second-highest points scorer.

As if to reinforce the dominance of the Americans in road racing, Kenny Roberts made his return to the track in fairytale fashion. At the opening round of the European season in Austria he stormed to a superb win, leaving the brakeless Barry Sheene floundering in his wake. To prove it was no fluke he took second place in the subsequent German GP, and then followed this up with a superb string of wins in Italy, Spain and Yugoslavia. Sheene had no answer to the flying Californian: even when Suzuki signed up Ulsterman Tom Herron to support Sheene, things did not improve. When Herron was tragically killed competing in the Ulster North West 200 it only compounded a disastrous season for the British-run Heron Suzuki team. Indeed, the team was not only being trounced by the Yamaha team, but was facing stiff opposition from the Italian Nava-Olio-Fiat-sponsored Suzuki team, run by Roberto Gallina with Virginio Ferrari as team leader. Ferrari's string of second places in Venezuela, Austria, Italy and Yugoslavia enabled the tousle-haired youngster to overtake Sheene in the points table, and a win in the Dutch TT set his sights firmly on the yellow Yamaha of Roberts; but, if Ferrari harboured any secret aspirations of winning the world title, they were to be dashed by the wily American. Although suffering a run of bad form towards the end of the season, Roberts finally put the title out of Ferrari's reach with a win at the British Grand Prix and a third place in France. Coming only nine months after his near-fatal accident in Japan, Roberts's second world title firmly established him as the world's number one rider.

In the smaller 250 and 350cc categories, another man was also establishing himself as being virtually unbeatable. This was South Africa's Kork Ballington who, on his works Kawasakis, earned himself both the 250 and 350 world titles with a string of impressive victories. Having won the same titles the year before, Ballington had also stamped his name as one of the greatest ever small-bike aces, although he himself was much more interested in getting to grips with the competition in the 500cc class, Kawasaki having announced the existence of a new square-four 500cc racer right at the end of the season.

Another 500cc Grand Prix machine which had been introduced during 1979 was Honda's new four-stroke contender, the NR500. It was a water-cooled V4 machine and it made its début in the hands of works riders Mick Grant and Takazumi Katayama at the British GP at Silverstone. This was a day that Honda would wish to forget, both bikes being well off the pace, but worse was to follow when the team took the machines to Le Mans for the French GP. Here the bikes were too slow even to qualify. The embarrassed Honda outfit quickly withdrew the machines from the fray and set about redesigning them, but although they continued to appear in various guises at race meetings during the next few years they were not successful. Nevertheless, much of the development work on water-cooled V4s was later put to good use by Honda in a series of production machines using vee-engine layouts.

In the other racing classes some familiar names emerged as

Below: Rolf Biland's radical sidecar designs of the 1970s gave the three-wheeled sport a very different look and, ultimately, a much-needed shot in the arm, although Biland was by no means the most popular man in the sport when he was running away from the opposition with monotonous regularity. In 1979, Biland won the controversially split world title in the category for what were regarded as 'conventional' outfits

304

Below: in 1979, on his way to the 500cc world motocross championship, Graham Noyce became the first Briton to win a mototcross GP for eleven years, in a branch of the sport which had once been British-dominated. After winning the 1979 title with consummate ease, Noyce was to have a frustrating season in 1980, dogged by injury and eventually losing his championship to his Belgian team-mate, André Malherbe

champions. The 125cc category saw Angel Nieto take his umpteenth world title, while the B2A sidecar world champion was Rolf Biland. In their infinite wisdom, the FIM had created two sidecar classes, B2A and B2B, one for conventional outfits and the other for the more radical machines for which Rolf Biland had earned such a controversial reputation. Ironically, it was in the B2A category that Biland scored his success; in B2B class Biland was forced into second place by Switzerland's Bruno Holzer. For 1980, however, the FIM once again returned the sidecar category to a single class, the two-class system proving both unpopular with spectators and too expensive for competitors. Highlight of the sidecar racing season, at least for British fans, was the victory of a young Scotsman, Jock Taylor, in the Swedish GP. This was the first British victory in the sidecar class for fourteen years.

Another reason why British fans remember 1979 was the emergence of Graham Noyce as the 500cc motocross world champion. When Noyce won his first Grand Prix – the Austrian GP – he became the first Briton to win a championship race for eleven years, Jeff Smith of BSA having been the last rider to achieve it. After this initial triumph Noyce simply went from strength to strength, eventually winning the title – fittingly at the British GP – by 47 points, from his nearest rival, Gerrit Wolsink of Holland. Noyce also won the 1979 British Motocross Championship to round off a superb season. In taking his world title, Noyce brought back to British motocross a degree of respect that had long been absent, and his influence inspired a number of younger riders, among them Neil Hudson and Dave Thorpe, who were to go on to international success.

Another success that pleased both British and Commonwealth fans during 1979 was New Zealander Ivan Mauger's victory in the World Speedway Final, held in Poland. Incredibly, in view of the stiff competition, it was Mauger's sixth world title win.

That year saw a further remarkable achievement when Mike Hailwood won the 500cc Isle of Man Senior TT on his works Suzuki. Hailwood had returned to the island the previous year to triumph after an eleven-year layoff, and his victory in the Senior simply reinforced the already proven fact that the man was a master of motor cycling. Sadly, his last-ever race, at Donington a few weeks later, was an anti-climax. It was to have been Hailwood's swansong, but he crashed in practice and on race day was too hurt to race. Instead he did a couple of laps of honour in a vintage Bentley, and received the kind of reception only motor cyclists can reserve for their chosen few.

As 1979 drew to a close it was the racing world which continued to attract the major headlines. This was because the sport had been drawn into a fierce political battle over something known as the World Series. This had first raised its head at the British GP in August, but the resultant row rumbled on into the winter months. Basically, the World Series was the brainchild of a breakaway group of top riders who planned to set up a series of events in opposition to the FIM-organised World Championship. Throughout 1979 a number of incidents had occurred which had angered the riders and which had set their plan into motion. Kenny Roberts had refused the victor's garland in Spain after a row with officials over start money. All the world's top riders had walked out of the Belgian GP at Spa after a row about circuit safety, and as a result Kenny Roberts and Virginio Ferrari had received bans, while the other riders received fines from the FIM. The bans on Roberts and Ferrari were subsequently lifted but the whole business, and the way it had been handled by the FIM, had encouraged the riders to take matters into their own hands – hence the World Series.

The trouble was that the World Series was born too early, before any real progress could be made with its organisation. The Press was also ambiguous in its feelings towards the movement, on the one hand sympathising with the riders over their problems with the FIM, but on the other being reluctant to promote anything that might divide the sport. Reportage in the Press was consequently both conflicting and confusing. The FIM retaliated by announcing that any track which ran a World Series event would lose its licence to operate international races, so that the race promoters were most reluctant to involve themselves in WS deals. In the meantime,

Right: few people disputed that Mike Hailwood was one of motor cycle racing's all-time greats, but in 1978 when Hailwood announced that he would return to the Isle of Man after an eleven-year absence, many thought that he would be embarrassingly out of touch with the new generation. He had not raced since his crippling four-wheeled accident at the Nürburgring in 1974 and he had not raced on two wheels for several years before that, but his fans needn't have worried; his emotional triumph for Ducati simply underlined the fact that he remained in a class entirely on his own. In 1979, Hailwood was back on the island with his works Suzuki to take yet another Senior TT win, but, tragically, it was to be his last victory. In March 1981, 'Mike the Bike' was killed in a needless road accident, robbing the sport of one of its greatest and most popular heroes

the various Japanese manufacturers sat back unable to make
much sense out of all the European political in-fighting.
Yamaha at first said they'd back Roberts whatever he did, but
later plumped for the FIM line. Kawasaki were always for the
FIM, while Suzuki and Honda played their cards close to the
chest before falling into the FIM camp. The projected series
was eventually put on ice after the riders themselves started
falling out. Wil Hartog, realising his works Suzuki ride was at
risk if he went with World Series, pulled out and eventually
became so embittered by the fighting that he gave up the sport
altogether. Australia's Gregg Hansford lost his Kawasaki
works ride because of the squabble and went back to Australia
to contemplate the future. In the end the FIM triumphed, but
at some cost to their pride. The riders had used the occasion to
air their grievances about conditions and pay and both these
areas were improved, although still not totally to the riders'
satisfaction.

So, as the winter of 1979 drew in, the sport was locked
into a confusing and complicated political row. In many ways
it simply mirrored the times. The world itself was plagued by
economic and political problems, many of them seemingly
insoluble. The industry itself was also becoming more and more
hamstrung by governmental and environmental demands, so
not suprisingly there were very few people involved in motor
cycling who were genuinely sad to see the back of the 1970s.

Chapter 16
Into the Eighties - a New Direction

The dawning of the 1980s brought the realisation that motor cycling would need a new direction if it was to survive. With the Western world locked into a recession, some drastic rethinking from the Japanese manufacturers was needed if they were to continue their phenomenal growth. In the past the Orientals had competed against each other simply by means of marketing one-upmanship: if one manufacturer built a 900cc, four-cylinder machine, its immediate rival would produce a 1000cc machine; the trick was in the timing of the launch. However, this system of business was no longer the answer. The bike-buying public had taken a good look at machines such as the Honda CBX six and the Kawasaki Z1300 six and decided that they represented too much of a good thing: they were too big and too expensive to run. So, from now on the Japanese would have to pay much more attention to the individual needs of the motor cyclist. The result was that the Japanese began to spread their tentacles into every nook and cranny of the market place. Eventually they would make everything from miniature motocross machines for children to mopeds, scooters and even street racers.

In planning their ranges, the Japanese were also forced to take two other factors into consideration. The first was that the economic recession in the West meant that the public was seeking cheap and economical alternative forms of transport. This was a godsend to the Japanese who, realising the sales potential, started to develop small, commuter machines designed not so much for the motor cyclist as for anyone who required cheap, reliable transport. The non-motor cyclist became almost as important to the designers as the traditional rider.

The second consideration to concentrate Eastern attentions was that of ecology and its attendant bureaucratic restrictions. Because of the world's growing fuel shortage and the continued pressure to reduce pollution and noise levels, the manufacturers had to produce engines more sophisticated than ever before. This, in turn, led them to explore avenues such as turbocharging and fuel-injection in their quest for more economical performance from smaller, cleaner engines. Vast quantities of money were required for research, which meant that the European manufacturers fell further and further behind in the engine development race.

These factors were therefore very much in evidence when the new model ranges for 1980 were announced. Only one

Above left: Honda's only real newcomer for 1980 was in the lucrative 250 class, the excellent, lightweight, single-cylinder CB250RS. It was as quick and agile as its twin-cylinder stablemate, the big-selling CB250N, but cheaper and less complicated

manufacturer launched what could truly be described as an old-style superbike. This was Suzuki, which introduced its new GSX1100, a bigger and faster version of the 1000cc model, with a four-valve head. Almost by way of an apology for this bit of overkill, Suzuki also announced a new GS1000GT, a milder, shaft-driven touring machine. There was also a new twin-cylinder four-stroke, the GS450 (this was a typical case of a manufacturer creating a new capacity class simply because the existing market – in this case the 400cc class – was overcrowded). While they were at it, Suzuki decided to add an odd capacity class to the trail bike world by introducing their SP400 four-stroke, single-cylinder model.

Honda kept a surprisingly low profile for their 1980 model launch. They beefed up their Gold Wing model by raising its capacity to 1100cc, and simply concentrated on refining the twin-cam 750 and 900cc fours they had introduced the year before. In fact, Honda's major newcomer was a machine typical of the new direction in which motor cycling was going. This was the CB250RS, a single-cylinder 250cc four-stroke. Economical to run and fun to ride, it was as quick as its more sophisticated brother, the CB250N twin. The RS was an excellent example of the degree of sophistication that could be achieved with what was basically a commuter/learner machine.

For a company as performance-orientated as Kawasaki, the 1980 model range additions were also surprisingly sober. True, they did launch a new lightweight version of the 750cc four – the new Z750E – but their main attentions were turned to a new 250cc four-stroke single, the Z250C. This was not as quick as Honda's CB250RS, but it was just as much fun to ride, and an ideal bike for the newcomer to motor cycling. Kawasaki's other new model was the Z1000H, the major talking point of which was its new fuel-injection system. Kawasaki had long been interested in fuel injection as a way of improving fuel feed control. Thus the new model sported a 'black box' in its rear tail section; in this lived the microchip-controlled computer responsible for feeding the injection system with the necessary information. Interestingly, Kawasaki promoted the fuel-injection system on the theme of economy as much as that of performance.

Yamaha, on the other hand, went totally for performance with their new range of 250 and 350cc two-strokes. Because the strict emission controls operating in America had meant an end

Above: also in the 250 class, but aimed at precisely the opposite end of the scale from the single-cylinder, four-stroke Honda, was Yamaha's exciting RD250LC two-stroke. The water-cooled 250LC (and its big brother 350) owed much to Yamaha's racing experience, both in the potent and (for a two-stroke) relatively clean engine and in its excellent monoshock frame. With 250s such as the Yamaha capable of a genuine 100mph, British legislators were beginning to look long and hard at learner regulations which allowed a complete novice on such machinery, all too often with disastrous consequences

Above right: with the shaft-drive XJ750 Seca, Yamaha made a huge leap forward from the elderly XS triple. The four-cylinder, four-stroke lightweight boasted 81bhp at 9000rpm, putting it well into the performance league, while the high-bar, stepped-saddle styling gave the bike a distinctly American look

to Yamaha's existing RD250 and RD400, the company set about designing a new generation of two-stroke machines. These were the RD250LC and RD350LC models, and a brilliant success they proved to be. Using technology developed in their racing machines, Yamaha produced two engines which used reed valves for improved power, but which now sported water cooling for increased efficiency and reduced noise levels. Monoshock rear suspension completed the specification, and the result was that boy-racers the world over took to the new generation RDs like ducks to water. The 250cc version was capable of a genuine 100mph, and its racer-like response made it a very exciting machine to ride.

Later in the year, Yamaha also announced two other, rather different, types of machine. These were the new XJ750 Seca model and the new vee-twin, four-stroke range of machines. The XJ750 was a lightweight four-cylinder, four-stroke model introduced as a timely replacement for the ailing XS750 triple. Like the XS it was shaft-driven, but its sporty performance put it right up with the other performance 750s. Unlike the little two-stroke RDs, it featured conventional rear suspension, but an innovative design feature of the XJ, and one which was to play an increasingly important role for all manufacturers in the times ahead, was its use of electronically operated, digital-readout instruments. This was one marketing gimmick exploited with glee by the Japanese, long expert in the art of electronics.

Yamaha's new vee-twin models, on the other hand, were typical examples of the Oriental ability to underplay their hand when necessary. For many years the European markets, particularly the British, had been complaining about the increasing complexity of the Japanese models. It wasn't the technical sophistication that bothered them so much as the fact that every time the Japanese launched a new model it made the old one obsolete. The continual flood of new machines was also creating a spares problem. Machines were being sold before the spares shipments had arrived from Japan, and by the time they did the machines were obsolete because new models had been announced. So, with a little bow to Europe, Yamaha set about making a range of simple machines the Europeans could live with. They chose an engine layout very popular in Europe – the vee-twin. This marketing tool was, in fact, a very useful double-edged sword as it also allowed Yamaha to take a sideswipe at a market in which they had never competed before – the Harley-Davidson-dominated tourer category in America.

When Yamaha eventually launched their vee-twin range, they clearly differentiated between the American and European markets. For Europe there would be the 980cc TR1 sports tourer, while for America there would be 920 and 750 'custom' versions. The engine was a 75-degree vee-twin, which was used as a stressed member of the frame and, as was now usual with Yamaha, monoshock suspension was fitted at the rear. In theory, therefore, the new Yamahas offered everything that the old 'let's keep it simple' school had been demanding. The only trouble was that the bikes didn't sell, in spite of very reasonable prices. Just as the old-fashioned SR500 single had flopped before it, so too did the new vee-twin. It seemed that, for all their protestations and their yearning for the 'good old days', British buyers actually preferred the new-fangled sophistication of the Japanese multis.

Two very interesting points were learned from the Yamaha vee-twin saga, however. The first was that the Japanese were now quite prepared to build different machines for the American and European markets. In the 1970s this had clearly not been the case, with a concentration on the American market and the Europeans having to settle for a like-it-or-lump-it situation. The second point was that the custom bikes, so popular in America, were not being accepted by the European – and particularly the British – markets. As support to Yamaha's roadster TR1, the European Yamaha importers had decided to offer for sale the American-inspired XV750 custom model, but if the TR1's sales were bad the XV's were downright appalling. Custom bikes, which featured high handlebars and stepped seats, were all the rage in America at this time and had been inspired by the customised 'chopper' machines. Choppers, of course, were one-off machines, usually using Harley-Davidson motors – and the idea of mass-producing customs was in itself a contradiction in terms. Nevertheless the Americans took to them, despite European rejection. The reason is hard to explain, but it's probably that in Europe a motor cycle is still regarded as a working tool rather than a plaything or status symbol. Consequently, Europeans demand complete efficiency from their machines. The customs, with their uncomfortable handlebars and restricted seat movement, simply weren't versatile enough, in spite of the fact that they invariably used the same motors as the roadster versions on sale in Europe. Interestingly, it was the smaller-capacity customs that proved more popular in Europe, indicating that newcomers to motor cycling, rather than traditional riders, were attracted to the custom styling.

Meanwhile, back on the racing front the 1980 season was kicking off with the traditional opener – the Daytona 200. This produced a win for the Yamaha-mounted Frenchman Patrick Pons, the reigning Formula 750 world champion who had won the title in 1979, the last year in which the formula was eligible for world championship status. By this time all the works teams had ceased to build F750 machines, and the entry list for Daytona's big event was once again made up of privateers, mostly on ageing Yamahas. Second in the 200 was Dale Singleton, the 1979 winner. Hero of the race, however, was yet another of America's teenage sensations, Freddie Spencer from Louisiana. Spencer led for most of the race on his Erv Kanemoto-prepared Yamaha, only to have machine troubles rob him of victory in the final stages of the event. Spencer also featured strongly in the Superbike event for large-capacity four-

Top: Plus ça change . . . *the 1980 Harley-Davidson Sportster and Roadster continued a line which had dominated the American touring scene for as long as anyone could remember, plugging dependability, durability and ease of maintenance as the Sportster passed its twenty-fifth birthday*

Above: in spite of Yamaha's obvious willingness to emulate traditional American styling and to offer the familiar and uncomplicated V-twin engine format, their TR1 roadster was an embarrassing flop in sales terms, both in America and in Europe

Above: Patrick Pons, the 1979 Formula 750 world champion, opened the 1980 season with a fine win in the Daytona 200, sadly against fairly minor opposition, since the F750 had lost its world status. Pons was killed later in the year at the British Grand Prix, at Silverstone

Above right: Jon Ekerold, leading Anton Mang at the 1980 Dutch 350 GP, was definitely one of the big finds of the season, combining skill and aggression on his private Yamaha to win the title. Mang went on to become the 1980 250 champion with his works Kawasaki

strokes, but here he was narrowly beaten by Suzuki's new signing, the Kiwi Graeme Crosby, who had come to prominence in Britain during 1979 with some quite spectacular performances on his Moriwaki Kawasaki. The 250cc event went to yet another young American wonderboy, Eddie Lawson, on his works Kawasaki.

By the time the racers arrived back in Europe most of the World Series wrangle had been buried, though not forgotten. There were quite a number of changes among the team personnel too. Barry Sheene had quit the British Heron Suzuki team to run his own team of works-supported Yamahas, bearing Akai sponsorship. Suzuki had replaced Sheene with Californian Randy Mamola and they then brought Graeme Crosby into the fold to give a very formidable appearance. Yamaha, as always, were backing Kenny Roberts while the Italian Nava-Olio-Fiat Suzuki organisation replaced Virginio Ferrari (lost to the team after a bitter argument over money with team boss Roberto Gallina) with Marco Lucchinelli and the promising Grazziano Rossi. Kawasaki wheeled out their new KR500 for Kork Ballington, while Honda still strove desperately to make the NR500 competitive.

The opening Grand Prix of the season, the Italian, saw Kenny Roberts pick up where he left off the previous year, scoring a very impressive win. He followed this with another win in France, which left no doubt that he would be the man to beat in 1980. France also saw the emergence of the aggressive South African Jon Ekerold as a potential 350cc world champion. Riding his private Yamaha he stamped his authority on the race, and as the season progressed he too became the pace-setter in his class. France was unfortunately notable for one other incident: Barry Sheene had to have the little finger of his left hand amputated after a crash.

Although Kenny Roberts made most of the early-season running, some good mid-season results enabled Suzuki teamster Randy Mamola to draw closer to his compatriot in the points table. By scoring a superb victory over Roberts at the British GP, Mamola ensured that the championship fight went to the last event, the German GP at Nürburgring, which in fact turned out to be something of an anti-climax. Mamola could only finish fifth and as Kenny Roberts came home fourth it meant that the little Yamaha rider had stolen his third consecutive 500cc world title. The event was won by Marco Lucchinelli who was by now emerging as a man to watch.

By this time the other championships had also been settled. The 250cc world title went to German Anton Mang who proved virtually unbeatable on his works Kawasaki. Jon Ekerold had gone on to win the 350cc title, a remarkable achievement considering his limited resources and lack of works support. Ekerold's victory was an inspiration to those many privateers who battle against almost overwhelming odds and diabolical conditions each season.

Highlight of the year for most British fans, however, came at Silverstone when Jock Taylor guided his Dennis Trollope-sponsored Yamaha outfit to victory. His win gave him sufficient points to claim the world title, and for the second time in five years a Briton had become world sidecar champion.

For British motocross fans, however, 1980 was a less happy year. They saw their hero Graham Noyce dislodged as world champion by his team-mate, the Belgian André Malherbe. Malherbe had made his mark on the championship as early as round one, when he won both heats at the Swiss GP in fine style. Noyce, who spent some of the season overcoming injuries, never recovered from this blow. Another Belgian took the 250cc motocross world title, this time a teenage newcomer, Georges Jobe, on his works Suzuki. Like his countryman Malherbe, Jobe won the opening round of the contest and never looked back. For Britain's Neil Hudson, however, the year was a total disaster. Regarded at the beginning of the season as Jobe's greatest threat, Hudson became embroiled in a messy legal battle between the Maico factory, for whom he had ridden prior to 1980, and the Yamaha company, for whom he signed at the beginning of 1980. As far as Maico were concerned, however, Hudson hadn't completed his contract and so they sued him – successfully as it transpired. After starting the year on Yamahas, a court injunction forced him to return to Maico, with whom he had a miserable season. Nevertheless, Hudson's tough 1980 season was to strengthen him for 1981, which turned out to be his most successful year.

A few other sporting events from 1980 are also worth recording. They include the incident on the Isle of Man when the Formula One win of works Honda rider Mick Grant was protested by fellow competitors. They believed the fuel tank on his machine to be too large, thereby contravening the regulations. However, Grant retained his victory when it was discovered that ping-pong balls and air bottles in his tank reduced its carrying capacity to the required amount! For British speedway fans 1980 was a very memorable year, the highlight of which came in Sweden when Michael Lee won the coveted World Speedway Final. To underline British supremacy, Dave Jessup, who earlier in the season had won the Commonwealth Final, finished second to Lee. On a less happy note, 1980 will also be remembered for the death of popular Frenchman Patrick Pons, killed in a tragic accident at the British Grand Prix at Silverstone.

In September, the world's attention was once again focused on the biennial Cologne Show. Cologne always seems to bring the best (or worst, depending upon your point of view) from the manufacturers and the 1980 show was no exception. A host of new models made their début and, unlike the model launches of the season before, it was all done with a great deal of razzmatazz. The Japanese appeared to be encouraging the West simply to spend its way out of the recession, and they certainly created a stir with their offerings.

It was hard to pick a star exhibit at the 1980 show, as there was something for everybody, but perhaps the most interest centred around Honda's new CX500 Turbo. For reasons they could not satisfactorily explain, Honda had chosen to turbocharge their middleweight vee-twin rather than one of their middleweight fours. The more cynical observers felt that the exercise was, therefore, little more than an ego-boosting operation for Honda. Of all the various engine layouts, the vee-twin is one of the most difficult on which to install a turbo unit, so if Honda could do it, it would not only have a demoralising effect on the opposition but would boost their own prestige. Whatever the cynics believed, there was no disputing the fact that the CX500 Turbo was a superb piece of work. Its styling was extremely attractive, and with its monoshock suspension it looked a million dollars. The trouble was that it literally cost a million dollars to develop, too. When production models eventually went on sale in Britain in early 1982, the price of a Turbo was around the £3500 mark, nearly £1000 more than machines such as Suzuki's GSX1100 and Kawasaki's Z1000. What's more, the Turbo was no quicker or cheaper to run than the ordinary superbike. As a flag-waving exercise the Honda CX500 Turbo was a runaway success, but translated into sales terms it flopped. The nett result was that the buying public still had some reservations about the usefulness of the turbocharger, and until that opinion was altered by the arrival of a machine which would not cost the earth, but which could outperform the larger-capacity machines, turbocharging would simply remain a marketing gimmick.

Another interesting innovation at Cologne was the appearance of a new range of Suzuki machines bearing the Katana model name. The range consisted of 1100, 1000, 750, 650 and 550cc machines, all wearing the most unusually shaped bodywork. The styling was the work of a West German company called Target Design, an organisation which had also been responsible for some earlier BMW styling exercises.

Featuring radical new tanks, seats and nose fairings, the Suzuki Katanas looked like something made for a lunar expedition. They met with a mixed reception, but, like them or loathe them, they were generally regarded as a welcome breakaway from the routine, almost jelly-mould, styling on offer from the majority of the Japanese designers. Indeed, over the next couple of years, styling was to play a much more important role than hitherto in motor cycle marketing. With so many manufacturers producing engines that were almost identical, it became important that individual models should establish some sort of recognisable identity.

One machine at Cologne with an identity all its own was the BMW R80 Futuro. Alas, it was not for sale, being merely a styling exercise by BMW of West Germany. Featuring all-enclosed bodywork and an ultra-low seating position it caused a considerable stir. The show, however, did mark the official debut of a new BMW model, the R80GS. This was an unusual machine, using the twin-cylinder 800cc BMW motor, and had been designed as a dual-purpose model suitable for both the road and the dirt. Surprisingly, BMW had dropped production of their R80/7 model to concentrate on the new GS. The bike itself was an attractive machine which featured shaft drive and only a single suspension strut at the rear. Another unusual aspect of its specification was that its tyres could cope with conditions either on or off the road.

In addition to their new CX500 Turbo, Honda wheeled out a remarkable new range of machines. At the top of their range

they introduced the new CB1100R. This was a bike whose engine had been developed from that of the race-winning CB900 and which featured a racing fairing and streamlined tail section. It was really nothing more than a pure street racer, having been designed to compete in the production racing events that were by now so popular in countries such as Australia, Britain and South Africa. Another faired Honda making its début was the beautiful CB900F2, intended purely as a touring version of the existing 900cc roadster and a typical product of Honda's ability to develop a single machine into a variety of guises. Further down the Honda range came new custom 750 and 500cc models, as well as a brutal-looking 500cc trail bike, the XL500S.

Kawasaki also produced a variety of new machines. These included two new 1100cc models, a fuel-injected, chain-driven sportster and a shaft-driven tourer version using carburettors. They also produced the neat-looking Z1000J model, a completely reworked version of their famous 900/1000 fours. In addition, new Z750 and Z550 models made their début, the latter being an improved version of the Z500 four. Towards the bottom of their range came the lovely little AR80 model, a racy sportster styled along the lines of the company's racing machinery.

Yamaha, in addition to their new XJ750 and vee-twin models, produced the neat little XJ550 model, while at the same time giving their venerable old XS1100 a new set of sports clothes. Known as the XS1100S, the new machine was intended as a rival for the new sports 1100s from Suzuki and Honda. Unfortunately, while it lacked nothing in the way of power, the XS1100S still wouldn't go round corners, and it was a dismal failure in the sales markets.

Overwhelmed by this flood of new models from the Orient, the European manufacturers' efforts paled into insignificance. Only BMW's brave showing with the Futuro and the R80GS could inject any life into the European scene, although Ducati's presentation of a 600cc version of their Pantah was well received. Poor old Triumph battled on, showing their TR7 Trail as well as a new custom Bonneville model, the Low Rider. As always, it was too little too late from the British company.

In fact, for British motor cyclists, once the excitement of the Cologne Show had died down, the remainder of 1980 was a fairly miserable time. For one thing, they were trying to digest a hotch-potch of new laws from the Department of Transport. These were mostly concerned with the learner rider who, according to the DoT, was killing himself off at an alarming rate. Consequently, the DoT announced a new scheme whereby learners would be restricted to machines of only 125cc (the current restriction was then 250cc) and they would have to undergo two tests before they could hold a full licence. These laws would eventually have the effect of wrecking the 250cc market, while causing chaos at the Driving Test Centres. Once again, the bureaucrats were making their presence felt within the motor cycle industry.

For once the off-season was relatively free of the rumour-mongering that so often causes confusion in the specialist press and friction between the riders and their respective employers. Most enthusiasts simply couldn't wait for the start of the 1981 season because it looked as though it ought to be the most exciting ever. For one thing, all the major Japanese factories were competing in the 500cc class.

Once again, Yamaha wheeled out Kenny Roberts, his machines now painted in the corporate Yamaha white, red and

Far left: Suzuki took the bold step of offering radical styling with their Katana range. In particular, the 750, 1000 and 1100 sported looks which were not really to the taste of all bikers, and Suzuki later offered mechanically identical versions with more conservative styling, for wider appeal

Left: the R80GS was a real departure for BMW and was their attempt to produce a dual-purpose, road/trail machine. Its weight proved a handicap off the road, however, and the bike would quickly bog down and stop when the going got muddy. Its on-road performance won general acclaim, though, and prospective buyers cried out for a genuine roadster version

Below: in 1980, Kawasaki launched the first production fuel-injected bike with their GPz1100 and unveiled a stunning middleweight performer with the GPz550; their performance was almost on par with the pace-setting Z1 of 1973

blue rather than the yellow and black of Yamaha America. Roberts was supported by Britain's Barry Sheene, now recovered from an unfortunate testing accident during the winter, who also ran a works Yamaha. Ranged against these Yamahas were the British Heron Suzuki team of Randy Mamola and Graeme Crosby, while from Italy came a works-supplied Suzuki run by Roberto Gallina for Marco Lucchinelli. 'Lucky', as he was known, would be Gallina's team leader, the unfortunate Grazziano Rossi having been ousted when he refused to race in the appallingly wet conditions at Nürburgring at the end of 1980.

From Kawasaki came the unproven new KR500 for Kork Ballington of South Africa. He was to have been supported by Gregg Hansford, but the big blonde Australian crashed even before the season had begun, breaking a leg in the process. He subsequently returned to Australia, to concentrate on a new career racing cars. Finally, from Honda came the underpowered Honda NR500, with which the factory was still persisting, for the Japanese pop star Takazumi Katayama.

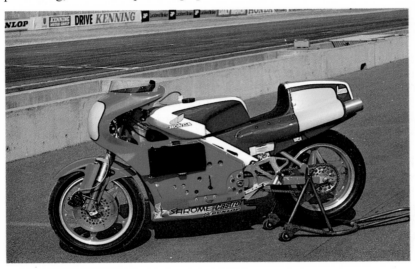

As always, however, the first entry on the calendar was for the Daytona event, in Florida, far from the pressures of European racing. Kenny Roberts was the man the Americans all came to see, the little Californian determined to win the one race that had always eluded him during his career. However, it seemed as though Roberts was jinxed at Daytona, because not only did he not win the 1981 event, but he didn't even get beyond lap two before machine troubles forced him to retire. Ironically, victory went to the one man who appeared to be able to win only at Daytona – Dale Singleton. Once again the Georgian piloted his obsolete Yamaha 750 to first place, aided largely by the unreliability of his major rivals' machines. Second favourite after Roberts to win the race was Freddie Spencer on a big 1025cc Honda four-stroke, but he lasted only nineteen laps, while the big Yoshimura-prepared Suzukis of Graeme Crosby and Wes Cooley also failed to go the distance. So Singleton sped to his second Daytona 200 win, while Marc Fontan, Richard Schlacter and Dave Aldana were runners-up.

Another big attraction at Daytona was the Superbike event. Since the 750 class had been abandoned, the big four-stroke Superbikes had begun to emerge as the top racing class in America. This was because they were based on production machines with which the fans could identify, a factor missing with the pure race-bred 500s from Europe and Japan.

Above left: for once, the mighty Honda group got their sums wrong when they decided to tackle the Grands Prix again. There was bitter argument at their research and development establishment as to whether a traditional four-stroke motor should be developed or whether they should go against company policy and produce a two-stroke which would be easier to develop into a race winner. In the end, a four-stroke was decided upon and the design brief was to produce a legal four-cylinder with as much eight-cylinder technology as possible built in. The NR500 featured a wide-angle, vee-four engine with oval pistons, twin plugs per cylinder, eight valves per cylinder and eight carburettors. In spite of being able to rev to 20,000rpm, the engine was always that precious few horsepower down on the works' two-stroke opposition. The two-stroke protagonists back at Honda built their three-cylinder machine anyway, and wondered how long it would be kept in the wings

Above: Marco Lucchinelli at speed on his Roberto Gallina-entered works Suzuki. 'Lucky' surprised everybody with his consistency aboard his mount, and took some fine wins to secure the 1981 world 500cc championship. There was little doubt that the Suzuki was the most powerful of the 1981 works' bikes, but where the Italian operation succeeded was in its organisation, in which the official Heron team failed. Gallina was able to develop machines much as he pleased from day to day, whereas Randy Mamola's outfit had first to get the go-ahead and, indeed, the parts needed from Japan. That across-the-world communication was something that not even Mamola's riding ability could make up for

Consequently the rivalry between the American outlets of the big four Japanese manufacturers was intense, the prestige of race wins being directly translated into showroom sales. 'What wins on Sunday sells on Monday' has long been a favourite American marketing truism. In fact, Honda were so determined to dominate the Superbike class that they had signed up the current wonderboy, Freddie Spencer, at quite considerable expense. To add even more weight to their thrust, they even restricted Spencer to racing only in America, so that any ambitions he may have nurtured about racing in Europe had to be abandoned for a year. In spite of Honda's 'big-buck' approach, the Daytona Superbike event was dominated by the two Suzuki teamsters, Cooley and Crosby, the former just beating his team-mate to the line.

For European racing enthusiasts the Daytona 250cc event also proved an eye-opener. They stood and watched as the current world champion, Anton Mang of Germany, on a works Kawasaki, was soundly hammered by two young American stars in the making – Eddie Lawson and the tiny teenage Jim Felice, yet another protégé from Kenny Roberts.

With the Americans having dominated at Daytona, the European campaign opened, and the Europeans discovered that they were still being beaten by the Americans, this time in the shape of Randy Mamola and Kenny Roberts. Mamola won the opening round of the championship in Austria and Roberts the second in Germany. At least British fans had the satisfaction of seeing their team trounce the Americans at the traditional Easter Transatlantic match races, although it had to be admitted that the US team was a very makeshift affair. With Kenny Roberts unavailable because of testing commitments, it was left to Mamola to make the running, but while the freckle-faced Suzuki star proved to be the quickest man on the circuit his team back-up was insufficient. Freddie Spencer, lured over for this one-off event, had borrowed a private Suzuki RG500 which proved to be more trouble than it was worth, while newcomers Dan Chivington, Jimmy Adamo and Nicky Richichi could not come to terms with the British circuits. In the end the score-line of 466 points to 345 was a fair reflection of the superiority of the British mid-field runners.

To add to their woes, the American fans had to watch while a new European threat emerged to tackle their twin spearhead of Roberts and Mamola on the Grand Prix scene. This threat went by the unlikely name of Marco Lucchinelli. Lucchinelli had been part of the European racing scene for a couple of seasons and had been one of Europe's quickest men, but his penchant for crashing had reduced his ability to score important points. Now, under the guidance of Roberto Gallina, 'Lucky' was emerging as a quick and safe rider.

Lucchinelli had surprised many observers with his remarkably mature win at the treacherous Nürburgring circuit at the the end of 1980. Many, however, simply shrugged it off as a flash-in-the-pan win, the kind that often happens at events plagued with poor weather as the 'Ring had been. By the middle of the 1981 season, however, Marco had been recognised as a real challenger. He opened his account with a win in France (the fourth round of the championship), thus breaking the stranglehold that the American duo of Roberts and Mamola had established early in the season. Mamola fought back with a win in the following round in Yugoslavia, but then Lucchinelli put together a superb string of wins in Holland, Belgium and the 'San Marino' race to sweep into the championship lead.

By now, any challenge that either Roberts or Mamola offered lacked any sting. Roberts had been plagued all season with an ill-handling machine, the Yamaha factory having supplied him with a new mount which, although it didn't lack for power, simply refused to corner properly. Mamola's end-of-season performances were also surprisingly disappointing. Rumour had it that there was friction within the Suzuki camp between team-mates Mamola and Crosby. To some degree the young Californian was being out-psyched by his aggressive team-mate, who was also proving consistently faster in practice – although he never reproduced this form during the race.

By the time the GP circus arrived at the detested Imatra circuit in Finland for the penultimate round of the championship, Lucchinelli was firm favourite for the title. Just to prove that his mid-season wins had been no fluke, the Italian triumphed in the Finnish GP to take the title. Having been dogged with the tag of 'the new Agostini' since his earliest days in GP racing, Lucchinelli had at last emulated his hero by bringing the 500cc title back to Italy. For the British-run Heron Suzuki team there was some consolation in that Randy Mamola's second place in Finland put him into second place in the title table, ahead of Roberts. Yamaha also enjoyed a brief end-of-season moment of glory when Britain's Barry Sheene won the final round of the year in Sweden.

In the smaller 250 and 350cc classes, one man had emerged dominant – Anton Mang. The German had ridden his works 250 Kawasaki to no fewer than ten wins out of a possible twelve, to annex the 250 title in no uncertain manner. In the 350cc class, however, Mang had a tougher struggle, the opposition this time coming from the previous year's holder Jon Ekerold. In the end, however, Mang's five GP wins completely overshadowed the South African's two, and the German took the title by 88 points to 52.

In the tiddler classes Ricardo Tormo of Belgium proved the man to beat in the 50cc class on his Kreidler, while the

Above: West German Anton Mang seen on his Kawasaki at the 1981 British Grand Prix. In 1981 Mang further proved what a competent rider he was and what a fast and reliable machine the Kawasaki had become. Its in-line tandem-twin motor with disc valves had the edge in power over the across-the-frame twin-cylinder Yamahas, and it only needed a rider of Mang's ability to guide it to two '81 world championships

320

125cc grade went to Angel Nieto of Spain on a Minarelli. The sidecar class was dominated by the Swiss Rolf Biland, who was followed home by Frenchman Alain Michel and Scotland's Jock Taylor.

All in all, the 1981 Grand Prix season provided a number of interesting talking points. The first was that Kenny Roberts's domination of the 500cc class had finally been broken, and by an unlikely combination. Until 1981, the reputations of Robert Gallina and Marco Lucchinelli were of men whose ambitions exceeded their achievements and whose performances were generally unreliable and unpredictable. Now they had both made their mark in the history books. The other, more troubled, observation was that the 250 and 350 classes were beginning to diminish in value. With the exception of Mang's works-supported Kawasaki, the 250 and 350 classes were usually made up of privateers or riders supported by small European manufacturers such as Ad Maiora, Sanvenero and MBA. The days when Honda clashed with Yamaha and Suzuki in the smaller-capacity classes seemed to have disappeared, perhaps for ever.

Away from the Grand Prix world, a number of racing events occurred which are also worth mentioning. For instance, there was the case of the two Isle of Man TT winners who weren't. Both Ron Haslam (Formula One) and Chris Guy (500cc Senior) were credited with victories in their respective events, only to have the cup of glory dashed from their lips. In Guy's case the ruling was particularly sad. He had been leading the Senior TT when, after two laps, the race was stopped because of bad weather. After first garlanding him as the winner, the race organisers then decided to declare the race null and void as it hadn't gone sufficient distance. The race was re-run and this time another privateer, Dennis Ireland from New Zealand, scooped the honours.

The Haslam incident was more controversial. As he approached the line to start the race, Haslam's great rival Graeme Crosby noticed that his works Suzuki had developed a puncture. He consequently rushed off to the pits where a new tyre was fitted. This completed, Crosby then rejoined the queue waiting to start the race, eventually setting off four minutes and fifty seconds after he should have. In the TT, of course, it's the rider with the fastest time who wins and Honda, believing Crosby to be nearly five minutes adrift, paced their team men accordingly. Imagine their dismay then when, after the race, the organisers decided not to regard Crosby's late start as a penalty but to consider his elapsed time as his race time. Crosby, who'd ridden like the wind to catch up, was therefore declared the winner. This so incensed the Honda team that they threatened to withdraw from the Isle of Man. They were persuaded against this, but as a protest their machines were painted black and their embarrassed riders told to appear in all-black leathers. It was a surprisingly childish protest from such a professional team and merely highlighted what a sorry business the Isle of Man TT had now become.

The saddest occurrences of 1981 were the deaths of two men whose names were synonymous with all that had once been good about the TT: Mike Hailwood and sidecar star George O'Dell. They both died over the same weekend, towards the end of March. Hailwood and his daughter, Michelle, were killed in a car accident, when a truck driver swerved across their path. It seemed ironic that the man who'd survived so many moments on the race tracks of the world should die in a stupid road accident. With his death, however,

Below: at the beginning of 1981, Neil Hudson finally freed himself of his Maico contract, a task which is said to have cost the British rider a sum well into five figures. It was a large gamble to take on his ability, and for a while the works' Yamaha-mounted Hudson thought that it wasn't going to pay off, until the last motocross of the season in Holland. In the end, he emerged victorious as 250 world champion, and looked forward to a year in the blue riband 500 class for 1982

Hailwood became established in legend as the greatest racing motor cyclist of them all. Even though Agostini may have won the majority of titles during their epic battles, 'Mike the Bike' is number one in the minds of the fans. Fittingly, one of the grief-stricken pall-bearers at the funeral was the great Agostini himself.

The O'Dell death was bizarre. The former world sidecar champion had had a series of unhappy seasons, culminating in a serious crash. With his health endangered by nervous problems, O'Dell was advised to give up racing. By now drink was playing an important part in his life and, when his new wife decided she could take no more and left him, O'Dell's mind became seriously unbalanced. Armed with a shotgun he invaded the house in which he believed his wife to be staying and set it alight. In the resultant conflagration O'Dell lost his life.

But while Britain lost two former champions in Hailwood and O'Dell, she gained a new one in the form of motocrosser Neil Hudson. At the beginning of '81 Hudson had finally become free of the Maico contract which had caused so many legal problems the year before, and he celebrated by signing a two-year agreement with Yamaha. Hudson's new contract stipulated that his initial year would be spent contesting the 250cc world championship and thereafter he might be promoted to the 500s. The season began badly for the quiet young Englishman, however: the new prototype water-cooled Yamaha 250s were plagued with reliability problems, and Hudson was forced to watch his great rival Georges Jobe of Belgium pile up an ever-increasing points lead. Yamaha then decided to abandon the water-cooled machines in favour of the old air-cooled models, and with this move came a change in Hudson's fortunes. He managed to pull back the points deficit, and by the end of the German GP his points stood at 168 to Jobe's 221. By winning the penultimate Russian GP, Hudson narrowed the gap to just 11 points, with Jobe on 233 and himself on 222. The title was eventually settled at the final round in Holland. Jobe tried all he could to hold off Hudson, but the Yamaha rider wasn't to be denied, and finished victorious.

Britain's other motocross star, Graham Noyce, didn't have such a happy season, however. Although he led the points table at several stages during the year, injuries reduced his effectiveness and by the end of the year he had been overtaken by his team-mate and great rival, André Malherbe of Belgium. When Noyce crashed his Honda at the Belgian GP at Namur at the end of the season, it virtually assured Malherbe of the title. To make absolutely certain, however, Malherbe won both legs of the final GP in Luxembourg, putting the contest firmly out of Noyce's reach.

Once the noise and fury of the road-racing and motocross competitions had subsided, the motor cycling world's attention turned to the end-of-year shows, in which the Japanese unveiled their new models for the 1982 season. The major showcases in 1981 turned out to be the Paris and Tokyo exhibitions and, true to form, there was a wealth of new machinery to gladden the eye and empty the pocket. The Paris Show was dominated by Honda and Yamaha, while the Tokyo Show was stolen, fittingly perhaps, by Kawasaki and Suzuki. It was Honda, who, as usual, provided the greatest number of surprises.

For openers, Honda launched a new version of the world-beating, top-of-the-range CB1100R. In 1981 this bike had completely dominated street racing around the world, and for 1982 it was further improved. Now known as the CB1100RC, it featured a full carbon-fibre fairing was well as improved handling and increased power output. As it happened, the RC proved so competitive that it virtually killed off all opposition in street racing and thus seriously damaged the credibility of the production-bike categories. In attempting to prove their superiority, Honda had bitten off the hand that fed them.

A far cry from the sophistication of the CB1100RC was the new Honda FT500. This was Honda's answer to Yamaha's SR500, a big, four-stroke 500 single, designed for easy maintenance and economic reliability. Unlike the SR, however, it was fitted with a self-starter, which made it a much more appealing prospect than the difficult-to-start Yamaha. It was also fitted with stylish bodywork, modelled on that of the short-track racers as used on American oval circuits, which was why, in America, it carried the Ascot name.

Yet another new, and very different, Honda was the VF750 model. This was a 750cc sports tourer, featuring a water-cooled V4 motor. Suddenly Honda's persistence in developing the V4 NR500 racer didn't seem so silly after all. What they'd learned then about V4s had been applied to the VF. With a 78bhp motor delivering its power to the road via shaft final drive, the VF was a competitive alternative to the 750 in-line fours on offer from rival manufacturers.

Another fascinating model on show in Paris was the CBX400 four. This was a twin-cam model with four valves per head, but, as it transpired, costs precluded the 400cc version from reaching the market. Nevertheless, British fans were not too heartbroken, for in its place they received a 550 version, the CBX550F, a superb little machine which soon won the

Below: by 1981, the middleweight market was being ever more fiercely contested by the Japanese factories. Honda's reply to Kawasaki's GPz550, which had been greeted with open arms by the public, was the CBX550. This diminutive machine featured a neat sixteen-valve motor in a Pro-Link frame which gave sensational performance. Available in faired or unfaired versions, the bike was an immediate success and, despite its greater capacity, took over where the famous Honda CB400F four left off. The CBX550's only failing was its enclosed disc brakes which, although they made wet-weather braking more secure, were prone to fade more than conventional items

admiration of everyone who rode it. Nimble, light and responsive, it was sheer pleasure to handle, and for riders interested in touring a faired version known as the F2 was made available.

Finally, Honda gave their venerable old CX500 a face-lift. The new version – the CX500E – sported much slimmer lines as well as Pro-Link monoshock rear suspension. It didn't go any faster, but it certainly looked a great improvement on the old 'ugly duckling' CX.

Yamaha also used the Paris Show to launch a number of new machines. The most interesting of these was the new XJ650 Turbo, based on the popular XJ650 in-line four, but with a small turbocharger mounted below and behind the engine crankcases. Surprisingly, it used a standard constant-vacuum carburettor instead of electronic fuel injection. The claimed power output was 85bhp. The XJ650T was also fitted with distinctive bodywork, fashioned in glass fibre-reinforced plastic, which had been wind-tunnel tested for high-speed stability and comfort. Unfortunately, when examples of the XJ650T became available for testing, it was discovered that the Turbo, in spite of its extra power, was little faster than the stock XJ650. To some extent this was because of the weight increase, but what Yamaha had really done was to concentrate on mid-range performance. The turbocharger had been designed in such a way that its major effect was on mid-range torque. Consequently, those riders expecting blinding acceleration or shattering top speed from the XJ650T were disappointed. Yamaha hadn't quite overcome the old problem of turbo lag, although on the XJ650T it was hardly cause for serious criticism. Nevertheless, the public was still dubious about the

turbocharged machine and, in spite of a much more reasonable price than that of its Honda CX500 Turbo rival, the XJ650T sales never really took off as Yamaha must have hoped they would.

By way of a change from multi-cylinder models, Yamaha also launched a new 550cc machine, the vee-twin XZ550. Yamaha completely surprised everyone with the introduction of this unusual motor cycle, which had for years been one of the best-kept secrets in the industry. Using a vee-twin motor set in line with the frame, the XZ550 also boasted such unusual features as water cooling and shaft drive. It had an impressive power output of 65bhp, and it was initially assumed that the XZ550 must be a direct rival to the sports machines coming from Honda and Kawasaki, the CBX550F and the GPz550. In reality, however, the XZ550 turned out to be more of a touring machine than a road-racer. For one thing, it was a large bike, and for another it simply didn't handle as well as the rivals from Honda and Kawasaki. Problems with flat spots in the rev range on early models merely reinforced the view that Yamaha had rushed the bike into production too soon.

But if the XZ flattered only to deceive, two Yamaha models which produced more than anyone expected were the two new 125s, the RD125LC and the DT125LC. The former was a road-going machine using a twin-cylinder, water-cooled engine, while the latter was an off-road equivalent. With 20bhp available from its tiny engine, the little RD offered performance approaching that of a racer, and it soon proved hugely popular, particularly with Britain's boy-racers. Another unusual machine from Yamaha was the XT550. Although an off-roader, it wasn't just an overblown XT500 but a completely redesigned machine, even though, like the XT500, it used a four-stroke, single-cylinder motor as its basis. The XT550 was intended primarily for the French market, where events such as the Paris–Dakar Rally had created a flourishing market for large-capacity four-stroke, off-road bikes.

At Paris, both Kawasaki and Suzuki put up fairly subdued performances in the new-bike stakes. Kawasaki showed a revamped version of their GPz1100, now fitted with mini fairing. Suzuki's major offering was also an 1100, the GSX1100E, which was simply an 1100 Katana without all the gaudy 'Star Wars' bodywork, but still using the powerful 111bhp engine. If Suzuki and Kawasaki exhibits were fairly low key, those of the major European manufacturers at Paris were practically invisible. Laverda showed their new Jota, now featuring a revised motor with 120-degree crankshaft throws, while BMW launched a sports version of the R65 model. Known as the R65LS, this machine used the existing 650 boxer motor but was fitted with radical (for BMW) styling. It had a nose cone not unlike that on Suzuki's Katanas, while the tank and seat unit was also reshaped. It was a pretty little thing, but not pretty enough to worry the Japanese.

Later in 1981, at Tokyo, Suzuki and Kawasaki revealed why their Paris efforts had been so downbeat. They had had a number of new machines under wraps, but had chosen to launch them in Tokyo so as to be sure of their share of the headlines. The main interest on the Kawasaki stand centred around their new KZ750 Turbo model. The existing four-cylinder 750 motor formed its heart, and the bike was fitted with a streamlined bodywork, not unlike that of its rival from Yamaha. As it happened, however, Kawasaki's Turbo prototype was just that: at the end of 1982, a full year after its show début, the KZ750T had still not gone into production.

One Kawasaki model which did find its way on to the streets, and which also made its début at Tokyo, was the revised 1982 version of the GPz550. The most noteworthy feature of this model was its Uni-Trak monoshock rear suspension. In the months ahead it was to prove enormously popular, particularly in Britain, where its reliability and performance won many friends.

Suzuki's main offering in Tokyo was also a turbocharged model, the XN85, a most attractive machine powered by the company's in-line, four-cylinder 650cc motor. However, as with Honda's CX500T, there was a long delay between the showing of the XN85 and the actual production. For all the attention they attracted at the various shows, it seemed that turbocharged machines, for the bike-buying public, were more for perusal than purchase.

So, for 1982, in spite of a wide-reaching economic recession in the West, the motor cycle enthusiast had a larger-than-ever variety of machinery from which to choose. Not only did the superbike enthusiast have a host of Japanese and even European machines to drool over, but two British manufacturers had now also launched new large-capacity models on to the market. These were Triumph, whose co-operative factory at Meriden produced the new TSS model – basically a Bonneville 750, but with an eight-valve head – and the new and exciting Hesketh company.

Hesketh took its name from its owner Lord Alexander Hesketh, a rich young Briton who had already made his name through Formula One car racing. It was Hesketh who had launched James Hunt on the F1 championship trail. Because of the style and pleasure with which they tackled F1, the Hesketh team soon captured the imagination of the racing public but, since Formula One car racing is such an expensive business, eventually even Lord Hesketh was forced to withdraw. Anxious to utilise its not-inconsiderable automotive talents elsewhere,

the Hesketh team eventually turned its attention to the world of two wheels. While James Hunt went off to McLaren to win a world championship, Hesketh settled down to design a superbike suitable for sale in the quality markets around the world.

It took several years for the prototype Hesketh to reach production but by the middle of 1981 sufficient models had been built for Hesketh to display the product at the NEC Motorcycle Show in Birmingham. The Heskeths were certainly worth a close look; they were beautifully made machines, featuring 90-degree vee-twin engines set in-line with the frames. The quality of the work was outstanding: the nickel-plated frames were made of Reynolds 531 tubing, and the paintwork was superb. However, even at that stage it was clear that there were two major problems with the Hesketh. The first was that, with an engine output of only 86bhp, it could easily be outperformed by many run-of-the-mill Japanese machines. The second, and more important, was that the fastidious production methods used by Hesketh in its new factory at Daventry were resulting in very high production costs. Consequently, when the Hesketh went on sale in late 1981 it was with an eye-watering price tag of £4495, at a time when a 130mph Honda 900 could be bought for less than £2500.

A third problem arose when a group of British journalists were invited to ride the machines for the first time. They nearly all agreed that, while the Hesketh handled well and performed quite adequately, its gearchange mechanism was unacceptably difficult to operate. Anxious to eliminate all design faults before the launch, the Hesketh delayed production of the model in order to eradicate the gearbox faults, but time was running out, debts were mounting up, income was non-existent and the company's creditors were getting nervous. By June 1982 the organisation was experiencing a severe cash crisis. Attempts to raise more capital had failed, and delivery dates weren't being met. Eventually the Receiver had to be called in. Attempts were made to sell the company as a going concern, but, with debts estimated at £600,000, few brave souls could be found who would consider carrying on.

Hesketh was closed down and its assets liquidated at an auction. Surprisingly, all of the machines auctioned were sold, many being bought purely for reasons of patriotism. Alexander Hesketh's dream had become a nightmare, but for once the age-old taunts of bad management and/or union problems, so often true of British industry, couldn't be levelled at the Hesketh company. The management had done everything in its power to produce a quality product and the workers had responded with a display of craftmanship hard to equal anywhere. The simple truth was that a £5000 motor cycle was a luxury the world neither needed nor wanted. The death of the Hesketh was a sad blow to British motor cycle enthusiasts anxious to see Britain return to the ranks of important world manufacturers. More seriously, however, it must have instilled serious doubts in the minds of on-looking potential manufacturers about the advisability of investing in the motor cycle industry. Had Hesketh been successful it might have inspired a resurgence of British builders, but with the company's demise it merely seemed to prove the hopelessness of tackling the Japanese at their own game.

So, while one brave venture was being buried, the Japanese factories returned to lock horns on the battle grounds of European and American race circuits – and what a battle the 1982 racing season promised to be. Once again, all four major

Above: by 1982, the Triumph co-operative at Meriden was starting to look like a healthy operation. Their latest variation on the venerable parallel twin was the use of an eight-valve head which gave the nimble roadster a fair turn of speed. The TSS was no match for the Japanese opposition in a straight line, even with revised valvegear, but its chassis had few peers when it came to bend swinging

Left: Hesketh tried to combine the best of two worlds with their V1000, a machine with all the inherent qualities of the vee-twin Ducati, finished with Japanese-perfect engineering. In the end the bike was overweight and under-engineered in spite of its pristine finish. After the demise of Hesketh, Lord Hesketh himself transferred production to his manor base and promised limited runs of bikes for 1983 onwards

manufacturers were fielding 500cc works teams, but this time
Honda had returned with a machine far more competitive than
their old four-stroke NR500. Their new bike was a two-stroke,
but instead of producing a square four, hitherto *de rigeur* in
GP racing, they had built a three-cylinder model, featuring disc
valves. While Honda weren't claiming any power advantage
over their more conventional rivals, the new NS500 had been
built low and light, giving its riders something like an 18kg (40lb)
advantage over the opposition. Just to show that they meant
business, Honda had also lured world champion Marco
Lucchinelli into their squad by the simple expedient of waving
a blank cheque under his nose.

   If the thought of damaging his reputation by riding
untested machines appeared not to worry the Italian, the
knowledge that his '82 team-mate would be Freddie Spencer
must have caused him some troubled thoughts. This deeply
religious youngster from Louisiana had long been considered
one of the hottest properties in racing, but, apart from a
spectacular showing in the 1980 Transatlantic series, he had
little experience of conditions in Europe. Nevertheless, anyone
who'd ever seen the lanky American knew him to be a
supremely gifted rider, who was likely to prove a threat not
only to his rivals but also to his celebrated team-mate.

   Another team that had undergone changes during the
winter of 1981 had been the British Heron Suzuki squad.
Personality conflicts between their star riders, Randy Mamola
and the popular but outspoken Graeme Crosby, had resulted in
Crosby being given his marching orders. The reason given at
the time was that Heron Suzuki intended to run only a single
bike for Mamola because of the huge expenses involved in
Grand Prix racing. Crosby then went off and negotiated himself
a ride with a private team which planned to use works-
prepared Suzukis, but this deal was quashed because, according
to the British motor cycling papers, Mamola had a clause in his
contract stipulating that only he should be supplied with works
bikes, a claim Mamola later vehemently denied. Needless to
say, this caused an enormous slanging in the press between the
former team-mates, so that by the time the season started
feelings were running high. In the meantime Crosby had
managed to land himself a ride with the newly formed Yamaha
team being run by former GP ace Giacomo Agostini. The team,
using works-supported Yamahas and heavily sponsored by the
Marlboro cigarette company, also signed another rider who'd
had his share of problems over the past season – Grazziano
Rossi of Italy. The combination of Ago, Crosby, Rossi and
Marlboro certainly looked an interesting and potent one.

   Ironically, Heron Suzuki then secured a wealthy new
sponsor in HB – yet another cigarette manufacturer. They also
signed a very interesting number-two rider, Virginio Ferrari of
Italy. Like Rossi, Ferrari had made his name with the Gallina
Suzuki team, only to fall foul of Gallina himself; the result was
that both riders had wasted precious seasons in a racing
wilderness. Now Ferrari was back, out of practice certainly, but
possessing enough natural talent to cause his new number one
problems. If nothing else, Ferrari's signing must have brought a
wry smile to Graeme Crosby's face.

   In Italy, Roberto Gallina was contemplating the 1982
season with some concern. Although he would be supplied with
works Suzukis, he had lost Ferrari, Rossi and now Marco
Lucchinelli. Casting his eye over the available talent, he settled
on two fellow Italians to make up his team – Franco Uncini
and Loris Reggiani. Uncini was a steady if unspectacular

Above: Randy Mamola pilots his Suzuki ahead of Barry Sheene's Yamaha in 1981. As well as contending with the likes of Lucchinelli, Sheene and Roberts in 1981, Randy had a distinct clash of personalities with his own team-mate Graeme Crosby. In a season when even Roberts had tipped Mamola to be his successor at the top of grand prix racing, things didn't work out as planned for the young Californian: he had expected to finish higher than second in the World Championship

privateer, while Reggiani was a virtual unknown whose previous experience had been on 125s. As history will relate, it was an inspired choice.

The works teams' line-up was completed by the lone Kawasaki KR500 of Kork Ballington. So dominant in the 250 and 350 classes in 1978/9, Ballington had struggled on the KR. The engine appeared to be competitive, but the chassis was proving too much of a handful for even this most professional of riders.

Before the Grand Prix circus got underway again, the annual pilgrimage to the Daytona 200 took place, and the big talking point here was the arrival of a new four-stroke racer from Honda. This was the FWS model, a V4 machine of 1025cc, destined to carry Freddie Spencer, Mike Baldwin and Roberto Pietri. Would this superb piece of equipment be able to beat off the two-strokes which had so dominated Daytona for the past five years? As an added attraction, Daytona also marked the first clash between those two mid-winter sparring partners Mamola and Crosby. On the first corner of lap one

the two found themselves side by side, fighting for the same piece of track. Crosby overcame the resultant collision, but Mamola was sent tumbling, fortunately without any serious damage. Whether the incident was purely accidental or a deliberate manoeuvre, only they will know, but it fuelled yet another verbal punch-up in the press. Crosby, having survived the first-lap pile-up, went on to win the race, but there's no doubt that luck was with him that day, because he really was not the quickest man on the track. That honour went to Freddie Spencer, whose ultra-powerful FWS Honda was chewing through its tyres at such an alarming rate that he eventually had to settle for second place. Baldwin and Pietri brought their new Hondas into third and fourth places, but for Crosby and the Agostini Yamaha team it had been a dream début, made especially sweet by Mamola's failure to finish. Honda did manage to salvage something from Daytona, however, when Spencer and Baldwin swept to first and second places in the Superbike race, vanquishing the Yoshimura Suzukis and the works Kawasaki of Eddie Lawson in the process.

A few weeks later, at the prestigious Imola 200 event in Italy, Crosby scored another victory, to establish himself and the Agostini team quite firmly on the racing map. Crosby's return to the big time, from having been unemployed just a few months before, was meteoric. Amazingly, and ironically, neither he nor arch-rival Mamola was to have very much influence on the Grand Prix season that lay ahead, although Crosby eventually finished in second place in the points table, by virtue of consistent high place finishes.

The 1982 Grand Prix campaign opened in Argentina, and the 500cc event proved little short of sensational. In all the to-ings and fro-ings of winter, two men had consistently been forgotten when it came to predicting winners for 1982 – Kenny Roberts and Barry Sheene. Roberts was still smarting from the loss of his title, while Sheene was determined to prove to the world that he was still a top-quality rider, and in Argentina it was these two, plus Honda's Freddie Spencer and Marco

Above: after an encouraging win at Sweden in 1981, Barry Sheene looked forward to the '82 season with greater relish than for many a year. He started the season the best of the bunch, but was increasingly worried that Roberts alone was given the task of perfecting the promising vee-four. In spite of his own square-four Yamaha's undoubted superiority in handling, Barry was anxious to get hold of the later version, if only to prove his superior machine-sorting ability. His wish granted, it was on the vee-four that Sheene suffered his horrific crash in practice at Silverstone. Responding to treatment in superhuman fashion, however, he was soon back in the saddle and announced a 1983 contract with Suzuki before the end of 1982

Above: with problems in the works camps of both Suzuki and Yamaha in 1982, it was left to another Roberto Gallina rider, Franco Uncini, to take the world title. Franco, here winning at Silverstone, was smooth and very quick and emerged as a worthy champion. Once again the Suzuki, carefully honed, proved the machine to beat in Gallina's experienced charge

Lucchinelli, who provided the fireworks. Lap after lap, they raced so close together that it was hard to tell them apart. Then Lucchinelli dropped back and it was left to Spencer to take on the two Yamaha teamsters, but his new and unproven Honda NS500 simply didn't have the legs for the task, and in the end it was the old war-lord Kenny Roberts who sneaked home three-fifths of a second ahead of Sheene. Sheene, incidentally, had secured considerable sponsorship from the John Player cigarette company and looked set for a competitive season. Indeed, at the following GP, the Austrian, Sheene finished second, to reach the top of the championship table. Austria, however, also provided a sensation, in that the winner was the unfancied Franco Uncini on the Gallina Suzuki. Had Gallina unearthed another Lucchinelli? Unfortunately, the following championship round at Nogaro in France provided no clues. The circuit proved so unsuitable for GP racing that the big-name stars all boycotted the event, which caused all kinds of repercussions from the sport's ruling body, the FIM. The FIM ranted on about bannings and so forth, but eventually settled on making examples of a number of riders by fining them heavily. Even this course of action backfired when the riders stood together and refused to pay their fines. Eventually the FIM relented and withdrew the fines, obviously deciding that perhaps the riders might have had a legitimate case in refusing to ride on a circuit that they considered dangerous.

If any critic thought that Uncini's Austrian win was a fluke, the quiet Italian soon silenced any doubts with yet another win at the Italian GP, followed with a victory in Holland. Suddenly, it looked as though Roberto Gallina was going to produce a carbon-copy version of his 1981 season – an unknown, unfancied Italian snatching a world title from the jaws of the more fancied runners.

The Belgian Grand Prix, however, saw the 1982 season produce yet another surprise, this time in the form of Freddie Spencer. Riding his Honda NS500 beyond its apparent limits, he romped home four seconds ahead of Barry Sheene, to score Honda's first Grand Prix win in fourteen years. So excited was he by the victory that he promptly dropped the bike on the slowing down lap! Appropriately, the date was 4 July.

So the circus arrived at Silverstone for the British Grand Prix. It was to prove the turning point of the season for a number of riders. For Franco Uncini it brought joy, as yet another victory earned him enough points to clinch the title. Even with three Grands Prix to be run, the Italian could not now be caught. For the two Yamaha teamsters – Roberts and Sheene – the British race meant the end of their title challenges. For Sheene, in particular, it was a disaster. All season long the British ace had been forced to use his outdated square-four Yamaha while the works technicians concentrated on perfecting Roberts's new V4, but for Silverstone Sheene was granted his wish and allocated a V4. Short of testing time, he elected to join a general practice session in order to get as much experience on the bike as he could. Unfortunately a slower rider took a tumble in front of him and Sheene was unable to avoid the fallen rider's machine. The resultant terrifying 150mph collision saw Sheene being rushed to hospital with dreadful injuries, which included two broken legs and a broken arm. For many it would have meant the end of their career, but for Sheene it marked just the beginning of a long and painful struggle back to the saddle. When, at the end of the season, Sheene was lifted out of his wheelchair and on to a road-going Yamaha for a couple of laps of the Donington circuit, his reception was rapturous, the kind only accorded to the most heroic of riders.

Below: another American to take Europe by storm in 1982 was 'Fast Freddie' Spencer aboard his vee-three NS500 Honda. Freddie, here winning the San Marino GP, put Honda back at the sharp end of the Grands Prix after a fourteen-year break. More than anyone else, Freddie was tipped to be the threat for 1983 and many seasons to come

Above: it was only a matter of time before one of the talented new band of Americans took motocross world championship honours. Brad Lackey had competed in Europe for several years, and was rewarded with the first world championship to go to the USA in the 500 class. Danny LaPorte, seen here at the British 250 motocross round, was contesting the class for the first year and won his title convincingly. If the USA needed to prove the worth of its riders even more, it was shown in the end-of-season Trophée and Motocross des Nations, where they scored resounding wins both times

For Kenny Roberts, a fall on the first lap of the race left him with a leg injury sufficiently serious for him to have to miss the remaining three GPs. Ironically, Uncini scored not a single point in those three remaining races, but his 103 points total was unbeatable. Nevertheless, the season still had a few touches of high drama to offer. The first was Takazumi Katayama's victory on the NS500 Yamaha at the Swedish GP. The former 350cc world champion had struggled for season after season to try and make the NR Honda competitive. Consequently the little Japanese had virtually been written off by the world's press as a no-hoper, riding now simply for the money. Sweden proved otherwise, and the race also saw the return to form of Randy Mamola, who finished in second place. Mamola's season on the HB Suzuki had been disastrous, so much so that after the initial five rounds of the championship the little Californian had scored only four points. By the end of the season, however, Mamola and the Suzuki team were beginning to get their act together again. At the San Marino GP, Mamola took a storming second place to Spencer's Honda, while at the final round in Germany Mamola scored the GP victory that had been eluding him all year.

So the season ended on a slightly strange note. Franco Uncini had taken the title with surprising ease, considering the opposition, but had faded badly towards the end. Graeme Crosby had finished in second place in the table but hadn't won a single GP in spite of his spectacular early season showings at Daytona and Imola. Spencer finished in third place, having carried off two GP victories in his first season in Europe. Sheene and Roberts finished in joint fourth place, both riders ending the season in hospital. Sixth came Randy Mamola after a truly weird season, while Honda teamsters Katayama and Lucchinelli took seventh and eighth spots. For Lucchinelli it had been a nightmare year: champion a year before, he'd been outridden by his young American team-mate and outscored by the supposed no-hoper Katayama.

If the 1982 Grand Prix season had seen some upsets in the 500cc class, those that occurred in the 250 and 350cc classes were equally remarkable. The major talking point in the two smaller categories was the emergence of two virtually unknown European riders, Jean Louis Tournadre of France and Didier de Radigues of Belgium. Tournadre proved the more sensational of the two, riding a privately entered Yamaha 250 prepared by his father, and snatching the world 250 title from Anton Mang by a single point. Although he scored only one GP victory to Mang's five, Tournadre's consistent placings eventually earned him the crown. For Mang there was some compensation when he won the 350cc class, but not before the young Belgian, de Radigues, had given him a considerable fright by winning two GP events – the Italian and Czechoslovak – outright. In the smaller capacities, the 50 and 125 categories, the world titles went to Swiss Stefan Dorflinger (Kreidler) and the Spaniard Angel Nieto (Garelli) respectively. For Nieto it meant an eleventh world title and put him second in the all-time title-winner table, behind fifteen-times world champion Giacomo Agostini. In the sidecar championship, the world title went to Germany's Werner Schwarzel, who narrowly defeated the former champion, Rolf Biland of Switzerland. Frenchman Alain Michel was third. For sidecar enthusiasts 1982 was a bad year, however, because it marked the death of one of the most popular sidecar racers of all time – Scotland's Jock Taylor. Racing at the unloved Imatra circuit in Finland, Taylor's outfit had run off the circuit and collided

with a trackside obstacle, killing the young Scot instantly. Taylor's passenger and close friend Benga Johansson was fortunate to escape with his life.

On the motocross scene, the 1982 championship trail could be summarised in just one word – America. During the late 1970s and early '80s, motocross had prospered enormously in America; indeed, it had become big business. Consequently, most of the top American riders preferred to stay in America where they could earn vast quantities of money while still enjoying the comforts of home life. Few could see the point of leaving America to live the gypsy life necessary to compete in the world championship, when all they would gain was prestige. However, by 1982, a few Americans had decided to broaden their horizons and tackle the Europeans on their home ground. Two such men were Danny LaPorte and Brad Lackey. Lackey had been a consistent performer in Europe, in fact, but had never won the world title, although he had come extremely close on several occasions. LaPorte, on the other hand, had little experience of Europe. He had crossed the Atlantic at the end of 1981 as a member of the victorious American Trophée des Nations and Motocross des Nations team and had liked what he'd seen. With Neil Hudson moving to the 500cc class, the Yamaha factory quickly signed the young American as his replacement in the 250cc category. LaPorte rewarded their faith by going on to win the championship title in his first year of racing in Europe. It was a remarkable achievement.

For Brad Lackey, 1982 also proved to be a golden year. He was teamed with Belgian André Vromans on works Suzukis, and the two riders made the early season running. By mid-season Lackey was championship leader, and when his major challenger for the title, André Malherbe of Honda, fell and broke his leg at Carlsbad in America, Lackey's last obstacle to the title was removed. Lackey had long been America's most important representative in Europe and it was only fitting that he should be rewarded with a world championship. Just to rub salt in European wounds, the American Trophée and Motocross des Nations riders again won their competitions with, it must be added, teams that most certainly weren't their strongest. America, incidentally, also won the world's major speedway honour in 1982, when Californian Bruce Penhall took the world individual speedway title after a controversial clash with Britain's Kenny Carter. Penhall then promptly retired from the sport to concentrate on his new career as a budding Hollywood film actor.

Top left: if domination of motocross and strong contention on the tarmac was not enough, America also provided Bruce Penhall on the shale, who took both the 1981 and 1982 world speedway titles on his Weslake. After his final win at his home town of Los Angeles, Penhall gave up competition bikes to concentrate on his new starring role aboard police bikes for the popular Chips *TV series*

Above: among the fifty new models which Honda unleashed on the public in 1982 was the VF400F-D, with a four-camshaft vee-four motor in Pro-Link chassis. This addition to the range meant that, in the 400cc class alone, Honda had single, twin, straight-four and vee-four versions. In early 1983 they announced that a 350cc vee-three (based on their NS500 racer) would be forthcoming. Was there any better example of market overkill?

Above right: the top-of-the-range Kawasaki for the third year running, the GPz1100 sported revised fuel injection, but for 1983 it also came complete with Uni-Trak monoshock rear suspension and smart bodywork. If that wasn't enough to tempt the buyer, bigger valves in the engine boosted power output to a staggering 120bhp, as much as the six-cylinder and much heavier Kawasaki Z1300 had four years previously. On the drag strip, it was expected that the '83 GPz1100 would be the first production roadster able to pull a ten-second quarter mile. On the road, one began to wonder whether there would ever be an opportunity to use the awesome performance of which the latest batch of super sportsters were capable

So, with the various sporting championships decided, the West settled down to await the approaching winter, while in the East the Japanese prepared to launch yet another onslaught of machines on to the world markets. And for 1983 they offered a remarkable selection.

From Honda came a flood of new models, many of them so different that one was left to marvel at the engineering resources of this astonishing company. Perhaps the most interesting of their offerings was the VF750 Super Sport, a chain-driven, fully faired sports version of their water-cooled V4 VF model, boasting a power output of 86bhp and a top speed of 135mph. Other new Hondas included the CB1100F, a larger version of their popular CB900 in-line four, as well as the VT500S. This was a vee-twin model, but with the cylinders set in line with the frame as opposed to across it as in the CX Honda model. The CX range also underwent some drastic changes: the capacity was now boosted from 500 to 650cc, and this included the Turbo version. For small-bike fans Honda also launched the VT250F vee-twin as well as a remarkable little 400cc V4, the VF400F. It was a truly bewildering display of engineering virtuosity.

Suzuki's range for '83 wasn't quite so dramatic, but did include the superb new GSX550F, a smart little 550 which was claimed to be the lightest in its class. Not quite so performance-orientated was the Suzuki GR650, a twin-cylinder, four-stroke model with monoshock suspension.

From Kawasaki came a revised GPz range featuring improved streamlining and with the 550, 750 and 1100cc models now all sporting monoshock Uni-Trak suspension. For off-road enthusiasts Kawasaki announced their amazing new KL500, which used a giant 564cc water-cooled, single-cylinder, four-stroke motor in a lightweight trail-bike chassis featuring monoshock suspension. It would take a brave rider to tame the KL500.

Yamaha's two new models for 1983 were both sports roadsters. These were the beautifully styled XJ900, which used a conventional in-line, four-cylinder motor and shaft final drive, and the 'boy-racer' RD350LC. The new LC sported bodywork modelled along the lines of the Yamaha GP racers, while the engine output had been boosted by the addition of electronically operated power valves, another feature of the racers.

It was obvious that the Japanese either wouldn't or couldn't slow down the production treadmill on which they

now found themselves. Super-successful they might have been, but observers were wondering just when the bubble would burst. It seemed impossible that the Japanese could keep up this pace; machine launches were occurring with such frequency that by the time production models had reached the showroom, rumours of improved models in the pipeline were already being heard. In addition, not only did models often go on sale long before sufficient spares shipments had been received, but the continual flood of new machines quickly rendered old ones obsolete and almost valueless. In countries like Britain, the economic recession had caused the large-capacity market virtually to dry up. Dealers were sitting with stocks of big bikes they simply couldn't move. For them 1983 would be a long, hard year.

To their credit, the Japanese were well aware of changes in the market. They had foreseen the demise of the large-capacity superbike and had responded by building smaller, sportier machines such as those in the 550cc class. They had also attempted to introduce new technology, such as the turbocharger, although market resistance to this manoeuvre proved tougher than they had expected.

The early 1980s were therefore a confusing and troubled time for the motor cycling industry, for whom there was yet one more cloud looming on the horizon. Governmental interference in the motor cycling business continued to grow: pollution and noise limits were being tightened all the time and in some countries, such as Britain, bureaucratic intervention had seriously disrupted marketing trends. For motor cyclists everywhere, the approaching mid-1980s would be a bubbling cauldron of confusion, fast-changing technology and a reappraisal of the very nature of motor cycling.

Top: Yamaha were quite late on the scene with their large-capacity sports bike (except for the touring-orientated XS1100), and it wasn't until late 1982 that they announced the XJ900. Design emphasis here was not so much on outright horsepower from the engine, but more on paring of weight and dimensions so that what performance there was would be more usable

Above: in late 1982 BMW launched the R80ST, as if by popular demand. A road-going version of the dual-purpose R80GS, the ST was the best-handling BMW yet, and probably one of the last variations on the boxer theme before the company got into production its much-rumoured longitudinal in-line four to take over at the top of the range

Index

338